Home Maintenance
FOR DUMMIES®
2ND EDITION

by James Carey and Morris Carey

WILEY

Wiley Publishing, Inc.

Home Maintenance For Dummies® 2nd Edition

Published by
Wiley Publishing, Inc.
111 River St.
Hoboken, NJ 07030-5774
www.wiley.com

WILEY

About the Authors

James and **Morris Carey,** known as the Carey Brothers, are nationally recognized experts on home building and renovation. They share their 60-plus years of combined experience as award-winning, licensed contractors with millions nationwide through a weekly radio program, daily radio vignette, syndicated newspaper column, and comprehensive Web site (www.onthehouse.com), all titled *On The House.*

These third-generation contractors have had broadcast careers in radio and television for 23 years. They deliver user-friendly, hands-on advice in their radio program, which is carried coast-to-coast weekly, via satellite, to a rapidly growing network of more than 250 stations. The program also is broadcast via live remote from home and building expos nationwide and on the Internet (www.onthehouse.com).

With a long career in television, the Careys have appeared as home-improvement contributors on CBS Television's *CBS New Saturday Morning.* In addition, the brothers were regulars on the Family Channel's *Home and Family* show, hosted by Cristina Ferrare and Michael Burger. They have also appeared as guests on national and local television programs.

Recognized for their efforts in answering immediate and constant structural concerns by the public in the hours and days following the devastating October 1989 earthquake, the Carey Brothers and KCBS radio in San Francisco received the George Foster Peabody Award, broadcasting's most prestigious honor, for their outstanding contributions toward "comprehensive, intelligent, and useful coverage."

Prior to becoming full-time journalists, Morris and James owned and operated a successful home-remodeling and -construction firm, Carey Bros., for over two decades. They have been named to *Remodeling* magazine's Hall of Fame "Big 50," which recognized top achievers in the industry. They have also been honored as one of the nation's top 500 companies by *Qualified Remodeler* magazine.

The Carey Brothers are the authors of *Home Remodeling For Dummies* (Wiley Publishing) and *Cost-Effective Home Upgrades* (Ortho Books) and are contributing authors to *Home Improvement All-In-One For Dummies* (Wiley Publishing) and *Living Well in a Down Economy For Dummies* (Wiley Publishing). They have also penned a monthly column for *The Family Handyman* magazine.

Homeowners can receive answers to their specific home renovation and repair questions by calling the Carey Brothers' toll-free number, 800-REPAIR-IT (800-737-2474), during their radio program, Saturday from 9 a.m. to 1 p.m. Eastern standard time or via e-mail at info@onthehouse.com and on the Web at www.onthehouse.com.

Dedication

Summer vacation had ended. It was my first day back to school and my first day as a sophomore. The morning air was warm, and I perspired as I anxiously rushed to chemistry class. I was excited and scared all at the same time. I shot into the room and made a beeline for a seat near the back wall. I slouched back in my seat in an attempt to appear relaxed. I wasn't. Not even a little bit.

As I glanced up toward the front of the room, I caught a glimpse of her for the very first time. Suddenly, the anxiety began to disappear. She had taken the first seat in my row. The desks between us were still empty. She was wearing a tight, gray-wool, calf-length skirt and a satiny white blouse. Her hair was sandy colored and she wore it short. She was tall and slender. I hadn't even seen her face, yet suddenly I knew that I had fallen in love. That was nearly 40 years ago.

We grew up, and she became my best friend. She became a woman of character and ambition. Even when she was a girl, she was wise and mature beyond her years. Yet, she has always been easygoing and fun to talk to. She is passionate about everything she does, and everything she does is tendered with great compassion. Our moments together are priceless pearls of happiness filled with mutual admiration and endearing love. In the morning, her smiling eyes get me going. In the evening, her calming voice puts me at ease. She is a loving mother, a sexy grandmother, and my partner in life. She is my wife, Carol.

Without her strength, this book would not have been possible. "Yo, Adrianne, Rocky loves ya baby!"

—Morris Carey

To Carol, my wife and partner for over 28 years: Thank you for the freedom, encouragement, and support to do my life's work. I am so blessed to be your husband.

To Chris, Jamie, and Chase, our three beautiful children; Never take the roof over your head for granted. There are so many people in so many parts of the world, including our great country, who either don't have adequate shelter or are without the means to maintain it so that it is both safe and sound. Always work hard to be good citizens and contribute to the betterment of society. Love, Dad.

—James Carey

Authors' Acknowledgments

We were thrilled when the folks at Wiley engaged us to give *Home Maintenance For Dummies* a new lease on literary life. We are delighted that the book has done so well in the nearly ten years since the publication of the first edition and we hope that this second edition will be equally popular and act as a valuable resource for people looking for help in maintaining their piece of the Great American Dream.

As we write this book, millions of Americans are struggling to survive one of the toughest economic times in modern history — certainly in our lifetimes. We hope that our book will, in some small way, help relieve some of the economic stress that you may be feeling when it comes to your home and its maintenance by empowering you to take on tasks that you might have previously, during more prosperous times, farmed out to a contractor or handyperson. If this is true, than our greatest hopes and dreams will have been satisfied.

There are many people who contributed both directly and indirectly to the success of this book. Although there are too many to list, we would be remiss without naming a few.

This second edition would literally have taken forever — certainly longer than our publisher would allow — had it not been for some very valuable writing assistance that we received from Tim Green and Tracy L. Barr. Tim, our longtime friend and a stellar writer, is an obedient husband, a loving father, and a frustrated do-it-yourselfer. He injects his unique perspective, which add both color and humor to this body of work. We were introduced to Tracy by the Wiley folks. She is a very talented writer and editor who has authored or coauthored several *For Dummies* books, including *Living Well in a Down Economy For Dummies,* to which we contributed. She did a marvelous job of helping us organize and prioritize content and was a pleasure with which to work. Thanks to you both for helping us make this book the best that it can be.

At Wiley, we want to thank Diane Graves Steele and Tracy Boggier for believing in this project and for giving us yet another opportunity to share the better part of our lives' work with you. A special thanks goes to our project editor, Elizabeth Kuball. This is our first opportunity to have had the pleasure of working with Elizabeth. She worked tirelessly to ensure that the second edition would contain the best of the first edition with lots of new and exciting material. We sincerely hope that she again will have the opportunity to transform our journalism into a finished project that is both professional and easy to understand and of which we are very proud.

Publisher's Acknowledgments

We're proud of this book; please send us your comments through our Dummies online registration form located at `http://dummies.custhelp.com`. For other comments, please contact our Customer Care Department within the U.S. at 877-762-2974, outside the U.S. at 317-572-3993, or fax 317-572-4002.

Some of the people who helped bring this book to market include the following:

Acquisitions, Editorial, and Media Development

Contributor: Tracy Barr

Project Editor: Elizabeth Kuball

(Previous Edition: Mary Goodwin and Sherri Fugit)

Acquisitions Editor: Tracy Boggier

Copy Editor: Elizabeth Kuball

Assistant Editor: Erin Calligan Mooney

Editorial Program Coordinator: Joe Niesen

Technical Editor: Roger A. Zona

Senior Editorial Manager: Jennifer Ehrlich

Editorial Supervisor and Reprint Editor: Carmen Krikorian

Editorial Assistants: Jennette ElNaggar, David Lutton

Cover Photos: © iStock

Cartoons: Rich Tennant (`www.the5thwave.com`)

Composition Services

Project Coordinator: Kristie Rees

Layout and Graphics: Carl Byers, Joyce Haughey, Christine Wiliams

Special Art: Shawn Wallace

Proofreaders: Melissa Cossell, Toni Settle

Indexer: Galen Schroeder

Publishing and Editorial for Consumer Dummies

Diane Graves Steele, Vice President and Publisher, Consumer Dummies

Kristin Ferguson-Wagstaffe, Product Development Director, Consumer Dummies

Ensley Eikenburg, Associate Publisher, Travel

Kelly Regan, Editorial Director, Travel

Publishing for Technology Dummies

Andy Cummings, Vice President and Publisher, Dummies Technology/General User

Composition Services

Debbie Stailey, Director of Composition Services

Contents at a Glance

Table of Contents

Introduction

*I*n our first *For Dummies* project — *Home Remodeling For Dummies* — we ventured with our readers down the sometimes rocky road of remodeling a home. Our goal was to prepare people for the many steps and potential pitfalls involved in planning and executing a home-remodeling project, regardless of its size or complexity. Throughout that book, "plan, plan, plan" was our mantra.

For this, our most recent offering, we've adopted an old cliché as our credo. In fact, had this not been a part of the best-selling *For Dummies* series, a more apt title may have been An Ounce of Prevention Is Worth a Pound of Cure. On the other hand, *Home Maintenance For Dummies*, 2nd Edition, does have a nice ring to it! What's more, chances are good that by the time you've had a chance to sink your teeth into this book, you'll be anything but a dummy when it comes to maintaining your home.

Your home is probably the largest investment that you'll make in your lifetime. So, it makes good sense to do everything that you can to protect that investment from deterioration caused by the forces of nature, wood-eating pests, and good, old-fashioned wear and tear. As you'll soon read, in addition to protecting the structural integrity of your home, regular maintenance will make it more comfortable, safer, and more energy efficient. And don't forget that a well cared-for home stands out in the neighborhood, and that's worth something — a bigger price tag when it comes time to sell, or simply the satisfaction of knowing that you're in charge of your home and not vice versa.

Few undertakings offer the pride and personal satisfaction that a home-maintenance job done well can. *Home Maintenance For Dummies,* 2nd Edition, is so full of information on how to care for your home, we guarantee that your cup of pride and personal satisfaction will forever runneth over.

Finally, if we've met our objective, your reading will be peppered with lots of laughter. Enjoy!

About This Book

Like most *For Dummies* books, *Home Maintenance For Dummies*, 2nd Edition, is a reference, meaning that it was written with the expectation that you would *not* read it from cover to cover over a couple of sittings. Instead, we think that you'll consider it one of the most important reference tools in your home-maintenance arsenal — like your prized hammer or wrench that you pick up and use whenever necessary.

Each chapter is divided into sections, and each section offers instructions on some home maintenance task, like

- How to fix those pesky floor squeaks
- What to do when you know you've got a leak but you don't know where it's coming from
- What cleaning solution is the best for removing mildew
- How to easily maintain those confusing machines that keep you comfortable, like your furnace, boiler, air conditioner, and water heater
- How to prevent a flooded basement and how to fix it if your last fix didn't work
- How to reduce your energy costs while improving your comfort — all in one fell swoop
- How to decide whether to do it yourself or hire a contractor

Who needs this book? Everyone — unless you're independently wealthy and you have no intention of lifting a finger to care for your home. Even then, this book could prove to be valuable. Who knows? You might just find it handy in rescuing one of your loyal servants. Seriously, if your home is an apartment, condo, single-family house, flat, co-op, cave, or hut; if you rent, own, or borrow; if your habitat is old, new, or somewhere in between, this book is for you.

Conventions Used in This Book

To help you navigate through this book and make maintenance as easy as possible, we've set up a few conventions:

- We use *italics* for emphasis and to highlight new words or terms that we define.
- We use **boldface** to indicate the actionable part of numbered steps.
- We use `monofont` for Web addresses and e-mail addresses.

In addition to these standard conventions, whenever a task takes more than a few tools, we provide a list so that you can gather everything you need before you start to work.

What You're Not to Read

We've written this book so that you can find information easily and easily understand what you find. And although we'd like to believe that you want to pore over every last word between the two yellow-and-black covers, we actually make it easy for you to identify skippable material — the stuff that, although interesting and related to the topic at hand, isn't essential for you to know. This text appears in *sidebars,* which are the shaded boxes that appear here and there throughout the book. They share personal stories and observations, but they aren't necessary reading.

Foolish Assumptions

You know what they say about the word *assume.* In any event, we've made the following assumptions about you:

- You care about the appearance and condition of your home and, hence, its value.

- You're not a home-improvement fanatic, nor are you particularly handy — you don't need to be.

- You have a song in your heart, a smile on your face, and an insatiable desire to see your home be the best that it can be.

- You don't have a warehouse full of tools and you're interested in getting only what you need. A few tools are of infinite value when it comes to home maintenance. However, the most complicated tool that you'll need is a cordless driver drill for sinking a screw here and there. The tools that you'll find yourself needing most often are a scrub brush, a paintbrush, and plenty of patience.

- You're the type who always seeks help when needed and always puts safety first when attempting a home-maintenance endeavor.

How This Book Is Organized

The chapters of this book are divided into the following parts so that you can easily find just the information that you're looking for.

Part I: Home Maintenance and You

This part introduces you to the benefits of home maintenance and to the major systems and components in your home. You can also find a series of lists to help you keep your home-maintenance tasks organized. Follow this schedule, and your home will love you for it.

Even though you don't have to read this book from cover to cover, we strongly recommend that you check out the three chapters in this part so that you have a clear understanding of what parts of your home require maintenance and why you should pay attention to them.

Part II: The Energy Envelope

Your home's envelope consists of all its exterior surfaces and associated components like windows and doors. And don't forget the attic, roof, basement, and foundation. To be comfortable inside your home, its exterior must be in secure and sound condition. Turn to this part to discover how easily you can maintain your home's exterior.

Part III: Key Systems: Plumbing and HVAC

Nothing is scarier than hearing a noise that wasn't there before emanating from mechanical equipment: a popping sound in the water heater, a faucet that suddenly sounds like it's running on a flat tire, or a screeching racket inside the deepest, darkest part of your furnace. If you want to prevent or repair these elements of your home, check out this part.

Part IV: Inside Home Sweet Home

This part contains information on the stuff that you come into contact with on a day-to-day basis within your home, such as the walls, ceilings, floors, interior doors, cabinets, countertops, and appliances, to name a few. If you never venture into another part of this book, and you accomplish a majority of the tasks contained in this part, you'll be light-years ahead of the home-maintenance curve. Part IV helps you patch walls, quiet floors, unstick doors, cure cabinet woes, and fix fireplaces. And, as an added bonus, we tell you how to keep your home and yourself safe and secure. If this book could be compared to a meal, this part would definitely be the main course.

Part V: Out in the Great Wide Open

If Part IV contains all the stuff that you see everyday *in* your home, Part V is all about what you (and others) can see *outside* your home, such as walkways, paths, patios, decks, and driveways. Think that the interior of your home takes a beating? Consider the abuse that your wood deck, concrete patio, or metal porch railing is subject to from constant exposure to sunlight, rain, wind, and snow. Wood oxidizes, cups, and cracks; concrete expands, contracts, chips, and cracks; and metal can become a full-blown science experiment when covered with rust. Fortunately, Part V is chock-full of money-saving and time-tested tips and recipes that will tame even the most ferocious home-maintenance predator in your great wide open.

Part VI: The Part of Tens

In this part, you find ten cleaning solutions you can make yourself. Not only will these recipes save you all kinds of money, but you'll actually know what's in the products you're using. We also tell you the ten home-maintenance skills you need to keep your home in tip-top shape.

Icons Used in This Book

Some information in this book is so important that we want to emphasize it by placing little pictures (called *icons*) next to certain points. Here's what the icons mean:

When we feel like telling you a little story, you'll see this icon.

We use this icon to highlight products that we've come to know and trust over the years.

This icon flags text that's important and not to be forgotten.

When we go out on a limb to suggest something you should do, we use this icon. It represents your basic good idea.

We use this icon to steer you clear of things that we don't want you to do. It points out dangers and health hazards you should be aware of.

Where to Go from Here

This book is organized so that you can go wherever you want to find complete information. Got a problem with your siding? Head to Chapter 5. Need to replace a toilet? Chapter 8 is for you. If you're not sure where you want to go, you may want to start with Part I — it gives you all the basic info you need, including vital safety guidelines and a home-maintenance plan to follow; plus, it points you to places where you can find more detailed information. You can also use the index to look up specific topics or the table of contents for broader categories. Or simply let your fingers do the walking until you find a topic that inspires you and let the games begin! This book makes for great armor — just don't get it wet!

Part I
Home Maintenance and You

The 5th Wave   By Rich Tennant

"Honey, I thought you checked with the homeowners' association before having the house painted magenta."

In this part . . .

Everyone knows that a bit of caulking or a coat of paint can make a home look better. What many folks don't know is that beauty isn't only skin deep. Both of these maintenance tasks, like most maintenance tasks, do much more than meets the eye.

In this part, we help you see beyond the obvious and show you what to look for when it comes to keeping your home fit. We also provide a home-maintenance schedule that suggests what you should do and when you should do it. Consider this a gentle reminder or two, or three. . . .

Chapter 1

Home Maintenance: What It Is and Why It Matters

In This Chapter

▶ Making your home a safer and more comfortable place to live

▶ Enhancing your home's value

▶ Saving money on repairs and energy

We grew up in house that was built by our grandfather shortly after the turn of the 20th century. Our family (all six of us) continually did maintenance on that house — painting, plastering, plumbing, repairing window screens, and a billion other tasks. Or so it seemed.

However, maintenance is not reserved for older homes. Home maintenance should begin the day the house is completed, and continue for as long as the structure exists. But please don't think that you've signed up for years of drudgery. In this chapter, we show you how home maintenance can be fast, easy, and even fun — and how it can save you money in the long run.

Keeping Up with Upkeep

Some homeowners think of maintenance as a challenge, something to take on, overcome, and, with luck, complete. Some see it as a learning experience, looking to master new skills, and, in the process, improve their home. Some get into the Zen of it, finding enlightenment in knowing — and truly understanding — the inner workings of their dwellings. And some focus on the bottom line, seeing maintenance as the preservation and enhancement of their huge home investment. Most just want their homes to look nice and work well.

However you approach maintenance (and regardless of whether you achieve insight into the meaning of your existence), you have to stay on top of your to-do list, because you need to keep little problems from becoming big trouble, because it's smart to keep everything looking good, and because keeping your home's systems working efficiently makes financial sense.

From little to big

Maintenance is not about big, time-consuming, and expensive projects. In fact, one of the most effective and worthwhile tasks — painting a room — requires only a couple of gallons of paint, a $10 brush, and a $3 roller cover. Changing the furnace filter takes two minutes. Caulking a drafty window frame is a five-minute, $5 job. Doing these little things, and doing them continuously or as needed, makes a huge difference in the appearance, comfort, and efficiency of your home.

Over time, there will be more little projects than big ones. Our advice: Do the little ones yourself. Most of them are easy to do. You'll save money, your home will look and work better, and you'll feel as though you've accomplished something.

Medium-size projects — like cleaning and adjusting your furnace, adjusting a sticking exterior door, or replacing a toilet — need to be evaluated on a case-by-case basis. To decide whether to do them yourself or hire a pro, ask yourself these questions:

✔ Do I have the right skills and knowledge?

✔ Do I have the necessary tools?

✔ Do I have the time?

If you have to say no to any one of these questions, you need to think hard before taking on the job. You may be better off hiring a pro.

Which brings us to the big projects, things like replacing the roof, re-siding, and pouring a new driveway. Unless you have some really awesome skills, solid experience, and know-how, as well as a workshop full of tools, hiring a pro is best. As a friend of ours says, "I know how to build a deck. But I've never done it before. There are people who build decks every day, people who know how to do the job right. It's worth the cost of hiring a contractor to be satisfied with the end product."

Many of our radio-show callers are homeowners who've taken on projects that are way beyond their expertise, require the purchase of expensive tools, and are taking much longer than expected. And they're not calling to share how wonderful the projects have gone. They need help putting things back together or advice on how to find someone who can get the monkeys off their backs, so to speak. Don't get caught in this trap. Be smart. Know your limitations.

All the chapters in Parts II through V contain many of the most common small and medium-size maintenance tasks that you can tackle yourself (with our help, of course). And when a task really should be left to a pro, we tell you that, too.

From inside to outside

Homes are complicated. They have many components and systems that need to be monitored and maintained (see Chapter 2). Inside, the systems include plumbing, electrical, and heating/air conditioning. Plus, you've got the foundation, structural framing, walls, floors, appliances, countertops, cabinets, sinks, bathtubs, fireplaces, and more to care for. It sounds like a lot (and it is), but you can find all the details you need in Parts II, III, and IV.

Outside, the components that require attention include windows and doors, roof, chimney, garage door, concrete, masonry, and siding. The key thing to know about problems on the outside of your home is that, if you don't attend to them, they can become problems on the *inside,* too. That's why we devote an entire part (Part V) to helping you prevent and address problems outside.

Benefiting from a Little TLC

There are five major benefits to maintaining your home well:

- Improved safety
- Increased comfort
- Enhanced home value
- Money savings
- Energy efficiency

Here's what this list tells you: that home maintenance literally pays off. To put it another way, these five big benefits prove that an ounce of prevention really is worth a pound of cure. And, as you'll soon discover, those are words to live by when it comes to your home.

To your health (and safety)

A poorly cared-for home is not just an aesthetic problem — it can hurt you:

- ✔ A rotted subfloor can result in an unexpected visit to the floor below — complete with bumps, cuts, bruises, and maybe a trip to the hospital.

- ✔ A poorly maintained furnace can leak deadly carbon monoxide gas, which is the leading cause of poisoning deaths in the United States.

- ✔ An air-conditioning system that fails in the heat of summer, or a furnace that takes a hiatus in the worst of winter, can lead to extreme indoor temperatures, which can be dangerous, or even fatal for the elderly and very young.

- ✔ A smoke detector with a dead battery doesn't work — it's literally playing with fire.

Simple home maintenance can prevent these disasters and make your house a safer place to live for you and your family. For example, the one 9-volt battery, vacuuming, and three minutes that it takes to maintain your smoke detector could prevent you from losing your home, a pet, or a loved one.

So how do you spell safety when it comes to your home? M-A-I-N-T-E-N-A-N-C-E!

Comfort: You'll miss it if it's gone

Your house contains a number of systems that make it a comfortable place to live (see Chapter 2). Most people take the comfort systems in their house for granted. They don't think about them until one of the systems breaks down. And then the result is a distinct *lack* of comfort.

You get what you pay for

Here's the first rule of home-maintenance materials: Buy the best that you can afford. Doing so gives your home the maximum benefit and protection. If you buy inferior materials, you'll likely be doing the job over again soon. Worse yet, you may end up spending a hefty sum to make repairs that otherwise wouldn't be needed had you spent a little more upfront. Not a bad proposition if you enjoy spending all your free time and spare change fixing up your home.

For example, your home's electrical system powers lights, your refrigerator, your water heater, and your washer and dryer, among other things. You may not think about your electrical system when you turn on lights; grab a cold can of soda from the fridge; take a hot, relaxing shower; or fold your freshly laundered clothes. But if that electrical system breaks down, you'll quickly realize how much of your day-to-day comfort depends on it.

Because many of these systems have motors and moving parts, they're especially vulnerable to wear and tear that, without preventive maintenance, could result in major inconvenience — and, at least at our houses, lots of swearing.

Money in the bank

Preventing a problem is almost always cheaper than making repairs after a problem occurs. And it's always less expensive to fix a little problem before it becomes big trouble. Use this as your home-maintenance mantra: "Ommmmm, smart homeowners are proactive, ommmmmm."

Avoiding more expensive repairs

Here's how the ounce-of-prevention thing works: The metal flashing that surrounds a chimney can be the source of a nasty roof leak if it's not maintained. The $20 it costs to caulk and paint the flashing is a fraction of the hundreds or thousands of dollars you would spend to repair water damage to ceilings, walls, and flooring. We bet you can't find a blue-chip stock that pays those kinds of dividends! Ka-ching!

Gaps in siding and trim around windows and doors allow cold drafts and moisture to make their way into the wood skeleton of your home. Aside from driving up utility bills, the moisture produces rot that, in turn, weakens the structural elements in your home, and provides a veritable smorgasbord for structural pests like termites and other wood ravagers, as well as creating a breeding ground for dangerous mold. These small gaps can result in thousands of dollars' worth of repairs and, if left unrepaired long enough, can actually lead to the demise of your home. The flip side: Spend five minutes and $5 to caulk the trim around a window. Your home will love you for it, and you'll love yourself for saving so much of your hard-earned cash.

Increasing efficiency

Most people know that the more efficiently a mechanical device works, the less it costs to operate. A well-tuned automobile engine, for example, delivers far better fuel efficiency than a clunker. The same holds true with many of the machines that you have around your home. Your furnace is a great example. A clean furnace filter, coupled with other preventive maintenance tasks, makes the furnace operate more efficiently, consuming less energy and making it less susceptible to breakdowns.

Energy savings equal money savings. Keeping the appliances in your home running efficiently also helps the environment — a major benefit for yourself and the planet.

Many times, improving efficiency requires the replacement of the system or appliance in question. A brand-new refrigerator is twice as efficient as one just 7 years old. A new water heater is significantly cheaper to operate than the one in your basement. (A tankless water heater is more efficient still.) Your 10-year-old air-conditioning system? Terribly wasteful! New ones must meet significantly tougher efficiency standards. The repair-versus-replace decision is complicated when it comes to appliances and energy-consuming systems. You need to consider whether it's worth repairing an old, inefficient unit and whether (and how long it will take) for the new one to pay for itself.

ANECDOTE

Roots: A good place to begin

Before there were the Carey brothers (or Carey sisters — there are two), there were the Carey parents: Morris and Alvera. We can attribute our interest in building, remodeling, and repair to our parents — a couple of dyed-in-the-wool do-it-yourselfers. Both gone now, they made one heck of a home-improvement and -repair team. They were hard working, creative, and industrious. If ever a sow's ear could be turned into a silk purse, Mom and Dad could do it.

Mom's favorite source for sprucing up the home was the local thrift shop, while the local landfill — we called them dumps back then — was Dad's hangout. After any given shopping spree, Mom would return home with unusual items, such as an old, metal milk can, an assortment of picture frames, and a light fixture or two. Armed only with her innate creativity and her infamous gold spray paint, she would convert trash into family treasures. The milk can became

a lamp, the ailing frames were transformed into sought-after antiques, and the light fixtures would rival those of Liberace. What they all had in common was their radiant gold finish, her trademark.

Meanwhile, Dad would be pulling an old piece of furniture off his truck that he "rescued" from the local landfill. His favorites were old console radios and television sets. Once, Dad took a vintage radio cabinet, tore out all the guts, and transformed it into an elegant glass cabinet that Mom used to showcase all her fine crystal and china. The hinged top that once served as the hatch to a turntable allowed convenient access to her treasures.

Be it painting, plastering, or plumbing, there was always something that needed to be done around our house. With some ingenuity, our parents showed us that these tasks could be fun. And that's something we want to show you, too.

Maintaining and increasing your home's value

If you're like most people, your home is the single largest investment of your lifetime. Besides having a place to live, you may have also made this investment with the hopes of making some money on it when you sell the house. Thus, it makes good sense (and big bucks) to keep your home in tip-top shape.

We learned a valuable term from real-estate professionals whom we encountered over the years in our building and remodeling business: *curb appeal.* This term refers to how the outward appearance of a home affects its value. A home with a roof, windows, doors, siding, fencing, and landscaping that are well cared for is more appealing to potential buyers and, hence, more valuable. Conversely, a poorly maintained home can be a real eyesore and worth significantly less than its well-maintained counterpart.

Even if you don't intend to sell your home in the near future, you need to maintain your home in order to maintain your initial investment. We've probably beat this message into the ground already, but simple repairs, like replacing a furnace filter, can make a big difference in maintaining this investment. How, you ask, can a home's value be affected by replacing a furnace filter? Seem like a stretch? Not in the slightest. With a clean filter, a furnace doesn't work nearly as hard; thus, it places less stress on the motor, fan belt, and other components. Consequently, the furnace has a longer life, and, in turn, you avoid having to replace the furnace prematurely.

Let the Games Begin!

Now that you have an idea of what it is about your home that needs to be maintained and why it's important to do so, you can use the information in this book to charge forward to tackle projects that have been on your to-do list. Keep in mind that, when it comes to project order, you should crawl before you walk and walk before you run. So as not to become discouraged or end up with a mess on your hands, we suggest that you attempt smaller, more doable projects first. This approach gives you the opportunity to get comfortable using tools and materials that may not be so familiar.

Safety first! Always have the right tools and equipment for the job and never be in a hurry. Haste makes waste and is a recipe for potential injury and poor results. We suggest that you have a look at Chapter 3 for suggestions on what projects to take on first and the basic tools that you'll need to accomplish most home-maintenance projects. Start with small projects and work your way up the ladder — literally and figuratively — to more-complex projects.

With time and experience, you'll grow increasingly more comfortable and confident wielding a hammer in one hand and a caulking gun in the other.

When all's said and done, the idea is to protect your home, save money, and have fun in the process. Who knows? You may just find that you like this home maintenance stuff. Yippee!

Chapter 2

Getting to Know Your House and Its Systems

Home maintenance reminds us a lot of the Monopoly board game. Both involve a bit of a gamble with real estate. In the game, dice decide your destiny. A favorable roll can turn you into a real-estate baron with holdings that rival those of Donald Trump. On the other hand, the wrong combination can land you straight in the pokey!

Each time you postpone a maintenance task, you're rolling the dice with your home's structural and aesthetic integrity and value. Plus, although it isn't very likely that failing to keep up your home will have you doing the jailhouse rock, sadly, there are occasions when such negligence can result in tremendous damage for which you can conceivably be held liable — not to mention the personal loss that you can suffer.

In this chapter, we show you that your home is more than just four walls and a roof; your house is actually made up of a group of systems and fixtures, all of which need your loving care and attention from time to time. We introduce you to each of these systems, which we examine in great detail throughout this book.

The Exterior: It's Nice to Fool Mother Nature

Every area of a home needs ongoing maintenance, but some areas require more care than others. At the top of the "needy" list is a home's exterior. The exterior is subject to constant deterioration thanks to the forces of Mother

Nature — the sun, wind, and rain. Consequently, it's no accident that you may find yourself spending a majority of your home-maintenance time on the exterior.

The following sections discuss the elements of a home's exterior that will, from time to time, require maintenance.

Your home's infrastructure: The foundation and floor frame

The foundation, which we discuss in detail in Chapter 4, is a key component of a home's infrastructure. The other key component of the infrastructure is the floor frame, also covered in detail in Chapter 4. Together these two support the walls, roof, and other structural elements of your home.

The foundation

Your home's foundation, whether it's a basement, a crawlspace, or a concrete slab, is the element of construction that helps a home stay put. A level foundation can usually contribute to a level floor, windows and doors that operate smoothly, and the absence of cracks in walls and ceilings. For homes with basements, the foundation also holds back earth and limits the intrusion of unwanted water.

Checking cracks before they spread and dealing with moisture control are among the most common maintenance tasks associated with a foundation.

The floor frame

The floor frame consists of floor joists and/or *girders* (beams) and the subfloor. The joists and girders travel horizontally and rest on the foundation. The subfloor consists of lumber or plywood that's fastened to the floor framing. Finish flooring (carpet, vinyl, hardwood, and so on) is installed above the subfloor.

The floor frame is notorious for the maddening creaks and squeaks that occur when traipsing across it. Aside from the fact that floor squeaks can drive you nuts, they're considered a sign of inferior construction, which can lower your home's perceived value. Although this can be true, the reality is that even the best-built homes can suffer from a squeak now and again. Thus, silencing squeaks is the most common maintenance task when it comes to the floor frame. Not far behind are preventing rot and leveling up an out-of-level floor before it damages the structure of the entire home. You can find all the information you need in Chapter 4.

Roofing and siding: Your home's protective coat

Most people think of *siding* as either vinyl or wood, but we use the term to describe a wider class of materials — whatever can be used as a finished, protective coat on the exterior walls of your home, such as brick, wood, vinyl, stucco, aluminum, or a composite siding.

Siding is, by design, expected to endure forces that simply aren't an issue with interior walls. In the children's story "The Three Little Pigs," the Big Bad Wolf didn't have a chance of blowing down the house with the brick walls. What the story failed to mention was that the Little Pig who lived in the house with brick walls made sure to keep the mortar joints in good condition, the brick well sealed, and all the gaps caulked.

Take a lesson from this smart Little Pig and follow the maintenance routines suggested in Chapter 5 for your siding. You'll discover that exterior wall maintenance is all about preserving the integrity of the siding.

We think of the roof as the fifth wall of the house. Because the roof is a horizontal surface, it's subject to all the same forces that siding is, and then some. Like siding, rain and sun are a roof's biggest enemies. Maintenance on your roof isn't much different from what you do to maintain your siding. So, we combine roofing and siding in Chapter 5.

Keeping a roof clean is one of the most important maintenance tasks. A debris-free roof improves watershed and prevents rot, mold, and fungus growth. Metal flashing at vents, chimneys, skylights, valleys, and other critical areas are most prone to leak, which requires special care. And although not officially a part of the roof, gutters and downspouts are essential to proper watershed and, when well maintained, can prevent everything from a roof leak to sticking windows and doors. Cleaning, caulking, and painting count among the most common gutter- and spout-related maintenance tasks.

Windows, exterior doors, and insulation

Without a doubt, windows and doors are two of the most important elements of a home. They give you access to the outdoors and, when armed with a key, access to the indoors! Windows and doors also provide natural light and ventilation — two of the most valuable commodities a home can have.

Keeping your eye on the doughnut

Although we were born 12 years apart, we shared many of the same teachers throughout school. One teacher who has a special place in both our hearts is Mrs. Roxie Gibbs. Mrs. Gibbs was our high school English and journalism teacher. She was your classic eyeglasses-sliding-down-the-nose, beehive-coifed, mid-length-skirted, prim-and-proper schoolmarm straight out of *Little House on the Prairie*.

One of Mrs. Gibbs's favorite adages was "Keep your eye upon the doughnut and not upon the hole." Although these words were initially a total mystery to us, we eventually discovered their meaning. What Mrs. Gibbs was so eloquently stating was to focus on the issue (the doughnut) and not the minutiae (the hole). What does this have to do with home maintenance? Plenty!

When dealing with home maintenance, concentrate on the root of a problem (the doughnut) instead of focusing on the symptom (the hole). For example, people often ask us how to keep a door from sticking. A door sticks for one reason and one reason only: The uniform gap between the door and the frame no longer exists. The gap (which should have been there at installation) allows the door to be opened and closed without interference from the frame.

The sticking door is a symptom of a larger problem, like an out-of-level floor. Accordingly, we don't want you to be stuck on the stick — rather, we want you to chew on what causes the door to stick. Are we making ourselves clear, or are you stuck? (Chapter 6 tells you all about unsticking stuck doors.)

Windows and doors

Unfortunately, windows and doors are frequently among the most maintenance-intense elements, primarily because, unlike siding and roofing, windows and doors have moving parts that suffer from wear and tear. What's more, in most homes, windows and doors are also responsible for the majority of energy loss.

Water leaks, air leaks, and condensation are a few of the most common window-related maintenance issues. As for doors, a touch of lubrication to hinges and hardware, shimming a hinge, and adjusting a strike plate or door bottom can be the saving grace to any door.

Chapter 6 offers tips on these window- and door-maintenance tasks.

An out-of-level floor can make doors and windows tough to operate and can be the cause of cracks in walls over windows and doors. If you're tired of patching cracks and wrestling with doors and windows, head to Chapter 4. Out-of-level floors have virtually nothing to do with the floor itself and almost everything to do with the foundation and soil that support it.

Insulation

Insulation is like a nice, warm blanket on a cold winter's night. It can make all the difference when it comes to comfort and energy efficiency. Insulation can typically be found in the attic, exterior walls, and floors above crawlspaces and basements. There are all kinds of insulation, ranging from treated paper to fiberglass. Over time, insulation can settle, becoming more compact and less effective. That's the bad news. The good news is that in Chapter 7 we show you what you can do about it.

Walkways, patios, and driveways

Walks and patios are to a home's exterior what halls and entertaining areas are to a home's interior. Can you imagine directing a houseguest down a hall with an uneven walking surface or trying to entertain a group of people in a room with chunks of carpet, tile, or hardwood missing? Doing so would inevitably result in a twisted ankle or a nasty fall — talk about putting a damper on a party! Why, then, would you be any less attentive to the condition of the walking and entertaining surfaces outside your home?

In the grand scheme of things, chances are good that the walks, paths, and patios that surround your home are subject to as much traffic as, or more traffic than, many spaces within your home. In addition to the safety aspects, these and other paved areas, such as a driveway or carport, can have a tremendous influence on the overall appearance (the "curb appeal") of your home. Accordingly, they should be given the same degree of attention when it comes to home maintenance.

Paths, patios, and other paved areas typically consist of concrete, brick, stone, or asphalt. None of these materials is immune to the need for periodic maintenance. Uneven surfaces, cracks of varying proportion, potholes, and staining are conditions that cry out for attention. Ironically, the need for many of these repairs can be prevented down the road with ongoing maintenance. For example, a driveway remains more resilient and water-resistant and, hence, is less likely to crack when a sealer is periodically applied.

If your driveway looks like an Indy 500 pit stop or your front walk looks like the San Andreas Fault, you can clean 'em, patch 'em, seal 'em, or even stain or paint 'em using the information found in Chapter 17.

Decks

Depending on what kind of deck you have — on grade or on the roof — the surface can consist of wood, vinyl, a composite, concrete, tile, roofing material, or a synthetic elastomeric product. (*Elastomeric* is a seamless paint or spray-on material that expands and contracts with the substrate. It's particularly popular for second-floor decks over living space where leak prevention is particularly important.) In any case, the biggest maintenance challenges are keeping the surface clean, preventing leaks, and prolonging its life by patching, painting, staining, or sealing. Chapter 18 is chock-full of information that you can use to make your deck the envy of your neighborhood.

Fences

Fences, like decks, come in all shapes, sizes, and materials. Wood, steel cyclone, ornamental iron, vinyl, concrete block, plaster, and the new kid on the block, composite fencing, are the materials most widely used. In spite of the vast array of material choices, most fences are constructed of wood, including wood posts, wood frame, and wood fence boards (or pickets).

Regardless of the material used to construct it, keeping a fence plumb (upright); preventing posts, framing, and fence boards from deteriorating or being ravaged by pests; keeping fence boards securely attached to the framing; and taking the sag out of a gate are the items that can be found on most homeowners' checklists. Chapter 18 tells you all about these tasks, and more. (If your fence is constructed of ornamental iron, go to Chapter 19 for care instructions; if it's constructed of brick, check out the tips for caring for masonry in Chapters 4 and 17.)

Retaining walls

If your home is built on anything other than a flat lot, you already know that a retaining wall holds back earth that would otherwise come crashing through your home. It can also keep your home or yard from sliding down a hill. You can also use a retaining wall to expand the "usable" area of your property by terracing a slope.

Although more and more retaining walls are being constructed of interlocking decorative block, the vast majority of residential, garden-variety retaining walls are constructed of wood posts and wood boards. The information in Chapter 6 about maintaining retaining walls can add years to the life of your retaining wall.

Ornamental iron

Ornamental iron is a fancy term for steel fencing, handrails, or other decorative steel elements. It's no surprise then that the biggest maintenance challenge associated with ornamental iron is *rust* — the reddish brittle coating that results from attack by moist air. Therefore, the key to preventing rust (and the damage it does) is to prohibit moist air and water from making contact with the steel. Painting, as you see in Chapter 19, is the most effective means of stopping rust dead in its tracks.

Unfortunately, rust may have already sunk its ruthless teeth into your helpless handrail. Before you pull out the old hacksaw to start cutting out bad spots, have a look at Chapter 19 for information on how to remove rust — chemically and mechanically — and what to do to patch the damage left in its tracks. You'll discover not only our secrets to getting rust off, but also how to prevent it from returning.

The Interior: Your Home's Insides

As with the exterior of your home, basic elements of the interior require maintenance from time to time. The following sections help you identify these elements and the ongoing maintenance they require.

The plumbing system

Of all of a home's systems, the plumbing system is likely the most demanding when it comes to maintenance. Leaking pipes, clogged drains, and a banging water heater are just a few of the many plumbing-related maintenance challenges that pop up.

Let us be the first to tell you that Chapters 7, 8, and 9 are all wet. That's because they focus on running water in the home. In these chapters, you can find out how to locate and shut off your water main, deal with your water heater, and care for wells and water softeners, as well as a bunch of other stuff.

Although the plumbing system is one of the most maintenance-intense, it really isn't particularly complex. Even beginners can easily perform the most common plumbing maintenance tasks: cleaning, lubricating, adjusting, and replacing worn parts. Make your plumber jealous by reading all about these simple maintenance tasks in Chapters 7, 8, and 9.

Pipes and water heaters

Indoor plumbing is one of the marvels of the last hundred years. It can also be the scourge of mankind when it isn't operating quite right. Banging or rattling pipes, water pressure that has been reduced to a trickle, and shower temperatures that fluctuate like the stock market — one minute it's nice and hot and the next you're playing freeze-out. Yikes!

Many factors can affect the performance of your water pipes: water pressure, scale buildup on the interior of the pipe, and a dreaded leak. Armed with the proper tools and the information in Chapter 8, all your water woes will soon be behind you. There, we tell you how to replace a clogged pipe, fix a leaking pipe, and increase water pressure. Who could ask for more?

When it comes to the water heater, what's on most people's minds is how long it'll last before it conks out. What most people don't understand is that, with a little care and maintenance, they can double or triple the life of their water heater — really! In Chapter 8, you learn that a little sediment removal from the bottom of the tank, replacement of a metal rod known as a *sacrificial anode,* and replacement of a broken dip tube (yes, there is such a thing) will keep your water heater going long after others have failed. And, as an added bonus, your utility bill will drop, and you'll get a good night's sleep if your water heater is rumbling in the middle of the night. We challenge you to find an undertaking that will have such a positive impact on so many facets of your life.

Fixtures

The best thing you can do for your sinks, faucets, toilets, tubs, and showers is to keep them clean. Chapter 8 offers straightforward guidance on this very topic.

The drain, waste, vent system

Chapter 9 discusses two essential elements of a plumbing system: running water and plumbing fixtures. Where does all the running water produced by faucets and all the waste produced by people and collected by fixtures go? Thankfully, it ends up in your on-site septic system or a municipal sewer system. The key is to get it from the fixture (tub, shower, sink, toilet, and so on) to one of these locations as quickly and as easily as possible.

The part of the plumbing system that performs this very important task is the drain, waste, and vent system. The drain and waste system uses gravity to carry wastewater and solid material to your home's main sewer line, located in the basement, in the crawlspace, or under the concrete slab.

The vent system prohibits dangerous sewer gases from making their way into your home. A "trap," or water door, at each fixture accomplishes this chore by being full of water at all times. You're probably familiar with the chrome or black plastic U-shaped pipe under your kitchen sink. What you may not know is that the same configuration exists below your bathtub and shower and is an integral part of the design of every toilet in your home.

If the foul odors don't make it into your home, where do they go? They're carried out vent pipes that are connected to drainpipes and go through the roof. The vents also serve another important function. They equalize pressure in the drain and waste system that facilitates drainage and prevents the siphoning of water from the traps.

What can go wrong? Plenty! Toilets, tubs, showers, and sinks can back up and cause chaos. What's more, slow-running drains and the foul odor that accompany them can drive you nuts. Don't wait another moment. Set yourself and your drains free with the information in Chapters 7, 8, and 9 . Don't waste another moment, because all your plumbing problems will soon be down the drain.

The heating, cooling, and ventilating systems

Heating, ventilation, and air conditioning (HVAC) — without these systems our homes would be little more than the caves that primitive civilization once occupied. How important are these systems? You tell us. Try turning off your heating system in the dead of winter or your air-conditioning system when a heat wave sends the mercury soaring above 100 degrees. It's no wonder that these systems are routinely referred to as "comfort systems" by heating and air-conditioning professionals. After all, their mission is to provide comfort, regardless of the climate or weather conditions.

There's more to a home-comfort system than heating and air conditioning, of course. Studies show that most Americans spend more than 90 percent of their time indoors, so the quality of the indoor air has as much to do with health as it does comfort. That's where ventilation comes in. Without adequate ventilation, heat, humidity, air pollutants, and odors can build up inside a home, causing serious health problems.

You can read about all these systems and find out how to maintain them in Chapter 10.

Heating

Home heating systems, also known as furnaces, come in various shapes, sizes, and configurations and are fueled by a host of different types of energy, including natural gas, oil, propane, wood, coal, and even the sun. The common system styles include forced air, *hydronic* (water), steam, gravity, electric resistance, radiant, and solar. One thing that all the systems have in common, regardless of the style or the energy that powers them, is their need for periodic maintenance.

Cleaning, lubrication, burner adjustment, and filter replacement, which we tell you about in Chapter 10, are among the most common maintenance tasks needed to keep a furnace running at peak efficiency. The more efficient a system, the less it costs to operate, the less energy it uses, and the longer it lasts.

Air conditioning

In 1902, Dr. Willis Carrier invented refrigerant air conditioning. Concerned that his new invention would receive a cool reception, he staged a boxing match to showcase this never-before-used technology. Although boxing remains a popular sport, it can't begin to compare to the phenomenon that air conditioning has become. Today, a whopping 30 million homeowners cool their homes with central air conditioning. In addition, another 18 million homeowners cool one or more rooms in their homes with a room air conditioner. That's a lot of cooling!

All air conditioners, whether window- or wall-mounted units or whole-house central air-conditioning systems, operate on the same principle. A fan sucks warm indoor air across a series of cool coils that contain a refrigerant. The cooled air is then blown back into the room. Amazingly, the refrigerant absorbs the heat and then exhausts it outdoors through another system of coils and fans.

The maintenance requirements for a home cooling system don't differ dramatically from those of its heating counterpart. In many cases, the systems are connected, sharing the same ductwork, blower, or other components. Cleaning, lubricating, and keeping the refrigerant level up are the most common maintenance tasks associated with a cooling system. (Many of these tasks should be performed by a professional, depending on what kind of system you have.) Maintain your cool by checking out Chapter 10.

Ventilation systems

There are two types of ventilation: passive and active. The former uses physics and natural air currents, while the latter incorporates some type of energized mechanical device. Passive systems can include a mechanical device so long as it isn't energized. A roof-mounted wind turbine is an example of passive attic ventilation.

Mechanically powered exhaust fans in the attic, bathroom, kitchen, laundry, and basement are active means of improving ventilation, reducing indoor humidity, removing pollutants, and improving indoor air quality.

Here, again, cleaning and lubrication top the list when it comes to maintaining a home's ventilation systems. After you read Chapter 10, you can breathe easy knowing that you can keep your home's ventilation system, and the people it serves, healthy.

Interior walls and ceilings

For the purposes of home maintenance, there isn't much that you can do to maintain interior wall structure, per se. It's the material that is on the interior walls that requires attention now and then. The same goes for the ceiling.

Drywall is the most common finish for walls and ceilings in homes built since the 1950s. Before that time, plaster was the material of choice for interior wallcovering.

Although drywall is a time- and cost-efficient building material, it doesn't have the rigidity and resistance to damage that plaster does. By the same token, maintaining drywall is a heck of a lot easier than keeping plaster in shape. A nick here, a gouge there, a hole here, and a crack there — these are, without doubt, sights that are seen on the walls and ceiling of almost any home. They're often the result of a doorknob crashing through the wall, a shift in the earth, foundation settlement, and the ever-present roughhousing by little ones.

Patching holes and cracks in walls and ceilings, cleaning grit and grime, and painting are by far the most pervasive maintenance tasks that folks encounter with their walls and ceilings. Cleaning, patching, and painting — it's all in Chapter 11.

Floors and interior doors

Floors. You can't live with them, and you can't live without 'em! Maintenance-starved floors can be summed up in three words: *squeaky, creaky,* and *dirty.* Sounds more like the members of a punk-rock group than a list of maintenance woes.

As for interior doors, they're particularly important elements in your home — particularly when they're located at the entrance to a bedroom or bathroom — if you get our drift. Do they close easily and securely? Do they stay open without the need for rocks or paperweights in their paths?

Floors

Floors get the most wear and tear of anything in a home. Cleaning is the single most effective means of cutting down on the deterioration of a floor. Frequent vacuuming and spot-cleaning can more than double a carpet's life span. And if you're looking for a way to keep the finish on your vinyl and hardwood flooring looking good, the answer is as close as a broom and dustpan. The grit and grime underfoot that we track into our homes acts like sandpaper that can turn a rich finish into a work in progress. The same holds true with ceramic tile and other types of flooring. Chapter 12 explains that when it comes to flooring, cleanliness is next to godliness.

Are squeaks in your floor driving you to the edge? You're not alone. They are, without a doubt, one of the most common home-maintenance issues and, aside from leaks, a contractor's biggest nightmare. Good news! Quieting a squeaking floor isn't brain surgery. Better news: We tell you how to do it in Chapter 4.

Doors

Open, close; open, close; slam shut! Interior doors get more than their share of use and the accompanying wear and tear. Beyond the occasional patch that needs to be made due to an errant clothes hanger or other hurling object that goes part in parcel with a disagreement between siblings (speaking from experience), door hinges can become loose, which can make a door really hard to open or close; the marriage between a latch and strike plate can become strained and prevent a door from being securely closed or locked; a pocket door can be jammed in its pocket; and it seems like sliding wardrobe doors are always coming off their tracks. So, if your home is experiencing some of these common door dilemmas, we suggest that you open the door to Chapter 12 for help on how to solve the problems once and for all. Door, er, case closed!

Cabinets and countertops

In the building trades, cabinets and countertops are referred to as finishes. We, on the other hand, like to refer to cabinets and countertops as your home's furniture. Like your home's furniture, aside from occasionally tightening a screw here or there, the biggest maintenance challenge that faces each is cleaning. Grit and grime from cooking and sticky fingers are the most common cleaning tasks with these things. The cleaning means and methods vary from finish to finish, as you can read about in Chapter 13.

Aside from keeping your cabinets looking good, cabinet doors, like interior doors, have hinges and hardware that, from time to time, need lubricating and adjusting, as do the cabinet drawer glides and hardware. After you read Chapter 13, your cabinets will, indeed, be like other fine furniture in your home.

In days gone by, countertops in most homes consisted simply of ceramic tile, plastic laminate, or linoleum with a metal edge. As with other home finishes, countertops have come a long way. Today, linoleum has all but disappeared, ceramic tile has remained strong, plastic laminate is enjoying renewed interest, and an array of solid surface materials are the rage.

Scratches in plastic laminate; stained, cracked, or mildew-laden grout; and grungy caulk are among the most common complaints that folks have about their counters. Accordingly, Chapter 13 offers solutions to all these problems and then some.

Appliances

A well-maintained appliance is both energy efficient and safe. In Chapter 14, we tell you how to maintain your cooktop, oven, range hood, microwave, dishwasher, refrigerator, freezer, washing machine, and clothes dryer, so that you get maximum efficiency and safety from them. As a bonus, we include a host of our special "people-friendly" cleaning solutions that require less elbow grease and are safer for you, your family, and the environment.

Fireplaces: Traditional and gas

Today, a fireplace is rarely used as a primary source of home heating due to its poor efficiency. Nevertheless, fireplaces remain popular because they provide a cozy atmosphere and romantic appeal. More than any other element of a home, a fireplace represents warmth and comfort.

Not all fireplaces are created equal. Fireplaces built 50 to 100 years ago were constructed of solid stone or brick. After World War II, the fireplace became more of a decorative feature than a viable source of heat. Consequently, solid stone and brick were replaced by less pricey variations, such as the free-standing metal fireplace and "zero-clearance" prefabricated models. The latter have been used almost exclusively in new construction in the last 20 years as a means of trimming building costs.

Cozy and romantic as it may be, a poorly maintained fireplace can be one of your home's most deadly elements. If you have a fireplace, following the advice in Chapter 15 is imperative. Regardless of the age or style of construction of your fireplace, you have to follow certain maintenance routines to ensure that the fireplace is safe.

The firebox, glass doors, screen, damper, spark arrestor, flue, and chimney require ongoing maintenance. Although all aspects of a fireplace are important, the integrity of the firebox and flue are of prime importance. *Creosote,* a byproduct of burning wood, can collect on the interior of a flue, and, when ignited, it can explode with the force of several sticks of dynamite. Consequently, one of the most important fireplace-related maintenance tasks is cleaning to prevent creosote buildup.

In addition to regular chimney inspection and cleaning, cleaning and adjusting the glass doors and screen, cleaning and lubricating the damper, and making sure the spark arrestor is in tip-top shape are the most common preventive maintenance tasks.

Feel like a fire? Check out Chapter 15 first! It may save your house — and your life!

Your home-safety systems

Repairing a leaking roof, quieting a squeaking floor, or making sure that your heating and cooling system is operating at peak performance are important and beneficial tasks. However, in the grand scheme of all things home, nothing is more important than making sure that your home is safe.

Home sweet home to most people consists of comfy surroundings and handsome finishes — cabinets, counters, flooring, and appliances. Yet the "bones" of a home consist of a complex system of pipes, wires, and ducts, which, often without warning, can go haywire and reduce your home to rubble.

A small electrical short can result in a disastrous house fire, and a poorly burning gas appliance not properly vented can produce deadly carbon monoxide.

If you don't have smoke detectors and carbon-monoxide alarms, install them! If you do and they aren't operating properly, fix them! A little maintenance can go a long way when it comes to smoke detectors and carbon-monoxide alarms. Vacuum them regularly, test them often, and replace the batteries at least twice a year or as needed.

The dangers associated with fire and carbon monoxide are clear. Less obvious is the devastating effect that a malfunctioning garage door or garage-door opener can have on you or someone in your home. Small children and pets can be seriously injured or killed by a malfunctioning system. Is the auto-reverse (anti-crush) function working properly? Does your system have electronic sensor beams, and are they doing their job?

Another concern for keeping your home safe relates to personal safety and security from prowlers and unwanted visitors. Have you stopped setting your burglar alarm due to repeated false alarms? The false alarms may be something as simple as a loose contact at a window or door or a failing backup battery.

Throughout this book, you can find out about maintenance tasks that will keep your systems running efficiently and safely to prevent disaster. However, in Chapter 16, we focus on some of the more common safety issues and specific steps that you can take that can save your home, your life, and the lives of your family should disaster strike. When it comes to home maintenance, maintaining your home-safety systems is job number one!

Chapter 3

Putting Together Your Home Maintenance Plan

In This Chapter

▶ Deciding what tasks to undertake now versus later

▶ Staying safe as you maintain your home

▶ Knowing when (and how) to hire a pro

*W*hen people think about owning a home, they picture warm summer afternoons relaxing on the patio, not a hot afternoon fixing the fence around it. Fortunately, there are far more fun days than workdays. But don't kid yourself: There will be work to do. Of course, we think it's the fun kind of work. And we're not alone. Many people get a great deal of enjoyment from maintaining and improving their homes.

Not a do-it-yourselfer? Not buying the work-as-fun concept? Let's talk money, instead. Maintenance is the work required to protect and maintain what is probably your single largest investment — your home. It's not optional. If it's not done (by you or by a professional), your home and its systems will slowly deteriorate, operate less and less efficiently, look worse, and, ultimately, lose real value. So, with those negative outcomes in mind, we're sure you'll agree that maintenance is necessary.

This chapter helps you prioritize your home-maintenance tasks and provides home-maintenance schedules you can follow. And if you're not a do-it-yourselfer? Well, we tell you how to find a pro, too.

Your What-to-Tackle List

Out of the enormous universe of potential projects, which ones are the most important and when should you do them? Let's talk about priorities. By setting priorities, you make sure that your most critical and financially sensible projects get done first. This may seem to be the obvious approach, but you'd be surprised by how many low-priority jobs get done before truly necessary projects.

We understand how that happens. Do-it-yourselfers are eager to get going, so they begin with whatever comes to mind first. And homeowners frequently confuse what they *want* to do with what they *need* to do. Sure, installing a pretty new granite countertop is a lot more "fun" than shoring up a crumbling foundation wall, but it won't be any fun when the kitchen starts sliding into the backyard.

We like to divide maintenance jobs into three categories:

- **Musts** are anything that threatens health and safety, violations of fire or building codes, structural weaknesses, and other critical needs.
- **Shoulds** are anything that cuts utility bills, reduces maintenance costs, or prevents a large repair in the future.
- **Coulds** are anything related to improving appearance and function.

For example, removing a dangerously obsolete (and probably overloaded), 60-year-old fuse box and replacing it with a modern circuit-breaker box (and more amperage for today's higher power demands) is, without question, a must. Reducing heating and cooling costs by adding another layer of attic insulation is a should. And wallpapering the bathroom is a could. *Voilà!* Intelligent priorities!

Musts: Safety and health

"Safety first" is more than a slogan. In all cases, safety and health issues are your number-one priorities. Don't even think about doing anything else until you:

- Install smoke detectors and carbon-monoxide detectors everywhere they should be installed — in bedrooms, in hallways, and on every level of your home.
- Purchase and install appropriate fire extinguishers for the kitchen, garage, and workshop.
- Replace all old and faulty electrical wiring. If your home was built before 1950, have the electrical system checked to make sure it isn't dangerously overloaded by the much higher power needs of a modern family.
- Install a ground wire throughout the electrical system to prevent electrical shock.

✔ Install ground fault circuit interrupters (GFCIs) on all outlets within 4 feet of a sink, on all exterior and garage outlets, and on all electrical fixtures over showers and bathtubs.

✔ Install or repair exterior lighting, for safety and security (aesthetics is just a bonus).

✔ Clean out the dryer duct and replace the lint-catching flexible duct with a smooth, rigid duct.

✔ Replace old, unsafe appliances.

✔ Have the furnace professionally serviced and repaired (or replaced) as necessary.

✔ Test for lead and asbestos, and perform any necessary abatement.

✔ Repair unsecure or wobbly handrails.

✔ Install a child-safe, auto-reversing garage door opener.

✔ Replace any untempered-glass sliding-glass doors and shower doors.

✔ Apply non-slip decals to the bottom of every bathtub.

✔ Eliminate mold and take steps to prevent regrowth.

✔ Replace or reinforce failing foundation components and broken or sagging structural members.

✔ Make any improvements — installing grab bars and ramps, widening doors, changing door levers, and so on — that are necessary to improve the safety of elderly or physically challenged people in your home.

It just makes sense to do these things before any others. After all, they're the tasks and projects that prevent fire, injury, and failure. Can you make a good argument for wallpapering the bathroom before completing every single one of these tasks? We didn't think so!

Shoulds: Reducing costs and preventing problems

Jobs that save energy and reduce utility costs come next. If you're looking to save big money and make your home significantly more efficient and eco-friendly, you should do the following tasks:

✔ Add attic insulation.

✔ Insulate heating and cooling ducts.

✔ Seal gaps around doors, windows, and pipes.

✔ Caulk around window and door frames.

✔ Install weatherstripping on exterior doors and windows.

✔ Insulate the water heater and hot-water pipes.

✔ Replace old toilets with modern, water-saving toilets.

✔ Schedule yearly furnace/boiler and air-conditioning service.

✔ Replace an old "gas-guzzling" furnace or power-gobbling air conditioner.

✔ Enhance attic and crawlspace ventilation.

✔ Replace old appliances with today's highly efficient Energy Star–rated appliances.

✔ Take steps to protect against termites and other structural pests.

✔ Replace energy-inefficient single-pane windows with new double- or triple-pane windows.

✔ Repair dripping faucets and constantly running toilets.

Doing things that prevent future problems is literally putting money in the bank. It's smart to fix a small problem before it can become a bigger, more expensive repair. If you want to do all you can to avoid trouble tomorrow, do these things:

✔ Seal any exterior gaps, including in siding and trim and around windows, doors, and pipes.

✔ Maintain and repair the roof and flashings.

✔ Monitor the condition of bathtub caulk and grout, and replace as necessary.

✔ Find and stop foundation, crawlspace, or basement seepage.

✔ Regularly clean and repair gutters, extend downspouts away from the foundation, and regrade the soil so water is directed away from the home.

✔ Repair driveway, walkway, and patio deterioration, and seal cracks.

✔ Paint exterior siding, trim, decks, and fences as needed.

✔ Repair exterior cracks as soon as possible.

✔ Trim bushes and trees away from the house.

✔ Tuck-point brick and block as necessary.

✔ Repair or replace leaking shower or tub walls.

Did you notice something about these projects? Most of them are about preventing water damage. The fact is, water and moisture are the number-one enemies of your home. Doing the jobs in this list, even if you do nothing else, will go a long way toward protecting your home's systems, structure, and value.

Coulds: Improving appearance and function

Many of the projects in this category are simple, inexpensive fixes or cleaning tasks that require what our grandfather called "elbow grease" — jobs like:

- Patching holes in wallboard
- Tightening up door hinges
- Shining up a kitchen sink
- Cleaning cabinets
- Getting rid of mildew

Others are cosmetic improvements such as:

- Painting the exterior
- Installing crown molding
- Putting in a new entry door
- Installing new carpet
- Adding a skylight
- Replacing cabinet and drawer pulls
- Installing new door hardware

And still others are practical, functional improvements such as:

- Replacing an old, tired cooktop or dishwasher
- Replacing shower tile
- Replacing a worn-out garage door
- Adding cabinet accessories like a pull-out rack
- Installing basement storage shelves
- Installing wardrobe organizational systems

Making your maintenance plan

After you know how to prioritize your tasks, it's time to make your maintenance plan:

1. **Grab a notepad and pen, and go through your home top to bottom and end to end, writing down everything you see that needs to be done, using the lists in this chapter to help you.**

    Be realistic. A 300-item list isn't going to get done. Focus on what you can do in the next six months. Promise yourself you'll make another plan at the end of the six months, and then do it.

2. **Mark each item with an M (for *must*), an S (for *should*), a C (for *could*), or an L (for *later*); then prioritize within those main categories by putting a number by the letter: M1, M2, M3, and so on.**

    Take a few minutes to make yourself a clean, easy-to-follow plan with every task or project listed in priority order. Put the *later* tasks on a separate sheet, and save them for the next plan.

Compiling your list on a computer using Microsoft Word (or a similar word-processing program) or in Microsoft Excel (or a similar spreadsheet program) will make it easier and faster to sort items and change priorities.

Done. Now get to work — and try to have fun!

Your Home-Maintenance Schedule

Maintenance performed regularly and on schedule provides optimum longevity and helps prevent potential breakdowns or malfunctions. Beyond maintenance procedures for operational sake, the primary (and most important) reason for checking, inspecting, and constantly tuning up your home is to ensure maximum safety for you, your family, and your friends.

Every home is different, so feel free to pick and choose from the following checklists. Whether you live in a typical suburban house, a condominium, a town house, a high-rise apartment, a farmhouse, or a palatial country estate, you're sure to find many items that pertain to your home.

Save manufacturers' instructions and product manuals for maintenance instructions and cleaning tips. If you don't have them, you can probably find them online at the manufacturers' Web sites.

Things to do annually

Make these tasks part of your annual schedule:

- ✔ Check for and repair bouncy or squeaky floors (Chapter 4).
- ✔ Repair insulation, weatherstripping, and air leaks (Chapter 6).
- ✔ Pressure-wash and oil or repaint wood fencing and check for rot (Chapter 18).
- ✔ Install or check termite flashing at decks and fence-to-house connections (Chapter 18).
- ✔ Inspect and test your landscape irrigation system.
- ✔ Clean and check irrigation anti-siphon valves and backflow-prevention devices.
- ✔ Check the water heater anode and the condition of the dip tube (Chapter 7).
- ✔ Check and clean water-heater burners, tank, and flue (Chapter 7).
- ✔ Clean or replace electric water-heater elements (Chapter 7).
- ✔ Clean toilet siphon jets (Chapter 8).
- ✔ Ensure that tub overflow is secure to avoid a leak at the tub (Chapter 8).
- ✔ Bleed air-logged radiators (Chapter 10).
- ✔ Professionally inspect and clean the fireplace and chimney (Chapter 15).
- ✔ Fill cracks, gauges, and nail pops in wallboard (Chapter 11).
- ✔ Repair sagging plaster at ceilings (Chapter 11).
- ✔ Scrub and touch up the paint on walls, ceilings, and cabinets (Chapters 11 and 13).
- ✔ Check and adjust the oven temperature (Chapter 14).
- ✔ Check and replace appliance lights (Chapter 14).
- ✔ Clean refrigerator-door gaskets and lubricate the hinges (Chapter 14).
- ✔ Vacuum refrigerator condenser coils (Chapter 14).
- ✔ Seal and protect tile and grout (Chapter 13).
- ✔ Update your emergency preparedness kit and provisions (Chapter 16).
- ✔ Vacuum dust off smoke alarms and carbon-monoxide detectors (Chapter 16).

✔ Check flexible gas-line connections at appliances (Chapter 16).

✔ Have your home inspected for termites or other structural pests.

✔ Have a professional check your septic tank and drain as necessary (Chapter 9).

Things to do seasonally

With different seasons come different tasks. Use the following to keep your maintenance up to date throughout the year.

Spring

Every spring, do these tasks:

✔ Check gutters and downspouts for debris and touch up the paint (Chapter 5).

✔ Check for *efflorescence* (white powdery mineral residue), fungus, and mold in the crawlspace or basement (Chapter 4).

✔ Pressure-wash and repair exterior siding (Chapter 5).

✔ Inspect exterior walls and roof for winter and seasonal storm damage (Chapter 5).

✔ Inspect the attic for signs of roof leaks (Chapter 6).

✔ Clean the roof and oil wood shingles (Chapter 5).

✔ Caulk and patch all exterior cracks and openings (Chapter 5).

✔ Caulk window trim and door frames (Chapter 6).

✔ Wash and repair holes and tears in window and door screens (Chapter 6).

✔ Adjust sticking doors (Chapter 12).

✔ Tighten and lubricate door knobs, locks, and latches (Chapter 12).

✔ Clean and preserve (or paint) your wood deck (Chapter 18).

✔ Replace the batteries in your irrigation controller and adjust the watering time.

✔ Clean, adjust, lubricate, and tighten sprinkler heads.

✔ Check for and replace damaged sprinkler head risers.

✔ Inspect railing and ornamental iron for rust and touch up the paint (Chapter 19).

✔ Clean and degrease exterior concrete surfaces (Chapter 17).

✔ Clean stained plumbing fixtures (Chapter 8).

✔ Clean faucet aerators (Chapter 8).

✔ Clean air-conditioning compressor fins and have your air conditioner serviced (Chapter 10).

✔ Clean lint from the dryer duct and from the interior of the dryer housing (Chapter 14).

✔ Inspect the washing-machine water-supply hoses and clean the filters (Chapter 14).

✔ Lubricate door hinges and drawer glides (Chapter 13).

Fall

Every autumn, do these tasks:

✔ Check gutters and downspouts for debris and touch up the paint (Chapter 5).

✔ Water-test the roof and flashings for leaks (Chapter 5).

✔ Repair (tuck-point) mortar joints around masonry surfaces (Chapter 4).

✔ Check for efflorescence, fungus, and mold in the crawlspace or basement (Chapter 4).

✔ Prepare for and prevent roof ice dams (Chapter 5).

✔ Look for loose shingles, siding, trim, or anything else that could become airborne in a winter storm (Chapter 5).

✔ Caulk and patch all exterior cracks and openings (Chapter 5).

✔ Caulk window trim and door frames (Chapter 6).

✔ Check the condition of heat-duct and water-pipe insulation (Chapter 6).

✔ Check roof decks for deterioration, damaged flashing, and waterproof integrity (Chapter 18).

✔ Clean and degrease exterior concrete surfaces (Chapter 17).

✔ Seal and protect all concrete and masonry surfaces (Chapter 17).

✔ Test the furnace, clean the burners, and lubricate pulleys (Chapter 10).

✔ Open and adjust the fireplace damper (Chapter 15).

✔ Clean and adjust the fireplace screen and doors (Chapter 15).

✔ Check the condition of the chimney spark arrestor (Chapter 15).

✔ Clean the lint from the dryer duct and from the interior of the dryer housing (Chapter 14).

✔ Inspect the washing-machine water-supply hoses and clean the filters (Chapter 14).

✔ Lubricate door hinges and drawer glides (Chapter 13).

Winter

Winterize your home by doing these things:

✔ Insulate water lines to prevent freezing (Chapter 6).

✔ Winterize your pool or spa.

✔ Turn off and drain your sprinkler system.

✔ Drain or insulate irrigation backflow-prevention devices.

✔ Install storm windows and doors (Chapter 6).

✔ Clean, oil, and store all garden tools for the winter.

✔ Clean, wrap, and store all garden furniture for the winter.

✔ Thin major trees and shrubs prior to winter to allow sunshine through during the cold months.

Things to do monthly

Every month, do these tasks:

✔ Check water-purification and water-softener filters (Chapter 7).

✔ Test the water-heater pressure and temperature-relief valve for proper operation (Chapter 7).

✔ Clean and freshen your drains (Chapter 9).

✔ Degrease and freshen your disposal using vinegar ice cubes (Chapter 14).

✔ Clean and replace furnace and air-conditioner filters (Chapter 10).

✔ Check the steam system safety valve and steam gauge (Chapter 10).

✔ Check the water level of your steam system (Chapter 10).

✔ Clean the filter on the interior of wall-mounted heat pumps (Chapter 10).

✔ Check air intakes for insect blockages and debris (Chapter 10).

✔ Clean the range-hood filter (Chapter 14).

✔ Clean your appliances (Chapter 14).

✔ Remove and clean range burners (Chapter 14).

✔ Wash and rinse the clothes-dryer lint screen (Chapter 14).

✔ Inspect, clean, and lubricate at least one major appliance per the manufacturer's instructions (Chapter 14).

✔ Deep-clean laminate surfaces (Chapter 12).

✔ Clean and brighten tile and grout (Chapter 12).

✔ Deep-clean all types of flooring (Chapter 12).

✔ Test fire-extinguisher pressure gauges (Chapter 16).

✔ Test smoke-detector sensors and alarms (Chapter 16).

✔ Test carbon-monoxide detectors (Chapter 16).

✔ Test the auto-reverse safety feature on garage-door openers (Chapter 16).

Shutting-down checklist

If you're leaving for an extended period of time, shut down your house by doing these tasks:

✔ Open outside faucets and wrap with a towel or cloth.

✔ Disconnect all liquid-propane gas tanks and safely store them away from the house.

✔ Wrap all liquid-propane regulator valves in plastic to prevent corrosion.

✔ Stop mail, newspaper, and magazine delivery.

✔ Arrange for a neighbor to check your property occasionally.

✔ Alert local police that you'll be gone.

✔ Arrange to have the lawn mowed or snow shoveled.

✔ If the electricity will remain on, put the lights and radio on timers.

✔ Remove valuables or place them out of sight.

✔ Draw the drapes and blinds to prevent people from seeing that you're not home.

✔ Turn off the well pump or close the water-main valve (Chapter 7).

✔ Open all faucets.

✔ Disconnect the *union* (pipe fitting designed to join two sections of pipe) or other quick-disconnect fitting near the water shut-off valve, to allow the maximum amount of water to drain out.

✔ Drain flexible spray hoses in sinks and hand-held showers.

- ✔ Use a plunger to push water out of all p-traps in sinks, tubs, toilets, and so on (Chapter 9).

- ✔ Turn off or drain the water heater (Chapter 7).

- ✔ Turn off washing-machine inlet hoses; remove the hoses and let them drain.

- ✔ Clear the washing-machine water valve by setting the timer for the fill cycle. Select the warm-water setting and let it run a few seconds.

- ✔ Remove the dishwasher inlet and outlet hoses. Operate the pump to clear the valve. Remove the drain hose.

- ✔ Unplug all electric appliances and electronics, both big and small.

If your home (or vacation home) is located in an unusually hot climate, be sure to do the following:

- ✔ Leave the air conditioner on and turn the thermostat up to 85 degrees.

- ✔ Leave toilet lids open to prevent condensation and mold.

- ✔ Place a tablespoon of mineral oil in toilet bowls, tub/shower drains, sink drains, and the dishwasher tub to slow evaporation and keep seals moist.

Other periodic maintenance tasks

Here are additional maintenance tasks that need to be done periodically:

- ✔ If your refrigerator is more than 10 years old, defrost and clean it every two months (Chapter 14).

- ✔ If you use your stovetop range often:

  - • Inspect electrical plug-in tips for grease or corrosion weekly (Chapter 14).

  - • Clean the removable gas burners weekly (Chapter 14).

- ✔ Run the dishwasher at least once a week to keep seals moist and prevent leaks and eventual failure (Chapter 14).

- ✔ Check and replace all exterior light bulbs.

- ✔ Put 1 teaspoon of Tang in the dishwasher soap dispenser once a week to keep the inside of your dishwasher clean (Chapter 17).

- ✔ Make sure that emergency shut-off wrenches are present at gas and water locations (Chapters 7 and 10).

- ✔ Replace smoke detectors if they're more than 10 years old or they've been operational for more than 87,000 continual hours (Chapter 16).

- ✔ Review shut-off procedures for electric, gas, and water mains (Chapters 7 and 10).

- ✔ Replace smoke alarm and carbon-monoxide detector batteries at least twice a year (Chapter 16).

- ✔ Test the backup battery on your burglar alarm at least twice a year (Chapter 16).

Paying Attention to Safety

Working around the house can be especially satisfying. It can also be extremely dangerous. Having the right safety gear (and using it), and practicing good work habits can prevent an otherwise pleasurable experience from becoming a nightmare.

The Boy Scout motto is "Be prepared." It should also be your motto when it comes to tackling home projects:

- ✔ **Know where the power, water, and gas shut-offs are, and how to use them.** Try them all at least once so you know if they're difficult to turn or hard to reach. You don't want to be figuring it out during an emergency!

- ✔ **Know where a fire extinguisher is.** Even better, keep a small one in your tool bucket. Fire is a possibility whenever you're working with torches, heat guns, electricity, or power tools, or when you're doing demolition. You never know what'll happen, and you want to be ready if you have a close encounter of the flaming kind.

Your clothing and safety gear

No one expects to look like a fashion plate when doing chores, but there's more to what you wear when you're tackling home maintenance than being comfortable. Make sure you do the following:

- ✔ **Always wear safety glasses!** And they go on your eyes, not on your head or in your pocket!

- ✔ **Wear gloves when you can.** Handling small screws and little parts is difficult with gloves on, but you can protect your hands most of the time — especially when using power tools or working with anything that can cut, puncture, scratch, burn, or squash your hands.

✔ **Always wear protective footwear.** Work boots are best. Absolutely no flip-flops or sandals. A dropped tool or falling two-by-four will truly and terribly hurt your tootsies.

✔ **Tie back your hair.** You really don't want it to get caught up in a drill or saw. Be safe and put it up in a ponytail.

✔ **Wear a shirt with short sleeves or sleeves that can be rolled up or buttoned snugly at the wrist.** Flowing sleeves are a lovely look for a garden party, and an oversized sweatshirt may be comfy, but they may get tangled in power tools, catch on corners, snag tools, and even catch fire.

Your work habits

If you don't work smart, the chances that you'll either hurt yourself or damage your home are significantly increased. Do the following to stay safe while you work:

✔ **Never work alone on dangerous projects, on ladders, or on the roof.** It's always good to have someone to help maneuver big materials, steady the ladder, or call an ambulance.

✔ **Use the right tool for the job.** Using a tool for something other than its intended use is asking for trouble. No wrench/hammers or screwdriver/drills! Remember that keeping your tools sharp and clean will produce superior-quality results. Plus, sharp and clean tools are safer to use.

✔ **Protect your work area.** A dropped hammer will mess up the floor. A spilled gallon of paint will take hours to clean up. Why risk damaging your home or its contents? Remove everything that doesn't need to be in your work area; cover whatever remains and every inch of the floor with dropcloths. A good-quality reusable canvas dropcloth will pay for itself many times over in preventing damage.

✔ **Work neatly and eliminate tripping hazards.** Keep your work area — especially the floor — free of tools, extension cords, and supplies. Put tools you aren't using in your bucket or out of the way. Bring in only the materials you need at the moment. Remove anything you no longer need for the job.

✔ **Follow basic ladder-safety rules.** Don't overreach. Position your ladder properly and on a stable surface. Never use a bucket or chair instead of a stepladder.

✔ **Keep a phone nearby while you're working.** If you break your leg falling off the ladder, you'll have to crawl only a few feet to summon help! Better yet, keep your cellphone in your pocket.

Do It Yourself or Hire a Pro? The $64,000 Question

Some jobs are either too big or too hard to do yourself, and there's no shame in hiring a pro to do them. But how do you know when you need to outsource a maintenance project? Simple! When you'll be in over your head. When you're crunched for time. When you don't have the specialized tools needed. When you won't be happy with your results. When you don't have the energy. When you don't want to be bothered. When the task requires specialized expertise.

Bottom line: If the job is going to be a pain in the butt and will exceed your skill/experience level, you're better off hiring someone who will do it right in a reasonable amount of time.

With that in mind, we think the jobs best left to experienced, expert pros include

- Furnace, boiler, and air-conditioner service and repair
- Major electrical or plumbing work
- Lead and asbestos testing and abatement
- Chimney cleaning and repair
- Foundation repairs and waterproofing and structural repairs
- Window or roof replacement
- Tuck-pointing
- Carpet and sheet-vinyl installation
- Garage-door installation

Everything else, pretty much, is up to you.

Finding a pro

The best way to find a qualified, reliable professional is to get referrals from your relatives, friends, and neighbors. Period. End of discussion. Every other way is a complete crapshoot. So ask! If someone you know has had a good experience (not just an okay one) with a particular professional, add that person or company to your referral list.

Also keep an eye peeled for trucks in front of homes in your neighborhood. Visit or call your neighbors and ask about their experiences with the contractors who've been working in their homes. Also, ask if they can recommend other types of professionals. Add the ones who receive good reviews to your referral list.

When you don't have a referral for a particular type of pro, improve the likelihood of a successful outcome by calling an established local company. Companies with roots in the community and a history of serving people in the community are unlikely to be unqualified hacks — they couldn't stay in business if they were. Plus, they'll be more familiar with homes like yours.

Check for licensing (where required), permits, and insurance. If you aren't sure what the licensing requirement is in your neck of the woods, check with your municipal and county offices. These folks can also tell you what type of insurance contractors are required to have and which permits you'll need.

When checking insurance coverage, always require certification directly from the insurance carrier, not the contractor.

For most maintenance jobs, that's the majority of the information-gathering you need to do. You're ready to move on to getting a price quote.

Getting a quote

If the job in question is really simple — such as a minor furnace service — the price is usually based on an hourly rate with a minimum service call or trip fee. The job isn't very complicated, and the price is based on a few hours of work. Often, such tasks are so inexpensive that it isn't worth getting lots of quotes — especially if you know that the company has a good reputation.

Comparing estimates for service work is a bit easier than dealing with large, complicated projects like extensive rot repair or a roof replacement. So, for most of these bigger maintenance jobs, you'll want to get extensive and detailed quotes.

After you've determined the scope of the job, ask your approved pros to estimate what the job would cost and how long it would take. Try to get two or three quotes, and make sure you're comparing apples to apples, that all the quotes encompass the same scope of work, and that all the quotes use essentially the same quality of materials.

Selecting a pro

With quotes in hand (which inevitably vary widely in price), you're ready to assess the professionalism, skill, and experience of the pros in question and evaluate their estimates.

Even small maintenance projects require the same kind of investigation and reference-checking as major remodeling projects. With your home and money at stake, you want to make absolutely sure that you've hired a reputable, professional, and qualified contractor.

Never make price the most important criteria — don't automatically choose the lowest bidder. Instead, all else being equal, you're usually better off selecting the contractor whose price is nearest the *average* of the bids.

Choose an individual or firm that you feel comfortable with. Home-maintenance projects involve a certain degree of closeness.

One final piece of advice: Never, ever, *ever* hire someone who comes uninvited to your door offering a "special deal" on driveway coating, roofing, carpet cleaning, and so on. These unsolicited visits almost always are scams, and the only thing they're going to do is take your money.

Part II
The Energy Envelope

The 5th Wave   By Rich Tennant

"I'm insulating two more houses after yours;
then I'm filling cannoli at an Italian bakery
down the block."

In this part . . .

I t's time to roll up your sleeves, put on your safety goggles, crawl on your belly, and sometimes stand on your head. It's you against one of the strongest forces imaginable — Mother Nature. Sun, wind, rain, and snow can give your home a real run for its money.

In this part, we show you how to protect your home's energy envelope: the foundation, roofing, siding, windows, and exterior doors that keep you warm (or cool) and dry.

It's not nice to fool Mother Nature. It's even worse to let her get the best of your house.

Chapter 4

Foundation and Floor Frame Fundamentals

"*A* home is only as good as its foundation." We couldn't agree more with this familiar phrase! A sound foundation keeps other parts of a home in good working order. In this chapter, we tell you how to care for this important component of your home. We show you how to keep cracks in concrete from spreading, maintain mortar surrounding brick, control excess water, and keep your basement or crawlspace dry.

The foundation bone supports the floor frame bone, and the floor frame bone supports the subfloor bone. Together the foundation and floor surround the crawlspace or basement. In this chapter, we tell you how to rid the floor system of squeaks, sagging, and unevenness and how to care for the underside to prevent fungus and rot.

Focusing on the Foundation

The foundation is a home's infrastructure. It supports the floor, wall, and roof structure. It helps keep floors level, basements dry, and, believe it or not, windows and doors operating smoothly. The foundation is also an anchor of sorts: It often travels deep into the ground, creating a structural bond between the house and the earth, which can be especially important if your home is built on anything other than flat ground or is in an area prone to earthquakes.

Interestingly, the origin of many leaks and squeaks can be traced to the foundation. A cracked or poorly waterproofed foundation, for example, can result in excess moisture in a crawlspace or basement. Without adequate ventilation, this moisture can condense and lead to, at best, musty odors, leaks, and squeaks, and, at worst, rotted floor framing.

There are different types of foundations and different foundation materials. The foundation of your house may be a slab, a basement, or a crawlspace, and it may be made of poured-in-place concrete, brick, concrete block, or stone. With each of these configurations come a host of specific maintenance routines that can safeguard your home's integrity.

Types of foundations: Slabs, basements, and crawlspaces

The area below the main floor and within the foundation walls can consist of a concrete slab, a crawlspace, or a basement.

Almost all houses have one of the following foundations; some have a combination — slab in one area, for example, and a basement in another. But only a very few homes in the developed world still lie directly upon the ground without the aid of a proper foundation.

✔ **Slabs:** Slab is short for *concrete slab*. A slab floor (see Figure 4-1) is one made of concrete poured directly onto the ground (poured in place). Slab floors are very rigid, so they don't give the way a wood floor does, making them prone to cracking. Unlike wood, concrete floors never squeak and don't rot.

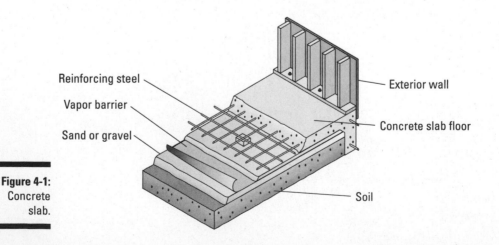

Reinforcing steel

Vapor barrier

Sand or gravel

Exterior wall

Concrete slab floor

Soil

Figure 4-1:
Concrete
slab.

✔ **Basements:** Today, basement walls are commonly constructed of concrete block or solid concrete (which is poured in place). In the past, basement walls were sometimes constructed of brick as well. We prefer solid concrete, but, with proper engineering, concrete block is every bit as strong as solid concrete.

✔ **Crawlspaces:** If you don't have a slab foundation, you have a wood-framed floor. And if you don't have a basement, the void between the ground and the underside of a wood-framed floor is known as the *crawlspace.* The clearance helps to prevent rot and termite attack that can occur when wood and dirt come into contact with each other.

Why the name *crawlspace?* Because you can stand up in a basement but not in a crawlspace. In a crawlspace, you have to crawl. We never admitted to being rocket scientists.

Foundation materials

The most common foundation materials are solid concrete, brick, concrete block, and stone. Each has its own advantages and disadvantages, as the following list explains:

✔ **Solid concrete (see Figure 4-2):** Solid concrete foundations are made of a mixture of cement, sand, rock or gravel, and water. When poured into forms and left to dry, this pancake-batter-like blend becomes unbelievably rigid. Steel reinforcing bars are used within the concrete to create added strength. Because of its rigidity, concrete can crack when the earth moves, which can lead to foundation shifting and cracks that can undermine the home's structural integrity. Water leaks also can result.

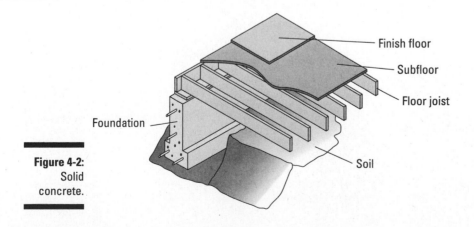

Figure 4-2:
Solid
concrete.

Finish floor

Subfloor

Floor joist

Foundation

Soil

- **Concrete block (see Figure 4-3):** Concrete-block foundations are very popular because they can be built by anyone who can lay one block atop another (making the concrete block the DIYer's foundation material of choice). Unlike brick, large holes within the blocks allow for steel reinforcing and mortar — both of which add super strength to the finished wall. Each block is joined with mortar on all four sides. Mortar has a tendency to deteriorate or crack (or both) over time and needs to be regularly maintained. Cracks in mortar can allow leaks.

- **Brick:** Brick foundations aren't common today. Their strength is inferior to that of other foundation materials, because they normally don't contain steel reinforcing. Old brick foundations still exist, but they're being replaced or retrofitted with concrete as they begin to fail.

If your foundation is built of brick (more likely if your house was built before the 1930s), be sure to read the sections of this chapter on dealing with *efflorescence* (lime buildup resulting from water evaporation), moisture control, grading and drainage, and especially tuck-pointing. If your brick foundation is not reinforced with steel (and it probably isn't) or it's crumbling, consult a structural engineer right away to determine what can be done to improve the integrity of the foundation.

Note: An unreinforced brick foundation in good condition can be reinforced by capping the foundation with concrete reinforced with steel.

- **Stone:** If a foundation is composed of massive chunks of granite, the foundation is probably incredibly strong — the Egyptians proved that. Other than granite, though, just about every other kind of stone foundation can be compared to brick. And, like brick, stone foundations usually lack a key element — reinforcing steel.

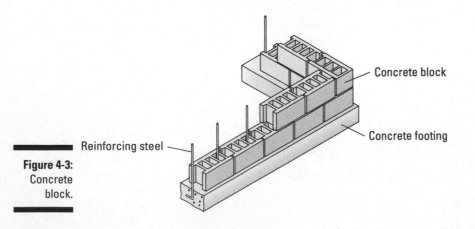

Figure 4-3:
Concrete
block.

Concrete block

Concrete footing

Reinforcing steel

Fixing Common Foundation Problems

A variety of maladies can occur on all the different types of foundations: efflorescence, cracks, seepage, *spalling* (chipping) and disintegration (caused by water getting into the foundation and freezing and thawing), and settling. Fortunately, we tell you how to deal with all these problems in the following sections.

Is there a fungus among us? Dealing with efflorescence

One of the most common foundation ailments is a white powdery substance that appears on the ground under your home, on the floor framing, or on your foundation or basement walls. Although most people mistake the white powder for a fungus (fungus is typically green or black), it's really efflorescence, a growth of salt crystals caused by evaporation of salt-laden water.

Efflorescence appears when mineral salts in the concrete or mortar leak to the surface. Although efflorescence is not particularly destructive, it is unsightly and can, in some cases, result in splintering or minor deterioration of the surface it grows on.

To remove efflorescence, follow these steps:

1. **Using a wire brush, remove as much of the efflorescence as you can.**

2. **Using a nylon brush, apply a vinegar solution (1 cup vinegar in 1 quart water) or, for really tough jobs, use a muriatic acid solution (1 cup of muriatic acid in 9 cups of water).**

   Muriatic acid is swimming pool acid. You can find it in swimming pool supply stores as well as many hardware stores and home centers.

    Working with acid can be dangerous. Always wear safety goggles, rubber gloves, and protective clothing, and always have plenty of ventilation. Add the acid to the water in a plastic bucket. Adding the water to the acid can produce a dangerous reaction.

3. **Allow the solution to stand for 10 to 15 minutes, but don't let it dry.**

4. **Thoroughly rinse the area with fresh water.**

   More than one application may be required to achieve the desired result.

Unless the soil in your area is particularly alkaline, efflorescence will usually cease to exist after the concrete or mortar is a couple of years old. If the efflorescence continues to rear its ugly head, check out the nearby sidebar.

Getting rid of the repeat offender: Efflorescence that won't go away

If the efflorescence continues to appear, you can usually solve the problem by sealing the concrete, masonry, or stone with a penetrating concrete sealer. Use a high-quality silicone concrete and masonry sealer. These sealers are generally clear and last for six months to a year depending upon the climate.

We don't recommend using inexpensive "water seals" because they don't offer the high level of protection that better-quality, pricier products do. Keep in mind that you need to apply the cheaper stuff more frequently, which generally ends up costing more money in the long run.

You can apply concrete sealers with a brush, roller, or a pump garden sprayer. Make sure that the concrete is clean before you seal it, though. A good power washing with a pressure washer or water blaster prior to application of the sealer offers the greatest penetration and lasting quality.

Being wise about cracks

Foundations are rigid and tend to crack over time. Minor cracks, though unsightly, are not normally cause for alarm. Major cracks, on the other hand, indicate substantial movement and can undermine the home's structural integrity. Therefore, you can't just ignore cracks in a foundation or concrete slab. Filling in these cracks and stopping them from spreading is essential to preventing serious structural issues in your foundation.

If your foundation or structural slab has an excessive number of smaller cracks or cracks that are larger than $1/4$ inch in width, have it examined by a structural or civil engineer to assess the extent of the damage and to determine the source. If the damage is severe, consult a geotechnical or soils engineer, who can suggest solutions to correct the problem once and for all.

Sealing cracks in concrete foundations and slabs

Even in the best of conditions, concrete moves a fraction of an inch here or there, not always resulting in a crack. And, believe it or not, concrete expands on hot days and shrinks when the weather is cold!

Therefore, when patching cracks in concrete, use a product that gives a little. The more elastic the product, the less likely a crack will reappear. One of our favorite patching products for cracks that are wider than $1/8$ inch is a vinyl concrete patch, which usually comes packaged dry in a box.

To repair a small crack, follow these steps:

1. **Clean the area and get rid of any loose chips.**

   For cracks wider than ¹/₈ inch, use a small sledgehammer and a cold chisel to chip away loose material, as shown in Figure 4-4.

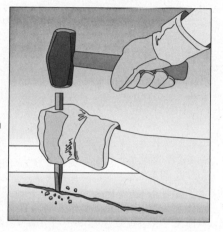

Figure 4-4: Chipping away loose material in a crack.

2. **Mix the concrete patch to the consistency of a thin paste.**

   We like to mix the dry patch powder with latex instead of water to give the product some added elasticity and adhesion. You can find latex additives, like patching compounds, at most hardware stores or home centers. Also, mix only a small amount of paste at a time because most products tend to dry pretty quickly.

3. **Mist the crack with water and then trowel the patching paste into the crack with a trowel.**

   Wetting the crack with water before installing a patching product prevents the moisture in the patch material from being drawn out by dry concrete, which causes the patch material to crack and not form a solid bond.

   If the existing concrete surrounding the patch is rough, you can match the finish by sweeping it with a broom.

4. **Use a trowel to scrape away any excess paste to create a smooth and uniform finish.**

5. **Clean up your tools and buckets immediately to avoid the patching compound drying in and on them.**

If you can't find vinyl concrete patch material, mix one part Portland cement to three parts sand; then add enough concrete bonding agent to make a stiff mixture about the consistency of mashed potatoes. Take a small part of the mixture and add more bonding agent so that it becomes a soupy consistency. Brush the soupy mixture into the crack using an old paintbrush, and then pack the stiff mixture into the crack with a metal trowel. Use the trowel to create a smooth finish.

To repair large gaps ($^1/_4$ inch or greater) in concrete (such as those between a concrete slab and foundation wall) that are not structural in nature and don't require advice from an engineer, use a latex caulk that contains silicone or a polyurethane caulk. You pump these products into the joint with a caulking gun; the caulking products remain pliable to allow for ongoing expansion and contraction. (Because most of these caulking products are self-leveling, no troweling is required.) Be sure to lightly spray the patch with water twice a day for a week to help it cure and prevent cracking.

Tuck-pointing brick and block foundations

Before the 1930s, bricks were used extensively to construct foundations. Today, however, if a foundation doesn't consist of solid concrete, it's probably constructed of concrete block. In either case, brick and block have one thing in common: They're both joined together using *mortar,* a combination of sand and cement.

Unfortunately, over time, mortar tends to deteriorate. Not only are cracked and deteriorating mortar joints unsightly, but they also diminish the integrity of the surface and can allow water to get behind the brick or block and cause major damage. You can avoid these problems by tuck-pointing the brick or block foundation, which means removing and replacing cracked or missing mortar.

If the area is manageable, any do-it-yourselfer can easily perform the task by following these steps (shown in Figure 4-5). *Note:* If the cracked or deteriorating mortar is extensive — an entire foundation, wall, or wainscot — leave the tuck-pointing to professionals.

1. **Chip away cracked and loose mortar using a slim, cold chisel and a hammer; remove the existing material to a depth of approximately $^1/_2$ inch.**

   Be sure to wear safety goggles to avoid catching a piece of flying mortar in the eye. Use the cold chisel slowly and carefully, to avoid damaging the surrounding brick. Clean up all the loose material and dust using a brush after you finish chiseling.

2. **Prepare your mortar and allow the mix to set for about five minutes.**

   You can buy mortar premixed, or you can create your own batch using one part masonry cement and three parts fine sand. In either case, add enough water to create a paste — about the consistency of oatmeal. It's best to keep the mix a touch on the dry side. If it's too runny, it'll be weak and will run down the wall, making it difficult to apply.

3. **Brush the joints with fresh water.**

   Doing so removes any remaining dust and prevents the existing mortar from drawing all the moisture out of the new mortar. Otherwise, the mortar can be difficult to apply and will most likely crack.

4. **Apply the mortar using a pie-shaped trowel called a *pointing trowel*.**

   Force the mortar into the vertical joints first, and remove the excess (to align with the existing adjacent mortar) using a brick jointer. The brick jointer helps create a smooth and uniform finish. After all the vertical joints are filled in, tackle the horizontal ones.

   Avoid applying mortar in extreme weather conditions because the mortar won't properly set up.

5. **A week or two later, after the mortar has had the opportunity to set up, apply a coat of high-quality acrylic or silicone masonry sealer to the entire surface (brick, block, and mortar).**

   The sealer prevents water damage, which is especially important if you live in an area that gets particularly cold. Unsealed brick, block, and mortar absorb water that freezes in cold weather. The water turns to ice and causes the material to expand and crack. Periodic sealing prevents this situation from occurring.

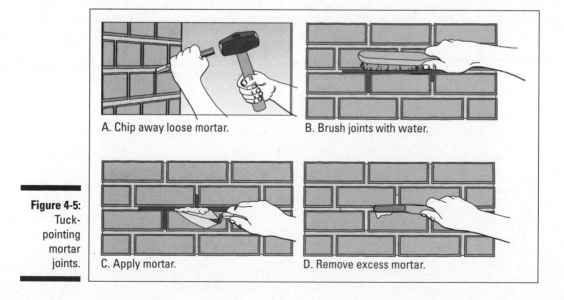

Figure 4-5: Tuck-pointing mortar joints.

A. Chip away loose mortar.

B. Brush joints with water.

C. Apply mortar.

D. Remove excess mortar.

Preventing moisture under your home

If you see efflorescence (see the earlier section "Is there a fungus among us? Dealing with efflorescence") on your basement walls and/or crawlspace and your crawlspace is perpetually damp and mildewy, you have a moisture problem.

What's a little water under the house going to hurt, you ask? Lots! Aside from turning a trip into the crawlspace into a mud-wrestling match or your basement into a sauna, excess moisture can lead to a glut of problems such as repulsive odors, rotted framing, structural pests, foundation movement, efflorescence, and allergy-irritating mold. We can't stress enough the importance of doing everything you can to keep excess moisture out from this area of your home.

Rooting out the cause of the moisture

A musty or pungent odor usually accompanies efflorescence and excessive moisture. Accordingly, a good sniffer proves invaluable in investigating the problem. Here are common causes of moisture:

- **Leaks in water and sewer lines under the home:** A failing plumbing fitting or corroded pipe is often the culprit. Fitting a replacement or installing a repair sleeve around the damaged section of pipe almost always does the trick. (See Chapter 8 for information on how to perform these maintenance tasks.)

- **A leaking toilet, tub, or valve located in the walls above:** Although a leaking toilet is often visible from above, most leaks must be searched out from below the floor. When it comes to finding the cause of a damp basement or crawlspace, leave no stone unturned.

- **Overwatering planters surrounding the house:** Adjusting watering time, watering less often, installing an automatic timer, and adjusting sprinkler heads are the simplest means of solving this problem. Better yet, for planters next to the house, convert the traditional sprinkler system to a drip irrigation system. Doing so not only helps dry things out under the house, but also makes for a healthier garden and conserves water as well.

- **Poor or nonexistent floor insulation:** Poor floor insulation can be another contributing factor to heightened condensation or dampness in a crawlspace or basement. (See Chapter 6 for more information on insulation and the importance it plays.)

Diverting water from the foundation

Keeping water out of the crawlspace or basement is critically important. You can acquire the necessary protection in several ways.

Making the grade

Be sure that the soil around your home slopes away from the foundation. The slope helps to divert most irrigation and rainwater away from the structure.

The earth within 30 inches of the foundation should slope down and away at a rate of $\frac{1}{10}$ of an inch per foot. We think that $\frac{1}{4}$ inch per foot is better.

If you're having a difficult time determining the slope, use a measuring tape and a level. Rest one end of the level on the soil against the foundation and point the opposite end away in the direction that the ground should slope. With the bubble centered between the level lines, use the measuring tape to measure the distance between the bottom of the level and the top of the soil. For example, if you're using a 3-foot level and you're establishing a grade of $\frac{1}{4}$ inch per foot, the distance between the level and the soil should be at least $\frac{3}{4}$ inch.

To grade the soil around your home, you need a pick, a shovel, a steel rake, and a strong back. You also need a homemade tamp that consists of a block of wood attached to a wood post that serves as a handle. Use the pick to loosen the soil and to break large clumps into smaller, more manageable soil that you can grade with the steel rake. Rocks and large clumps should be removed and replaced with clean fill dirt that can be well tamped. After you complete your grading work, use a garden hose to wet down the area to further compact the soil. Wetting down the area also gives you an opportunity to test how the soil drains.

Build up your grading with well-tamped dirt and not loose topsoil, which easily erodes.

Paths and patios should slope away from the foundation, too. A patio or path that slopes *toward* the home discharges water into the basement or crawlspace, a condition that breeds foundation problems and structural rot. Unfortunately, the only sure way to correct this problem is to remove and replace the patio or path, and that can get really pricey.

Using gutters

Contrary to what you may think, rain gutters are more than a decorative element for the roofline of a home. Their primary purpose is to capture the tremendous amount of rainfall that runs off the average roof. Without gutters, rainwater collects at the foundation and, consequently, ends up in the crawlspace or basement. So, if you don't have gutters, install them. And if you do have gutters, keep them clean. (See Chapter 5 for more information on cleaning gutters.)

Make sure that your gutters and downspouts direct water a safe distance away from the house. Even worse than not having gutters and downspouts is having downspouts that jettison water directly onto the foundation. We recommend piping the water 20 feet away from the foundation. You can use a length of rigid or flexible plastic drainpipe (without perforations) to carry water away from the downspout outlet to a safe location. Better yet, to avoid an eyesore and a potential trip hazard, bury the drainpipes below the ground.

Giving the problem some air: Automatic foundation vents

Ventilation is another effective means of controlling moisture in a crawlspace or basement. You can use either passive or active ventilation:

- ✔ **Passive ventilation** doesn't use mechanical equipment. Foundation vents (metal screens or louvers) and operable daylight windows for basements are the best sources of passive ventilation.

- ✔ **Active ventilation** involves mechanical equipment, such as an exhaust fan.

Passive ventilation should always be your first choice because it allows nature to be your workhorse and doesn't necessitate the use of energy to drive the mechanical device. You save on your utility bill and help the environment by not relying on fossil fuels.

If you use passive ventilation, you must keep the vents clean to allow maximum airflow. You may need to thin nearby shrubbery, vines, and ground cover from time to time. If vents are clear and moisture is still a problem, you may be able to add additional vents. Because adding vents can affect the aesthetic and structural elements of the home, consult a qualified engineer for this project.

All the passive ventilation in the world may not be enough to dry out some problem basements. In this case, install an active source of ventilation, such as an exhaust fan. Installing an exhaust fan requires some minor carpentry and an electrical source. (See Chapter 10 for more information on ventilation.) Never hesitate to use active ventilation when your crawlspace or basement needs it.

Installing a vapor barrier: Crawlspace finishing systems

Excessive dampness in a crawlspace or basement can condense, causing floor framing to become damp and covered with fungus, efflorescence, and rot. To avoid this damage to the floor framing, you can install a vapor barrier consisting of one or more layers of sheet plastic (6-mil Visqueen) on top of the soil in the crawlspace or basement (see Figure 4-6).

If you'd rather have someone else take on this less-than-desirable-job, an entirely new industry has cropped up consisting of firms that specialize in crawlspace finishing systems. The average system consists of a sheet plastic that is about ten times thicker than the DIY 6-mil stuff. They also use industrial-strength tape, caulking on the walls, and an assortment of other tools and techniques that will make your crawlspace almost livable. Check in your local Yellow Pages or search online for "crawlspace finishing systems."

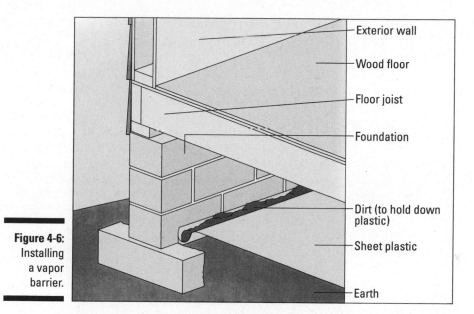

Figure 4-6: Installing a vapor barrier.

Labels on figure:
- Exterior wall
- Wood floor
- Floor joist
- Foundation
- Dirt (to hold down plastic)
- Sheet plastic
- Earth

Lap the plastic a minimum of 6 inches and seal the seams with duct tape. Cut around piers and along the inside edges of the foundation. In severe cases, you can run the plastic up the sides of piers and the foundation and secure it with duct tape or anchor it with a line of soil at the perimeter.

Just because you installed a vapor barrier doesn't mean that your work under the house is done. With the plastic in place, you have a nice, dry surface on which to work to remove efflorescence or mold that has propagated on wood framing. Wearing safety goggles, use a wire brush and a putty knife or paint scraper to clean the affected areas. (Also, see "Is there a fungus among us? Dealing with efflorescence," earlier in this chapter.)

As you remove efflorescence or mold, have a blunt tool handy, such as a flat-head screwdriver, to test for evidence of rot. If you can insert the blade of the screwdriver into the wood fibers using moderate pressure, it's time to call in a pest-control specialist to make an inspection and suggest needed repairs.

Wood framing that was previously damp but not severely damaged should be treated with a wood preservative that contains a pesticide such as copper or zinc naphthenate. This wood preservative is a liquid that you can brush on with a disposable paintbrush.

Use extreme caution when working with wood preservatives that contain pesticides. They can be hazardous to your health — not to mention the fact that they have a fierce odor for the first week or so. Follow the manufacturer's instructions on the label to the letter.

Saying oui to a French drain

If the advice we give in the previous sections doesn't help, and you're still faced with a crawlspace or basement that looks like the La Brea Tar Pits, it's time to call in a soils engineer to determine whether the condition requires the installation of a *French drain,* an elaborate drainage system that consists of a trench filled with rocks and a perforated drainage pipe. The rock-filled trench, acting like a drainage ditch, collects water that easily travels through the rock and down to the pipe. The holes in the bottom of the pipe allow it to collect the water and direct to a point where it can be safely discharged.

If you already have a French drain, it needs maintenance. Clean the inside of the pipe once a year using a *pressure cleaner,* a high-powered water blaster with a hose and nozzle for specific use within drainpipes; you can rent this equipment from a tool-rental company. If you don't want to clean the French drain yourself, have a plumbing contractor or a sewer- and drain-cleaning service do the job for you.

Tackling spalling and disintegration

Spalling, or chipping, occurs when water gets into the foundation, freezes, expands, and breaks away small pieces of the surface. Disintegration occurs for the same reason or can be due to attack by salt. Poorly mixed concrete is another cause of both of these conditions.

You can repair both spalling and disintegration with a latex patching compound. Prevent spalling from happening in the future by applying a protective sealant, which helps to prevent salt air, water, and snow melt from attacking the foundation surface.

Not settling for settling

When the earth moves, so does the foundation — and so will the entire home. The result can be as simple as a squeaking floor, or it can cause major cracking in the foundation and every other part of the home. Doors and windows can stick, glass in windows can break, and even sinks can chip.

Minimize damage by contacting a structural engineer as soon as you notice one of these symptoms. Repairs of this nature are always expensive, but if left unchecked, they can end up costing ten times more. With proper intervention, you may be able to slow and even prevent future shifting.

Keeping Your Basement Dry

Finished or not, one place you don't want water is in your basement. Besides yucky dampness, smelly mold, and funky fungus, there's rust. Don't worry about being all wet — we have solutions.

Basement water collection systems: The sump pump

The most common and effective basement water collection system is the sump pump. Basement water is directed, via drainage trenches and/or sloped floors, to a recessed cavity in the floor known as a *sump*. The sump cavity is outfitted with a drainage pump that draws water in the sump and pumps it up and out of the basement (or in some cases a crawlspace) to a safe discharge location. The sump pump is activated by a float valve; when the water in the sump rises, so does the valve, activating the pump. The pump continues to discharge water from the sump until the level drops enough to turn the float switch off.

Be sure to frequently check the float to ensure that it's clean and moves freely. Every fall, check it by filling the sump with water.

Sump pumps run on 110-volt power, which often fails in heavy rains. If your system has a battery backup, make sure the battery is in good condition by running the sump a second time with the house power off. (Replacing a battery is a lot less expensive than a flooded basement.)

Check your owner's manual for motor maintenance. Older sump-pump motors require minor lubrication.

The discharge line that travels up and out of the basement contains a *check valve,* which prevents discharge water from traveling back into the sump. This valve can occasionally become frozen shut. If, during your test, everything seems to be operational, but water remains in the sump, the check valve may need to be replaced.

What to do when it floods

Try as you might, the day may come when your basement actually floods. When that happens, you need to minimize the damage by doing the following:

- ✔ Turn off the electricity and call your electric company to report the flood.

- ✔ Turn off the gas to the water heater and furnace.

- ✔ Call your insurance company and report the circumstances.

- ✔ Arrange for remediation and cleanup immediately.

- ✔ Remove salvageable items as quickly as you can, and discard items that you can't clean or that are contaminated.

  Protect yourself from sewage and other types of deadly contamination with hip boots, gloves, and goggles. And limit traffic in contaminated areas.

- ✔ If your basement flooded because of a sump-pump failure, call a plumber.

- ✔ After the water is gone, run dehumidifiers and fans until the units collect only a small amount of water over the course of a few days. Initially, the dehumidifiers will collect buckets of water. It may take several days — or longer — for the majority of the moisture to be collected.

Prematurely draining a basement that was fully flooded due to a natural disaster could cause a collapse. The flood waters in the saturated soil exert a tremendous amount of pressure on your basement walls, and the water within the basement is needed to resist that pressure. You have to allow the water in the soil to evaporate and seep deeply into the ground before your basement can be pumped dry; this evaporation can take a week or more, depending up how saturated the soil is.

The Floor Frame

If plywood were strong enough, we wouldn't need a framed structure beneath it for support. Even better, there wouldn't be anything beneath the plywood to go squeak in the night. Despite all the strength that the floor frame provides, it's plagued with inherent problems. Builders have two fears in a newly built home — leaks and squeaks. A one-story home with a slab floor solves half the problems. Does that tell you anything about how inherent the problem really is?

Floors that go bump in the night

No matter what kind of finish flooring you may have — carpet, vinyl, tile, or hardwood — unless your home is built on a concrete slab, underneath it's wood. And it's that wood that causes the squeaks — well, sort of. Usually, the squeak is a loose nail rubbing inside the hole it was originally driven into.

Lumber used to build homes contains a certain degree of natural moisture, which makes the wood easy to cut and minimizes splitting when it's being nailed together. Unfortunately, as the wood dries, it shrinks — a natural process that can take years. When the wood shrinks enough, once tightly seated nails can loosen and rub when the wood flexes below the pitter-patter of foot traffic, creating the familiar irritating sound: a floor squeak.

Boy, have we got good news for you: Floor squeaks aren't difficult or expensive to repair, and with a little guidance, you can avoid the frustrating part of the task: actually finding the cause of the squeak.

If you have company coming or you're expecting houseguests for a week and you don't have time to make the repair, try this temporary fix: talcum powder. We've found that talcum powder works particularly well in quieting a squeaky hardwood floor or wood stairs. Sprinkle a generous amount of the stuff wherever the floor makes noise. Work the powder into the joints and around any exposed nail heads. Make sure that you completely remove the excess powder, because it can make the floor dangerously slippery. The relief lasts for a few weeks or months.

First up: Finding the squeak

The first step in repairing a floor squeak is to find the nail that's rubbing up against the wood floor — a task akin to finding a needle in a haystack. Here's a trick that we use to pinpoint a floor squeak so that we can make a repair: Use a short length of garden hose as a stethoscope. Hold one end of the hose to your ear and the other end on the floor while someone else walks across the floor to make it squeak (see Figure 4-7).

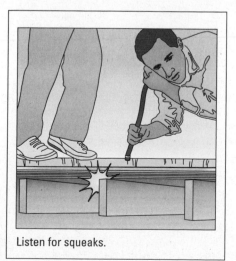

Figure 4-7:
Finding floor squeaks.

Listen for squeaks.

If you can listen to the floor from a basement or subarea, the makeshift stethoscope yields more accurate results.

Fixing the squeak

If the problem is a loose *subfloor* (the wood floor beneath the carpet, vinyl, hardwood, and so on), the repair can get sticky depending upon the type of finish flooring you have. However, if access below is available (that is, you can get to the subfloor through the basement or crawlspace), installing a wood shim shingle between the subfloor and the floor joist is a quick and easy means of preventing the subfloor from flexing, and it quiets the squeak. Just squirt some carpenter's glue on the thin end of the shingle and tap it in with a hammer (see Figure 4-8).

Figure 4-8:
Tapping in a shingle with a hammer.

Tap in shingle with hammer.

Another means of quieting a squeaking floor by preventing it from flexing is a nifty gadget called a Squeak-Ender. It consists of a metal plate and threaded-rod assembly that's screwed to the underside of the subfloor and a steel bracket. You slip the bracket beneath the joist and over the threaded rod; then you tighten a nut onto the rod to pull down the floor and close the gap. For more information on the Squeak-Ender, go to www.squeakender.com or call 800-854-3577.

If access below is not available, after you locate the culprit nail, the next step is to create a better connection. Don't use nails to make the repair — use screws. Just follow these steps:

   1. **Locate the squeak using the method discussed in the preceding section.**

2. **Near the existing squeaking nail, drill a small pilot hole through the carpet, pad, and wood subfloor and into the floor joist.**

   The *floor joist* is the horizontal floor framing member that the wood subfloor is attached to. Drilling a small pilot hole makes the job easier. You can leave the old nail in place, or, if it's loose, remove it using a nail puller or pry bar.

3. **Drive a construction screw into the pilot hole, through the carpet, pad, and so on (see Figure 4-9).**

   When working on a hardwood floor, *countersink* (recess) the screw head so that it can be concealed with hardwood putty. Use a putty knife to install hardwood putty. Touch up the floor finish with 400- to 600-grit wet/dry sandpaper.

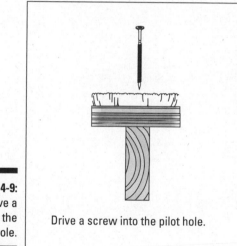

Figure 4-9:
Drive a
screw in the
pilot hole.

Drive a screw into the pilot hole.

We recommend construction screws because they're easy to drive and they grip like crazy. You can purchase ones with a finish head (like a finish nail), which makes them a particularly good choice when working on a hardwood floor. You simply countersink them slightly and putty over them. You can also drive them directly through the carpet, pad, and subfloor and into a floor joist. A construction screw's course threads and really sharp tip make it the perfect fastener for old, dry wood. The sharp tip gets through harder lumber easier, and the course screw threads go in faster and hold better.

If you do decide to use nails, choose a ring shank nail, which has a barbed shank for superior holding power. (Ask a clerk at the hardware store to help you find these nails if you don't know what they look like.) Like construction screws, ring shank nails can be driven through the carpet and pad; however, due to the size of the nail head, they aren't a good choice for hardwood flooring.

If the squeak persists, it may mean that your foundation has settled, in which case pier post shimming may be required. This process is similar to installing a shim shingle (discussed earlier). Instead, the shingle is inserted between the top of the pier post and the bottom of the girder (see Figure 4-10). Coat the end of the shingle with glue and tap it in snuggly using a hammer.

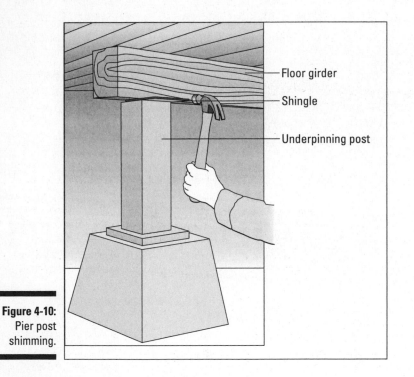

- Floor girder
- Shingle
- Underpinning post

Figure 4-10:
Pier post
shimming.

Still struggling with a squeaking floor? Major foundation settlement or an out-of-level floor could be the problem; see the following section for more information. Because this is a more expensive repair, you may want to consider the positive aspects of owning your own floor squeak. Think about how different the movie Psycho would've been if Janet Leigh had heard Anthony Perkins coming.

Getting on the level with your floors

Is a stroll across the floors in your home like negotiating the decks of a ship upon the high seas? If so, it's probably time to consider leveling the floor. Out-of-level floors are not only nuisances to go across, but if severe enough, they can also become a real safety hazard. Out-of-level floors can also cause cracks over windows and doors or make doors and windows stick and tough to operate. Thus, by repairing your out-of-level floor, you may find the windows and doors in your home are a whole lot easier to operate and last longer. Talk about preventive maintenance!

Not sure whether your floor is out of level and by how much? Don't head to the workshop to pull out a fancy level just yet. Simply swipe a marble (we like peeries) out of the little tyke's toy box and place it in various locations on the floor throughout the home. If the marble doesn't stay put, your floor isn't level.

If the marble test proves that your floor isn't level, be prepared to venture into your basement or crawlspace to investigate and make the necessary repairs. Unfortunately, floor leveling can't be done from above, unless you're willing to tear out the finish flooring to install a troweled-on floor leveling compound. This alternative is rare and is typically only performed when flooring is being replaced. Furthermore, you'll want to leave this one to the pros because the required material dries pretty fast — if you don't know what you're doing, you could end up with a bigger problem than you had before you started.

The majority of homes with floors not on the level probably didn't start out that way. Poorly compacted soil, excessively damp or excessively dry soil, and shrinking support posts under the floor are a few of the most common causes of this condition. Homes constructed on a hillside, on soil that expands when wet, or in earthquake country fall into a totally different category. Although some of the fixes suggested in this section may indeed apply to these homes, chances are, the services of a licensed soil engineer and structural engineer will be required.

Plan A: Trying some easy fixes first

Before embarking on the floor-leveling project we describe in the next section, we suggest that you take a simpler approach first: Start by stabilizing the moisture content of the soil near the foundation. Installing gutters and downspouts (and keeping them clean), installing downspout diverters (splash blocks), installing underground drainage systems, controlling landscape irrigation, and grading soil to shed away from the foundation are all effective means of controlling excessive moisture. (See "Preventing moisture under your home," earlier in this chapter.)

Don't expect miracles. This isn't one of those conditions that will straighten itself out overnight. Depending upon the climate and temperature (based on the time of year that you take action), this passive stabilization process could take anywhere from a few weeks to the better part of a year. Try the marble test every month or so to see if your work is making a difference.

If controlling the moisture near your foundation doesn't help or if there was a change for the good, but it simply wasn't enough, you need to move to Plan B.

Plan B: Giving the support posts some support

If the easy fixes didn't work, you can whip out that fancy level you've been dying to use.

All bubble levels are read the same way, regardless of length. True level is established when the bubble in the glass tube is located equally between the centermost lines on the glass vial. Lifting one end of the level will send the bubble in one direction while lifting the opposite end will send the bubble the other way. Playing with the level, raising and lowering one side or the other, will familiarize you with how it works.

Start your floor-leveling project with a 6-foot level and a Sherlock Holmes approach. Walk the floors of your home to identify the areas that appear out of level. Place the level over the floor in various directions and read the level to determine how far out of level it is. Repeating this process enough times in various locations will reveal where the high and low spots exist.

Now comes the fun part: Here's where you get to work on your belly, side, or back in a space similar to that of graves in ancient times. Seriously, working under the house can be no fun, so make sure you wear coveralls, carry a *drop light* (what a mechanic uses when working under the hood of your car), and have the tools you'll need with you:

- A few feet of replacement post material
- A couple metal connectors (see the following section)
- A handful of 8-penny nails
- A hammer
- A nail puller
- A sledgehammer
- A circular saw
- A hydraulic jack
- A screw jack and an adjustable wrench (if you're installing a screw jack — see "Installing a screw jack," later in this chapter)
- Some patience and, if you're the least bit claustrophobic, some anti-anxiety medication
- A helper topside to assist (because crawling in and out of the subarea can get old mighty fast)

Most crawlspaces are accessed in one of two ways: through an access door in the foundation (an opening in the foundation with a door or removable panel) or through a trap door somewhere inside the home (typically in the floor of a closet). If your house is on a concrete slab or has a full basement, you don't have a crawlspace. Lucky you: No spiders to do battle with. Plus, if the support post that needs adjustment runs from your basement floor to the support framing of the floor above, you don't have to work in a dark crawlspace on your belly; you can work upright in a well-lit basement.

However, if you're among the unfortunate, after you get into the crawlspace, you get to have a look around. Here's what you'll see: At the perimeter of the crawlspace is the foundation. The various piers are scattered about the interior. Atop these piers, which vary in depth from home to home, are support posts called underpinning posts. The bottoms of underpinning posts are attached to wood blocks embedded into the tops of the concrete piers. The tops of the underpinning posts are also fastened to floor support beams called girders. Sometimes the subfloor is attached directly to these girders; other times, for a more "beefy" floor, *floor joists* (horizontal floor framing) are installed above and perpendicular to the girders. The subfloor is then attached to the floor joist. In either case, the repair to the support posts is the same. Over time, the piers may either sink or rise depending upon the type of soil in which they're embedded and how moist it is.

Installing new support posts

To install new support posts, follow these steps:

1. **At those locations where the floor is high, place the floor jack atop a block of wood and directly under the support beam, a couple of feet from the pier.**

2. **Jack up the floor slightly (just enough to relieve any pressure on the existing support post) and knock out the existing post (see Figure 4-11).**

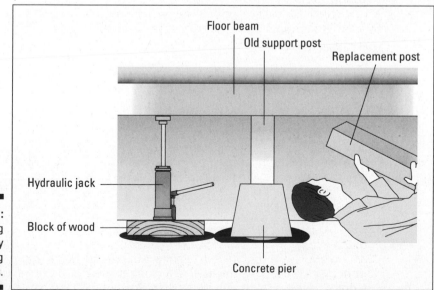

Figure 4-11:
Leveling
the floor by
replacing
piers.

Floor beam

Old support post

Replacement post

Hydraulic jack

Block of wood

Concrete pier

3. **Cut a new support post (shorter than the one removed by the amount calculated with your level from above) and place it between the pier and the support beam just like the one that you removed.**

To determine the length of the new support post, from above, place one end of the level on the high spot and direct the opposite end to a predetermined level area on the floor. Hold the level so that the bubble is between the centermost lines in the glass vial. Then, measure the distance between the bottom of the level and the level area of flooring. The new post should equal the length of the old post less the measurement taken with the level.

4. **Slowly lower the jack until the support rests firmly on the new support post, and attach the new support post to the pier and the support beam with metal connectors held with 8-penny nails.**

Metal connectors are made of galvanized sheet metal fabricated to accommodate a specific size framing member. For example, the metal connector that would be used to anchor an underpinning post to the wood cap on a pier block is called a *post bottom*. In the case of a four-by-four post, the post bottom is square (slightly larger than the size of the post and about $2^1/_2$ inches high) and has holes in all sides through which nails are driven. You drive nails through the holes in the bottom of the connector into the pier cap.

A *girder-to-post connector* is used at the top of the underpinning post. This connector consists of two straps that attach to opposite sides of the post and two straps that attach to either side of the girder. As with the post bottom, this connector has holes in all the faces for nailing.

Both connectors must be in place before the new post is installed. Use a short level to make sure that the post is *plumb* — at a right angle to horizontal. **Remember:** The bubble in the glass vial needs to be centermost between the lines.

At the locations where the floor is low, the process is the same with one exception: The new support posts being installed need to be cut longer by the amount calculated with your level from above.

In some severe cases where the condition has existed for a long period, a deep saw cut may be required at the underside of the support beam in one or more locations to make the timber more yielding and to facilitate movement of the floor up or down. The saw cut should penetrate approximately two-thirds the thickness of the timber. So, if the timber is 6 inches thick (measured vertically), the cut should be about 4 inches deep. For added strength, a splint consisting of short pieces of two-by-six should be glued and nailed with 16-penny nails onto either side of the support beam at the locations where cuts are made.

Installing a screw jack

If your home is built on expansive soil and, thus, subject to regular movement, a screw jack is the ticket (see Figure 4-12). Screw jacks, also known as *adjustable floor jacks,* are used in lieu of solid wood posts between the concrete piers in the crawlspace and the *girders* (horizontal beams) that support the floor joists.

A screw jack is a metal support post that can be adjusted to level the floor. It consists of two heavy steel pipes, one inside the other. The inside pipe is threaded and adjusted up and down by turning a large wing nut. The screw jack is attached with nails to the underside of the girder and to the wood block atop a concrete pier.

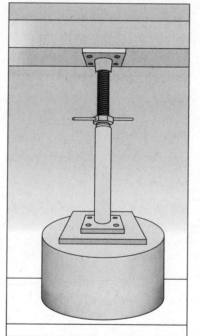

Figure 4-12:
Using a screw jack to shore up your floor.

Screw jacks can generally be found at local hardware stores and home centers. Here's how to install a screw jack:

1. **Use a hydraulic jack and a short post to shore up the floor during this process.**

2. **Use a hammer, a nail puller, and a sledgehammer to remove the existing underpinning wood post and nails.**

3. **Center the screw jack below the girder and on top of the wood block on the concrete pier.**

4. **Adjust the screw jack so that the top and bottom plates are flush to the wood surfaces above and below.**

5. **Drive 16-penny nails through the holes in the plates and into the wood framing.**

6. **Lower the hydraulic jack to transfer the floor load to the new screw jack.**

7. **Adjust the screw jack up or down to achieve a level surface.**

In some cases, when radically adjusting a floor, don't be surprised if windows crack and doors stick. On the other hand, besides not having to take motion-sickness medicine anymore, don't be surprised if a few of those once-sticking doors and windows now operate just fine. It's amazing what a little trek under the house can do!

Chapter 5

Roofing and Siding

. . . .

In This Chapter

▶ Stopping leaks before they begin

▶ Discovering the destructive side of icicles

▶ Getting into gutters

▶ Painting for more than appearance

▶ Caring for siding

. . . .

Your entire home and its contents depend on the integrity of your roof and exterior walls in the same way that you depend on protective clothing to keep you dry in foul weather. Getting temporarily stuck in bad weather can make you slightly uncomfortable and maybe even ruin your hairdo, but left unchecked, a roof leak — even a tiny one — can end up costing a fortune in damage to a home's interior and its precious contents. Damage to flooring, plaster, wallboard, furniture, important papers, and more is no small matter. To avoid problems like these, you need to keep your roof and siding in good condition and repair. This chapter tells you how.

Your Roof: The Fifth Wall of Your Home

Most folks are pretty conscientious about maintaining the exterior walls of their homes. On just about any day during good weather, you can drive through a neighborhood and find the sides of at least one home under siege by painters. But rarely do you see anyone on the roof of a home unless the roof is being replaced. For some reason, people just don't pay as much attention to their roofs, which we think is a mistake.

The whole idea of maintenance is to ensure longevity, reduce costs, and improve value. We think this concept should apply to the roof in the same way it does to the walls. In fact, we like to think of the roof as the fifth wall of the home — and we think the roof should be maintained with the same regularity as the walls that support it. With proper care and maintenance, a roof can outlast its warranty without leaking a drop or suffering any ugly damage.

Staying safe on the roof

A pitched roof is an alien plane. No, not a spaceship from another planet. Rather, it's an unfamiliar surface to walk upon. And for the novice, an angled surface can be even more dangerous than the dastardly spaceships that tried to destroy the Earth in the movie *War of the Worlds.* To stay safe, follow this advice:

- ✔ **If you aren't agile or athletic, or if you have a fear of heights (or falling), think about hiring someone to maintain your roof.** Your best bet would be a roofing contractor. He has the equipment, the know-how, and, best of all, the experience of working up high on an unlevel plane.

- ✔ **If you do go up there, be sure to wear rubber-soled shoes.** They grip better than leather.

- ✔ **Wear a safety harness.** Safety harnesses have fabric straps that wrap around your legs, your waist, and the trunk of your body, and you connect them to a rope that's securely anchored to a tree trunk — or other fixed and secure object — located on the other side of the roof. These harnesses could prevent broken bones or even save your life. You can find them online, at construction-supply stores or at a sports-supply or camping store that sells products for rock climbing and repelling.

   Be sure to adjust the slack in your safety line as you work your way up the roof. The less slack, the less sudden the stop!

- ✔ **If you're cleaning your roof, applying a preservative, or doing some other similar task, never stand downhill of your work.** You can very easily slip on the wet surface. Always stand uphill of your work (see Figure 5-1).

- ✔ **Use binoculars to inspect your roof.** If you want to take a close look at your roof but don't want to climb up there to do it, get a good pair of binoculars. Then you can stand on the ground and see what there is to see! Split wood shingles, shingles with holes, cupped and curling asphalt shingles, stains, mold, mildew, and other damage and wear will be as easy to spot as if you were standing right next to them.

Cleanliness is next to godliness

Streaking or discoloration can cause a perfectly good roof to look old, tired, and tattered. So, for appearance's sake, keep your roof clean. You can use our Universal Roof-Cleaning Formula (see Chapter 20), which not only cleans off dirt but also gets rid of mildew, moss, and algae, all of which can cause extensive damage if left unattended.

Figure 5-1:
When cleaning or applying a preserva-tive, always stand uphill of your work.

If you prefer not to make your own, you also can use one of dozens of com-mercial roof cleaning solutions available. Although many of them simply con-tain detergent and bleach like our recipe, others contain peroxide, fungicides, mildewcides, disinfectants, and other fancy fluids. Some are better at killing mold and mildew. Some are better at removing stains. Some are easier on your landscaping. In the end, though, they all work pretty much the same. To find out more about the options, visit your favorite home center or hard-ware store.

To clean your roof, you need these supplies:

- Cleaning solution
- Safety glasses or goggles
- Pump garden sprayer
- Stiff-bristle broom
- Tall ladder (how tall depends on the height of your roof)
- Garden hose
- Safety harness

Choose a cool, humid, overcast day to make sure that the cleaner doesn't dry too fast on the roof and then follow these steps:

1. **Pour your cleaning solution into the garden sprayer.**

2. **While standing on the roof, spray the cleaner on a strip about 3 feet high and 10 feet wide and let it sit for about 15 minutes.**

   Begin cleaning the lower portion of the roof, moving up as you clean each lower section. That way, you always stand on dry ground and reduce the chance of slipping (refer to Figure 5-1).

3. **If the cleaner begins to dry out, spray on a bit more.**

A few uplifting words about ladders

There are as many different ladders as there are tasks that require one. They range from the small two- and three-rung step-stool type to the common 6- and 8-foot folding models to the big daddy of them all, the extension ladder. If your home-maintenance budget can afford only one ladder, get a 6-foot stepladder. It gives you the length you need when tackling most home-maintenance and repair projects. You can change light bulbs at ceiling-mounted fixtures and paint ceilings and walls. However, if your ceilings are 10 feet or greater, you need an 8-foot ladder instead. If your project involves a multistory roof, you need an extension ladder. (Whichever type of ladder you choose, be sure to check its posted weight capacity. The ladder must be able to carry your own weight plus your payload.)

Don't try to save money by purchasing a cheap ladder. Cheap ladders fall apart in no time — usually with someone on them. When buying a ladder, look for secure connections, metal-supported steps, and superior hinges. As the ladder gets older, keep an eye out for loose connections, splits, cracks, and missing rivets.

Follow these tips to help you avoid any unplanned downward trips off your ladder:

✓ When working on dirt or turf, stabilize the ladder by placing the feet on boards or on a sheet of plywood to prevent them from sinking into the earth. For added stability, place the bottom of the ladder away from the wall one-quarter of the ladder's length; if you have an 8-foot ladder, place the bottom of the ladder 2 feet away from the wall.

✓ When working on the roof, make sure that the ladder extends a minimum of 2 feet above the edge of the roof.

✓ Never climb onto a roof from the gable end where the roof crosses the ladder rungs at an angle. Instead, mount the roof from a horizontal side. The plane of the roof should be parallel to the ladder rungs at the point where you leave the ladder to mount the roof.

✓ To maintain proper balance, keep your hips between the side rails when climbing the ladder or when reaching out. Keep one hand on the ladder and the other free for work.

4. **Use the broom to gently scrub the area as needed to get it clean.**

   You don't want to scrub off the granules from your asphalt shingles, or scrub your wood shingles loose.

5. **Rinse the cleaned area with fresh water.**

   Repeat the process until the roof is clean.

A wood-shake or shingle roof covered with pine needles, leaves, moss, and other debris may retain water, causing the shingles to rot prematurely. An annual sweeping with a stiff-bristle broom cuts down on fungus damage by enhancing proper watershed. Cleaning to promote proper watershed is important with other types of roofs as well. Built-up debris can create a dam, which can cause a leak.

Replacing an asphalt shingle

Asphalt and fiberglass shingles, sometimes called *composition shingles,* are by far the most popular roofing material. Made of asphalt (tar), reinforced with fiberglass or other organic materials, and covered with mineral granules, they're good looking, long lasting, and need very little maintenance. Composition shingles are more flexible and, therefore, somewhat more forgiving than wood shingles (see the next section).

Because composition shingles become more flexible when warm, replacing a shingle is best saved for a sunny day.

Here's all you have to do to replace a composition shingle (see Figure 5-2):

1. **Fold back the shingle(s) that are above the one you want to remove.**

2. **Use a flat pry bar to remove the nails that hold the damaged shingle in place.**

3. **Slip a new shingle in position to replace the one that was removed.**

4. **Nail the new shingle in place using a flat pry bar as a hammer extension.**

   Using a flat pry bar as a hammer extension, you can drive the nail in from beneath an overlapping shingle. First, press the nail into the shingle by hand; then position the bottom of the flat pry bar so that the straight end rests atop the nail head; then strike the flat pry bar with a hammer. The offset below drives the nail home.

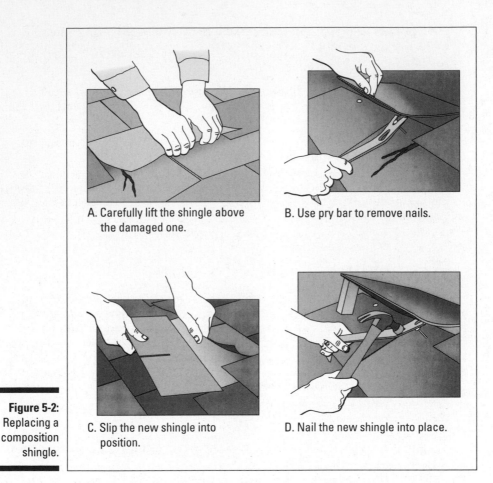

A. Carefully lift the shingle above the damaged one.

B. Use pry bar to remove nails.

C. Slip the new shingle into position.

D. Nail the new shingle into place.

Figure 5-2: Replacing a composition shingle.

Preserving a wood-shake or shingle roof

If your wood roof-covering members are machine-sawn on both sides, they're known as just plain *shingles*. If they're hand-split (having a rough, ribbed surface), they're known as *shaked shingles* or *shakes*.

Regardless, no matter how clean you keep your wood roof, it usually starts looking a little worn out after only a few years. Good Old Mr. Sun causes the majority of the damage, drying out shingles, causing them to split, and literally burning holes into them. These shingles can lose virtually all their moisture (water and natural resins) in as few as five years, which can result in cupping, curling, splitting, and an almost certain early demise. However, with proper care and maintenance, you could double or even triple the life of a wood-shake or shingle roof.

Most preservative applications last three to five years depending upon the climate. Keeping the roof clean and debris-free helps extend the lasting quality of the preservative and, therefore, the life of the roof.

For more information on wood-roof maintenance, contact the Cedar Guild (phone: 503-897-2541; Web: www.cedar-guild.com/contact) and order its terrific "Double the Life of Your Roof Manual."

Super-cleaning to open the pores

Preserving your roof begins with an even more thorough cleaning than the general roof-cleaning technique that we describe in the "Cleanliness is next to godliness" section, earlier in this chapter. It completely exposes all the pores of the wood so that the preservative you apply later can penetrate deeply and completely into every pore. This super-cleaning also cuts through grime and makes your wood-shake or shingle roof look almost as good as new.

Step 1: Pressure-washing

The first step in super-cleaning your roof is to pressure-wash it. We recommend a *pressure washer,* a small device that converts water supplied from a garden hose to a high-pressure mix of air and water that comes through the hose with enough force to cut through soft wood. Talk about eliminating elbow grease! When using the pressure washer, hold the spray tip approximately 8 to 12 inches from the roof's surface while working backward from the lowest part of the roof up to the highest part.

Step 2: Getting rid of mold

When mold is present, follow the pressure-washing with an application of mold-killing bleach (1 quart bleach to 1 gallon hot water) to eliminate remaining spores that may reside deep within the pores of the wood. Place the mixture in a garden sprayer and thoroughly wet the entire roof. Keep it wet for at least 15 minutes and then rinse with fresh water.

Replacing damaged wood shingles

After super-cleaning the wood roof, let it dry and then follow these steps to replace any damaged shingles (see Figure 5-3):

1. **Using a hacksaw, cut the nails anchoring a damaged shingle and carefully slip it out.**

   Attempting to pry nails loose or pull a shingle out may damage surrounding shingles and make it more difficult to install the new one.

2. **Using the shingle you just removed as a pattern, custom-cut a replacement shingle.**

3. **Slip the new shingle up and under the building paper until the butt end (the fat end) is within 1 inch of the ends of the shingles on either side of the new one.**

4. ***Toenail* (nail at an angle) two barbed roofing nails as high up as possible without damaging the butt end of the overlapping shingle.**

5. **Finish the repair by driving the shingle until it aligns with the surrounding shingles.**

Place a wood block against the butt end of the new shingle and strike the block firmly with a hammer. This process conceals the new nails, providing a more watertight installation.

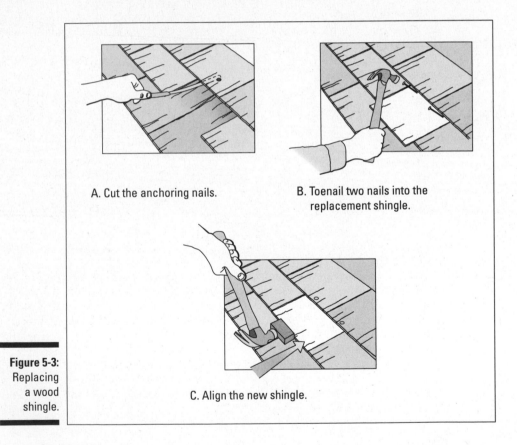

A. Cut the anchoring nails.

B. Toenail two nails into the replacement shingle.

C. Align the new shingle.

Figure 5-3:
Replacing
a wood
shingle.

What about other types of roofs?

A number of alternative roofing materials simulate traditional roof coverings. Synthetic and fiber-cement slate look like the real thing but are considerably cheaper and lighter — an important consideration in retrofitting. Metal, polymer, fiber-cement, and even rubber shakes offer a top fire rating and are an alternative for homes in areas where wood roofing is banned.

Of these alternative materials, metal is the fastest-growing. Here's why: Unlike asphalt or wood shingles, metal doesn't rot, crack, or grow fungus or algae. It can last more than 50 years. And if it's installed properly, metal requires very little, if any, ongoing maintenance. All you can really do is screw it up by walking around on it. Be aware that metal roofing is more than just those big, flat, shiny panels you see on houses in the southeastern United States. Today, metal comes in profiles that mimic virtually every type of roofing material. You won't believe what you can find — and you should see the colors available!

Sometimes we forget about tile roofs. They're terribly expensive, and their use is virtually limited to homes with Mediterranean architecture. But they never need repair, and a well-installed tile roof can last up to 75 years. If a tile roof is appropriate for your home, it's actually a good value when you spread the cost out over the life of the roof.

And that's not all. Chemists, engineers, and wizards continue to work to develop new higher-performance, eco-friendly roofing materials. Reflective shingles, heat-reflective roof underlayment, systems that create an insulating airspace beneath the roof covering, advances in waterproofing underlayment membranes, and so on are just the beginning. Although most of these new products are years away from being available to the public, we think their "green-ness" will help them succeed in the marketplace.

Applying preservative to wood shingles

The preservative restores the natural oils to the wood fibers, safeguards the roof from fungus and rot, and protects the roof from the harmful ultraviolet rays of the sun. You see both oil-based and water-based preservatives at the stores; we prefer the oil-based type because it penetrates deeper, combats weather stress better, and lasts longer.

You can add pigments to non-pigmented preservatives to improve ultraviolet protection. An added benefit is that the pigment evens out the surface colors so that you can't tell the difference between the older shingles and the new ones that were used to make patches.

To apply the preservative, choose a calm, breeze-free day (to ensure that the majority of the product ends up on the roof and not on your neighbor's new car). Then just spray the oil onto the roof, being sure to work backward from the low end to the high end and careful not to walk on an already treated area, which could be very slippery (refer to Figure 5-1). When the surface becomes shiny, stop spraying in that area and move on.

Although you can apply preservative with a garden-type pump sprayer, you can perform the task more professionally and in less time by using an airless paint sprayer, which you can rent from a paint store or tool-rental outlet.

The naked truth about flashing

Most apparent roof leaks are really flashing leaks. You can take super-good care of your roof and still get leaks if you don't also take care of your flashing. Here's why: Roof flashing creates a watertight connection where the roof joins a wall, as when a first-story roof connects to a second-story wall. Roof flashing also creates watertight connections between the roofing and items that penetrate it, including plumbing pipes, furnace flues, skylights, and chimneys. Good, tight flashings around chimneys, vents, skylights, and wall-roof junctions are the key to preventing water infiltration — and damage to walls, ceilings, insulation, and electrical systems.

Caulking around the flashing

The most effective way to prevent leaks is to keep a close eye on the places where flashings meet vertical surfaces. Prone to gaps where old caulk fails, those meeting points always must be well sealed. Use a good-quality exterior-grade caulk and then follow these steps:

1. **Scrape and wire-brush away any loose caulk, flaky paint, old adhesive, and rust, if there is any.**

   You can find rust-removal steps in the next section.

2. **If the flashing is no longer stuck to the vertical surface, use a scraper to slide a smear of flashing adhesive on the back side of the flashing. Bend the flashing as little as possible. Hold until firmly adhered.**

3. **Caulk the edges to prevent water infiltration.**

4. **If desired, paint when dry to match the flashing color.**

Removing rust

Although some flashings are made of lead or copper, most are made of galvanized sheet metal or aluminum. And that means rust or corrosion. And rust or corrosion can mean leaks. So another way to prevent flashings from leaking is to keep them from rusting. Applying a good coat of paint every few years generally does the trick.

You need the following items:

- ✔ A box of trisodium phosphate (TSP), mixed to the manufacturer's specifications
- ✔ Sandpaper or a wire brush
- ✔ A paintbrush
- ✔ A can of rust converter
- ✔ A can of latex paint

Follow these steps to eliminate rust on your flashing:

1. **Wash the surface with the TSP.**

   The TSP *etches* (chemically roughens) the painted surface.

2. **Use the sandpaper or the wire brush to remove all rust.**

3. **Clean away the dust and use the paintbrush to apply the rust converter.**

   The rust converter acts as a primer while converting leftover rust to an inert material.

4. **When the rust converter is dry, apply the latex paint as a finish coat.**

   To make your roof flashings, vent pipes, and flue caps less obvious and more aesthetically pleasing, make them the same color as the roofing material.

One type of roof flashing, called *vent pipe flashing,* incorporates a rubber grommet held by a sheet of metal that seals the connection between a plumbing vent pipe and the roof. This grommet is located at the centermost portion of the flashing and presses evenly all around the plumbing vent pipe. *Do not paint the rubber section — ever.* You can keep this rubber grommet in good condition by applying a rubber preservative every year or two.

Dealing with all that dam ice

If you have icicles, you may have an ice dam. And if you have an ice dam, you may soon be fighting a roof leak. Here's why: When snow falls on a roof, it seals the roof, which becomes almost airtight. As the house warms to a nice toasty temperature, heated air escapes into the attic. As the attic gets warmer, it melts the snow on the roof, and water rushes downward toward the overhangs. The moment the liquefied snow hits the cold (uninsulated) overhang, it begins to freeze. The water that freezes *after* it rolls over the edge becomes icicles. Water that freezes *before* it rolls over the edge builds up to create a barrier known as an *ice dam,* which becomes larger and larger as runoff continues to freeze. Finally, the ice on the overhang widens to the point where it reaches the edge of the attic. At this point, the water remains liquid and the ice dam causes it to back up over the attic where it can leak into the home.

Ice buildup can also damage rain gutters, causing the need for costly repairs. By preventing ice buildup, you might be able to save your house from being flooded during a freeze and add a little life to your gutters as well.

To prevent an ice dam, you need to keep the underside of the roof in the attic cold. If the attic is cold, the snow on the roof won't melt, and ice dams won't form. Here's how to make it happen:

✔ **Don't close off eave and roof vents during the winter.** Sealing the vents traps the warm air that can melt the snow on the roof.

✔ **Fill all penetrations between the living space and the attic area with foam sealant.** You can buy expanding foam sealant in a spray can. Look for penetrations in the ceiling in the following places (many may be hidden beneath attic insulation):

  • Plumbing vents

  • Ventilation ducts

  • Heat registers

  • Electric wiring

  • Ceiling light fixtures

Any hole that can allow heat from the home into the attic is a bad thing.

Don't caulk around furnace flues. A flue that contains hot gases should not come into contact with combustibles such as wood or foam sealant. Contact your local heating or sheet-metal contractor and have a metal draft stop installed. The metal draft stop can be sealed to the pipe and the house frame without creating a fire hazard.

✔ **Check your attic insulation.** Be sure that your attic insulation is loose (as opposed to compacted) and that there is a more-than-sufficient amount of insulation up there. Look for gaps in insulation — especially at corners and at the perimeter where the walls and roof framing meet.

✔ **Consider installing an eave-heating device such as heating tape or heating wire (see Figure 5-4).** These devices prevent water from freezing on your eave.

✔ **Install special metal flashings at problem eaves.** Ice doesn't stick to the metal as readily as it does to most types of roofing. Metal flashings can be made to order by your local heating or sheet-metal contractor.

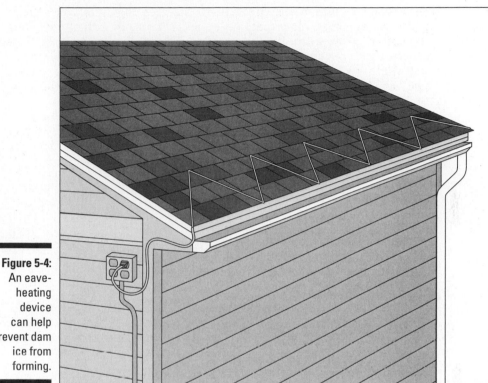

Figure 5-4:
An eave-
heating
device
can help
prevent dam
ice from
forming.

Finding a roof leak

The first step in repairing a leak is finding its point of origin. Finding a leak can be extremely difficult on a flat roof, so we recommend that, if you have a flat roof, you hire a roofing professional to find the leak and repair it. If you have a pitched roof, you can find the leak yourself. You'll still probably need to hire a contractor to repair the leak, but being able to tell the contractor where the leak is saves time and shows the contractor that he's dealing with an informed homeowner.

To find the origin of a leak on a pitched roof, you conduct a water test. Although it's not difficult, water testing can be time-consuming and tedious. Be prepared to exercise a bit of patience. The process requires two people — one on the roof and one in the attic (or living space below if no attic exists). You also need the following tools:

  ✔ Ladder

  ✔ Garden hose

  ✔ Flashlight

Then follow these steps (see Figure 5-5):

1. **Station your partner in the attic and tell her to holler at the first sign of water.**

   Where's the water coming from, you ask? From you, or, more precisely, from your garden hose, as explained in Step 2.

2. **Use the garden hose to run a modest amount of water over the roof at a point below the area where a leak is suspected.**

   Don't run the hose full-blast, don't use a spray nozzle, and don't force the water between the shingles. Doing so may force water into the home, creating the illusion that you've found a leak when, in fact, you did nothing more than temporarily create one.

   Work from the lowest point of the roof (near the eaves or gutters) in an area of about 4 to 6 feet wide. Work your way up the roof a couple of feet at a time.

3. **Have your helper in the attic let you know the moment he sees water, and mark the spot with chalk.**

   A loud yell will do the trick, but an inexpensive pair of kids' walkie-talkies allows you to communicate clearly without yelling. Better yet, just have your cellphone with you and have her call you from her cellphone when she sees the water.

Figure 5-5:
Water-
testing a
pitched roof.

Getting Your Mind into the Gutter

Gene Kelly probably wouldn't be remembered as well for his part in *Singin' in the Rain* if the movie set had been equipped with rain gutters. As a matter of fact, the producers probably would've changed the title of the film to something like *He Stayed Dry while Singing near the Rain*.

Gutters are important. Because you'll be singing in the rain indoors if you don't properly maintain your gutters and downspouts.

Cleaning gutters and downspouts

Gutters and downspouts that are filled with debris can back up, causing roof leaks, rot at the overhang, and structural damage. At least once a year, you need to get up on the ladder and give those gutters and downspouts a good cleaning. Gutters that haven't been cleaned for a while may be filled with a gross, mud-like muck, which you can scoop out with a small garden trowel or a medium-width putty knife. You may even want to invest $7 in a *gutter scoop* (a plastic trowel-like scoop made especially for cleaning gutters).

After you remove the majority of the debris, flush the rest away using a garden hose with a spray nozzle. If the water pressure at your place is weak, you can use a pressure washer to blast out debris. We both own pressure washers just for this purpose.

Patching up leaks

When galvanized sheet-metal gutters aren't properly maintained (regularly cleaned and painted) they tend to rust. As we mention in the "Flashing" section, earlier in this chapter, unpainted metal rusts, and rust results in leaks. The same technique used to maintain roof flashings can be enlisted on gutters.

When a rusty area turns into a leak, you can make a quick repair. To do so, you need the following tools:

✔ Wire brush (or a wire wheel mounted on an electric drill).

✔ Disposable paintbrush.

✔ Strips of tin foil or plastic (for pinhole leak repairs) or small strips of galvanized sheet metal (for larger hole repairs). Whether the strips are made of foil, plastic, or metal, they need to be just slightly larger than the hole being repaired.

✔ Rust converter.

- Paint.
- Roofing cement.
- Putty knife.

If the gutter is sagging, replace the mounting brackets before fixing leaks. You don't want the gutter shape to change after the leak has been fixed — if the gutter changes shape, a patch could open.

With your tools assembled, follow these steps to patch the leak:

1. **Use the wire brush or a wire wheel on a drill to remove as much rust from the area as possible.**

2. **Apply a coat of rust converter over the repair area.**

   The converter renders any minute remnants of rust inert. With rust, you can't be too careful. Allow the converter to dry completely.

3. **Apply a $^1/_8$-inch-thick coat of roof cement around the leak and, before the cement dries, add a strip of tin foil to the repair area (kind of like taping a Band-Aid to your arm). Use a putty knife to gently flatten the foil and squeeze out the excess cement.**

   The total thickness of the repair should not exceed $^1/_{16}$ inch. If you use too much cement, you may inadvertently create a dam.

   For larger repairs (bigger than a pinhole), use a piece of sheet metal instead of tin foil.

   For badly damaged areas, you can pop-rivet the sheet metal plates into place and seal them with gutter caulking, or you can leave this maintenance task to the sheet-metal contractor.

4. **With the foil (or a strip of sheet metal) in place, use a putty knife to add another thin layer of roof cement, completely covering the patch.**

If the repair area is too large, then you should consider replacing the damaged sections. The style you have is probably still available. But if, for some reason, the gutter profile on your home no longer is made, a sheet-metal contractor can fabricate a perfect match.

Rust isn't the only cause of leaks. Occasionally, a gutter seam or joint will open. Catching this problem early on reduces the chance of rust and, possibly, the need for a major repair. You can caulk seams in aluminum and galvanized sheet-metal gutters with a high-quality gutter caulking. Use polyurethane caulk for plastic gutters. In both cases, be sure to thoroughly clean and dry the area before applying the caulk.

Maintaining gutter-protection systems

The whole idea of gutter-protection systems is that you don't have to get up on a ladder and scoop the gloop out of the gutters every fall. But that doesn't mean your "protected" gutters don't need a little TLC every now and then. Some leaves, pine needles, and crud still get in. So instead of an annual cleaning, you probably can get away with cleaning them every two years.

Other, newer gutter-protection systems, including a product that resembles a bottle brush on steroids, are inconspicuous and easy to install. But don't be fooled into thinking you'll never need to do anything.

Siding: A Raincoat to Keep You Dry

Water can attack and damage wood siding. Stucco walls crack when the house shifts as winter rains expand soil. Metal siding dents easily. Vinyl siding pits as it oxidizes. Even bricks chip and crack with winter freezes and summer ground settlement. No surface is perfect; no material perfectly withstands the rigors of nature and the force of the elements. But you can do a thing or two to add life and beauty to your home's siding.

Aluminum siding

Think of aluminum siding in the same way that you think of a car body. It's a smooth metal surface covered with paint that needs to be regularly cleaned, polished, and waxed. Really, think about it. Aluminum siding is metal that is formed and polished and given a factory paint job just like a car body. So what automobile paint job do you know of that will last forever? The fact is that aluminum siding, like all the others, needs to be maintained and occasionally painted.

Taking care of chalked paint

If you want to see a good case of *chalked* (oxidized) paint, then get up close and personal to a 20-year-old home sided with aluminum that has never been cleaned or painted. So, how do you prevent chalking? You can't, but you *can* make light work of getting it to disappear. All you have to do is attend to it on a regular basis.

Pressure-wash regularly (once or twice a year), and don't forget the laundry detergent. (Most pressure washers have a plastic "suction tube" that can draw the contents out of any container and blend it with the pressurized water. It's a great accessory for incorporating cleaning chemicals and detergents into the jet spray. Follow the pressure-washer recommendations for diluting the detergent — it's usually one part detergent to one part water.) Your aluminum siding will remain bright and shiny for years. And the task won't ever seem overwhelming.

Painting aluminum siding

When your aluminum siding begins to look worn and tattered, painting is in order. Follow these tips:

- **Don't scrape aluminum siding.** Aluminum has a smooth surface and should be sanded with a finer 400- to 600-grit sandpaper.

- **For bare aluminum, prime with a zinc-oxide primer (metal primer).**

- **Spray-paint the aluminum surface for best results.**

- **If you have to patch the surface, use a filler made especially for metal (like Bondo, which is made for cars).**

Vinyl siding

Vinyl siding doesn't warp, split, or buckle and, according to what several manufacturers espouse, it doesn't ever have to be painted. Actually, it can't be painted — paint simply will not stick to vinyl in the same way it sticks to wood or aluminum.

Like all types of exterior siding, vinyl does have its shortcomings. Over time, its surface oxidizes. As the surface deteriorates, the pitted result causes the material to become dull and prone to stain. The only way to combat this problem is to regularly clean the siding. Twice a year is good — once in the spring and then again in the fall. Use a pressure washer with laundry detergent to get the surface sparkling clean.

Keeping the surface of the vinyl clean won't prevent it from oxidizing, but it will prevent corrosive chemicals in the air from attacking the surface.

Stucco

Stucco is cool stuff. It doesn't rot, and compared to other types of siding, it's relatively easy to maintain. Stucco is very porous and holds on to paint better than most other kinds of siding. Also, it's one of the easiest surfaces to prepare and paint. So, if you have stucco, count your blessings.

Caring for cracks

The most challenging stucco maintenance is crack repair. Stucco's tough but brittle surface sometimes can be a drawback. When the house shifts, rigid things crack.

You can turn your home into an interstate road map of ugly, obvious crack repairs if you aren't careful. When it comes to stucco crack repair, less is more. Don't try to patch every crack. Hairline cracks and those that you can't get your fingernail into should not be patched; in fact, paint usually will fill those cracks. Wider cracks (those up to ¼ inch wide) should be filled with a high-quality, exterior-grade, acrylic latex caulk. Have a damp sponge handy to wipe away excess caulk that escapes.

Just follow these simple steps:

1. **Clean all loose debris from the crack.**

   The V end of an old-fashioned can opener and a vacuum cleaner work wonders here.

2. **Use a paintable silicone caulk — and your finger — to make an invisible repair.**

   Don't use a putty knife, because it prevents you from matching the existing texture. And don't use just any caulk; use the 50-year kind, which really does hold better and longer than the other types.

3. **With a damp sponge, wipe off the excess caulking in all directions.**

4. **While the caulk is still wet, place fine texturing sand into the palm of your hand and, holding your hand in front of the caulking, blow across the sand to scatter it onto the surface of the damp caulk.**

   The sand makes the patch less obvious and prevents the road-map effect by helping the caulk blend into the surrounding finish.

Taking a chunk out of gouges

You can repair wider cracks and gouges with a stucco patching compound. Follow mixing instructions carefully because the amount of water you use can change the properties of the compound. If the properties of the compound change, it may not hold as well.

Follow these steps:

1. **Clean all loose debris from the crack or gouge.**

2. **Use a latex patching product and a putty knife or trowel to fill the area.**

3. **Apply a second coat to match the surface texture.**

   Thin the patching compound to a pancake-batter consistency. Dip the end of a paintbrush into the mixture. Holding your hand between the wall and the paintbrush, slap the handle of the brush against your hand. The patching compound splatters onto the surface, matching the texture of the stucco. If the texture is flat, wait for the splattering to become slightly firm and then wipe it to the desired flatness with a putty knife or a trowel.

Painting stucco

To paint stucco, use a roller for small jobs; for larger jobs, use an airless sprayer. A brush is not recommended for painting stucco, but you can use one to add texture: After you spray the paint onto the surface, use a deep-nap roller ($^3/_4$ inch to 1 inch) to work the paint into the surface and to achieve a uniform texture.

Although one coat may do the trick, stucco usually will require two coats, due to its high level of absorption and to conceal cracks and other repairs.

Really porous stucco absorbs gallons of paint. If you're painting stucco for the first time, save paint by using a water hose to completely wet the surface of the stucco before painting. The water fills the pores in the stucco and prevents the stucco from absorbing excess amounts of paint. Wait for surface water to evaporate first and then begin painting.

Wood siding

When wood's moisture content reaches 20 percent to 30 percent, fungi deep within its fibers begin to grow and flourish, causing dreaded wood rot. To prevent wood rot, treat your wood siding with an application of oil, stain, or paint. These materials act as a barrier, preventing water from coming into direct contact with the wood.

Which finish you choose is mostly an aesthetic choice, although practicalities like ease of application, how long lasting the finish is, and so on are also factors:

  ✔ **Oil,** a clear finish, is absorbed into the wood and fills all pores and voids, displacing water that would otherwise be absorbed. It's easier to apply than paint, and if the oil is clear (or almost clear), mistakes are nearly impossible to detect. In addition, oil doesn't split, chip, or blister. Unfortunately, oil has a tendency to evaporate and doesn't last as long as paint.

✔ **Oil stain** is the same as oil except that a pigment has been mixed into the oil. The added pigment makes application of oil stains slightly more difficult (mistakes show more readily). But the pigment also helps to filter out more of the sun's damaging ultraviolet rays. Like oil, oil stains don't split, chip, or blister.

The more wood that you can see when the job is complete, the more often you can expect to redo the finish.

✔ **Paint** penetrates and protects in the same way that oil does. Additionally, paint coats the surface of the wood with a thin, durable waterproof hide. Paint certainly lasts longer, but it is the most difficult to apply and is more prone to chipping, splitting, and blistering.

Everything's a trade-off. With oil you won't ever have to sand, scrape, or chisel the surface to prepare it for another application. But be ready to reapply a new coat every several years. With an oil stain, figure about three to five years of lasting quality. A good grade of paint, applied to a properly cleaned surface, lasts seven to ten years or more.

Paint experts agree that 80 percent of a good oil, stain, or paint job is in the preparation. But the exterior of your home is no small area, so when it comes to preparation (removing old layers of loose paint, a tattered layer of stain, a discolored layer of wood, or just plain dirt), you can expect to do some major work. Fortunately, tools like sand blasters, soda washers, and pressure washers are available at home centers, paint stores, and rental outlets; these tools help make cleanup and removal an almost fun job. All these tools involve some degree of work on your part, but they're a breeze to use compared to a hand scraper, a hand chipper, or a blowtorch. Our personal choice is a pressure washer.

Preparing painted surfaces

To prepare surfaces for repainting, follow these steps

1. **Completely remove all old loose paint and sand the spots where a painted surface meets a bare spot.**

   A new coat of paint won't stick any better than the old paint below it; that's why removing all loose paint is so important, and tapering or feathering these transition points makes them less visible and guarantees a nicer looking finished product.

2. **Prime all bare spots with a high-grade oil-based primer.**

   Tinting a standard white primer a shade or two lighter than the finish coat can improve coverage. For example, a light-brown finish coat covers a beige primer more effectively than it covers a white primer.

3. **Caulk all joints with a high-grade, 50-year, paintable silicone or polyurethane product.**

   Doing so prevents water from getting behind the siding.

Now you're ready to paint.

Preparing oiled surfaces

To prepare an oiled surface for refinishing, clean the wood with a pressure washer, apply a coat of wood bleach, let it stand (following the manufacturer's instructions), and pressure-wash again. At this point, the wood is ready for a fresh coat of oil or oil stain. Your oiled siding will look so good, you won't believe you did it yourself!

Chapter 6

Windows, Exterior Doors, and Insulation

In This Chapter

▶ Maintaining the comfort of your home through insulation

▶ Caring for windows

▶ Getting the most out of your doors, inside and out

Most home-maintenance projects save you money over time. But only a few of them produce an immediate and measurable return. Maintaining your home's energy envelope is one such project. The floors, walls, ceilings, doors, and windows of your home combine to make up its *energy envelope*. When the energy envelope is properly maintained, your personal comfort level reaps the benefits by better protecting you from the elements. And your wallet also notices a difference when you aren't paying such high heating and cooling bills.

Saving Energy with Insulation

If your home is like most, your attic and exterior walls are insulated. If you're really smart, you also have insulated floors. But if your home is at least 20 years old, you may need to perform a little maintenance on your insulation. How will you know? Well, if you're freezing, your furnace is running full bore, and there isn't a window open in the house — well, you know. The good news is that insulation is pretty easy to maintain, as the following sections explain.

Looking at different types of insulation

Before you start adding insulation everywhere, take a few minutes to find out what kinds of insulation exist so that you can make a good decision about what you need and understand what you currently have.

Here are the basic categories of insulation:

- **Loose-fill insulation:** This kind of insulation is made out of small individual chunks of fibers. It's also known as *blown insulation* because it's installed with a *blower,* a giant vacuum cleaner that works in reverse.

- **Batt insulation:** With batt insulation, insulative fibers are woven together to create a continuous blanket of material. Batt insulation is available in 16- and 24-inch-wide rolls (or 8-foot strips) to fit standard spacing between ceiling and wall framing members. A paper or foil moisture barrier is glued to one side of this type of insulation.

  When installing batt insulation, always place the side with the backing toward the inside of the home. For example, with ceilings, the backing goes down, and for floors, the backing faces up.

- **Rigid insulation:** Insulative fibers are tightly sandwiched together between two layers of foil, creating a solid insulative material that looks a lot like a thick sheet of plywood. Rigid insulation, typically used between the roof sheathing and the roof covering when no attic exists, is available in different thicknesses and insulative values. It can be used anywhere the batts or loose-fill insulation can be used, but rigid insulation isn't always practical because of its rigidity and high cost.

- **Spray-foam insulation:** Spray-foam insulation works in the most convoluted and irregular places, expanding into places that other types of insulation can't reach. The expanding foam also acts as an excellent water seal. Unfortunately, this type of insulation can only be installed into an open wall, so it's an option only when you're remodeling a room or adding on.

- **Radiant-barrier insulation:** Radiant-barrier insulation is nothing more than a lightweight aluminum fabric that blankets existing attic insulation. Radiant barriers have hundreds of thousands of teeny-tiny holes that allow vapors to pass and prevent condensation from occurring at ceiling level. These barriers also reflect heat from above during summer, while at the same time holding in heat during winter. You install the barrier as a single sheet.

- **Duct insulation:** The fabric of duct insulation is soft and pliable like so many other types, but it's only 1 inch thick, comes in 1-foot-wide rolls, and is specifically made to be corkscrew-wrapped around ducting.

- **Pipe insulation:** Preformed, tubular, foam-pipe insulation has a specific use: to insulate water piping. This material is most available for $1/2$ inch, $3/4$ inch, and 1-inch piping; is usually sold in 6-foot lengths; and is easy to cut with scissors or a razor knife. Each section of insulation is split lengthwise to ensure quick installation.

Getting the lowdown on insulation materials

Many of the categories of insulation noted in the preceding section are available in a number of insulation materials: fiberglass, rock wool, cellulose, and more. They all work. And you can mix and match them. If you have cellulose insulation, for example, and need more, you can add any type of fiber you want. You can also use batts over loose-fill material and loose-fill material over batts.

Here's what we think about each type of insulation material:

- ✔ **Fiberglass:** Fiberglass insulation is the most popular and widely available type of insulation. You can buy it as either batts or loose fill. It's relatively inexpensive, and the batts are very easy to install. It's nonflammable and resists damage from water.

  The fibers can irritate your skin and lungs, so take precautions while handling it. In addition to wearing protective clothing and goggles, take a cold shower after working with fiberglass insulation to help remove tiny fibers that make their way to your skin and cause you to itch. (Why a *cold* shower? Because a hot shower opens your pores and allows the pesky fibers more opportunity to make you uncomfortable.)

- ✔ **Rock wool:** Although it's similar to fiberglass insulation, rock wool (also called mineral wool) is a little more expensive and somewhat more difficult to find, but it doesn't usually provoke the same itchy reaction that fiberglass does. It looks a lot like dryer lint and can be just as dusty when handled. Rock wool can be blown in or poured in place. Rock wool can cake when wet and naturally settles over time, conditions that diminish its insulative value.

- ✔ **Cellulose:** Cellulose insulation is an organic, loose-fill material made from recycled paper chemically treated to resist moisture and pests. Moisture absorption can make cellulose heavier, causing it to pack down and lose its insulative value.

  If you have cellulose insulation in your walls or ceilings, the insulative value has probably diminished substantially since it was first installed. When loose-fill insulation compacts in walls, it should be vacuumed out so that fresh insulation can be added. Cellulose in the attic can be left in place and simply covered with new insulation.

Many insulation materials can irritate your skin and lungs, so whenever you work with any type of insulation, be sure to use gloves, a fabric mask, protective clothing, goggles, and a hat to reduce exposure. In addition, some insulation is manufactured with formaldehyde — when buying insulation, check to ensure that the insulation you choose does *not* contain this nasty chemical.

Understanding R values

Insulation value is measured using what is known as *R value*. The higher the R number, the better the insulative value. R values vary widely between climate zones. Whereas an R value of 11 (R-11) may be recommended for your floor, your walls may need R-13, and your attic may need R-38.

Over the years, insulation requirements in homes have changed. R-19 was once sufficient for use in attics. Today, in moderate climates, R-30 is required. In extreme climates, R-60 may be necessary.

Check with the building department in your area to determine the correct R-value for each area of your home.

Adding insulation all over your house

We had been away from home for over three weeks. Before we left, we shut down all the mechanical systems — the water heater, air conditioner, and so on. The day we returned, the temperature was 104 degrees. But when we walked in the front door, we discovered that that house was cool and comfortable. We turned to each, making the same comment at the same time: "Good insulation."

When it's done well, nothing keeps on working — for free — like insulation. In this section, we walk you through all the parts of your home that should be insulated and tell you how to fill in the gaps.

Where to start: The attic

When you've got a problem with your insulation, the attic is the first place you should look. Believe it or not, most heat is lost through the ceiling — 60 percent or more. Properly maintained insulation can significantly reduce this heat loss.

The nice thing about attic insulation is that it doesn't have to be glued, nailed, stapled, or otherwise held in place. All it does is lay there.

So if all it does is lay there, why would you ever need to do anything with insulation after it's installed? Powerful air currents are created in your attic as air enters through eave vents and exits through higher vents. Natural air currents can actually move loose-fill insulation as if it's being swept by a broom, resulting in piles of insulation in some areas and none in others. If you have loose-fill insulation, check to see if the insulation in your attic has shifted; if it has, you can use a plastic lawn rake to gently move the insulation from high spots onto the bald areas.

Notice that we said a *plastic* rake. With electrical wires present in the attic, you don't want to use a metal rake.

You also can use a piece of batt insulation to fill a gap or a hole. Hey, it would save raking, and it can't be easily blown out of place again. Just measure the approximate area to be filled, use a razor knife or a pair of scissors to cut pieces of batt insulation to the approximate length required, and lay the material in place.

If your insulation appears to be in good shape, but you still feel a chill, you may need to add more. Check with your local public utility or your local building department for advice on what to do.

Whether you're filling holes or adding more, be sure to keep attic insulation clear of light fixtures. Light boxes covered with insulation can overheat and result in a fire. And don't plug your attic vents. An attic must be able to breathe; otherwise, hot air trapped in the attic can convert even the best-insulated home into a sweatbox on a hot summer day. Plus, a buildup of humidity can occur, which, over a long period of time, can result in wood rot, mildew, mold, and fungus growth.

If you have traditional wood-framed skylights in your home, then you have skylight chases. A *skylight chase* is the walled area that immediately surrounds the skylight between the roof and the ceiling — it's a vertical tunnel that runs through your attic from the ceiling to the roof. Skylight chases should also be insulated.

The walls

If mildew is growing on the inside surface of your exterior walls or if your exterior walls are *sweating* (you see excessive condensation), it may mean that there is no wall insulation or that the insulation has settled and is no longer effective. In either case, you need to add insulation.

Adding insulation to a wall is a bit more difficult than adding it to an attic (see the preceding section) because in a wall, the insulation is hidden between the interior and exterior wallcoverings. Removing the wallcovering to insulate the wall cavity just isn't cost effective. It's cheaper and easier to create small penetrations in the wall so that the insulation can be blown in. For that reason, blown insulation is usually the preferred choice when you have to re-insulate a completed wall.

Insulating a completed wall is easy. You need an insulation blower (kind of like a giant tank-type vacuum cleaner that blows instead of sucks). You can rent insulation blowers, but some stores provide the machine at no charge when you purchase your insulation from them. In addition to an insulation blower, you need these tools and materials:

- A stud finder
- An electric drill
- A hole saw (slightly larger in diameter than the tip of the insulation blower)
- Blue masking tape (which is easier to remove than the regular kind of masking tape)
- Several bags of blown insulation

Should you blow the insulation in through the inside or outside walls of your home? It depends. Attacking the project from the interior is a bit messier but also less expensive. Plus, a perfect repair normally can't be made to the exterior wallcovering — regardless of type. However, if some portions of the interior side of the wall are covered with tile or other expensive finish, your next best bet is insulating from the outside.

Follow these steps to blow in insulation:

1. **Use the stud finder to locate each stud and any horizontal blocks that exist at or near the center of the wall's height; then mark each stud center and horizontal blocks with a piece of blue masking tape.**

   Some homes have a horizontal block midway between the top and bottom of a wall cavity. Some have a diagonal row of blocks. Others have none.

2. **Use the drill and hole saw to make a penetration (on center between each pair of studs) into the top of the cavity approximately 6 inches below the ceiling.**

   Because studs are spaced every 16 inches or so, penetrations to add insulation must be made at the same intervals, filling one cavity at a time.

   Save the discs of wall-covering material removed by the hole saw. When the project is complete, you (or a wallboard contractor) can use them to quickly patch the holes.

3. **If the wall has horizontal or diagonal blocking, make an additional (second) penetration (on center between each pair of studs) an inch or so beneath the block.**

4. **If you find old compacted insulation within the wall, remove it with a vacuum.**

5. **Blow in the new insulation.**

6. **Repair the holes and clean up the mess.**

Consider hiring a wallboard contractor to repair the holes. In an average home, they can be repaired for a few hundred dollars, and you'll never be able to tell that the holes were there.

The floor

An insulated floor substantially reduces the loss of heat (thank you, energy gods), helps to eliminate mildew- and rot-causing condensation, and generally helps to keep your tootsies warm when you go barefoot through the kitchen. If you have hardwood floors, you should be especially interested in maintaining your floor insulation because lack of floor insulation can cause planks of hardwood flooring to twist, buckle, and curl.

Periodically (at least once a year), crawl beneath your home with a flashlight to check the condition of the floor insulation in your basement or sub-area to ensure that it's properly positioned. Here, sagging is the biggest problem.

Floor insulation is normally held in place with netting or bailing wire attached from one joist-bottom to another. If the insulation netting sags, you need to reattach it or replace it:

- **To reattach insulation netting,** you can use nails or staples. Nails hold better but are hard to drive in tight spots. Staples are easier to install, but you may need to buy a tool (a construction-grade staple gun — known as a *hammer tacker,* which you can find at your local hardware store or home center). If the paper has become brittle and tears, staple or nail directly through the insulation.

- **To replace insulation netting,** lightning rods (named for their speedy installation) are a handy alternative to netting or bailing wire. These lightweight, flexible steel rods hold the insulation in place by spring tension. Just place one end of the rod against the side of a floor joist and bend it slightly so that the other end is forced into place against the face of the opposite joist (see Figure 6-1). Use one hand to hold up the insulation and the other hand to whip the lightning rod into place. Lightning rods are available at hardware stores and home centers.

Pipes

Putting insulation around all accessible water pipes (see Figure 6-2) saves energy, prevents freezing during most moderate to medium chills, and reduces condensation when pipes flow through attics and crawlspaces. It's also cheap insurance. A pipe that bursts in the crawlspace is no joy to experience or repair, but it's bearable. A pipe that bursts in the attic is an altogether different story. We know. Years ago, long before we were old enough to spell *contractor* (let alone be one) a pipe in our attic burst. What a mess!

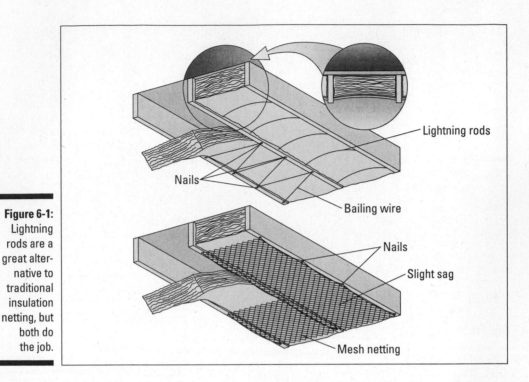

Figure 6-1:
Lightning rods are a great alternative to traditional insulation netting, but both do the job.

Lightning rods

Nails

Bailing wire

Nails

Slight sag

Mesh netting

Be sure that the tape that holds the insulation in place and the insulation itself are in good shape. If either the insulation or the tape crumbles to the touch, replace it. You can remove crumbling insulation with nothing more than a gentle tug. With the insulation removed, all you have to do is slip a new piece in place.

If you live in an area where temperatures frequently reach below freezing, and you've installed pipe heaters (wire or tape), don't insulate these pipes without first getting the approval of the company that manufactures the pipe heaters. By the way, pipe heaters also deteriorate. If you see signs of deterioration or fraying, it may be time for replacement.

Heat ducts

As with other kinds of insulation, the material that surrounds your heat ducts reduces energy costs while improving the effectiveness of your central heating and cooling system. It also helps prevent unwanted condensation in attics and crawlspaces, thereby reducing the chance for mold, mildew, and the foul odors associated with them.

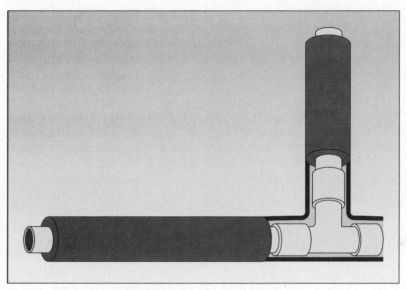

Figure 6-2:
Insulate your pipes to prevent them from bursting in cold weather.

Reattaching and adjusting insulation

Insulation is wrapped around and around the duct in a corkscrew fashion (see Figure 6-3). Air currents, rodents, house movement, and vibration in the heating system can cause the insulation to loosen and fall away from the ducting. Reattaching or adjusting the insulation to cover the ducting is a good thing. While you're there, add an extra layer — it couldn't hurt.

You can "stitch" a nail into insulation to hold it together. You do this in the same way that a seamstress uses a sewing pin to hold two pieces of fabric together.

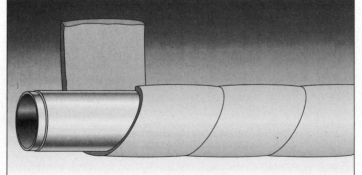

Figure 6-3:
Heat-duct insulation keeps your energy costs low.

A thin layer of plastic, which acts as a vapor barrier, surrounds modern insulated ducts and prevents moisture from attacking the insulation and the ducting. If rodents or sloppy workers damage the thin plastic vapor barrier, use plastic sheeting (any kind) and metal tape to fix the barrier.

Metal tape looks like duct tape, except it's shiny and won't rot in moist areas where duct tape can. Actually, for small tears, just tape over the damaged area in the same way that you'd cover a cut with a Band-Aid. For areas of larger damage, use a piece of plastic as a patch held in place with metal tape. Make sure the tape seals all four sides of the patch.

Performing a duct leak test

Those same workers, house shifts, and pesky rodents also can cause duct damage that creates air leaks. This condition can result in major heat or cooling loss and can substantially increase your energy bill. Therefore, checking for duct leaks can pay off big time. Because most ducting is covered with insulation, leaks can be hard to find.

Here are a few signs that may indicate a leak:

- Ducting that is crushed or badly bent
- Insulation that has darkened
- An area around the ducting that is warmer than normal in the winter or cooler than normal in the summer

If none of these conditions exist and you aren't happy with your energy bill, hire a home-comfort specialist — a heating contractor — to perform a duct leak test. He'll cap off all register outlets and pressurize the duct system. If pressure loss occurs, the contractor will search out the leak using smoke and then repair it.

Controlling air leaks in your ceilings, walls, and floors

There's more to the energy envelope than maintaining insulation. You also need to perform another maintenance step, known as *infiltration control* (controlling air leaks through penetrations in ceilings, walls, and floors). No matter how much insulation you have in your home, if major air leaks exist, your insulation won't work effectively.

Locating leaks

Unwanted air can leak into your home from all sorts of places: at weather stripping, door and window frames, attic and sub-area plumbing and electrical penetrations, heat registers, yes, and even electrical switches and receptacles.

Infiltration also occurs where pipes and wires in walls penetrate into the attic or sub-area.

Here are tips for finding leaks in different areas of your home:

- **In an attic or crawlspace:** Finding a penetration in an attic or crawl-space isn't terribly difficult when it comes to plumbing pipes, flues and ventilation, and heating ducts. Just check the point where a pipe or duct penetrates the ceiling or floor and look for gaps.

- **Around wiring:** Finding penetrations around wiring — especially in an insulated area — is a challenge. Short of removing the insulation, you can't see where penetrations exist because the wiring normally doesn't stick up beyond the insulation like a pipe or a flue does. Therefore, you have to search through insulation until you find a point where a wire travels down through the top of a wall.

- **In walls, ceilings, and floors:** The amount of infiltration from walls, ceilings, and floors is simply amazing. Fortunately, you can easily locate these leaks in the myriad of places that they occur: around light switches, electric plugs, drain and water pipes, heat registers, thermostats, wall and ceiling light fixtures, smoke and carbon monoxide detectors, floor plugs, door bell chimes, doors, and windows. Just light a smoky incense stick — if leaks exist near the stick, the smoke flickers.

- **Around windows and doors:** When it comes to leaks, doors and windows are major culprits. Even the slightest amount of house shift can cause a previously well-maintained and properly adjusted door or window to leak like a sieve. Check the weatherstripping on doors and windows twice each year: once during mid-spring when the soil around the house dries out and begins to shrink and the house begins to shift, and again during mid-winter when the soil around the house swells from moisture retention and the house begins to shift. Here's an easy way to check for air leaks at the bottom of a door. At night, and from the outside of the door, point a flashlight toward the bottom of the door. If light can be seen from inside, an adjustment is needed.

Stopping infiltration

In the days when we were the maintenance men aboard the ark, we filled small cracks (no wider than 1/4 inch) with caulking. For larger openings, we stuffed insulation or steel wool into the gaps. For the largest and most gaping of holes, we used tin plates or wood covers.

Today, things have changed. Expanding polyurethane spray foam in a can is now available. No more time-consuming tin-plate installations or replacing insulation or steel wool that has fallen out. Simply spray a little expanding foam into the gap, and it immediately expands to permanently seal the hole (see Figure 6-4). Home maintenance in a can. What a country!

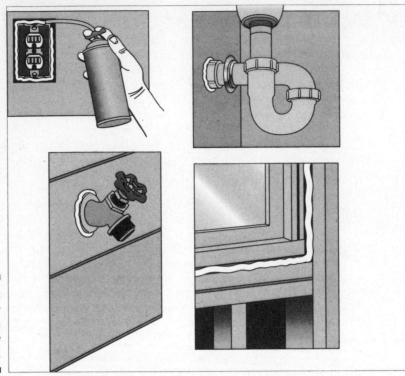

Figure 6-4:
Stopping air
infiltration
with spray
foam.

Where polyurethane spray is now best for large gaps, then and now, caulking is still best for narrow cracks. The kind of caulking to use depends on the area being caulked. Glass, metal, wood, plastic, and other surfaces respond differently to caulk. Read the manufacturer's label carefully before making your purchase.

Another infiltration-control method is installing precut gasketing into electrical switches and outlets. The gasket material consists of a thin foam that fits neatly between the plug or switch cover and the wall. Each gasket is precut to match either a plug cover or a switch.

If your electrical boxes aren't gasketed, we suggest that you add them. An entire home can be done for under $50. Cover outlets on interior walls, too. Don't forget that air can get into interior walls via wire and pipe holes that penetrate through to the attic and crawlspace.

Windows: See the Light, Feel the Cold

As beautiful as they are, most windows aren't as energy efficient as an insulated wall. Unfortunately, you can't see through a wall. The R value (insulative value) of a typical wall is about R-13. (See "Understanding R values," earlier in this chapter, for more information.) The R value of a typical window is about R-2. Even triple-pane windows have a low insulative value.

None of the window types or brands on the market today can compare to the recently developed highly energy-efficient windows that are available. Where current window brands offer an R value of R-2 or R-3, a new line of truly energy-efficient window offers R values of R-5 to R-13. (A solid wall in a moderate climate has a rating of R-13.) Wouldn't you like to have a window in your home that has the exact same insulative value as a wall? Manufactured by Serious Materials, these windows come in a range of insulative values from R-5 to R-13 — depending on your budget. For more info about these windows, go to www.seriousmaterials.com or call 800-797-8159.

If highly efficient window replacement isn't in your immediate future, here are a few maintenance suggestions for your windows that will make them a bit more energy efficient, add longevity to their existence, and make them easier to operate.

Dealing with water and air leaks

A window that leaks air can also mean excessive energy loss and cost. Summer or winter, you don't want your house to leak air, especially if you spend your hard-earned dollars warming or cooling it. Test a window for leaks by burning an incense stick near all its joints and connections. If the smoke flickers, you have an air leak. Check:

✔ Where one section of the window meets another

✔ Where the windows meet the frame

✔ Where the frame meets the wall

You seal air leaks and water leaks in the same way — by caulking and replacing weatherstripping. You can also inject foam sealant between the frame of the window and the frame of the house.

Caulking

Often water leaks at a window result from a breakdown in the connection between the window frame and the wall. To prevent leaks, caulk the window where it meets the exterior siding (see Figure 6-5). If the window is surrounded by wood trim, use a high-grade polyurethane caulk to seal all gaps between the trim and the siding (and the trim and the window).

Take special care to seal the top side of the top piece of trim. Puddling water at this location causes many window leaks.

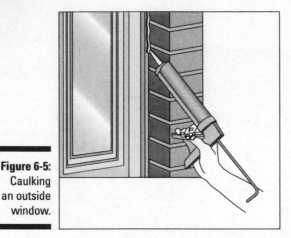

Figure 6-5:
Caulking
an outside
window.

Expanding spray foam

If you're willing to remove either your exterior or interior window trim, you can do a much better job of sealing window and door leaks — permanently! — than you can with just caulk. Using expanding foam not only prevents air infiltration, but it also makes the treated area watertight too.

Here's how to do it:

1. **Use a pry bar and a hammer to remove the window trim (either inside or outside — not both).**

2. **Fill the void with expanding spray foam in a can.**

   Don't worry about overfilling. Let it bulge out of the wall. What you don't want to do is touch the foam while it's wet; you'll make a huge, hard-to-clean-up mess.

3. **After the foam dries (it'll take several hours), use a razor knife to cut off the excess.**

   We like to use a serrated knife from the kitchen. However, "borrowing" a knife is only possible when the boss isn't home.

4. **Replace the trim in the reverse order in which you removed it and touch up paint as necessary.**

Weatherstripping

Leaks also occur when weatherstripping wears out. You may have to remove the operable portion of the window to find the weatherstripping:

- ✔ **For sliding windows,** open them halfway and lift the window out of the bottom track. Then pull the window out of the opening bottom first.

- ✔ **For single-hung windows,** usually you just release a lever on the side track(s) of the window frame. Contact the manufacturer for specific instructions.

After you remove the operable portion of the window, it becomes pretty obvious where the weatherstripping is and how it has to be replaced. Most home centers offer replacement weatherstripping in peel-and-stick rolls. If you aren't sure about what to do, take the section that you removed to the store with you or photograph the area that needs attention. A picture is definitely worth a thousand words!

You may need an adhesive solvent to unstick old weatherstripping. Adhesive solvent is available in spray cans for easy application.

Adhesive remover can be pretty caustic stuff. Read the can to be sure that it won't damage your window frame.

If you have metal or vinyl frame windows, check the drain holes at the outside edge of the bottom portion of the window frame. During rains, water can fill the bottom track, leak to the inside of the home, and literally flood the area surrounding the window. Drain or weep holes allow water to escape from the frame, preventing flooding. You can use a piece of wire or a small screwdriver blade to ensure that the holes are clear.

Preventing condensation

Condensation around windows can result when a window leaks air. Cold outside air mixes with warm inside air and creates a wet layer of condensation over the entire window. Condensation can actually form enough moisture to cause wood to rot. And don't forget mildew. Condensation is a feed bag for mildew.

You can reduce condensation by:

- Sealing air leaks around windows (see the "Dealing with water and air leaks" section, earlier in this chapter)
- Replacing single-pane windows with double-pane "insulated" glass
- Using wood-frame windows
- Using storm windows

 If you have insulated windows and you see rainbows or condensation between the two sheets of glass, then your window has failed and should be replaced. The frame can remain, but the glass must be replaced. Be sure to shop for the best guarantee. A failed insulated window is expensive to replace at $250 and up.

Maintaining storm windows

Storm windows are necessary when you have old, single-pane windows. A *storm window* is nothing more than a second window that adds insulative value to the window that it covers. We wouldn't be surprised if yours are 50 years old and tired. When storm windows are right, and when they don't slip down and make gaps because of "tiredness," they reduce heat loss and cold-air infiltration. But dealing with them, no matter how old they are, can be a challenge.

As far as maintenance goes, here's what you need to do:

- **Take down the storm windows in the summer so that you can open your windows.** Leaving them up year-round can cause rot to occur in the area between the storm window and the house. Also, ventilation is a must to reduce fungus growth in a home.

- **Put the storm windows back up in the winter.** Make sure that storm windows are properly sealed at their edges when they're installed. Air leaking through the edges of a storm window can allow condensation to occur between it and the window it protects.

- **Replace cracked panes.** Leave this task to a pro.

- **Clean the panes every time you take the windows down or put them back up.** Use standard glass-cleaning methods.

✔ **Wipe the frames with lacquer thinner.** Lacquer thinner cleans off the weird aluminum corrosion and shines up the frames.

✔ **Periodically (at least once a year), caulk the area between where the frames meet the walls and the sills.** Be sure not to block the weep holes!

Why not replace storm windows? Cost. New storms for a house with 28 custom-size windows will cost thousands of dollars and are probably only the second-best solution anyway. Many homeowners have done away with their storms and just replaced the windows entirely — but that costs $15,000 to $20,000.

Maintaining screens

Newer, more energy-efficient homes don't allow for the passive exchange of air through cracks, gaps, and penetrations as older homes did. Unfortunately, this condition creates stale trapped air within the home. In addition, some of the components used in the fabrication of construction materials emit gases that cause health problems, which can range from a minor case of the sniffles to a full-blown allergic reaction. Air in the home must be continually exchanged with a fresh supply from the outside, which makes screens really important.

Cleaning screens

In order to get a good exchange of air, you have to keep your screens clean. Grit and grime can also hasten deterioration, thereby diminishing the life of a window screen. As if that weren't enough, dirty screens also prevent light from making its way into your home. Finally, a gust of wind can blow dust from a screen straight into your home, aggravating allergies and increasing housekeeping chores.

To clean your screens, lay them flat on a smooth, cloth-covered surface, such as an old sheet on a picnic table. Scrub them gently with a soft nylon brush, rinse with a hose, and shake off excess water. We recommend pressure-washing your screens once in the spring and again in the fall.

Patching a screen

Screen patch kits are available at hardware stores and home centers. They're inexpensive and easy to install (the process takes less than a minute). You can also use any of the following methods to repair small holes in window screens, depending upon the type of screen material:

- ✔ **Apply a small amount of clear nail polish to a small hole or tear in a vinyl or fiberglass screen.** The polish acts as an adhesive, sealing the damaged area.

- ✔ **Mend small tears in metal or fiberglass screens with a dab of clear silicone adhesive.** If necessary, dab it on in successive layers until the tear is completely filled.

- ✔ **You can darn small holes in metal screening.** Simply unravel a strand or two from a piece of scrap screening and sew the hole shut, weaving the strands through the sound fabric with a needle (see Figure 6-6).

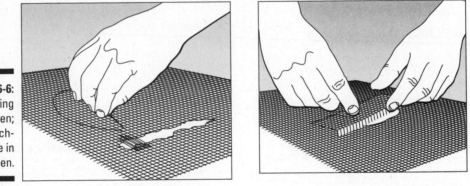

Figure 6-6: Left, darning a screen; right, patching a hole in a screen.

Large holes in metal screen material take a little more effort. Follow these steps:

1. **Neatly trim the damaged area to a ravel-free square or rectangle using tin snips (metal shears).**

2. **Cut a piece of patch screen material that measures about 1 inch larger (in both directions) than the damaged area.**

3. **Unravel a couple of strands of material around the entire perimeter of the patch; then bend the unraveled ends at each side of the patch at 90 degrees.**

4. **Place the patch over the damaged area and carefully thread the bent wires through the sound fabric (refer to Figure 6-6); then bend the wires flat again to hold the patch in place.**

For large holes in fiberglass screening, simply cut a patch of similar material and affix it to the good material using transparent silicone glue.

Replacing a screen

Whether it's a window or a door, rescreening is easy. There are two types of screen available: metal (copper, steel, aluminum, and so on) and fiberglass.

Rescreening with metal is slightly more difficult than with fiberglass (metal is not as flexible as fiberglass), but metal seems to stretch tighter, and it does last longer. However, where fiberglass screen material is not as strong as metal and often sags slightly once in place, it's much easier to install. In either case both metal and fiberglass install in exactly the same fashion. You need the following tools and materials:

- ✔ The screen material of your choice — a few inches larger than the screen to be repaired in both width and height.

- ✔ A roll of screen spline of a size that matches the size you currently have. The *spline* is the rubber gasket material located all around one side of the screen's frame that holds the screen in place.

- ✔ A *spline roller* (a tool that is composed of a grip with a rolling wheel at each end).

- ✔ A razor knife.

- ✔ An awl or ice pick.

- ✔ A large, flat work surface. The kitchen table covered with an old blanket or a piece of cardboard works well.

Replacement is pretty easy. Lay the screen spline side up on the work surface and then follow these steps:

1. **Poke the awl into the old rubber spline and pull it out of its recess.**

   When enough of the spline has been removed, you can pretty much do the rest by grabbing and pulling.

2. **Remove and discard the old screen.**

3. **Lay the replacement screen centered over the frame.**

4. **At one corner, use your fingers to press the spline material into the spline groove in the frame.**

5. **When an inch or two of the spline is started, use the spline roller to steadily push the spline into its groove around the entire frame (see Figure 6-7).**

   Keep the edge of the screen aligned with the frame and do one side first, and then the opposite side. Then do the top and finish with the bottom. Make sure to keep the screen taut. A helper may be in order here.

6. **With the spline in place, cut the end and use the razor knife to remove the excess screen material.**

   Place the razor knife in the outside edge of the spline groove, pointing the tip away from the spline. Gently wipe the razor knife along the groove. It will easily cut away the excess.

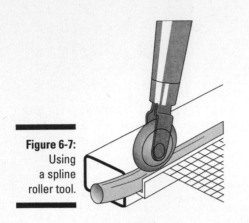

Figure 6-7:
Using
a spline
roller tool.

Buying new windows

Sometimes repairing or maintaining an old window isn't worth the trouble.
When replacement is the only alternative, it's good to understand how
window components differ to have a strategy for deciding what kind of
window is best for you. When we get calls about windows on our radio program, most people want to know "What brand?" That's not the way we recommend approaching the decision. When we need a window, we choose the
frame type first, then the glass configuration (how many layers), and finally
the energy options (low-emissivity, gas filled, and so on).

Choosing a frame

Some frames are more energy efficient than others, some last longer than
others, and some are just plain easier to maintain. Here's a list of the frames
in order from our most to least favorite:

- **Clad wood frames:** These are wood frames covered on the exterior
  with either a thin coat of aluminum or a thin coat of fiberglass. A frame
  made of wood is by far the most energy-efficient type. But, by itself,
  wood is a pain to maintain — painting, scraping, yuck! With a coating
  on the exterior, maintenance is reduced to almost nothing, offering the
  best of both worlds: energy efficiency and low maintenance. We prefer
  fiberglass over aluminum because fiberglass doesn't dent as easily as
  aluminum.

- **Composite and fiberglass frames:** These frames are next best in energy
  efficiency and low maintenance. They won't last half as long as clad
  wood, but they're far less expensive.

- **Metal frames:** Metal frames are lowest on our list because they're not at
  all energy efficient and they corrode faster than the others combined.

Choosing the glass

Choosing the correct glass configuration isn't so easy. Here it's more about money than anything else. Three panes are more energy efficient — and more expensive — than two panes.

Our advice? Select as many sheets of glass as you can possibly afford (with windows, more is better) and have the glass coated with ultraviolet (UV) inhibitors. These protect carpets, drapes, and furniture and are well worth the investment.

Choosing energy options

Always be sure to ask for a window with a *low-emissivity* (low-E) coating or layer. Low-E windows are somewhat more energy efficient than windows without this coating.

Installing windows

There are two basic types of window installation:

- ✔ **Replacement windows that fit inside the frame of the old window and that are designed to fit on top of the exterior wallcovering:** These types of windows can be installed in just a few minutes and are sealed with caulking. In our opinion, they're the *worst* choice. They're a leak waiting to happen. No matter how much these windows are caulked, some of them always leak.

- ✔ **Windows that are replaced in the same way as those that were originally installed:** These windows look better, are more airtight, and usually don't leak. This type of installation is three times as expensive as common replacement window installation, but it's worth every penny. When a window frame is laced into surrounding siding paper and flashings, it doesn't need caulking to prevent leaks. With this type of installation, caulking is an added precaution, not a waterproofing must.

Don't try to save money on window installation. If you do, it'll come back to haunt you. And when the window contractor tells you that his caulking is the best and that it'll hold for 60 years, call him a liar and throw him off your property.

Getting In and Out: Maintaining Exterior Doors

An exterior door may be more energy efficient than a window, but a door can leak just as much water and air. As the moisture content changes in soil, your home shifts. Your doors also shift, creating gaps large enough for a dump truck to pass through. Finally, doors can deteriorate and need to be regularly painted or varnished.

 If you get tired of the often backbreaking maintenance that you have to perform to keep your wood front door looking presentable, look into a fiberglass or steel door and frame. They look better longer, are far easier to maintain, and are more secure than most wood doors. Where steel is not nearly as energy efficient as wood, fiberglass is far more energy efficient than both steel and wood.

With doors, you need to regularly caulk the exterior trim even if the exterior door in question is protected by a covered porch. (**Remember:** Caulking is designed to keep out air as well as water.) Caulk the doorframe to the door trim and the door trim to the exterior wallcovering.

Fixing leaks between the threshold and door bottom

If you find moisture on the entry floor, it could be a leak between the threshold and the door bottom. The *threshold* is the wood or metal platform at the base of the doorway. It usually tilts outward (to shed water). The bottoms of most exterior doors are fitted with a metal door bottom, or *shoe,* that houses a rubber gasket. The door shoe is attached to the bottom of the door with screws driven through oblong slots. The oblong slots allow the door bottom to be adjusted up and down as the house — and consequently the door — shift up and down. When the door is closed, the rubber gasket is supposed to rest tightly against the full length of the threshold, preventing the influx of air and water.

No matter how successfully the door shoe and threshold work to prevent air and water leaks, there could be yet another problem: The threshold itself might leak. Exterior door thresholds are normally laid in a thick bed of caulk when they're installed. Occasionally, the caulk shrinks, and the threshold leaks.

The only way to prevent future leaks is to remove the threshold screws and force caulking into the area between the threshold and the floor. Make sure to heat the caulking first so that it'll flow freely — a hairdryer works great. When the caulking begins to ooze out of the edges, stop the caulking process.

Stopping air leaks with weatherstripping and sealant

An air leak in a doorframe is pretty common. You can eliminate leaks by adding foam sealant between the frame of the door and the frame of the house. Simply remove the wood trim that covers the joint between the doorframe and the wall. (Use a flat pry bar to slowly remove the trim to avoid damaging it.) With the door trim removed, fill the void with expanding spray foam. (Don't worry if it expands beyond the surface; once it dries — in a few hours — you can easily remove the extra with a knife.) With the excess foam trimmed, replace the trim and touch-up paint as necessary.

Leaks also can occur between the door and the doorframe. Check the condition of your weatherstripping to make sure that it's in good condition and fits tightly to the door when closed. If your existing weatherstripping is tattered and in bad shape, replace it. We like the kind of weatherstripping that consists of a rubber bead attached lengthwise to a strip of metal.

Here's how to install new weatherstripping:

1. **While standing outside the door, with the door in the closed position, gently press the rubber portion of the weatherstripping against the door and the metal strip against the frame — both at the same time.**

2. **While holding the weatherstripping in place, attach the metal section to the frame of the door with the nails or screws provided.**

3. **Oblong holes allow the weatherstripping to be adjusted back and forth during installation and later as house movement causes the door to shift.**

Caring for wood and painting

Wood and water don't mix. For that reason, exterior doors must be protected (painted or varnished) on a regular basis. Whether painting or varnishing, follow the same process:

1. **Clean the door with TSP.**

   TSP not only cleans but also etches the finish, creating a surface that the new paint or varnish will readily bond to.

2. **Lightly sand imperfections and clean the entire door with a clean, lint-free rag and paint thinner.**

   You can also use a *tack cloth* (a cloth with a sticky substance that readily collects dust). Tack cloths are great for pre-paint cleaning.

3. **Prime bare spots on painted doors and follow with your chosen finish coat as soon as the primed areas are dry.** And don't forget to paint all four edges of the door — top, bottom, hinge side, and strike side. The paint will thoroughly seal the door and prevent it from swelling, which can cause the door to rub or stick.

There is no perfect paint for an exterior door. Some experts say varnish, others say marine varnish (used for boats), others say water-based paint, and others say oil-based paint. We think they all work well. As long as you regularly maintain your exterior doors, they'll look good and last a long time.

Showing some love to your sliding glass doors

Did you ever reach out to open a sliding glass door, give it a tug, and feel like the door was pulling back? Unlike conventional exterior doors that swing on hinges, a sliding glass door moves on rollers. Little wheels made of neoprene or metal. Little wheels that wear out with use. Because the wheels on the bottom of a sliding glass door run in a threshold often filled with dirt and sand, it's a wonder that they last more than a year or two.

If you have sliding glass doors, here's how to convert loving care into lasting quality and a door that opens and closes as easy as pie: Keep them clean and lubricated, and adjust (or replace) the rollers as necessary. In the following sections, we explain how.

Keeping them clean and lubricated

Always keep the bottom track of the door clean and free of dirt and sand. In addition, regularly spray the track and the wheels with a waterless silicone spray. The absence of water in the spray reduces the chance for rusty wheels, and the silicone is a colorless lubricant that won't stain or attract dust.

Adjusting (or replacing) the rollers as necessary

Just like other doors in the home, a sliding glass door can be knocked out of whack when the house shifts. Adjusting the wheels at the bottom of the door can compensate for this problem. Raising or lowering opposing wheels (located at the underside of each end of the door) can straighten a crooked door, allowing it to close parallel to the doorframe. Raising both wheels evenly can prevent the bottom of the door from rubbing on the track as the wheels wear out and become smaller.

For wheels that are adjustable, simply turn the adjacent screw. In most cases, you'll find a hole at each end of the bottom track of the sliding door through which a screwdriver can be inserted. Use a pry bar to slightly lift the door to take pressure off the wheel while you turn the adjustment screw. If the door is lowered when you wanted to raise it, simply raise the door and turn the screw in the other direction. How's that for getting the best bang for your sliding door buck?

Rollers that are completely worn out (or those that can't be adjusted) can be replaced. Open the door about halfway, raise it 1 inch by forcing it into the top track, and, at the same time, pull out on the bottom. With the door out of the opening, snap the old rollers out and pop in a pair of new ones.

Depending upon the size (and weight) of the door, you may need a helper. Otherwise, you may be repairing a sheet of glass and your back.

Part III
Key Systems: Plumbing and HVAC

The 5th Wave   By Rich Tennant

"Oh, Dave is very handy around the house. He manually entered the phone numbers for the electrician, the carpenter, and the plumber on our speed dial."

In this part . . .

Plumbers pride themselves on "bringing water to the world." However, the fact is that plumbers run water and sewer lines at the very same time. We've always wondered what their saying would be if they didn't do the water portion. Think about it!

In this part, we show you how to maintain your plumbing fixtures and trim, as well as your heating, ventilating, and air-conditioning (HVAC) systems. Each of these "mechanical" systems has moving parts, and, as such, all of them, from time to time, require attention. Don't worry — we've got your back.

Chapter 7

Plumbing, Part I: Pipes, Water Heaters, Water Softeners, and More

This chapter is devoted to the water delivery system — the water pipes, if you will. They're the thin pipes that run through the walls, basement, and attic, carrying water in and out. In contrast, drain, waste, and vent pipes are fatter and are not *pressurized* (filled with water under pressure); you can find out about them in Chapter 9. For the most part, water pipes are hidden in walls, attics, crawl spaces, basements, and below cabinets, and they require little or no maintenance — that is until they spring a leak or become so clogged that they deliver little more than a trickle. In this chapter, we help you deal with both of these issues along with a few other challenges that may spring up from time to time. We also tell you about getting the most out of your water heater and water softener.

Don't confuse gas lines with water lines. They sometimes resemble each other — gas lines are often made of the same material as water lines, but gas lines travel from the gas main to fuel-burning appliances such as a water heater, range, furnace, or gas-powered dryer.

Thar She Blows! Turning Off Your Water Main

If you don't already know where your water main is, read this section, and then put down this book and go out and find it. Don't wait until an emergency to hunt for your water main — if you do, the consequences could be catastrophic.

The water main is typically located in a precast concrete vault in the front yard near the curb or below the sidewalk in front of your home. It has a concrete or metal lid that you have to remove to access the main water valve. In general, you can remove the lid by wedging a screwdriver into the slit in the top of the lid. If the lid hasn't been removed in a while, you may need a small pry bar to free it from the vault.

Turning off the main water valve can sometimes be quite a chore. Although most main water valves can be turned using an adjustable crescent wrench (also known among friends as a "knuckle buster"), using a water-main wrench is easier, more effective, and safer. You can find a water-main wrench at your local home center or hardware store.

To prevent the main water valve from becoming difficult to operate, periodically turn the valve on and off.

Replacing a Damaged Section of Pipe

If your hardwood flooring is buckled and your crawl space is like a steam bath or your drywall is damp and covered with mold, chances are good that your water pipes have sprung a leak. The bad news is that even a pinhole leak can cause lots of damage. The good news is that you generally won't need to tear up walls and rip out vast amounts of plumbing pipes. You can save the day (and lots of time and money) by replacing a damaged section of pipe.

Copper pipe

To remove and replace a piece of copper pipe, you need these supplies:

- A measuring tape
- A pencil

> ✔ A copper-pipe tubing cutter
>
> ✔ Fine sandpaper or emery paper
>
> ✔ Flux and a flux brush
>
> ✔ Solder
>
> ✔ A propane torch
>
> ✔ A short length of replacement copper pipe and two couplings (***Note:*** The total length of the replacement piece of pipe and the two couplings, when fully assembled, must be about ³/₄ inch *longer* than the length of the damaged pipe.)

To remove the damaged piece of pipe, follow these steps:

1. **Turn off the main water shut-off valve; then open a faucet at the lowest point in the home (either the ground floor or, if you have one, the basement) to allow the line to empty.**

2. **Use a measuring tape to determine the length of pipe needed and use a pencil to transfer the measurement to the pipe.**

   When figuring the overall length of the replacement piece of pipe, make sure to take into account the ends, which will slide into fittings.

3. **Place the blade of the tube cutter over the mark on the pipe and gently clamp down on the pipe by turning the grip clockwise while rotating the cutter around the entire circumference of the pipe.**

   The cutter should move freely. Applying too much pressure too fast will bend the end of the pipe and damage the cutting blade. A bent end can result in a leak.

4. **Use the deburring blade located at the end of the tube cutter or a small file to remove any burrs at the cut end.**

5. **Polish the outside of the end to be soldered with emery paper until it has a bright finish. Do the same with the interior of the fitting to which it will be joined.**

   This polishing cleans the material and provides the necessary tooth for a solid connection.

6. **Apply a thin layer of flux to the outside of the pipe and the interior of the joint.**

   Flux is an acid that further cleans the pipe and causes the solder to flow more evenly.

7. **Assemble the pieces and rotate the pipe in the fitting to distribute the flux and ensure a secure fit.**

8. **Solder the connection.**

Soldering is *not* like welding, where the flame is placed directly on the connection. When soldering, the tip of the blue flame should be directed at the fitting, not the pipe, which allows the heat to radiate to the joint. When the flux begins to bubble, touch the end of the solder to one point of the joint and let capillary action do the work. The solder will automatically form a tiny bead around the joint. Remove the flame as soon as the solder begins to flow. Be careful not to move or jiggle the pipe or fitting for about a minute after the flame has been removed — you want to allow the solder enough time to cool.

9. **When the soldering is complete, remove the excess flux by wiping off the pipe and fittings with a clean, dry cloth.**

10. **Turn the water back on and check for leaks.**

Using a torch can be dangerous, especially if you're not experienced in its use. So keep these safety tips in mind when soldering:

- ✔ Wear safety glasses and gloves, as well as long pants and a long-sleeved shirt to avoid being burned by hot flying flux or solder.

- ✔ Have plenty of ventilation, especially if you're working in tight situations.

- ✔ When working near wood, use a metal shield between the flame and the combustible surface to avoid causing a fire. *Never* use a torch around natural gas or gasoline, and always have a working fire extinguisher nearby.

Threaded pipe

Galvanized pipe is notorious for rust, corrosion, and leaks. When this happens, the most prudent solution for a permanent repair is to remove the damaged section and replace it with a new section of threaded pipe. There are other stopgap emergency repair methods that may be used (mentioned later in this chapter), but we consider them temporary at best.

Replacing a section of threaded pipe is not nearly as difficult as you might imagine, thanks to the wide assortment of threaded sections of pipe that are now standard inventory at most hardware stores or home-improvement centers. These prefab sections come in various diameters and lengths. Many stores will custom-cut and thread a section of pipe if a stock item is not available.

To remove and replace threaded pipe, you need these supplies:

- ✔ Two medium-size pipe wrenches
- ✔ Hacksaw or reciprocating saw

✔ Penetrating oil or lubricant, like WD-40

✔ Two sections of replacement pipe and a union (***Note:*** The total length of the two pieces of pipe and the union, when fully assembled, must equal the length of the damaged pipe.)

When calculating the overall length of material needed, measure from the face of one fitting to the face of the opposite fitting and add 1 inch. This accounts for $\frac{1}{2}$ inch of threads at either end, which overlap into the fittings.

Removing the old pipe

To remove the old pipe, follow these steps:

1. **Turn off the main water shut-off valve so that no water flows into your home.**

2. **Open a faucet at the lowest point in the home to allow the line to empty.**

3. **Cut through the damaged section using a hacksaw or a reciprocating saw so that the two pieces that remain can be unscrewed from the adjacent fittings.**

4. **Remove the existing pipe, using two medium pipe wrenches, one gripping the pipe and the other gripping the fitting), and then pry in opposing directions.**

   Removing the old pipe from the fittings may prove difficult. Prying the two wrenches in opposite directions enhances the leverage needed to break the connection.

   If at first you don't succeed in loosening the connection, spray the area with a penetrating oil or lubricant, such as WD-40, to break down some of the rust and corrosion that prevents the pipe from budging.

5. **With the pipe removed, spray the threads within the fittings with more of the penetrating oil, and allow the oil to sit for approximately 15 minutes.**

6. **After 15 minutes, use a small wire bottle brush to remove any residue, preparing the area for a new leak-free connection.**

Picking up the pieces

With your replacement pieces (the two sections of pipe and the union) gathered, follow these steps:

1. **Apply a pipe joint compound to the threaded ends and the threads in the fittings, pressing the compound into the threads with a fingertip.**

2. **Insert the ring nut over one of the sections of pipe.**

   The union is a fitting that consists of three components: two union nuts and a ring nut. The union nuts attach to the replacement sections of pipe where they join together. The ring nut acts to join the two pieces.

3. **Screw both sections of pipe into their respective fittings (where the previously damaged sections were removed).**

4. **Tighten both sections of pipe and then the ring nut.**

   Just as with the removal process, using two pipe wrenches makes reassembly easier and safer.

After the section is replaced, complete the process by turning the main water supply on and checking for leaks. Your iron pipe will be as good as new — that is, until the next leak!

Protecting Pipes in Frigid Weather

When the mercury drops, your water pipes become increasingly vulnerable and may freeze and burst. When water freezes, it expands, and the pipes rupture. A burst water line can cause tens of thousands of dollars in damage and forever destroy personal possessions in the path of the raging water. The good news is that you can take steps to help prevent a burst pipe and the chaos that it causes.

An ounce of prevention

The following tips reduce the chances of your pipes freezing and help keep water running in your pipes all winter long:

- **Turn on your faucets just a little.** A faucet left dripping at the fixture farthest from the main water inlet allows just enough warm water movement within the pipes to reduce the chance of a freeze.

- **Insulate your above-ground pipes.** Insulating pipes that are above ground (those that are most susceptible to freezing) prevents them from freezing during most moderate-to-medium chills — even when faucets are off. Be sure to insulate pipes in the crawl space, basement, attic, and especially any that are located at the exterior, such as a main water line and shut-off valve. (See Chapter 4 for more information on insulating pipes.)

- **Open your cabinets.** If the pipes that supply water to your kitchen or bathroom sink faucets are prone to freezing, leave the cabinet doors open at night. The open doors allow warm air to circulate in the cabinet and warm the cold pipes.

✔ **Install electric pipe cable.** If you're in an area where temperatures frequently drop below freezing, think about purchasing pipe heating cable. They're easy to install, inexpensive to operate, and can save a lot of heartache. Pipe heaters plug in to a standard outlet, and the temperature is controlled with a thermostat. All you have to do is wrap a wire around your water pipes — the heater does the rest.

Quick fixes for burst pipes

Being prepared to defend your home's plumbing system against a sudden burst pipe can save you thousands of dollars in damage. Think of these quick, easy fixes as plumbing first aid — they slow or stop a leak long enough to give you time to enlist the services of a qualified plumber during business hours.

To temporarily stop a pinhole leak, you need to apply pressure to the opening. The solution? Wrap duct tape around the pipe. In many instances, it supplies the necessary pressure. Unfortunately, duct tape doesn't always give you enough pressure. In that case, you need to move to a more robust fix (see the next section).

Using a C-clamp when you need more pressure

Another way to temporarily stop a small leak involves a C-clamp, a block of wood, and a piece of rubber. *Note:* Because the block of wood is flat (and the pipe is round), it can only create pressure along a very narrow area of the pipe.

Follow these steps:

1. **Turn off the water at the main shut-off valve.**

2. **Place a piece of rubber over the area where the pipe is leaking.**

3. **Put the block of wood on top of the piece of rubber.**

4. **Open the C-clamp wide enough to surround the pipe, the gasket material, and the block of wood.**

5. **Place the stationary part of the opening of the C-clamp against the pipe (opposite the location of the leak) and the screw part of the C-clamp against the block of wood. Tighten the screw clamp until it's snug.**

Junkyards are filled with rubber that can be had for pennies. Old automotive radiator and heater hoses are just what the doctor ordered. If you have a friend who works on cars, he'll probably be glad to give you all you need.

Using a sleeve clamp for larger leaks

A sleeve clamp stops everything from pinhole leaks to larger leaks. (Forget searching out a piece of rubber for this one — a sleeve clamp comes with its own gasket.) A sleeve clamp consists of two semicircular pieces of metal that, when put together, completely surround the pipe — hence, the name *sleeve*. The clamp is about 3 inches long, but you have to buy one to fit your specific pipe size — a sleeve clamp made to repair ½-inch pipe is smaller than one needed to repair ¾-inch pipe.

Other than the sleeve clamp, you only need a screwdriver. Here's how it works (see Figure 7-1):

1. **Wrap the damaged section of pipe with the gasket material provided.**

2. **Surround the gasket-wrapped pipe with the two semicircular clamps.**

3. **Tighten the screws that connect the two halves of the sleeve clamp.**

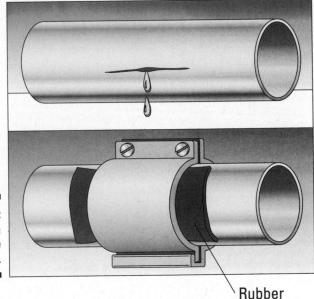

Figure 7-1:
Using a
sleeve
clamp.

Rubber

No one relishes the idea of spending money on plumbing repair items on the off chance that they may be needed. But if you think about it, things like hose clamps, C-clamps, duct tape, and rubber are pretty cheap, especially when you consider how much money they can save you if your pipes do spring a leak. These simple items are good junk to have in your workshop.

Quieting Noisy Water Pipes

Imagine a fast-moving stream of water traveling down a narrow pipe. Suddenly and unexpectedly, the water finds a closed valve in place of what, moments earlier, was an escape point. All of a sudden, the water has nowhere to go. As it comes to an abrupt stop, a loud thud results, and it can be heard throughout the entire house. This deafening sound is known as a *water hammer*. The hammering action that creates the horrible racket is actually capable of damaging joints and connections in the pipe.

Combating water hammers with air chambers

An *air chamber* is a vertical pipe located in the wall cavity at the point near a faucet or valve where the water-supply pipe exits the wall. Air chambers act as cushions to prevent water from slamming against the piping. Because air compresses, it absorbs the shock of the fast-moving water before it has a chance to slam against the end of the pipe. Many household plumbing systems have air chambers built in to them at critical locations — like the clothes washer and dishwasher — where electric shut-off valves close rapidly. In some homes, air chambers exist at every location where water is turned on and off — even the toilet.

To eliminate a water hammer, you need to replenish all the air chambers with air. You can't inspect the air chambers, so this procedure is a must whenever you notice a faint noise in the pipe. Here's how:

1. **Shut off your home's main water supply valve.**

2. **Open the highest faucet inside your house.**

3. **Find the lowest faucet on the property — it's usually on the first floor somewhere outside or in the basement — and turn it on to completely drain all water from the pipes.**

   As the water drains from the pipes, air automatically replaces it.

4. **The moment the water is completely drained from the piping, turn off the lowest faucet and reopen the main valve.**

   Air pushes out of the horizontal and open vertical water lines, sputtering as it exits the faucets inside. However, air remains in the air chambers, eliminating water hammer.

Tightening loose mounting straps

Sometimes a water hammer can occur when a pipe-mounting strap is loose. These straps consist of metal plumber's tape or the vinyl-coated nail-in hooks and hangers that attach pipes to roof, wall, and floor framing. A loose pipe strap allows the pipe to freely vibrate against framing members as water is turned on and off. Check all accessible pipes to ensure that they're properly and tightly connected.

Never use galvanized plumber's tape or galvanized straps on copper pipe. When different metals contact one another, electrolysis can occur, which can lead to a plumbing leak.

Adjusting too-high water pressure

Another reason for banging pipes is excessively high water pressure. You can adjust water pressure with a water-pressure regulator or pressure-reducing valve. Most modern homes have a regulator mounted at the location where the main water supply enters the home.

If you don't have a regulator, consider having one installed. A professionally installed pressure regulator can cost several hundred dollars, but it's a good investment in the long run. (Only do-it-yourselfers with some serious plumbing skills should try to install a pressure regulator themselves.)

Not only is high water pressure wasteful, but it can damage dishwashers, ice-makers, washing machines, and other water-supplied automatic appliances. In fact, many appliance warranties are voided when water pressure exceeds 100 pounds per square inch (psi). Testing water pressure is important regardless of whether you have a pressure regulator.

You can test the water pressure yourself using a water-pressure gauge that screws onto a hose bib; in most communities, the water department will conduct the test at no charge. Normal water pressure runs between 30 and 55 psi. If you already have a regulator, use a screwdriver or wrench to adjust it so that the pressure doesn't exceed 50 psi (see Figure 7-2).

By the way, if you have low water pressure, consider adding a booster pump.

Some Like It Hot: Your Water Heater

Thanks to the water heater, it's been a while since our modern civilized society heated water for daily use over an open flame. Instead, the dilemma facing most folks is one of short showers and high utility bills. If this situation sounds familiar, it's time to take action! A bit of preventive maintenance on the water heater can provide hot water longer, result in energy savings, and even extend the life of the water heater.

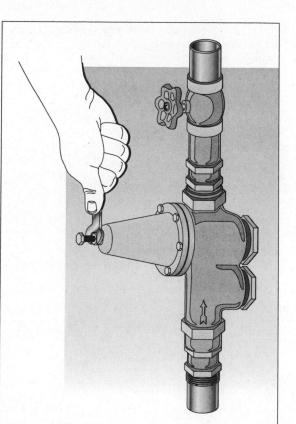

Figure 7-2:
Adjusting
the water
pressure.

Maintaining your water heater

A water heater, shown in Figure 7-3, has three basic parts: the enclosure, the water tank assembly, and the burner and control assembly. The enclosure holds everything together and protects the tank and other fragile parts from damage. The water tank stores water that arrives cold and leaves heated. The burner and control assembly are responsible for heating the water, discharging combustion gases, and adjusting the temperature. An electric water heater varies slightly. It has an enclosure and a tank, but instead of a burner, it contains one or two electric elements that heat the water. Consequently, there is no need for a flue to exhaust combustion gases. Aside from these fundamental differences, gas and electric water heaters function essentially the same and require essentially the same tender loving care.

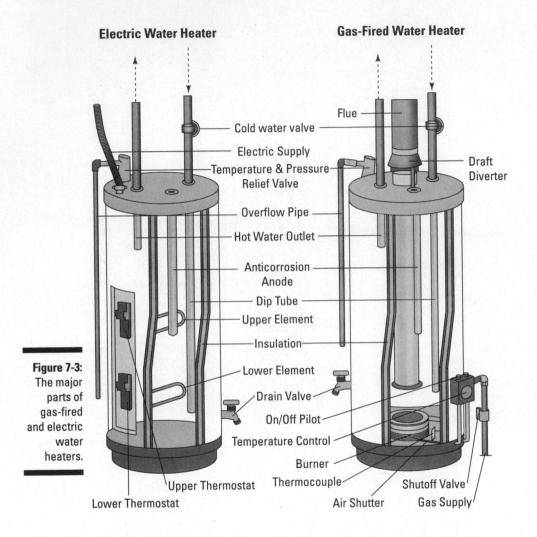

Electric Water Heater

Gas-Fired Water Heater

Cold water valve

Electric Supply

Temperature & Pressure Relief Valve

Overflow Pipe

Hot Water Outlet

Anticorrosion Anode

Dip Tube

Upper Element

Insulation

Lower Element

Drain Valve

On/Off Pilot

Temperature Control

Burner

Thermocouple

Upper Thermostat

Lower Thermostat

Flue

Draft Diverter

Shutoff Valve

Gas Supply

Air Shutter

Figure 7-3: The major parts of gas-fired and electric water heaters.

Insulating for improved efficiency

An insulation blanket can make some water heaters more energy efficient. If your water heater is located in unconditioned space (a garage, basement, or attic) or you don't want added heat, install a heavy blanket — R-11 or better. The higher the R value, the thicker the blanket and the more insulating horsepower.

An insulation blanket is not recommended for a water heater located where its lost heat could be utilized. Nor is a blanket necessary if you have a new water heater that is factory insulated with R-16 or better. (The factory-installed insulation is located between the metal shell and the tank, so don't worry if you can't see it.) The manufacturer's label will tell you how much insulation your water heater contains.

You purchase a water-heater insulation blanket as a kit based on the size of the heater — 30 gallons, 40 gallons, 50 gallons, and so on. The kit contains a blanket that's finished with white vinyl on the outside and raw insulation on the inside and enough adhesive tape to finish the seams.

Here's how to wrap your water heater with an insulation blanket:

✔ **If you have a gas water heater:** Wrap your gas water heater all the way around and from the top to just below the controller. Don't worry if the blanket seems a bit short. *Remember:* The bottom of the tank is several inches above the very bottom of the water heater — a couple of inches below the drain valve.

Don't wrap the top of a gas water heater because the insulation could catch fire from the heat being exhausted. Also, the blanket should not cover the controller, the anode, or the pressure and temperature relief valve.

✔ **If you have an electric water heater:** Because electric water heaters have no exhaust, you can insulate the sides and the top. But to prevent electrical components from overheating, don't cover the heating-element access panels.

Keeping your water heater clear of sludge

If the bottom of your water heater fills with sludge, the heater won't operate at peak performance. Aside from being a breeding ground for bacteria, sediment at the base of a tank significantly diminishes the efficiency of a gas water heater and can cause it to rumble like a freight train. Sediment buildup also causes the water at the base of the tank to super-heat and turn to steam, resulting in mini explosions that blast small amounts of sediment off the bottom of the tank.

To clean the sediment out of a water heater, follow these steps:

1. **Turn off the power to the water heater and the cold-water inlet valve at the top of the water heater.**

2. **Unscrew the cold-water supply line at the top of the water heater and remove the nipple screwed into the cold-water port.**

3. **Pour a citric-acid-based cleaner into the open hole and wait about eight hours for the acid to dissolve the minerals at the bottom of the tank.**

The citric-acid-based cleaning product we recommend is called Mag-Erad, but it can sometimes be hard to find at local plumbing supply stores. If you have trouble finding it, call the Mag-Erad manufacturer, Tri-Brothers Chemical Corporation at 847-564-2320, or contact A. O. Smith Distributors at 800-845-1108 or 800-527-1953.

4. **After the cleaning agent has had time to work, flush the tank.**

Connect a garden hose to the drain valve located at the bottom of the water heater and run the hose out into the garden. Open the drain valve, reconnect the cold-water supply line and then turn on the cold-water supply to the water heater. The cloudy water and sediment that comes out of the end of the hose will amaze you.

5. **When the water runs clear, close the drain valve, and remove the hose.**

6. **Bleed air from the system by turning on the hot-water faucet farthest from the water heater; when water runs from this faucet, turn it off and repeat this process at other faucets throughout the house.**

7. **Turn the power to the water heater back on.**

Hopefully, you'll be in hot water now.

Avoiding rust

Most water-heater tanks are made of glass-lined steel. If water gets through imperfections in the glass, then you can count on rust and eventually a leak. But because the tank has no inspection ports, it's hard to tell when it's dirty or beginning to rust. Actually, tank rust usually isn't discovered until after a leak occurs — and then it's too late. You're not totally without recourse, though.

A special rod called a *cathodic anode* (or sacrificial anode) is built in to the water-heater tank assembly to prevent rust. As long as the rod is in good condition, deterioration of the tank is drastically reduced.

Unfortunately, you can't determine the condition of the anode by just looking at your water heater. You have to turn off the power and the water to the water heater and remove the anode with a wrench. Check the anode for deterioration at least twice a year; this will give you an idea of how long the anode will last. You can then include its replacement in your maintenance schedule accordingly.

To prevent damage to the tank, simply replace the cathodic anode, a $15 item that takes about 30 minutes to install. Cathodic anodes are often not readily available in hardware stores — you'll probably have to buy one from a plumbing-supply company. Because anodes come in all shapes and sizes, be prepared to give them the make and model of your water heater so that you get the right one. You can find this information on a label located on the water-heater housing.

To replace the cathodic anode, follow these steps:

1. **Turn off the power to the water heater and the cold-water inlet valve at the top of the water heater.**

2. **Unscrew the hex bolt holding the cathodic anode in place and remove the rod — or what remains of it.**

   You may discover that only a short piece of rusted metal rod remains — definitely a sign that a new anode is desperately needed.

The cathodic anode is about 3 to 5 feet long, about $^3/_4$ inch in diameter, and has a hex bolt welded onto one end. The hex bolt screws into the top of the tank, holding the rod in place inside the tank, and, when tightened down, the nut also makes a watertight seal at the same time.

3. **Install the new anode.**

   Insert the new anode in the reverse order that the previous one was removed. Be sure to use Teflon tape on the threaded fitting to prevent a leak.

4. **Turn the water and power to the water heater back on.**

Most factory-installed anodes are magnesium, which can produce a sulfite-reducing bacteria that makes your water smell like rotten eggs. Using a replacement anode made of zinc or aluminum will prevent this problem. Peeeww!

When things get too hot

Water temperature is another important factor in controlling energy costs and extending a water heater's life span. Water-heater manufacturers recommend a lower water temperature setting whenever possible — 130 degrees or less. On a gas water heater, you can adjust the temperature by turning the dial located on the front of the controller. On an electric model, the thermostat is located behind an access panel adjacent to a heating element.

Don't set the temperature below 120 degrees. A temperature setting less than that could allow potentially fatal bacteria to propagate within the tank.

Testing the temperature and pressure relief valve

The temperature and pressure relief valve (TPR valve) opens to release pressure buildup in the water heater when the temperature or the pressure get dangerously high, preventing a possible explosion.

A buildup of mineral salt, rust, and corrosion can cause a TPR valve to freeze up and become nonoperational. To test the valve to ensure that it's working properly, simply raise and lower the test lever several times so it lifts the brass stem that it's fastened to (see Figure 7-4). Hot water should rush out of the end of the drainpipe. If no water flows through the pipe or you get just a trickle, replace the valve.

Some water-heater experts recommend testing every six months. More frequent testing can reduce the chance of a leak caused by mineral and corrosion buildup. However, if a leak results immediately after a test, simply operate the test lever several times to free lodged debris that may be preventing the valve from seating properly. If the valve is doing its job and hot water is dripping or spewing out of the TPR drain valve, turn down the temperature on the water-heater controller and/or turn down the water pressure (see "Adjusting too-high water pressure," earlier in this chapter), if necessary.

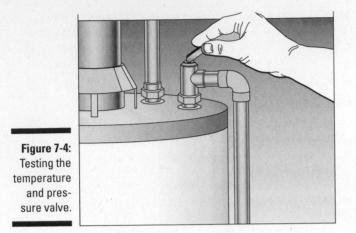

Figure 7-4:
Testing the temperature and pressure valve.

Here are other things to pay attention to:

- **The pipe leaving the relief valve should be the same diameter as the exhaust port of the valve — usually ³/₄ inch.** Moreover, the pipe should be made of a material that is not adversely affected by heat, such as copper. If the pipe is undersized or not heat-resistant, replace it with copper or have a plumber do it for you.

- **The TPR drainpipe should travel in a slightly downhill direction from the valve to the point where it terminates.** It should end outside the house at 6 to 24 inches above the ground. If the drainpipe moves uphill and then downhill, water could get trapped against the outlet of the valve and corrode it shut. If the drain line had a trap or a low spot, water could freeze. And even if the valve works, pressure would be captured and an explosion might occur. If the drainpipe isn't properly configured, call in a plumber to correct it.

Dealing with a sudden blast of cold water

When the hot water in your shower suddenly turns ice cold, you have the right to be frustrated and confused. (That is, if the hot-water supply hasn't been drained due to recent use.) If you receive this rude wake-up call, the culprit may be that your dip tube or the water-heater nipples need a little TLC.

Caring for a broken dip tube

The dip tube consists of a plastic pipe that travels vertically within the water-heater tank from the cold-water inlet to within a few inches of the bottom of the tank. The dip tube brings cold water in the bottom of the tank where it can be heated. If the dip tube is cracked or broken, the cold water mixes with the hot water at the top of the tank (heat and hot water rise), resulting in your unwelcome early-morning shock. When this condition arises, a cracked or broken dip tube is usually to blame.

Changing a dip tube is easy:

1. **Turn off the power to the water heater.**

2. **Turn the cold-water inlet valve off and use a wrench to disconnect the cold-water supply line at the top of the water heater.**

3. **Remove the *nipple* (a short piece of pipe threaded at both ends) to expose the top of the dip tube.**

4. **Remove the dip tube by inserting a screwdriver at an angle and using friction to pry the tube out of the opening.**

5. **Drop a new tube into the opening and replace the nipple and supply line.**

6. **Turn on the water and restore power to the unit.**

Nipples: A sensitive subject

Nipples are short pieces of pipe that are threaded on both ends. They come in various lengths and diameters and are made of a host of materials. Most water heaters have two nipples that are used to connect the cold-water supply line and hot-water outlet line at the top of the water heater. These nipples are subject to corrosion and a buildup of solids at the interior that can bring your supply of hot water to little more than a disappointing drip.

You can solve this problem by installing PVC-lined nipples, galvanized iron nipples lined with plastic or PVC that prevents mineral buildup on the inside. The galvanized finish helps prevent rust on the outside. Use Teflon tape on the threads for a leak-free seal. Also, make sure to use dielectric unions to connect all dissimilar metal water pipes to prevent electrolysis — a deterioration that occurs when unlike metals come into contact with one another.

The cold-water shut-off valve

If you discover rust at the top of your water heater — aside from the nipples — it may be due to a leaking pipe fitting or a leak at the cold-water shut-off valve. If all the fittings are in good shape, and the valve is the culprit, try to stop the leak by using a wrench to tighten the packing nut.

The controller: The brains of the operation

The *controller* is the device you use to light the pilot and turn the unit off and on. It's also used to adjust the temperature setting. The controller is usually pretty reliable and doesn't require much maintenance other than an occasional dusting. However, if you have too little hot water, water that is not hot enough, or water that is excessively hot, it may be time to replace the controller. This is a job best left to a pro.

Securing your water heater to a wall

A water heater thrown over during an earthquake or other disaster can cause both broken gas lines and broken water lines. You can prevent such a scenario if you strap the water heater securely to an adjacent wall.

Metal straps around the belly of the heater can be screwed to the housing and then anchored to wall framing. You can also install a special anchor that attaches to the water pipes at the top and to wall framing. In either case, your best bet is to check with your local building department for recommendations and a diagram on how best to anchor your water heater.

If you have a gas water heater

The burner, thermocouple, and venting system are components that are fundamental to the safe and efficient operation of a gas water heater. Keeping them clean and in good working order will keep you safe and help manage utility costs.

The burner: Just an old flame

On a gas water heater, the burner assembly is located at the bottom of the unit below the tank (refer to Figure 7-4). When the water temperature in the tank drops below the desired temperature, a thermostat activates the burner. The same process occurs with an electric water heater, but instead of a burner, electric heating elements are activated.

Periodically inspect the burner to make sure that it's burning safely and efficiently. A dirty burner chamber can cause a fire and can make the burner less efficient. (If your burner is operating at peak efficiency, you'll see a blue flame. If the flame is orange, adjust the shutter until it turns blue.)

To clean the burner, first turn off the gas shut-off valve (located on the gas supply to the water heater), remove the access panel, and vacuum the burner and chamber. Use a stiff wire and a wire brush to clear clogged burner ports and removes rust. If you aren't successful in getting a blue flame, call in a service rep from your utility company or a plumber or heating specialist.

The thermocouple

If you have a gas water heater with a pilot light that won't stay lit, it's probably due to one of two things:

✔ **There is a blockage in the tiny tube that supplies gas to the pilot.** If the tube is blocked, you can clear it by inserting a thin piece of wire or blowing air through it.

Make sure that the gas controller is in the off position before attempting this repair.

✔ **The thermocouple has failed.** The *thermocouple* is a thermoelectric device that shuts off the gas if the pilot light goes out. In simple terms, it's a short piece of tubing that runs from the gas controller to the pilot. The pilot end of the thermocouple and the pilot are held side by side in a bracket that's anchored to the burner. If your pilot light won't stay lit, the thermocouple probably needs to be replaced. A new one costs about $5 to $10 and is easy to install.

If the thermocouple has failed, follow these steps:

1. **Turn off the gas supply.**

2. **Remove the whole burner and thermocouple assembly.**

   Unfasten the three nuts that hold the thermocouple and the two gas tubes to the valve. The burner typically sits loosely — or under clips — in the burning chamber and just slides out.

3. **Detach the thermocouple from the burner.**

   The thermocouple is usually attached to the pilot gas supply tube with one or more clips that snap into place. The end of the thermocouple is inserted into the pilot assembly and can simply be pulled out.

4. **Take the detached thermocouple with you to the home center or hardware store and buy a new one.**

5. **Install the new one the same way that you removed the old one.**

   Attach the end of the new thermocouple into the pilot assembly and reattach the thermocouple to the pilot gas supply using the clips previously removed, reinstall the burner and, using a small open-end or adjustable wrench, reconnect the thermocouple lead, the gas tube to the main burner, and the pilot gas tube to the valve.

6. **Turn the gas back on and follow the lighting instructions on the water heater.**

7. **Check for gas leaks by applying soapy water to joints and looking for bubbles while the main burner is firing.**

The venting system

The venting system of a gas water heater consists of a flue that runs up the center of the water heater from the burners, out the top of the water heater, and through the rooftop to vent deadly gases created by combustion. At least twice each year, inspect the venting system to ensure that it's properly aligned at the top of the water heater and that the connections are secure.

Here's a quick test you can use to see if your gas water heater is venting properly: With the water heater running, hold a match near the *draft diverter* (the opening at the top of the water heater where the vent pipe connects to the unit). If the flame on the match leans in toward the vent pipe, your draft is good.

If the flame leans back toward the room, or worse yet, if it blows out the flame, your unit may be back-drafting, a potentially dangerous situation. If this happens, immediately turn off the unit and call the gas company for assistance. Chances are, your vent pipe or chimney is blocked somewhere, and your house may be filling with deadly combustion gases.

If you have an electric water heater

Electric water heaters have no burners to clean, no thermocouples to replace, and no venting systems to be concerned with. However, an electric water heater is not without its own set of maintenance tasks.

Cleaning your water heater's electric elements

An electric water heater contains one or two heating elements similar to what you might find in your oven, except that they're short and narrow. These electric elements can become laden with lime and mineral deposits that reduce their effectiveness or cause them to overheat and short out.

To clean your electric elements, follow these steps:

1. **Turn off the power to the water heater.**

2. **Drain the tank by turning off the cold-water valve at the top of the water heater, attaching a garden hose to the drain valve at the base of the water heater, and opening the drain valve.**

   To facilitate draining, open a hot-water faucet somewhere in the home.

3. **After the water heater empties, use a screwdriver to remove the access panels to the elements.**

   Depending upon the number of elements, one or more access panels will have to be removed. You may need to move a piece of insulation to expose the element.

4. **Using your screwdriver, remove the elements and any electrical wires that power them.**

   Elements are generally attached with a series of bolts, or they have a threaded base that screws directly into the tank.

5. **Clean or replace the element.**

   To clean the removed element, use a solution of vinegar and water or sodium carbonate and water (2 tablespoons of vinegar or 2 tablespoons of sodium carbonate in 1 quart of hot water) and a scouring pad.

   If an element has begun to corrode, replace it with a new one. Many different element types and styles are widely available; simply take the old one to the hardware store and find a match. Cooler-than-normal water, sporadic hot water, and a short supply of hot water are all telltale signs of a corroded element.

6. **Reconnect the wires and refill the water heater.**

   To refill the water heater, close the drain valve and turn the cold-water supply valve on, making sure that the hot-water faucet farthest from the water heater is left open to express all the air from the system.

7. **Check for leaks around the elements.**

8. **After you're sure that there are no leaks, replace the insulation and access panels and turn on the power.**

Hard water and an electric water heater are a disastrous combination. You will forever be cleaning and replacing electric elements. We suggest that you consider installing a water softener if you have an electric water heater.

Fixing a defective thermostat or tripped limit switch

If you still have a problem getting hot water out of your electric heater, it may be due to a defective thermostat or a tripped or defective high-temperature limit switch. The limit switch cuts off power to the element when the water temperature exceeds a certain limit — usually 190 degrees. You can reset a tripped high-temperature limit switch with the push of a button behind the access panel.

If the switch continues to trip, it may be due to either a defective limit switch or element. In either case, one or both need to be replaced. To replace a thermostat, follow these steps:

1. **Turn off the water and power to the water heater and remove the access panel and insulation.**

2. **Use a screwdriver to remove the wires from the thermostat.**

3. **Loosen the bracket bolts that hold the thermostat in place and slide the thermostat out.**

4. **Slide the new thermostat into place, tighten down the bolts, reconnect the wires, and press the Reset button.**

5. **Reinstall the insulation and access panel; then turn on the water and power.**

Caring for your tankless water heater

Tankless water heaters are the newest kids on the water heating block. Beyond the fact that they're more energy efficient, they don't have the cleaning and maintenance woes associated with traditional tank-style units. However, a few tasks will ensure that your tankless water heater has a long, prosperous, and energy-efficient life:

✔ **Keep control compartments, burners, and circulating air passageways of the appliance clean.** First, turn off and disconnect electrical power and allow the unit to cool. Then remove and clean the water inlet filter. Using pressurized air, clean dust from the main burner, heat exchanger, and fan blades. Finish by using a soft, dry cloth to wipe the cabinet.

✔ **Inspect the vent system for blockages or damage at least once a year.**

✔ **Flush the heat exchanger to get rid of lime and scale build up.** Consult the owner's manual for specific instructions on how to flush the heat exchanger.

✔ **Visually inspect the flame.** The burner must flame evenly over the entire surface when operating correctly. The burner must burn with a clear, blue, stable flame. Consult a pro to clean and adjust the burner for an irregular flame.

Softening Your Water

With the exception of adding salt to the brine tank on a regular basis, a water-softening system is reasonably maintenance-free. Every now and then, the brine solution becomes clogged at the base of the brine tank, which prevents the solution from being siphoned into the resin tank. You know that this is the case if your brine tank is full of salt, yet your water doesn't have that "slick" feel of softened water.

You can correct this problem by removing all the salt from the brine tank and flushing the bottom of the tank with a garden hose and water. Before replacing the salt in the brine tank, manually cycle the unit to ensure that it's operating properly. Individual units will have either a lever or a button that, when pressed, manually cycles the system. Check your owner's manual to determine where the manual cycle button is on your water softener.

Wishing Your Well Is Working Well

If you don't get your water from a municipal water source, it probably comes from a private well. Water is pumped from the source with a submersible pump that's usually about 10 feet from the bottom of the well to a pressure tank in or near the house. The tank, in turn, feeds the water-supply lines. In a standard pressure tank, incoming water forces air into the upper third of the tank, where it forms a spring-like cushion. When the air pressure reaches a preset level — usually between 50 and 60 psi — the spring action of the compressed air triggers a pressure switch, which shuts off the pump. As water is drawn from the tank, pressure diminishes. When it reaches a preset level — 30 to 40 psi — the switch turns the pump on again.

When the pressure tank loses too much air pressure, it can become "waterlogged," which causes the pump to switch on and off frequently. You can solve this problem by doing the following:

1. **Turn off the power to the pump; then attach a garden hose to the drain valve at the bottom of the tank and open the valve and leave it open until there's no more pressure in the tank.**

2. **Open a faucet in the house to drain all the water out of the tank.**

3. **When the tank is empty, turn off the faucet, close the drain valve on the tank, remove the hose, and turn the pump back on.**

A leaking tank is another prevalent problem. If a leak develops, it usually appears first as an oozing rusty blemish. Although tank plugs are available, they're only a temporary measure. The tank should be replaced as soon as possible.

Occasionally, the pump may stop working. If this is the case, first check for a blown fuse or tripped breaker. A loose wire may also be the source of the problem. If all these check out, your best bet is to call in a well service technician.

Chapter 8

Plumbing, Part II: Fixtures

....

....

*Y*ou may be able to live with peeling paint, a squeaking floor, or doors that won't shut properly. But, when it comes to your toilet and the woes that it encounters — not flushing properly, overflowing, or looking like a full-blown science experiment — that's where you draw the line! Fear not! Armed with this chapter, a closet auger, a pumice stick, vinegar, turpentine, a wax ring, and other assorted paraphernalia, you'll not only tame your toilet, you'll transform your tub, shape up your shower, and make your faucets sparkle like Dorothy's ruby red slippers. Oh my!

Maintaining Fixture Surfaces: Stainless Steel, Cast Iron, Fiberglass, and More

A home dweller eventually becomes intimately familiar with the various plumbing fixtures in a home — the sinks, tubs, toilets, and shower pans. It's no fun when these fixtures become tattered. In many situations, cleaning is all it takes to make a worn-out fixture look brand-spanking-new!

Stainless-steel fixtures

Vitreous china and porcelain fixtures are great, but when it comes to sinks, one made of high-quality stainless steel wins hands down. Stainless steel sinks are light and easy to install, they don't chip, and they're easy to keep clean.

To clean a stainless steel surface, use one of the following:

- ✔ One drop of liquid dish soap in 1 quart of hot water
- ✔ Baking soda mixed with water until it forms a paste
- ✔ One part vinegar to one part water

Clean and then dry with a soft cloth. For tougher cleaning tasks, look for a commercial, stainless-steel cleaning product that contains oxalic acid. Regardless of the cleaner, a nylon scrubbing pad will help.

When caring for stainless steel, follow these two simple rules:

- ✔ **Never use steel wool.** Steel-wool fibers can lodge in the surface of the stainless steel and eventually rust, giving the appearance that the *stainless steel* is rusting. What a mess!

- ✔ **Don't use abrasive cleaners.** They can scratch the surface over time.

If you really want to make your stainless-steel sink — and anything stainless steel (appliances, barbecue, and so on) — look like new, consider investing in a stainless-steel refinishing kit. Kits retail for about $50; can be found at appliance retailers, hardware stores, and home centers; last for years; and can make a tired, old, stainless-steel sink look like new.

Porcelain-on-steel and porcelain-on-cast-iron fixtures

Porcelain on steel and porcelain on cast iron are both used primarily for kitchen sinks, laundry sinks, and bathtubs. Although cast iron is a stronger base, making porcelain fixtures generally more durable, porcelain does chip, and the finish is every bit as easy to scratch as vitreous china.

When porcelain is new, its surface gleams and glistens, but over time, it can lose its luster, especially if you use abrasives for cleaning. Plus, if you drop a heavy object onto a porcelain fixture, you may not shatter it, but you may chip the enamel. Fortunately, some companies do specialize in making such repairs. Look in the Yellow Pages under "plumbing fixture refinishing." Here's what the pros can do:

- ✔ **Repair chips.** A chip can be professionally repaired for about $75 to $125. Chip touch-up kits are available at your local home center or hardware store, but we think they're useless — they don't last, and the finished result usually looks terrible.

✔ **Reglaze.** Porcelain and ceramic sinks, tubs, and other bathroom fixtures that are badly scratched, are chipped, and have lost their luster can be *reglazed* (refinished) by a professional porcelain refinisher. The fixture must be removed and sent to the reglazing house where a porcelain finish is applied. It's then returned and reinstalled — hopefully without chipping it in the process.

Reglazing is very expensive. In fact, reglazing a porcelain fixture isn't worth the cost or effort unless it's a valuable antique or a family heirloom, because replacing the fixture is far less expensive.

✔ **Refinish.** Refinishing — a paint-like coating — is a far less expensive alternative to reglazing and can produce finishes with varying degrees of durability. The least durable refinishing method involves paints or epoxies similar to what you can buy in a home-improvement store. The best materials are the industrial systems designed specifically for porcelain refinishing. Plan to spend $250 to $750 for a professionally refinished tub, depending upon the size, color, and condition. Refinishing typically takes as many as two days. Make sure to ask the refinisher how long your sink, faucet, or tub will be out of commission.

As you investigate refinishing companies, look for a reputable one with references. Also ask about the warranty: Anything less than a five-year guarantee makes this process a bad bet. Some companies offer longer guarantees.

Fiberglass fixtures

Fiberglass fixtures are popular because they're competitively priced. Fiberglass has been around for a long time and is used most commonly in tubs and shower pans. Fiberglass fixtures aren't as durable as other types of fixtures and must be treated with care. However, given such care, they'll last as long as any other.

A stained fiberglass tub or shower pan is a breeze to clean. Simply wet the entire surface to be cleaned with water, sprinkle on a thin layer of automatic dishwashing powder, and let it sit for about an hour. Keep the surface wet by spraying it with clear water. After an hour, use a nylon bristle brush to scrub away stains. Finish up by rinsing the entire area with fresh water.

For severely stained tub or shower floors, plug the drain and fill the tub or shower pan with about an inch of water. Sprinkle the automatic dishwashing powder over the entire surface and allow it to sit overnight. Use the nylon brush to scrub away stains and thoroughly rinse with fresh water. You'll be amazed by its like-new appearance!

Composite fixtures

Although fiberglass is a resin painted onto a backing, composite fixtures are great thick hulks of plastic also known as *solid surface* material. What you see on the surface goes all the way through to the other side of the fixture. Composite fixtures are long lasting and far more durable than fiberglass. However, they aren't as damage resistant as stainless steel.

Ordinary spills on composite require only a damp cloth for cleanup. You can eliminate tougher stains with a paste made of turpentine and salt: Mix 2 or 3 tablespoons of turpentine into $\frac{1}{4}$ cup of regular table salt, use a nylon bristle brush to apply the cleaner and scrub away the stains, and wipe up the excess with a paper towel. (Let the towel air-dry before disposal.) Then finish up by using a mild detergent and water followed by a freshwater rinse.

If a composite sink ever becomes really grungy, try filling the sink with a solution of bleach and water. The bleach works very well and will bring back the sink's original color.

Most composite fixture manufacturers have product cleaning, repair, and maintenance kits or recommend specific cleaning products. Check with the manufacturer or contact the dealer who installed the fixture.

Because the finished look of a composite fixture goes all the way through, light sanding can remove burns, stains, or minor scratches. Polish the sanded area with fine 400- to 600-grit wet-dry sandpaper lubricated with turpentine to restore the surface to its original beauty. Wipe up the excess turpentine with a paper towel and finish the job by cleaning with a mild detergent and a freshwater rinse.

Vitreous china fixtures

Vitreous china — a smooth form of baked clay with a shiny or glassy look — is used primarily for bathroom sinks, toilets, and bidets. Although it's strong, it can be chipped or broken if hit with a hard object, such as a tool. The bottom line: Be careful around vitreous china, especially during repairs and maintenance.

China is easily scratched, so for most cleaning, leave your scouring powder and abrasive pads in the cupboard. ***Note:*** A variety of commercial products claim to clean china without causing damage, but proceed with caution. Abrasive cleaners slowly wear down china's brilliant surface, although the process can take years. Make sure that the cleaner you select states that it is nonabrasive.

For lime deposits, try a pumice stick — like the one our mom used on her feet to remove calluses — dipped in turpentine. Pumice is an extremely fine abrasive used for polishing. It comes in four grades with 4/0 being the finest. Don't use hand cleaners; the grade of pumice used in them is too coarse.

Shopping for recycled or vintage fixtures

When it's time to replace fixtures, either because you're ready for a change or because the old ones are beyond repair, before you run out to buy new, think about buying used. Using recycled fixtures can have several benefits: Beyond achieving the desired look (usually something vintage or retro), recycled fixtures are usually less expensive than new ones. Plus, using recycled fixtures is very "green" and environmentally friendly — it reduces what goes into landfills and, in the big picture, saves on the manufacture and shipping of new products.

Salvage and recycling centers sell used and surplus building materials at a fraction of normal prices. Although plumbing fixtures are among the most popular product categories, doors, windows, lumber, siding, trim, roofing, finish hardware, cabinetry, counters, flooring, lighting, radiators, and just about anything you can think of can be had.

An entire network of salvage and recycling centers and retail outlets has sprung up across the land. An excellent resource for recycled fixtures is the Building Materials Reuse Association (www.bmra.org), which has several hundred affiliate members throughout the United States.

Keep in mind that many vintage fixtures — particularly toilets and faucets — don't meet current water conservation codes and, thus, can't be used. Fortunately, there is no shortage of brand-spanking-new replica vintage plumbing fixtures and accessories that look just like the real McCoy. The difference is that these products are new and comply with current water conservation codes. Plus, their valve construction is more reliable, and the finishes are more durable. Check out Historic Houseparts (phone: 888-558-2329; Web: www.historic-houseparts.com), Ohmega Salvage (phone: 510-204-0767; Web: www.ohmegasalvage.com), and Vintage Plumbing Bathroom Antiques (phone: 818-772-1721; Web: www.vintageplumbing.com) — or just type **vintage plumbing fixtures** into your favorite search engine. You'll be amazed at what you find!

Remove tea or coffee stains with a solution of 2 tablespoons chlorine bleach per 1 quart of water. Soak for just a minute or two; then rinse promptly.

Never mix bleach with a solution containing ammonia. The combination can release a poisonous gas.

Cleaning Your Faucet Works

When a faucet becomes dull, it makes an otherwise bright and shiny decorating accessory look tattered and worn. It isn't worn out — it's just dirty. The bad news is that dirt that has built up for a long period of time can be difficult to remove. The good news is that you can remove it without damaging the faucet if you know a few tricks.

Cleaning a faucet is a two-part operation:

- ✔ Cleaning the aerator
- ✔ Cleaning and polishing the exterior finish

Cleaning the aerator

The aerator, a thimble-size accessory consisting of a very small disk filled with tiny holes, screws into the end of a faucet spout. It mixes the water with air and controls the amount of flow. When the aerator is operating normally, the water comes out of the spout in a smooth, gentle, even flow. If the water flow from your faucet is slow, if the water sprays out in random streams, or if a once-smooth flow has become sporadic and now sputters, then you probably have a clogged aerator.

Cleaning the aerator is really easy. Here's all you have to do:

1. **Unscrew the aerator from the spout by turning it counterclockwise.**

2. **Disassemble the aerator parts.**

   The parts simply sit one atop another inside the aerator housing.

   As you disassemble the aerator, note exactly how the parts are assembled. If you make a mistake during reassembly, the aerator won't work.

3. **Use an old toothbrush and a toothpick and some vinegar to clean each part.**

   If you can't remove lime-deposit buildup easily, soak the parts in straight vinegar overnight. Then scrub them clean.

4. **Reassemble and reinstall the aerator.**

   Be sure to align the threads correctly to avoid stripping them, which could cause a nasty spray leak every time you turn on the faucet.

Cleaning and polishing the outside of a faucet

To keep a faucet clean, regularly wipe it down with a damp cloth followed by a clean, dry towel. Built-up debris is a bit more difficult — especially when it's a thick layer of lime deposits. Several different cleaners are available that remove hard-water stains and other mineral-deposit buildup:

- ✔ **Pure sodium carbonate:** Pure sodium carbonate (also known as *washing soda* or *soda ash*) is nothing more than laundry detergent. No fillers, no anti-bubbling agents, no odor eaters, nothing except pure cleaning power. It's available at swimming-pool supply stores. To use pure sodium carbonate, mix ½ cup sodium carbonate with a few drops of warm water. Then, using a soft clean cloth, rub the paste onto the faucet surface, and keep rubbing until it shines. To finish, rinse with fresh water and towel-dry.

- ✔ **White vinegar and baking soda:** To use this foamy cleaner, mix equal parts of baking soda and white vinegar, wipe the concoction onto the surface of the faucet with a clean, soft cloth and rub until the surface is clean and shiny. Then rinse with clear water and towel-dry.

- ✔ **Calgon:** Calgon is a common household product that acts as a really neat faucet-cleaning agent. To clean your faucets with Calgon, mix 1 teaspoon of Calgon into 1 gallon of hot water. Soak a rag in the concoction and very gently wring it out; then place the soaked rag onto the faucet, pressing the rag against all parts of the faucet, and cover it with plastic wrap (the kind you use with leftovers in the kitchen) so that it doesn't dry out. Come back in one hour, remove the rag, and use it to briskly wipe away the mineral buildup. Finally, rinse the Calgon away with fresh water and pat dry with a soft clean cloth. ***Note:*** For long-time buildup, you may have to soak the rag in the solution and place it back onto the faucet several times.

- ✔ **Plain vinegar:** Plain vinegar is great for removing a major mineral-salt buildup. You use it the same way you use the Calgon solution: With a vinegar-soaked rag, wipe down all the faucet areas; leave the rag on the faucet for an hour covered with plastic wrap; then wipe it down again, rinse, and towel-dry.

Don't use abrasive cleaners on a faucet. Liquid cleaners work best without damaging the finish. Be sure to test a cleaner on an out-of-the-way spot to ensure that it doesn't remove or damage the paint.

Removing copper residue

If your plumbing pipes are made of copper, or if the faucet entrails are made of copper, chances are that a dark green cast will appear at the faucet spout. The patina color indicates oxidation of copper. If left unattended, this condition will destroy the finish on a polished brass faucet in no time.

If you see green at the tip of your faucet, reach for a metal cleaner such as Brasso or Flitz. Both products are used in the same way: Pour a small amount of the cleaner on a soft, dry cloth and rub the cleaner onto the corroded area and keep rubbing until the ultra fine polishing compound eats away at the bad finish. Let the remaining compound form a white haze and use another soft, clean cloth to wipe away the last remnants of the polish.

Toilet Training 101

What follows is a bit of toiletology that we hope will bring you and your family even closer to your bathroom and, specifically, your toilet.

When you clean or repair your toilet, you often need to empty the water out of the *tank* (the reservoir that holds the water that enters the bowl when the toilet is flushed) and/or the bowl. Here's how to perform these very basic tasks:

- **To empty the tank:** Turn off the water to the tank (at the shut-off valve) and flush the toilet. With the wall valve off, the tank will not refill. (The shut-off valve is the knob located below and behind the toilet.)

- **To empty the bowl:** Turn off the water to the tank (see the preceding bullet) and then fill a large container with 1 gallon of water and pour the water into the toilet bowl. You can remove any water that remains with a small cup and/or a sponge.

Until you turn the water on and flush the toilet, the bowl and tank will remain empty.

Some of the problems associated with toilets also apply to bidets, including slow water flow and mineral deposits. Obviously, a bidet doesn't have a tank, but the bowls are similar, so if the problem fits, so does the solution.

Cleaning the toilet

Toilets that aren't cleaned regularly can become a mess, and toilet-bowl cleaners don't always do the job. The strong ones can be dangerous to work with, and the others aren't always strong enough to get things really clean.

Because bacteria love to live in toilets, pour 1 cup of bleach into the tank and mix it into the water. Let it set for a few minutes; then flush the toilet a few times. You've just sanitized your toilet.

Bleach is great for killing bacteria, but it can also kill your flapper. Some toilet bowl cleaners that are designed to be placed in your toilet tank and give the water in your bowl that ocean blue color contain chlorine, which, with prolonged exposure, can prematurely deteriorate the rubber flush valve (also called a *flapper*) and result in a leaking toilet. That's why we recommend the occasional shot of chlorine bleach followed by a full flush.

Cleaning the siphon jets

The *siphon jets* are the small openings under the rim of the bowl that help rinse the bowl and assist with the flush. If these jets become clogged, your toilet won't flush properly. If, when you flush the toilet, the water comes straight down rather than swirls, the holes are probably plugged. Discolored vertical lines in the bowl are another telltale sign that the holes need cleaning.

Inspect the rim openings with a pocket mirror. It they're clogged with mineral deposits, first empty the tank and the bowl and then use a hanger as a "pipe cleaner" to ream out the holes at the rim (see Figure 8-1). If the scale that exists is too hard to remove, try this trick to soften things up:

1. **Use a towel to completely dry the underside of the rim.**

2. **Apply a layer of duct tape to the underside of the rim to seal all of the holes.**

    If it doesn't stick, the rim is wet.

3. **Fill the tank with 1 gallon of pure vinegar (any kind).**

4. **Flush the toilet.**

    The vinegar travels from the tank into the rim of the toilet. Let it sit there for as long as possible — 24 hours is ideal.

5. **Remove the tape, scrub away the softened scale, turn the water back on, and flush the toilet.**

    This solution should work beautifully.

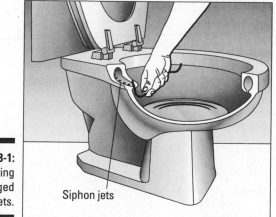

Figure 8-1: Clearing clogged siphon jets.

Siphon jets

Removing a ring around the bowl

If a white or brown ring forms in the bowl, place a couple of denture tablets in the bowl. The tablets will effervesce in the water and dissolve. Let the mixture set over night. (We recommend a separate container for your dentures.) The next morning, just flush the toilet and wipe away the softened buildup.

If some of the stains remain, empty the bowl; then dip a pumice stick (which looks like a large, dark gray piece of chalk) into some turpentine and scrub. (For lighter buildup, use a nylon scrubbing pad in place of the pumice stick.) Turpentine is a great cleaning agent, and the pumice is a super-fine abrasive. Together they make cleaning a breeze.

Pumice is abrasive — don't use a pumice stick on chrome or painted finishes.

Unclogging plugged toilets

A clogged toilet is always an accident. No one ever intends to cause the disgusting mess associated with a toilet backup. If you do experience a blockage, try clearing the obstruction with a plumber's helper (a plunger). If that doesn't work, cut a coat hanger and bend a hook in one end. Force the coat hanger into the neck of the toilet and try to hook the blockage. If you're still not successful, it's time to use a closet auger, also called a *closet snake* (see Figure 8-2).

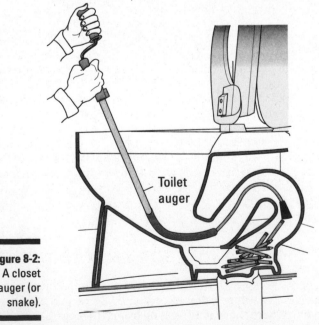

Toilet auger

Figure 8-2:
A closet auger (or snake).

To use a closet snake, follow these steps:

1. **Pull the handle of the closet auger all the way out of the hollow tube so that the hooked end is up against the end of the tube and none of the cable is released.**

2. **Insert the auger end of the snake into the throat of the toilet.**

   Make sure that the vinyl sleeve is up against the porcelain to prevent damage.

3. **Turn the crank slowly while, at the same time, pushing the rod and snake into the toilet trap and down into the sewer line; continue to turn the crank when retracting the snake.**

If the snake doesn't work (or you aren't interested in getting this up close and personal with your toilet), call the plumber.

Preventing a sweaty tank

A toilet tank sweats when the cold water inside chills the tank in a warm bathroom. The sweat is actually condensation. The condensation can become so profuse that it can result in puddles on the floor that can damage floor covering, trim, and other finishes. One way to reduce sweating is to make sure that the water entering the tank isn't cold, by having a plumber add a mixing valve at the tank inlet to introduce warm water into the tank. Unfortunately, this fix is relatively expensive.

A less expensive solution is one you can do yourself: Just fit sheets of polystyrene or foam rubber against the inside of the tank walls. You can either use a toilet tank liner (available at hardware stores, home centers, or plumbing-supply wholesalers), or you can cut the foam to fit the bottom of the tank and the walls. Glue the foam or liner in place with silicone cement and let the adhesive dry for at least 24 hours before filling the tank (see Figure 8-3).

Decorative (typically shag-style) cloth tank covers are supposed to insulate the tank and reduce the chance for condensation. However, if the temperature difference is great enough, a certain amount of condensation will still occur, which can be a problem. If the cloth cover gets wet, mold and mildew can result. Yuck! We never did like those cloth covers anyway.

Looking for leaks in and around the toilet

Some leaks occur outside the toilet. If the floor is wet around the toilet, you obviously have a leak (or a sweating toilet, as explained in the preceding section). The trick is finding where the leak is coming from (there are several places to look) so that you can take the proper steps to solve the problem.

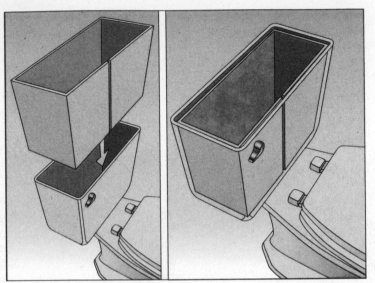

Figure 8-3:
Lining the
inside of
your tank.

The shut-off valve at the wall

Use a towel to dry the floor around the toilet; then lay a piece of toilet paper on the floor beneath the valve and wait for about 15 minutes. If the toilet paper is wet, the shut-off valve (or the supply tube connected to it) leaks. Try tightening the valve fittings. If that doesn't work, you need to replace the valve and/or supply line.

If the shut-off valve is leaking, replace it using the following steps:

1. **Turn off the main water supply to the house and open an exterior water faucet at the lowest point of the home.**

2. **Flush the toilet to remove all the water from the toilet tank. Remove any remaining water with a sponge.**

3. **Use adjustable pliers to loosen the nut that attaches the water-supply line to the shut-off valve.**

4. **Use an adjustable wrench to grasp the shut-off valve's hex-shaped body and carefully turn it counterclockwise to remove it from the *nipple* (the short piece of threaded pipe) that is stubbed out of the wall.**

5. **Wrap Teflon tape around the threads on the nipple, place the new shut-off value onto the nipple, and gently turn it clockwise to thread the shut-off valve onto the nipple. Use the adjustable wrench to snug the valve into place.**

If the nipple is copper, call a plumber to replace the leaking shut-off valve. These can be very tricky to replace because of the compression ring used instead of the threaded connection you find on galvanized pipe.

6. **Reattach the supply line, being sure to first use Teflon tape on threads on the shut-off valve to prevent a leak.**

7. **Turn on the main water valve and the toilet shut-off valve and use the toilet paper investigation technique mentioned earlier to check for leaks.**

Where the supply tube connects

Use a small clump of toilet paper to wipe the bottom of the tank where the *supply tube* (the thin, flexible tube that carries water from the shut-off valve to the toilet tank) connects. If it's wet, the leak is there. Tighten the nut and the supply line at that location. If that doesn't work, replace the supply line.

When choosing a new supply line, get a braided stainless steel one instead of the copper or vinyl hoses, which are not as durable and can burst under excessively high pressure or exceedingly cold temperatures. A few extra dollars can prevent a flood that could save thousands of dollars and lots of heartache.

To replace the supply line, follow these steps:

1. **Turn off the shut-off valve that supplies water to the toilet.**

   Simply turn the little valve that is located below and behind the toilet clockwise until it stops.

2. **Flush the toilet to remove all the water from the toilet tank. Remove any remaining water with a sponge.**

3. **Use adjustable pliers to loosen the nut that attaches the water supply line to the underside of the tank and the nut that attaches the supply line to the shut-off valve.**

   The supply line is now free of the toilet and shut-off valve and can be replaced with a new one.

4. **Install the new supply line, being careful not to over-tighten the nuts at either end.**

   Use Teflon tape on the threads of the shut-off valve and the fitting at the underside of the toilet to prevent a leak.

5. **Turn on the main water valve and the toilet shut-off valve and use the toilet paper investigation technique mentioned earlier to check for leaks.**

The area where the tank connects to the bowl

Two bolts hold the tank to the bowl. If either of them leaks, try tightening the bolt slightly. Don't over-tighten — you can crack the toilet. If tightening the bolts doesn't stop the leak, replace the rubber gasket that is on either bolt within the tank: Empty the tank, remove the bolts, replace the gaskets, and reinstall the bolts.

The toilet's exterior surface

Check the entire exterior surface of the toilet for hairline cracks. If you find any, the toilet needs to be replaced. Replacing a toilet may not be one of the most exciting ways to spend a Saturday, but then that's the nice part about this particular project; you should be able to perform this little task and still have time to enjoy your afternoon.

Gather the following tools:

- An open-ended wrench ($\frac{1}{4}$ inch or $\frac{3}{8}$ inch)
- An adjustable wrench
- A pair of adjustable pliers
- A flathead screwdriver
- A hacksaw

Then follow these steps to replace the toilet:

1. **Turn off the shut-off valve to the toilet (see Figure 8-4).**

   Turn the valve that is located below and behind the toilet clockwise until it stops.

2. **Disconnect the water-supply line.**

   Flush the toilet and remove any water that may remain in the tank or bowl with a small cup and a sponge. After all the water has been removed, disconnect the water-supply line at the base of the tank; use adjustable pliers to turn the nut in a counterclockwise direction.

3. **Unfasten the toilet from the floor (see Figure 8-5).**

   Most residential toilets are anchored to the floor with a couple of fasteners called *closet bolts,* which are concealed by plastic caps. Pry the caps off by wedging a flathead screwdriver between the bottom lip of the cap and the porcelain. Remove the nuts that remain with an open-ended wrench turning counterclockwise.

4. **Remove the toilet and as much of the wax ring as you can (see Figure 8-6).**

   We suggest that you have one other person help you lift the toilet and carry it out because it's as awkward as it is heavy.

   Grasp the toilet by the rim and the underside of the tank and lift directly upward. Don't be alarmed by the gooey mess on the floor where the toilet once sat. It's some of the wax ring, which forms a seal between the toilet and the toilet flange that's connected to the sewer. Use a putty knife to remove the wax that remains; doing so improves the odds of a new leakproof seal.

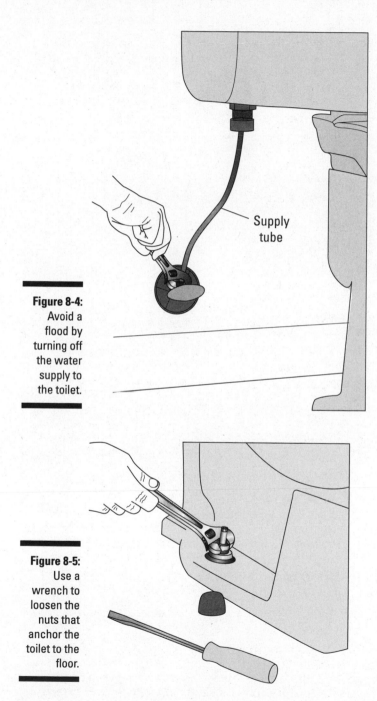

Figure 8-4:
Avoid a flood by turning off the water supply to the toilet.

Supply tube

Figure 8-5:
Use a wrench to loosen the nuts that anchor the toilet to the floor.

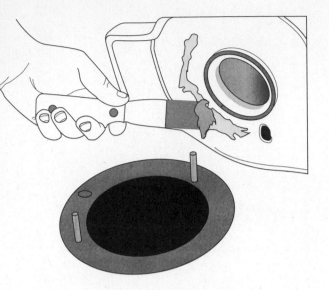

Figure 8-6:
The ring acts as a seal between the toilet and the flange. When reinstalling a toilet, make sure to remove as much of the old wax ring as possible for a good seal.

5. **Install the new toilet (see Figure 8-7).**

   With the toilet lying on its side, install the new wax ring (sold separately) by placing it wax side up against the underside of the toilet. The wax ring will be slightly larger than the hole at the base of the toilet. Install new closet bolts (typically provided with the toilet) in the slots on the closet flange in an upright position, just as you found the old ones. Next, with the help of a friend, stand the toilet up and, without allowing the bottom to touch the floor, align the holes in the base of the toilet with the closet bolts, and then gently lower the toilet until it completely seats.

6. **Connect the closet bolts.**

   Install the washers and nuts onto the closet bolts, being careful not to tighten them too tight, which could result in a broken toilet. Ugh! Then place the bolt caps over the nuts. If the bolt caps don't properly seat, chances are that the bolts are too long. Shorten the bolts by cutting off the excess with a hacksaw.

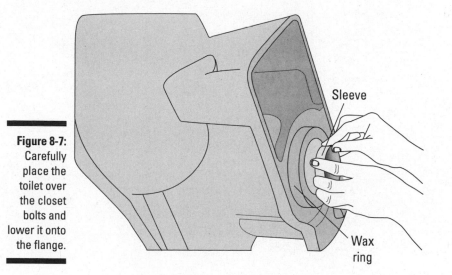

Sleeve

Figure 8-7: Carefully place the toilet over the closet bolts and lower it onto the flange.

Wax ring

7. **Install the water-supply line (see Figure 8-8).**

See "The shut-off valve at the wall," earlier in this chapter, for instructions on removing and reconnecting a supply line.

The easiest way to remember which direction tightens and which one loosens is the old axiom "righty-tighty, lefty-loosey." Turning most threaded things right, or clockwise, tightens them (righty-tighty); turning them to the left, or counterclockwise, loosens them (lefty-loosey). There *are* exceptions to this rule — for example, left-handed threads on things that are used to secure things that also turn clockwise (like the blade on a table saw). So, if you run into a nut that just won't give, before muscling it any more, try switching direction.

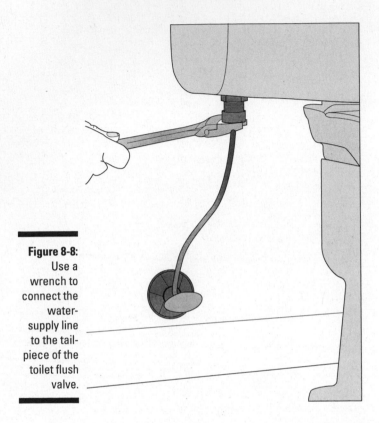

Figure 8-8:
Use a wrench to connect the water-supply line to the tail-piece of the toilet flush valve.

Between the base of the toilet and the floor

If water is seeping out between the base of the toilet and the floor, then the wax ring has failed. Remove the toilet (see the preceding section), replace the wax ring, and reinstall the toilet.

Even if the floor is dry, if you have access to the area beneath the toilet (like in the basement or crawlspace.), occasionally check to see if the toilet has developed a hidden leak. Look for damp wood or evidence of dripping water. If you find this telltale evidence, replace the wax ring.

Maintaining Tubs and Showers

Most people make at least one trip a day to the tub or shower. We don't know anyone who wants to perform a morning scrub-down in a mildew-lined fixture with a dangerously slippery floor. Our tub and shower tips show you how to easily maintain these fixtures so that your movie called *Showering and Bathing* will be a love story — not a horror flick.

Keeping your tubs and showers clean

How you clean your tub or shower depends on the material they're made of:

✔ **To clean a porcelain tub:** Use the same methods described for cleaning vitreous surfaces (see the "Vitreous china fixtures" section, earlier in this chapter). You can also remove soap scum and dirt using automatic dishwasher detergent and hot water. Rinse with fresh water and towel-dry.

✔ **To clean fiberglass:** Use a mixture of ¹⁄₄ cup of salt mixed with 2 to 3 tablespoons of turpentine. Scrub the concoction onto the surface with a nylon bristle brush. Wipe up the excess with paper towels. Follow by washing with a mild detergent. Rinse with fresh water and towel-dry.

To minimize major cleaning chores, try these tips:

✔ **Apply a coat of lemon oil or a coat of car polish (but not both) to your tub, shower walls, and shower door.** These products reduce surface tension and cause water and soap residue to drain off instead of sticking to a surface.

✔ **Squeegee wet surfaces or wipe them dry with a towel after each use.** It only takes a moment.

Re-caulking

If you have tile shower walls, there is a very good possibility that a leak could develop between the tile and the tub. As the house moves (a natural process that occurs in every home), a hairline crack can occur that allows water to get into the joint. Once water gets in, there is no telling how much damage can be done. That's why it's important to annually caulk the connection between your shower walls and the tub or shower pan.

Here's another good reason to re-caulk. If you've tried to remove the black mildew stains from caulk, you know it's sometimes hopeless. That's because the stains are often behind the caulk — between the caulk and the wall. The answer, of course, is to remove the caulk, kill the mildew, and then replace the caulk.

To remove old caulk

Removing what exists and then caulking from scratch are the way to go. Fortunately, removing the caulk isn't as hard as it may seem.

Caulk-Be-Gone and Adhesive & Caulk Remover are two commercial products that can assist you in the job. These products are specially formulated to soften caulk for easy removal.

To remove caulk, simply apply a caulk remover and allow it to sit until the caulk has softened (it may take a few hours). Then remove the softened caulk with a plastic putty knife. Finish up by cleaning the joint with paint thinner and wiping the area dry with a clean rag.

To get rid of mildew

After you've removed the old caulk, you can get rid of mildew by cleaning the joint with our Easy Mildew Remover (see Chapter 20). Just spray the mixture onto the mildewed area. Let it sit until the black mildew turns white. Rinse with fresh water; then use a hair dryer to thoroughly dry the area. The joint can now be re-caulked.

Although our Easy Mildew Remover mixture is mild, don't forget to wear gloves and eye protection and make sure the area is well ventilated.

Improve the odds of preventing mildew from returning by wiping down the joint with denatured alcohol just before applying the new caulk.

To apply new caulk

For a professional-looking job, follow these steps:

1. **Apply blue painter's masking tape to the tub ¹/₈ inch from the joint; then apply another strip of tape along the wall, ¹/₈ inch from the joint.**

   Now the caulking will go between the two pieces of tape, making straight, smooth lines.

2. **Apply tub and tile caulk into the joint and smooth it with your finger, an old teaspoon, or a caulking spreader.**

3. **Immediately remove the tape.**

   Pull it out and away from the freshly caulked joint. Be careful not to touch the caulk.

4. **Let the caulk dry.**

   Caulk can take varying amounts of time to dry, depending upon the type being used and the temperature and humidity in your home. In general, your best bet is to allow the caulk to dry overnight before getting it wet.

You simply won't believe how beautiful your job will look.

Avoiding overflow leaks

The tub overflow is the device located at the end of the tub just above the drain. It derives its name from the purpose it serves: preventing a tub from overflowing. Sometimes the overflow assembly holds the lever for a built-in drain stopper. (Sinks also have overflows — a hole beneath the front edge — but with sinks, the overflow is built in; no hardware is attached that can fail and leak.)

What you see when you look at a tub overflow is a decorative metal cover. Behind the cover and on the outside surface of the tub is a gasket. Behind the gasket is the pipe that directs overflow into the sewer system. The two screws located in the overflow plate hold together the decorative cover plate, the overflow gasket, and the overflow pipe. When the screws become loose, the gasket can leak.

To avoid leads, check the screws every year or two to ensure that they're snug. If you overfill the tub and the gasket isn't tight, it can leak behind the tub, causing problems that can be hard to detect.

Chapter 9

Plumbing, Part III: Sewer and Septic Systems

In This Chapter

▶ Getting to know your sewer system

▶ Keeping your sewer or septic system running clog-free

▶ Eliminating the most common clogs

Sanitation is one of the single most important systems in your home. A cracked window pane or a broken fence board can wait until you have time to make the necessary repair. However, when it comes to your sewer or septic system, time is of the essence. Think about it; what could be worse than a toilet that won't flush, a sink that won't drain, or an overflowing tub? Okay, a house fire is obviously more urgent, but beyond that you'll be hard pressed to find a more time-sensitive maintenance emergency. So, kick up your feet and delve into this chapter before one of the kids calls out for help in the bathroom.

Sewer-System Basics

Every plumbing fixture in your home is joined by the same drainpipe — that means the kitchen sink, the dishwasher, the washing machine, the toilets, and so on. The waste from each of these fixtures exits the house through this one drainpipe. A problem caused by one fixture can easily become a problem for all the other fixtures.

Your common, everyday household sanitary sewer system consists of three basic elements (see Figure 9-1):

- **The waste lines and drainpipe:** The waste lines carry sewage from each of the fixtures in your home down through the walls and under the floor, and then outside the home to either a public sewer system beneath the street or a septic tank somewhere below ground on your property. A clog in any of these pipes stops waste from reaching its destination away from your home — and it can back up into your home.

- **The vent pipes:** Vent pipes travel from each plumbing fixture (or group of plumbing fixtures), upward (inside walls) and out through the roof. These pipes are the typically black ones that stick up out of your roof. The vents allow air into the sewer lines so that they drain freely. A clogged vent pipe can be a serious problem, preventing good drainage of waste.

- **The p-traps:** You have one of these traps in every fixture: sink, toilet, washing machine, you name it. If the fixture drains into the sewer system, the water or waste first travels through a p-trap. The trap allows water and waste to enter the sewer system while at the same time preventing sewer gases from backing up into your home. A clogged p-trap can inhibit the flow of waste from the home and can allow stinky gases to back up into the home through the fixtures.

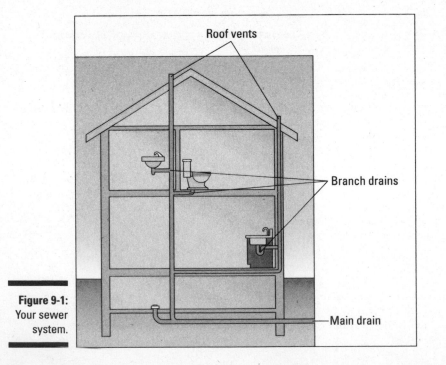

Figure 9-1: Your sewer system.

Roof vents

Branch drains

Main drain

Keeping Your System Clog-Free

When we were just a couple of youngsters, one of our dad's favorite sayings was "An ounce of prevention is worth a pound of cure." Dad was right — especially when it comes to the drain and sewer system. Trapping hair and soap scum in the tub or shower, using a lint filter at the clothes washer, and being careful about what you throw into the kitchen sink — including the garbage disposal — can prevent minor clogs that can cause major headaches and repairs. Take it from our dad and do everything you can to prevent a plumbing disaster. You can be a real hero and keep your home's lower GI tract in tip-top shape by taking advantage of the following advice. Thanks, Dad!

Being careful what you put down the drain

One of the absolute best ways to prevent slow or clogged drains is to be careful about what you put into them. Clever, eh?

Cooking grease, coffee grounds, hair, and soap scum are four of a drain's biggest enemies. Do whatever you can to avoid introducing any of these items into a drain. Here's how:

- **Save cooking grease in an old coffee can or cardboard milk container.** Then dispose of it in the trash.
- **Throw coffee grounds away in the garbage or add them to your mulch pile.**
- **Use a screen or drain-grate to cover the drain's opening and minimize problems with hair and soap scum.** Stop by your local plumbing-supply store to study the choices appropriate for your particular fixture. Take along a picture of the drain system to better explain your needs. Most filters and screens can be simply laid in place.

Preventive pipe cleaning

Regular cleaning has its merits. To keep drains in your home running freely — and absent of odor — try these methods:

- **Run hot water through the sink after each use.** Hot water keeps oils in food products running down the drain, rather than building up on the interior surface of pipes, which can make drains sluggish and lead to clogs.

> ✔ **Throw a handful of baking soda into the drain and follow it with hot water.** Baking soda is a terrific cleaning agent, and it's also great for absorbing foul odors and leaving your drain pipes smelling like a rose. Okay, maybe not like a rose, but a lot better than they otherwise would.

> ✔ **Pour 1 cup of vinegar down the drain and let it sit for 30 minutes; then chase it down with very hot water.** Vinegar is a wonder cleaner (as Chapter 20 explains). It contains acetic acid, which acts as an excellent organic solvent in removing organic buildup of crud in pipes.

If clogging is a regular problem at your place, try this one out for size. It works on drains in sinks, showers, and tubs. You need $1/2$ cup each of baking soda, salt, and vinegar and a couple quarts of boiling water. Just before going to bed (to allow the solution to sit overnight, giving it more cleaning horsepower), do the following:

1. **Pour the salt and the baking soda into the drain.**

2. **Add the vinegar and let the concoction foam for about a minute.**

3. **Chase with at least 2 quarts of boiling water.**

For additional tips on cleaning your sink, toilet, tub, and shower, turn to Chapter 8.

For sinks with garbage disposals, you can also try this trick:

1. **Fill an ice-cube tray half-full with vinegar and top it off with clear water.**

   Vinegar alone won't freeze well. Be sure to mark the tray clearly — you wouldn't want an unsuspecting family member to end up with a mouthful of vinegar. Can you imagine how that martini would taste?

2. **Turn the disposal on and then throw in the cubes.**

   Vinegar is a mild acid that cleans the disposal and the drain while the ice literally chills and scrapes grease off its walls (see Figure 9-2).

   If you don't like the smell of vinegar, you can chase the cubes with one sliced lemon. Your disposal and your kitchen will smell great!

A word about commercial drain cleaners

Lye is the active ingredient in most popular store-bought drain cleaners. It dissolves soap scum and hair in a heartbeat. All you have to do is pour some down the drain, chase with a small amount of water, and wait for the chemical to do its job.

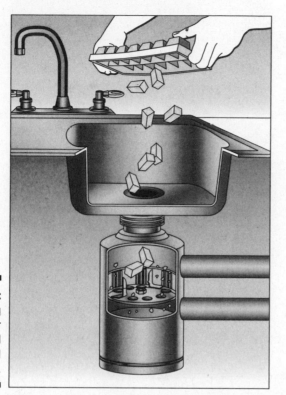

Figure 9-2:
Cleaning
your
disposal
with ice and
vinegar.

Small amounts of lye are reasonably safe. But too much of a good thing could suddenly turn nasty. Strong drain cleaners aren't safe when used in large quantities. Make sure to follow the directions on the label to the letter.

Unclogging the Waste Lines

The clean-out system in your sewer provides access to the waste lines for easy cleaning, which can save you hundreds of dollars in plumber's bills. A *clean-out* is a port with a removable cap that provides access to the inside of the sewer line.

So where are your clean-outs? The National Plumbing Code requires clean-outs to be placed in your waste lines at least every 100 linear feet of horizontal travel. Clean-outs must be even closer together when the total angle of all bends in the horizontal sections of line exceed 135 degrees.

The tell-tale sign of a clean-out is its cap. It's a flat, threaded disk fitted with a hexagonal protrusion at its center, which allows it to be easily removed (or replaced) with a wrench or a pair of pliers.

Clean-outs can be found under sinks, sticking out of exterior walls, and randomly in the area beneath the floor — but not buried below the soil. When you know where all your clean-outs are, you can use that knowledge to keep your sewer clean on your own. And you can give your plumber a rest — at home, not in Tahiti with your money!

To clear a clog through the clean-outs, follow these steps:

1. **Using a wrench or pair of pliers, remove the clean-out cover.**

2. **Use a plumber's auger, or "snake," to clear a clog at the first sign of a drainage problem (see Figure 9-3).**

   Most good do-it-yourselfers own a small version of a plumber's auger. Not only is a small auger inexpensive, but it's easy to store as well. (See Chapter 8 for information about snakes that are made especially for clearing toilet clogs.)

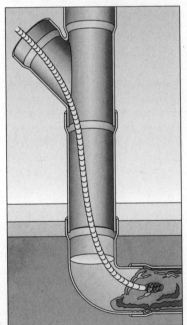

Figure 9-3:
Using a plumber's auger or a snake to clear a line.

Keeping Vents Free from Debris

When a sink isn't draining properly, and the waste line isn't clogged, you may need to take a look upward to find the culprit — up toward the vent system. You know, the black plumbing pipes that stick up out of your roof. When a vent becomes clogged, it shows up within the home as everything from "ghost flushes" at the toilet to sinks that simply won't drain properly.

One or more of the following can collect in a vent line and completely clog it. Here are a few things that we've found:

- ✔ Birds (usually deceased, but sometimes nesting)
- ✔ Rodent carcasses (once we found just the skeleton)
- ✔ Leaves, trash, and other rubbish, which are sometimes almost impossible to remove
- ✔ Tennis balls and baseballs (we're still waiting for our first water balloon)

Because clearing vent-pipe blockages can be a real pain in the you-know-what, we suggest that you take the preventive steps. You won't be sorry.

Getting rid of blockages

Unfortunately, the best place to clear a blockage in a vent pipe is from the roof.

Working up on the roof can be a dangerous task, to say the least. So, you may want to have this job done by someone who has experience working up high. If you feel confident about performing the work yourself, be sure that the roof is dry, wear rubber-soled shoes, and use a safety harness to prevent yourself from falling off the roof if you slip. (See Chapter 5 for more tips on working on the roof.)

Dealing with clogs

You'll need a flashlight, a plumber's snake, and a garden hose. Use the flashlight to shine a bright light down the vent pipe to look for leaves, nesting materials, or other debris you may be able to remove from above. Then try the following:

- ✔ **Remove any items you can reach.** For those items you can't remove from above, run the plumber's snake down the vent pipe.
- ✔ **Feed the end of a garden hose down the vent pipe and have someone on the ground turn on the water.** Listen carefully for water backing up

and a sudden whoosh when the weight of the water forces the clog into and down the drain.

You can also feed the hose down into the vent pipe as you would a plumber's snake to dislodge a clog that's not solid enough to dam water.

Dealing with frozen plumbing

Blockages caused by frozen plumbing vents can be a problem for homes located in extremely cold climates. The best way to clear a frozen vent is by pouring really hot water into the vent pipe. But climbing up a ladder with a bucket of hot water can be dangerous. A simpler way of doing this is to connect a rubber hose — rated for use with hot water — to the hot-water spigot at your washing machine. Works every time!

Putting preventive measures in place

One of the most effective means of preventing plumbing-vent pipe blockages is with the use of vent pipe screens. These nifty devices fit snugly onto the top of vent pipes and prevent blockages from animals, bugs/insects, and debris such as leaves. You can find these screens at hardware stores, home centers, plumbing wholesalers, and online.

Is your ghost flush friendly?

About five years ago, we were on the air doing our radio show. A caller phoned in with a most unusual question. "My toilet flushes all by itself," she said. She went on to explain that no one was near the toilet when it flushed. It did it all by itself. "Do I have ghosts," she asked? Naturally, we decided to run with it. We excitedly told her that Casper the Friendly Ghost was on a toilet-flushing rampage and, well, you can probably figure out the rest.

After a few minutes of horsing around, we returned to serious diagnosing. The flush that our caller described was not a conventional one. The flush-lever never moved — not once. And water wasn't released from the tank. Each time, the tank remained full and undisturbed. But the toilet was flushing. Every once in a while, the water in the bottom of the toilet bowl would simply be sucked right down the drain! Fllluuuusssshhh!

As we continued to diagnose, we found out that each time that the toilet had flushed, someone was taking a shower. We surmised that the shower and toilet were connected to the same vent pipe (often, two or more plumbing fixtures are connected to a single vent pipe) and that the vent had clogged.

When the shower drained, the water moving down the sewer line acted like a piston, causing suction. Apparently, air could not be drawn in from the clogged vent to offset the increasing negative pressure, so the next best place — the toilet — became the ventilation intake port. Casper had nothing to do with it.

Preventing a frozen vent can be a bit trickier. In general, the easiest way to prevent a vent pipe from freezing is by increasing the size of the vent by two to three times the diameter where the pipe travels vertically in the attic. The added volume of air makes freezing more difficult.

An alternative is to install a vent pipe that has a built-in heater, such as the ArticVent by Heat-Line (www.heatline.com). It's a heat tape for your eaves, gutters, and pipes, except the heating element is built in to the vent pipe. You simply remove about 3 feet of the uppermost portion of vent pipe, install the ArticVent, and plug it into an electrical outlet in the attic. Not a bad alternative if you live in a really cold climate and frozen vents are a recurring problem.

Avoiding Problems with P-Traps

The *p-trap* is that strangely curved pipe that you see beneath any sink in your home. Actually, a p-trap can be found at every single plumbing fixture — whether you can see it or not. If you can't see it, you can be sure it's either inside the fixture (as it is with toilets), beneath the floor (in the case of showers and tubs), or inside the wall (for washing-machine drains).

The name of this special piece of drain comes from the letter of the alphabet that it resembles, and also from the fact that it actually traps water. Essentially, the trap holds enough water in its curved base to act as a "water door," preventing unpleasant waste and sewer gases from backing up into the home.

Unfortunately, the trap's water-trapping ability extends to hair, grease, debris, and soap scum. This makes a p-trap the number-one location of clogs in the sewer system. If the p-trap becomes only slightly clogged, then you experience slow drainage in the fixture. Oh, you say the toilet is the place where all the clogs occur at your house. The toilet has the largest p-trap of any fixture in the home. Had to pull any toys out of yours lately?

You can prevent drain clogs by being careful about what you put in the drain and by performing monthly preventive cleaning, as explained in the earlier section "Keeping Your System Clog-Free." But if these measures don't work and you experience slow draining in your fixture, try cleaning the p-trap to avoid a full-blown blockage. You need:

- 1 small plastic bucket
- 1 rag
- 1 large pair of pliers or a pipe wrench
- 1 portable light

Before beginning, remove everything from under the sink so that you have ample room to work. Then follow these steps:

1. **Position the plastic bucket directly under the p-trap.**

2. **Using the pliers, remove the two coupling nuts that attach the trap to the sink tailpiece and to the adjacent wall fitting.**

   If these nuts won't budge, or if they simply fall apart when you try to move them, it's time to purchase a replacement trap.

3. **Clean the interior of the trap with a straightened wire coat hanger or a large nylon bottle brush.**

   Make sure that all the parts are completely clean inside and out. A piece of debris lodged between a drain washer and the drainpipe can cause a leak.

   Use the cleaning as an opportunity to inspect all the washers — they should be soft and supple. (Don't you just love that description? Go to the hardware store or home center and ask for "soft, supple drain washers.") If they aren't soft, you need to replace them.

4. **If you discover that the trap is clean and clear (and not the reason for the clog or slow draining), then insert a small retractable drain snake directly into the drain or, if the p-trap has been removed, directly into the pipe in the wall.**

   Work the snake in and out while rotating the handle clockwise.

5. **Reassemble the trap.**

   Make sure that each washer is properly seated. Twisting can be a real problem. Don't over-tighten the connections. At first, the coupling nuts should be no more than hand-tight. If a leak persists, continue to tighten a little at a time until the leak disappears. If increased tightening doesn't do the trick, chances are, the washers are dirty, twisted, or defective. Try again!

If cleaning doesn't solve your p-trap problems, pick up the telephone and call a plumber or sewer-and-drain specialist who has the expertise and proper tools to get things flowing freely.

If all the drains in the home are running slowly, the main sewer line may be the problem. Skip all these steps and go straight to the plumber.

Your Sewer System's Fall

If you repeatedly have drainage problems, and you've determined that all waste lines, vents, and p-traps are clean and clear, then the *fall* (the downward slope of the pipes), or actually the lack of fall, could be the problem.

One thing you don't want is a sewer system that looks like a set of roller-coaster tracks — up and down, up and down. Sewers work best when the waste lines slope downhill. In fact, they don't really work very well at all otherwise.

The National Plumbing Code requires sewer lines to fall (slope downward) at a rate of $1/8$ inch per foot (which equals 1 inch every 8 feet). We think the minimum should be twice as much. There is no maximum fall — the more the better.

If fall is an issue, call a plumber to correct the problem. We don't recommend major sewer work as a DIY project.

Maintaining Your Septic System

If you live in a rural area or have vacation property in the middle of nowhere, you're no doubt familiar with the form and function of a septic system (see Figure 9-4). In brief, a septic system is your very own onsite sewage treatment facility. It's used primarily where access to a municipal sewer system is neither available nor economically practical. A septic system is out of sight and is odorless (when properly maintained).

A septic system is reasonably maintenance-free. A well-constructed, properly maintained tank could last indefinitely. However, the *leach field* (the underground area where all of the sewage drainpipes are located) will most likely require some treatment or perhaps replacement after about 15 to 20 years of service.

Following a few simple rules — like not using too much water and not depositing materials in the septic tank that bacteria can't decompose — should help to make a septic system trouble-free for many years. But don't forget that the septic tank does need to be cleaned out when too many solids build up.

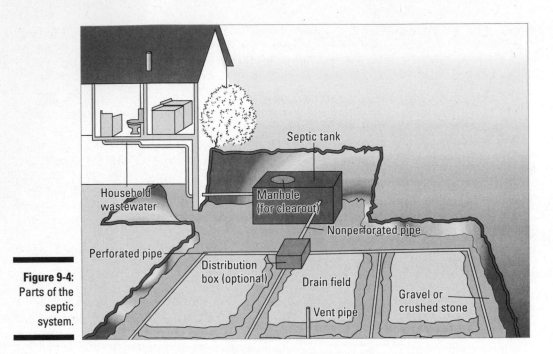

Figure 9-4:
Parts of the
septic
system.

Being careful about what goes in

Be mindful about what you and your family put into your septic system. It doesn't take much to upset the delicate biological balance within the tank. You can extend the life of a septic system by watching everything that's introduced to the system.

Keep in mind the following recommendations:

- ✔ **Too much water can upset the delicate biological balance within the tank, thus defeating its ability to work wonders.** Moreover, discharging more water into the system than it can handle can cause it to back up — not a desirable occurrence.

- ✔ **Don't use excessive amounts of any household chemicals.** You can use normal amounts of household detergents, bleaches, drain cleaners, and other household chemicals without stopping the bacterial action in the septic tank. But, for example, don't dump cleaning water for latex paintbrushes and cans into the house sewer.

- ✔ **Don't deposit coffee grounds, cooking fats, *wet-strength towels* (paper towels that don't dissolve easily, like the heavy-duty kind), disposable diapers, facial tissues, cigarette butts, and other non-decomposable materials into the house sewer.** These materials won't decompose, will fill the septic tank, and will plug the system.

Use a high-quality toilet tissue that breaks up easily when wet. One way to find out if your toilet paper fits this description is to put a handful of toilet tissue in a fruit jar half-full of water. Shake the jar, and if the tissue breaks up easily, the product is suitable for the septic tank.

✔ **Avoid dumping grease down the drain.** It may plug sewer pipes or build up in the septic tank and plug the inlet. Keep a separate container for waste grease and throw it out with the garbage.

According to the Environmental Protection Agency, because of the presence of significant numbers and types of bacteria, enzymes, yeasts, and other fungi and microorganisms in typical residential and commercial wastewaters, the use of septic-system additives containing these or any other ingredients is not recommended.

Cleaning and pumping your septic tank

You need to have your septic tank pumped and cleaned by a professional every one to three years. A septic tank in a northern climate will need to have the solids removed more often than a tank farther south. (This geographic variance is primarily because cooler temperatures inhibit bacterial action and provide less decomposition of the sewage solids.) How often you need to have your septic tank pumped also depends on the size of the tank, the volume of wastewater, and how many solids go into it. Constant foul odor, slow drains, and drains that back up are all telltale signs that your septic tank needs pumping. When in doubt, call in a septic pro.

Chapter 10

Heating, Ventilating, and Air-Conditioning Systems

In This Chapter

▶ Keeping your furnace and boiler happy

▶ Ventilating your home from top to bottom

▶ Keeping your air-conditioning cool

We can describe heating, ventilating, and air-conditioning (HVAC) with just four words: *hot, cold, in,* and *out.* Or, more specifically: heating the interior when it's cold outside; cooling the interior when it's hot outside; drawing fresh air into your home to moderate temperatures and humidity; and venting moist, smoky, greasy, or stinky air from inside to outside.

And this brings us to the paradox of HVAC: These seemingly simple processes actually rely on some complex technology. As a result, there are very few maintenance tasks that don't bring with them a high likelihood of killing the furnace, the air conditioner, or yourself. But the tasks that *can* be done by a do-it-yourselfer are easy and non-threatening. We're confident you can do them without difficulty or danger — and they'll make a huge difference in the efficiency, performance, and life of your system, whatever kind it is.

Making Friends with the Monster: Your Furnace

Most grown-ups never would admit it, but they're terrified of their furnaces. A furnace is a big, complicated piece of machinery. But we're here to tell you that there's nothing to be afraid of. Your furnace is less mysterious and scary than you think. It heats up air or water, and then moves hot air, water, or steam around the house. It's really that simple. In this section, we tell you what you need to do to maintain your furnace.

Taking care of a forced-air system

In a forced-air system, air is heated as it passes through the furnace (shown in Figure 10-1). A blower and a system of ducts take the warmed air throughout the house, and then cooled air is sucked into return ducts back to the furnace. You need to take care of your forced-air system to keep it running safely at peak efficiency.

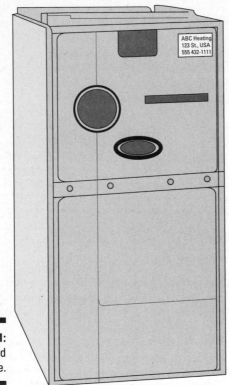

Figure 10-1:
A standard furnace.

The parts of your furnace and their locations may be different from the illustrations in this book. For specifics on your furnace, consult the owner's manual that came with the furnace. (You probably filed it under "Manuals I'll Never Look At.") You may be able to get more information, a diagram, or even the manual, from the manufacturer's Web site.

Inspecting and servicing a forced-air furnace

Forced-air furnaces must be inspected and serviced every year before the heating season begins. Follow these steps:

1. **Look for the sticker that the last serviceperson affixed to the outside of the housing.**

2. **Hold a flashlight between your chin and shoulder while you write down the company name and phone number located on the sticker.**

   If you're young and have great vision or if your furnace is located in a basement, attic, or garage that is well lit, you may be able to do without the flashlight.

3. **Call that company to arrange for a professional inspection and service.**

Kidding aside, it's critically important to have a *qualified, licensed* heating contractor (or, euphemistically, a "home-comfort specialist") inspect and service your forced-air system. Sure, you could save $90 by not having your furnace inspected at all, but a dirty, inefficient furnace costs you ten times that much per year in wasted fuel.

Even more important, a cracked heat exchanger or dislodged flue could fill your home with deadly carbon-monoxide gas. Plain and simple, an under-maintained or failing furnace is a danger to you and your family.

So what will the furnace serviceperson do? First, he'll carefully inspect and check every critical component. Then he'll perform dozens of maintenance tasks (lubrication, adjustment, and so on) that will help maintain, and even improve, your furnace's efficiency and go a long way toward keeping it running well year after year.

Replacing the filter

The easiest furnace-maintenance task is replacing the filter. During the heating season, you should replace your furnace filter every month. If an air conditioner is part of the same system, you should change the filter every month year-round.

The filter, typically fiberglass or pleated fabric, is designed to take dust, dirt, pollen, lint, carpet fibers, and pet hair and dander out of the air, which keeps your home cleaner and keeps allergies at bay. Without all that stuff in the airflow and inside the unit, the blower motor lasts longer, and other parts of the heating system work better. The filter also prevents the air-conditioner evaporator coil (hidden within the unit) from becoming clogged — that's a good thing, because when the evaporator coil is clogged, the air conditioner's efficiency is reduced, and your utility bill runs sky-high.

If your furnace uses a standard 1-inch disposable filter, don't bother buying fancy, ultra-high-efficient filters. The pleated kind is fine. The filter is tightly woven and won't let large particles pass, and the pleats double the filtration area, resulting in less stress on the system blower. Unless your home is hermetically sealed, you never open a window or a door, and you've removed all inside allergy sources (which is extremely unlikely), those mega-filters don't provide benefits commensurate with their significantly higher cost. And they may reduce airflow and cause the blower to strain to push air through their thicker, tighter filtering medium. Don't believe us? Ask your serviceman. He'll back us up on this.

Why do we like pleated filters better than the typical spun-fiberglass filters? Because they actually work. You can see for yourself: Lay a standard fiberglass filter flat on a table, and shake some table salt onto it. If the filter allows salt to pass through (which it will), how can it snag a microscopic grain of pollen? Now, perform the same experiment using a pleated filter. Look mom, no salt! A pleated filter does add some resistance to airflow, but not enough to make a difference.

Don't buy 1-inch filters one at a time — get a whole case. They're cheaper by the dozen. What's more, the box sits by the furnace and reminds you to do the monthly change. And you'll never miss a change because you don't have a filter on hand. Want to make extra-sure you don't forget? We have a friend who opens the box as soon as he gets home from the store and labels each one with the month in which he'll install it. We think that's smart. Try it!

To replace the filter, follow these steps:

1. **Locate the filter slot.**

   You can usually find the filter near where the cool air enters the furnace — in the cold-air return duct, or at the entrance to the blower chamber. Though redundant, sometimes you'll find filters in both locations — typically a washable filter at the furnace and a replaceable fabric filter at the cold-air return. (If it's not where the cool air enters the furnace, look in the main return air register, which is on the wall or ceiling somewhere in your home.)

2. **Slide out the old, dirty filter.**

   You may have to jockey it back and forth a bit.

3. **Remove the wrapping from the new filter (if any), and locate the airflow arrows on the side.**

4. **Position the filter so that the airflow arrows point toward the blower and with the flow of cold air.**

5. **Slide in the new filter, being careful not to dent, deform, or tear the cardboard frame.**

6. **Check to make sure the filter is snugly in place and all the way in its slot.**

Some furnaces have more-complicated, wider filters that slide into a plastic housing that, in turn, slides into a wide slot. Follow the manufacturer's instructions for replacing the filter, and then slide the housing into place.

Other furnaces have permanent filters. These filters usually don't need to be cleaned as often as the less sophisticated fabric filters. Cleaning instructions usually are affixed near the filter on the side of the furnace or in the owner's manual. Consult a pro when in doubt.

Cleaning the blower compartment

The blower is a large "squirrel cage" fan (see Figure 10-2) that pushes air out through the ducts to the registers throughout the home. The blower also draws air through return registers into the return ducts and into the unit to be reheated or re-cooled and recirculated. You need to clean it twice a year. Here's how:

1. **Before you do anything, turn off the power to the unit.**

    A service/emergency switch may be mounted on the furnace itself or near it. If you can't find the switch, turn off the power at the circuit breaker or fuse box.

2. **Open the access panel on the front or side (if it isn't already open to change the filter).**

    You may need a screwdriver or socket wrench to do this.

3. **Locate the blower, and remove the blower access panel.**

    The blower will have an access panel that is held on by slip-fit hooks or retaining screws.

4. **Use the vacuum cleaner with the upholstery brush attachment on it to remove any dirt, lint, and dust bunnies you find.**

5. **Replace the blower access panel.**

6. **Replace the access panel, making sure it's in correctly and tightly closed.**

7. **Turn on the power to the unit.**

Whenever you're poking around inside your forced-air unit, be careful not to disturb any of the small wires inside the unit. Most systems have low-voltage controls, so you can't get zapped, but if you inadvertently dislodge a control wire, the system may not come back on.

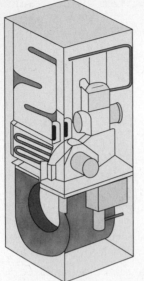

Figure 10-2:
Inside your
furnace.

Checking, replacing, and adjusting the blower-fan belt and pulleys

If your furnace is not a newer model, you need to keep your eye on the blower-fan belt. (If you have a newer furnace, you won't be able to find the belt or a fan — the blower is driven directly by a motor.) A worn, wimpy belt can fail at any time, and it always seems to do so at the most inconvenient time — like midnight on Christmas Eve. A loose belt won't fail, but it will make a squealing noise that can drive you crazy. More important, a loose belt costs you money because, if the belt is slipping, the blower doesn't turn as it should. Plus, if the blower isn't blowing hard enough, you're getting weaker airflow and less hot air for your money.

To check the fan belt, turn off the power to the unit, remove the access panel, and look for fraying, cracks, slippage, and so on. If the belt is frayed, cracked, or otherwise worn-looking, you must replace it as soon as possible. If the belt is loose (with more than $1/2$ inch of give), you must tighten it.

You can also inspect and adjust the pulleys. The belt rides on two pulleys: one connected to the motor and the other connected to the blower. The pulleys often have lubrication points that should receive a few drops of oil each time the system is serviced.

You can address all these problems by taking the steps in the following sections.

Replacing the belt
To replace the belt, follow these steps:

1. **Turn off the power to the unit.**

 2. **Remove the access panel (if you haven't already done so).**

 3. **Loosen the adjusting bolt on the motor just enough to get some slack.**

 4. **Slip the belt off the pulleys.**

 5. **Go to your local hardware store or home center and buy two replacement belts.**

   Take the old belt with you to make sure you get the right replacement. Keep the extra belt in a plastic bag on a nail by the furnace. That way, you have one on hand when you have a middle-of-the-night, all-the-stores-are-closed, the-house-is-freezing, blower-fan belt emergency.

 6. **Put the new belt back on the pulleys and tighten the adjustment bolt until the belt has only ¹/₂ inch of give.**

 7. **Replace the access panel and turn on the power to the unit.**

Tightening and adjusting the belt

The belt should have no more than a ¹/₂ inch of give when you press on it with your finger. If it gives any more than that, you need to tighten it.

To tighten the belt, follow these steps:

 1. **Turn off the power to the unit.**

 2. **Remove the access panel (if you haven't already done so).**

 3. **Slightly loosen the motor adjustment bolt.**

 4. **Slide the motor a little bit at a time to increase tension on the belt until you have about ¹/₂ inch of give.**

   Don't over-tighten the belt. A too-tight belt will damage the motor and fan bearings.

 5. **Double-check to make sure the belt has ¹/₂ inch of give.**

 6. **Tighten the bolt.**

 7. **Replace the access panel and turn on the power to the unit.**

Checking and adjusting the pulley alignment

When the pulleys aren't aligned, they can twist the fan belt and cause it to wear quickly or even break. To check and adjust the pulley alignment, follow these steps:

 1. **Turn off the power to the unit.**

 2. **Remove the access panel (if you haven't already done so).**

 3. **Place a ruler against the pulley faces.**

 4. **Check to see that the pulleys line up perfectly and that the belt travels between them without twisting even a little.**

5. **If the pulley alignment is off, slightly loosen the motor-pulley mounting bolts, adjust the motor pulley to align it with the other pulleys, and then retighten the mounting bolts.**

6. **Recheck the alignment using the ruler and readjust as necessary.**

7. **When the alignment is perfect, replace the access panel and turn on the power to the unit.**

Taking care of your ducts

Ducts are square or round metal tubes in the ceiling, walls, and/or floors that transport air from the furnace to each room in the house. A leak in a duct can allow massive amounts of heat into the attic, crawlspace, or basement. Keeping the ducts tightly sealed ensures that all the expensive heated air coming from the furnace gets to where it belongs.

Leaks aren't the only issue with ducts, though. Even with a serious commitment to filter replacement, the inside of ducts eventually get a coating of fibers, lint, dirt, allergens, mildew, grease, and even bacteria.

Checking the ducts for leaks

If you have access to your ducts, checking for leaks is easy:

1. **Follow each duct from the furnace to its termination, paying special attention to the joints between segments.**

2. **Look for fuzz that has been forced through joints, or feel for warm air coming through gaps.**

   You may need to pull insulation away from the joints and visually inspect them. Dark stripes in the fiberglass insulation is a telltale sign of a duct leak below the insulation. Other big leak locations are around the *boot* (the piece where the duct penetrates your wall, floor, or ceiling).

If you really want to identify how leaky your ducts are, bring in a pro to perform a duct pressure test. This test involves pressurizing the entire duct system, which determines how much of your heated or cooled air is being wasted. A duct pressure test usually runs in the neighborhood of $100 to $200, depending on the size of your home and where you live.

Sealing leaks

If you find any leaks during your inspection, seal them:

✔ **If your leak is below the duct insulation,** seal it with metal duct tape. (*not* the fabric duct tape that you're used to using and that you can use on just about anything other than ducts).

Alternatively, use an elastomeric duct sealant (available at most home centers or hardware stores). When dry, the elastomeric duct sealant provides a rubbery, airtight seal at all joints and seams; it bonds flexible ducts to metal duct fittings.

You can also call in a heating pro to do the job for you.

✔ **If your leak is around the boot,** remove the register cover and caulk the joint between the boot and the wallboard.

As an alternative, you can use a butyl-backed tape to seal the gap — this method is the one that the pros use. Be sure that you position the tape in the right place because, after it's applied, this stuff sticks like heck. Use a utility knife with a sharp blade to trim any tape that may be exposed after replacing the register cover.

Got a big duct dent? Have damaged duct segments come completely apart? Call an HVAC pro to fix them. The pros know all kinds of tricks for repairing damage, large and small. They even have a metal patch that they slip in and affix to the damaged area with an elastomeric sealant.

Cleaning the ducts

Checking and cleaning your ducts every few years is smart. Why? Because clean air is healthy air.

But cleaning ducts is not a job for a do-it-yourselfer — access is difficult (you have to take apart the ducts in several places), and duct cleaning requires specialized equipment (a mega-vacuum!) and skills. Call a pro. The pro will have all the tools and high-tech equipment that'll scrub the inside of your ducts and suck up the dirt without putting it right back into your home.

Balancing a central heating system

Are some rooms in your home too hot, some too cold, and some just right? You need to fine-tune your system for maximum efficiency, minimum energy consumption, and even temperatures in every room. It's about airflow, and dampers and registers help control the airflow in the ducts.

Here's how to balance your central heating system:

1. **Start at the furnace unit and follow the main ducts outward, looking for small levers on the side; these are the handles for dampers.**

   When the handle is horizontal, the damper is fully open, allowing maximum airflow. When the handle is anywhere between horizontal and vertical, the damper is reducing airflow.

2. **Place thermometers in the rooms in question, away from registers and cold-air returns, and all at about the same height from the floor.**

3. **Turn on the heat and open all the dampers, wait about an hour, and then check the thermometers.**

   Is one room warmer than others? Is hot air roaring out of the register?

When to replace a forced-air furnace

How do you know when your furnace is on its last legs? When its old technology makes it unacceptably inefficient and expensive. In general, if your system is more than 15 years old, replacing it with a new Energy Star–rated system will save you money, prevent maintenance headaches, and keep you warmer and more comfortable. (If your system is less than 15 years old, regular maintenance probably is the way to go.)

Money talks. By replacing an older furnace (which is typically 60 percent efficient) with a new furnace (typically 90 percent efficient, or better), you can cut your heating bills in half! Don't believe it? Furnace manufacturer Web sites offer calculators that help determine energy savings and payback timeframes.

For more on the Energy Star program, go to www.energystar.gov.

4. **Partially close the damper in the duct that feeds that room by moving the handle one-third of the way between horizontal and vertical; wait an hour and recheck the room.**

5. **If the room seems cooler, you're done. If it doesn't, close the damper another third, wait another hour, and check the room again.**

   You also can fine-tune airflow by adjusting the register.

6. **Repeat steps 2 through 5 for each room until you have the temperature balanced.**

   By the way, *balanced* may mean that the main living areas and bathrooms are warmer than the bedrooms, or vice versa. It all depends on what you prefer . . . or how cold your spouse claims to be.

7. **After you've achieved balance, go back to the ducts and use a permanent marker to write a *W* (for winter) where the damper handle should be positioned for the heating season.**

Repeat the process for the cooling season, except write an *S* (for summer) where the damper handle should be positioned.

Hot-water systems

Hot-water, or *hydronic,* systems use a gas- or oil-fired burner to heat a tank of water to near boiling, and then circulate it with a pump throughout the house to radiators or baseboard convectors, and then back to the boiler to be reheated and make the round-trip again (see Figure 10-3).

Seems simple? Not so much, actually. As with forced-air systems, most maintenance tasks are beyond the skills of the do-it-yourselfer. Call in a qualified, licensed heating contractor to do an annual inspection and cleaning.

Forced Hot-Water Heating

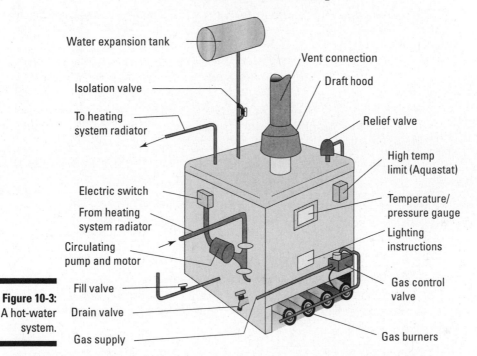

Water expansion tank

Isolation valve

To heating
system radiator

Vent connection

Draft hood

Relief valve

High temp
limit (Aquastat)

Temperature/
pressure gauge

Lighting
instructions

Gas control
valve

Gas burners

Electric switch

From heating
system radiator

Circulating
pump and motor

Fill valve

Drain valve

Gas supply

**Figure 10-3:
A hot-water
system.**

Don't be penny-wise and pound-foolish. A dirty, inefficient boiler costs you far more than a service call. The serviceman will catch little problems before they become big trouble. And a neglected system will fail many years before a well-maintained one.

Gauging the pressure

Most hot-water systems have only a single gauge, located on the main unit, which measures three things: pressure, temperature, and *altitude* (the height of the water in the system).

To monitor the performance of your hot-water system, keep an (occasional) eye on the pressure. Most boilers run at 12 to 15 pounds per square inch (psi) of pressure. If the pressure is lower or higher, something is wrong.

Low pressure most often is caused by a low water level. The system's automatic filling system should maintain the proper water level. But if yours doesn't, you can manually fill the boiler by opening the water feed valve on the incoming supply pipe. Just open the valve and keep it open until the pressure gets to 12 psi. Then call a repairman.

High pressure usually is caused by too much water in the expansion tank; read on to find out what to do in that case.

Draining the expansion tank

Located overhead near the boiler, a conventional expansion tank is cylindrical and has a drain valve at one end. To drain excess water from the expansion tank:

1. **Turn off the power, turn off the water supply to the boiler, and let the tank cool.**

2. **Attach a garden hose to the drain valve, open it, and let water out until the levels of the pressure gauges on the boiler and the expansion tank match.**

3. **Close the valve, turn the power back on, and reopen the water supply.**

If you have a diaphragm expansion tank, the pressure problem isn't too much water; it's too little air. You need to recharge the expansion tank. Use an ordinary tire-pressure gauge to check the air pressure. If it's lower than the recommended psi (look on the tank for the correct reading), use a bicycle pump to juice it back up.

When the expansion tank has been drained or the diaphragm tank refilled, restart the system and carefully monitor it. If the pressure goes back up, turn off the system and pick up the phone. You've done all you can do — it's time to call an expert!

Boilers must have a proper pressure-relief valve, located at the top of the unit. This important valve opens when the pressure reaches 30 psi — to prevent the boiler from exploding. If you ever see water draining out of the relief valve, chances are, the system is operating under excessively high pressure and should be shut down immediately — and stay shut down until it can be checked by a professional.

Bleeding the radiators

Bleeding radiators is sometimes necessary in even the best of systems. If you have a radiator in your system that just won't heat, chances are, it's air-locked. Bleeding the air out of the radiator relieves the pressure and allows the system to fill normally.

To bleed the radiators, look for a small valve at the top. When you've found it, turn it about a quarter-turn counterclockwise and keep the screwdriver or radiator key in the valve. If you hear a hissing sound, that's good — it's air escaping. As soon as the hissing stops and you see a dribble of water come out, close the valve.

Don't open the valve more than is necessary; hot water will come rushing out before you can close it. At the very least, you'll make a wet mess. At the worst, you could be scalded. Don't forget to wear eye protection and rain gear when working with water that's under pressure.

Steam systems

As with forced-air and hot-water systems (see the previous sections), it pays to have a professional, licensed contractor check your steam system every year. Not only will you save money in the long run through greater efficiency, but you'll also have peace of mind knowing that your system is operating safely. We cannot emphasize this point enough.

Most adjustments to your steam boiler should be performed by a pro. But there are three important things you can do by yourself:

- **Check the steam gauge on a regular basis — every couple of days.** Make sure it's within the normal range. If it isn't, shut down the system immediately and call for service.

- **Check the safety valve once a month.** Located on the top of the boiler, this important valve vents excess pressure if the boiler goes crazy and exceeds safe levels. When the system is hot, push down on the handle to see if steam comes out. Make sure to stand away from the outlet, because the steam is boiling hot. If no steam comes out, call a service-man to replace the valve immediately.

- **Check the water level once a month.** The water-level gauge has valves on each side. Open them both and make sure that the water level is in the middle, and then close the valves. If you didn't see any water, shut off the boiler, let it cool down, and add water.

Because steam systems occasionally need water added, consider adding an automatic water valve to your system. The valve will monitor water levels and, if the system needs it, add water ever so slowly to avoid damaging the boiler.

Maintaining your radiators

You also can do a few things to keep your radiators working well:

- **Make sure that every radiator slopes slightly toward the steam inlet pipe (the one that comes out of the wall or floor).** If one doesn't, slip a little $1/4$-inch-thick rectangle of wood under the feet at the vent end (as shown in Figure 10-4). This helps prevent those irritating knocking and clanging noises.

- **Check the vents to make sure they aren't blocked.** Corrosion and paint can keep the vent from venting, and then air trapped in the radiator prevents steam from entering the radiator. If your vent is blocked, replace it. Your local hardware store probably carries a vent. The vents simply screw off and on, so they're easy to replace.

- **Check the position of the inlet valves.** The valves should be either all the way closed or all the way open. A partially open or shut valve does nothing to regulate the heat, and it causes knocking and clanging.

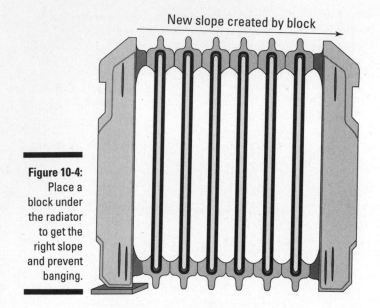

New slope created by block

Figure 10-4:
Place a
block under
the radiator
to get the
right slope
and prevent
banging.

Fixing leaks at the inlet valves

If your inlet valve is leaking, chances are, it's actually leaking at the *cap nuts* (the big nuts at the vertical and horizontal connections). Luckily, a leak there can be cured with a little retightening. Get two big wrenches — use one to hold the valve and the other to tighten the cap nut. If the leak seems to be coming from under the valve handle, take off the valve head and tighten the topmost nut, which (amusingly) is called the gland nut.

If neither of those solutions fixes the leak, the valve adapter — the double-ended/ double-threaded clunk of brass that connects the valve to the radiator — is probably the culprit. Once again, you need two wrenches to remove the valve, remove the adapter, and install a replacement. Open the valve, check for leaks, and make extra-sure that everything is properly tightened.

Electric systems

In an electric heating system, electrical resistance creates heat, which is radiated into rooms using baseboard units, or in cables in the ceiling or floor. Installations of electric heating systems hit their peak in the 1960s, when electricity rates were low. But now, at least in areas of the country not near a hydroelectric dam, the cost of electricity makes these systems very, very expensive to operate. If you have one, you're probably paying twice as much to heat your house as a neighbor with a gas-fired furnace or boiler.

That's the bad news. The good news is that electric heating, whether delivered via baseboard convectors or radiant floor or ceiling systems, requires you to do virtually nothing to maintain it. The only two things you have to do:

- ✔ Vacuum the convectors once a month (if you have them).
- ✔ Pay the big electricity bill.

Ventilation: Letting Your House Breathe

When we talk about ventilation, we're actually talking about two different things: interior ventilation and structural ventilation. Proper interior ventilation is vital to the health and comfort of your family; it helps your home rid itself of moisture, smoke, cooking odors, and indoor pollutants. Good structural ventilation controls heat levels in the attic, moderates dampness in the crawlspace and basement, and keeps moisture out of uninsulated walls.

Interior ventilation

Kitchens, bathrooms, and laundry rooms are the biggest sources of moisture and odors. The secret to having a dry, stink-free home is to have three key exhaust units — a range hood, and bathroom and laundry exhaust fans — all of which should be exhausted to the exterior.

Range hoods

Many kitchens have a range hood that doesn't actually vent to anywhere — it just "filters" and recycles stovetop air back into the room. But it's much better to get the greasy, smoky, steamy air outside, and that requires ductwork to an exterior vent.

So, if your kitchen is perpetually stinky, and the walls are covered with a thin film of grease, take a two-pronged approach to fixing the problem:

- ✔ Stop eating so much fried food.
- ✔ Get an exterior-venting exhaust fan. (Your favorite appliance retailer can make it happen for you.)

If you just can't give up Mama's Special Sunday Fried Chicken and Homemade Hash Browns, you should know that airborne grease makes exhaust fans sticky, which in turn attracts dirt and dust. The key to preventing this process from getting out of control is regular cleaning:

✓ **Clean the grill and fan blades twice a year, or whenever they start to look bad**. Use a spray-on nonchemical degreaser. (Test it first to make sure it won't remove paint.) Follow with a mild soap and water wash. Finally, flush with fresh water and towel-dry.

✓ **Clean the filter in a recycling range hood every couple of months or so (depending on how or what you cook).** We clean our range hood filters in the dishwasher — works great! If your filter has charcoal pellets inside, you need to replace it annually.

✓ **Clean the fan and housing every six months.** Lots of grease and gunk can build up on the fan housing. Over time, it can produce a foul smell that will rival anything cooking in Mama's kitchen. Use a spray-on nonchemical degreaser and a sponge to clean the housing. Rinse with fresh water and towel-dry.

Bathroom exhaust fans

Bathrooms generate huge amounts of moisture and some unpleasant odors — especially at my brother's house. If you've got incurable mildew in the shower, wallpaper peeling off the walls, or a lingering funky smell, you need to either install an exhaust fan or get a bigger, higher-capacity fan. Exhaust fans can be installed to vent the bad air through the wall or through the ceiling and attic. Call an electrical contractor, not your brother-in-law, to do the work.

Steamy air, hairspray, and other grooming products create a tacky surface that attracts dust, dirt, and fuzz at an alarming rate. Clean the housing, grill, and fan at least twice a year, using the same techniques for cleaning that we suggest in the preceding section.

Place a bath fan on a timer. It allows the fan to run for several minutes after you've left the space to fully remove odors or excessive moisture from showering. A timer is a must for the kids' bathroom!

Laundry exhaust fans

Laundry exhaust fans and bathroom fans are one and the same — as is the care and maintenance. The only difference is that a laundry fan doesn't usually have to deal with odors, and the moisture content isn't as high in a laundry room as it is in a bathroom, so a laundry exhaust fan doesn't need to be quite as powerful.

Quieter fans cost more than fans that are not so quiet, but a less expensive, not-so-quiet model will do just fine.

Structural ventilation

There are two kinds of structural ventilation:

- ✔ **Passive ventilation:** Passive ventilation uses the natural airflow generated by convection (hot air rising, cold air falling).

- ✔ **Active ventilation:** Active ventilation uses fans to do the work.

To keep heat and moisture from roasting and rotting your home over time, you need adequate ventilation in the attic, crawlspace, and (if it's unfinished) the basement:

- ✔ **Attic:** In the attic, passive ventilation creates an upward flow of air. Warm air rises and goes out through vent(s) near to, or at the peak of, the roof, drawing cool air through vents in the eaves or soffits.

- ✔ **Crawlspace:** In the crawlspace, where upward flow is impossible, passive *cross-ventilation* (the movement of air from one side of a space to the other) is created by placing vents on each exterior wall.

- ✔ **Basement:** In the basement, the HVAC system moves air around (active), and operable windows enable cross-ventilation (passive) when weather permits.

Ventilation — passive or active — won't work if insulation, crud, or dead squirrels block the vents, or if you don't have enough vents. Poor ventilation can result in an attic and subarea that are damp and "tropical." Rot can develop in the wood framing and do great damage over time. Condensed water can soak insulation, making it ineffective and mildewed. Condensation from above and below can make its way into the house, ruining ceiling, floor, and wall finishes, and short-circuiting electrical wiring. If you notice that your vents are clogged, clear them immediately.

 Building codes specify how much ventilation you need. As a general rule, have 1 square foot of vent area for every 150 square feet of attic area or crawlspace. We think more is better.

Attic ventilation

If your attic space is hot and humid in the summer, you may need to install additional vents at the eaves and at the ridge of the roof. Assuming you're not a trained carpenter or roofer, we think it's best to leave this kind of work to a professional, someone who knows her way around the roof structure and knows how to install leak-free roof penetrations.

Make sure that each vent and screen is painted (to prevent deterioration) and that the screens are secure to the frame of the vent. Animals, baseballs, and other common household missiles have a way of dislodging vent screens. Replace badly damaged vents. Solid vent screens prevent varmints of all sorts from settling in your attic.

Cardboard or prefab Styrofoam baffles can be used to prevent insulation from being blown into piles, leaving bare spots. Alternatively, they can prevent blown insulation from blocking air flow from eave vents. You can buy insulation baffles from home centers or insulation companies. The baffles are easy to install. They fit between rafters where eave vents are located and are held in place with staples. When installed properly, air passes over the baffle and up the underside of the roof sheathing, and the insulation stays put!

Crawlspace ventilation

If your crawlspace is damp, moist air can cause rot in the wood frame, attacking your home from below. Just like the attic (see the preceding section), a crawlspace needs a good flow of fresh air. If your crawlspace feels clammy, or you see mildew on the walls or structure, you need better ventilation — called *foundation vents*.

Extra vents are difficult to install and require special tools to cut through lumber, concrete block, concrete, stucco, and brick. Don't go poking holes in your foundation on your own — call a carpenter or masonry contractor to do the work. They have the know-how, tools, and experience to do the job right.

Foundation vents can be damaged in the same way as eave vents. In fact, because they're closer to the ground, there is greater potential for damage. Critters that can't get into your attic will settle for the area beneath the floor. Establish a no-holes policy. Maintain foundation vents in the same way that we suggest for eave vents: Make sure they're painted and securely attached, and replace any that become badly damaged.

Does your crawlspace have a dirt floor? If so, you may be able to avoid adding vents by installing a plastic vapor barrier. See Chapter 4 for instructions on how to do this.

Basement ventilation

A basement can get mighty musty, especially when moisture can make its way in through cracks in basement walls and floors. For this reason, ventilation is particularly important to eliminate moisture and odors.

Ventilation in a basement can be had in a variety of ways. If your furnace is located in your basement, you can introduce a small amount of air through a supply duct that moves the air and provides a little bit of heat — assuming the space is not occupied. A finished basement can have all the comforts of home — supply and return air ducts, exhaust fans, and moisture-control systems, such as a dehumidifier or water-collection and sump system.

If your basement has a window and it doesn't work, fix it! There is no substitute for natural light and ventilation. A little bit of sunlight throughout the day can create natural air currents that can help control moisture and odors.

Troubleshooting thermostats

Is your house too hot or too cool? Your problem could be the thermostat. Some potential causes:

✔ **It's in a bad location.** The thermostat shouldn't be located over a lamp, over a TV, or near any heat source. Drafts will read as lower temperatures and send wrong commands to the air conditioner or furnace.

✔ **It needs cleaning.** When older mechanical thermostats malfunction, those with lever-set temperatures and contact switches usually need cleaning only. To clean your thermostat, remove the cover and dust inside with a soft brush. To clean contacts, slip a piece of paper between them, moving the paper very lightly back and forth.

✔ **Its anticipator needs adjustment.** If your air conditioner or furnace cycles on and off too seldom or too frequently and you have a mechanical control, try adjusting the anticipator — usually a flat metal pointer on a scale. If heat starts and stops too often, move the anticipator a smidge higher. If it starts and stops too seldom, adjust it a tad lower. Wait a few hours to see if the adjustment was enough.

✔ **You need new batteries.** Electronic thermostats with digital readouts and keypads rarely fail. Just put in new batteries when the low-power light comes on.

With simple maintenance and light cleaning, thermostats, whether electronic or mechanical, will function best and as they should — for comfort.

Today's programmable thermostats are so "smart" that they will not only make your home more comfortable, but conserve energy and save money, too. How, you ask? Simple. You can program a smart thermostat to turn the heating system on just before you get out of bed in the morning, turn off about the time everyone leaves the home, turn on again just in time to have the home toasty for your return after a long day, and finally turn off just about the time you snuggle into bed. Some electronic models can be programmed day to day or for weekdays versus weekends, or to raise and lower the temperature several times a day. What's more, as technology improves, the product becomes more affordable. Programmable thermostats range in price from $35 to more than $100, depending on features. They can be installed by most do-it-yourselfers and come complete with step-by-step instructions for easy installation. Some manufacturers even offer toll-free installation help lines that will walk you through the installation process. Yippee!

A wall-mounted mechanical exhaust fan is another great means of improving air circulation in a basement. Keep in mind that an exhaust fan will create negative pressure in a basement where there is no air intake, so you'll want to be sure to have a window or a screened vent (such as a foundation vent) to provide for air intake.

Negative pressure can starve your furnace or gas-fired water heater of necessary oxygen for efficient combustion. In addition, negative pressure can prevent toxic gases from properly exhausting through vent flues.

Big or Small, an Air Conditioner Cools Y'all

When it comes to air conditioning (AC), people don't care *how* it works, just *that* it works. It's all about being cool. Fortunately for sweat-averse folks, AC technology has advanced tremendously in recent years. And, even better, the energy efficiency of central-AC equipment had improved along with it. In fact, if you have an AC unit that is more than 10 or 12 years old, today's ultra-energy-efficient units can cut your cooling costs in half.

The efficiency of window units has improved a great deal, too, as has the performance of AC/heat-pump units. Even the old-style evaporation systems (sometimes called *swamp coolers*) have received an infusion of advanced technology.

With all this new technology, are there any maintenance tasks a do-it-yourselfer can do? Not very many.

Central air-conditioning systems

Maintenance-wise, you can take care of a central-air system just by changing the furnace filters monthly, and periodically hosing off the fins of the exterior *condensing unit* (that's the large cube that sits outside in a flower bed and contains a fan that blows hot air) to remove dust and debris. The most important thing you can do is call a licensed heating/cooling contractor every spring for a thorough inspection and comprehensive maintenance.

Regular maintenance aside, if you're getting to know your serviceman a little too well because of frequent and repeated repairs, it's time to replace your system. According to Energy Star, a government-backed program that helps businesses and individuals protect the environment through energy efficiency, if your air-conditioning system is ten years old or older, you should replace it with a new, significantly more energy-efficient Energy Star–rated model.

Replacing a central air-conditioning system is not a do-it-yourself project. Contact a qualified heating and air-conditioning contractor who will be able to discuss the various decisions you have to make when purchasing and installing a new system.

Among these considerations is size. In the past, the general rule for sizing a central air-conditioning system was 1 ton of air-conditioning capacity for every 500 square feet of living area. Today, sizing an air-conditioning system takes into consideration many factors and is far more complex.

When it comes to central air-conditioning, bigger isn't necessarily better. An oversized unit will operate with short run times, not allowing the unit to reach efficient operation or deliver even temperatures throughout the home. Another disadvantage to an oversized unit is that it won't run long enough to adequately remove excess humidity. What's more, an oversized unit will experience increased operating costs. Conversely, an undersized system will run much longer than it should, and will likely never do an adequate job of cooling your home.

Studies show that summertime operation at 78 degrees and 30 percent relative humidity provides the same level of occupant comfort as 74 degrees and 70 percent relative humidity. This lower humidity level will provide increased comfort, lower utility bills, and less risk of health issues associated with high humidity.

To reduce wasted energy, the U.S. Department of Energy has established minimum efficiency standards for air conditioners. Every unit is given an efficiency rating, called a *seasonal energy-efficiency rating* (SEER). The higher the SEER number, the more efficient the unit, and the lower the cost to provide a given amount of cooling. The minimum SEER for a new central air conditioner is 13. Ultra-efficient models have a SEER of 15 to 18. (**Note:** Window AC units are exempt from the SEER requirements — their rating is around 10.)

Don't be confused by terminology. Ignore marketing words like *high-efficiency, super-high-efficiency,* and *ultra-high-efficiency,* and focus on the SEER number.

If your air conditioner seems dead or if it's blowing only *hot* air, check the circuit breakers before you call for service. Nothing makes you feel more stupid than paying a serviceman $75 to flip the breaker back on or replace the fuse.

Window air-conditioner units

As with a central AC system, there's not much you have to do to maintain a window air-conditioning unit:

- ✔ **Clean the filter on the interior face every month.** Unplug the unit. Pull off the front panel and remove the filter, or slide the filter out the side. Then wash the filter gently in mild detergent, rinse, and dry.

- ✔ **Clean the condenser coil fins on the exterior face at least once a year.** Gently vacuum or brush the fins and then straighten any bent fins with a comb.

Never remove the cover and clean inside the unit. You could get a shock (even when it's unplugged), and all you can do is bend or break something. If you goof up something inside, you won't have a window unit anymore; you'll have an ugly doorstop.

Got a 10-year-old window air conditioner? Throw it out! A new unit will be 25 percent to 50 percent more energy efficient. But don't buy just any air conditioner; get one that works efficiently — one with an Energy Star label, one that does all it can to help you keep your electric bill in check. Also, you'll want to

- ✔ **Buy the right capacity unit.** Measure the room you want to cool and bring the width, length, and height measurements to the store so that the salesperson can help you choose a unit that's efficient for the space.

- ✔ **Get a unit with an energy-saving thermostat that cycles the unit on and off.**

- ✔ **Make sure you get a three-speed fan (high to cool the room quickly and medium or low to maintain the temperature).**

- ✔ **Choose a model with a timer to turn the unit on before you get home.**

Part IV
Inside Home Sweet Home

The 5th Wave · By Rich Tennant

WALLPAPER PATTERNS

"Hellfire or brimstone — which one's it gonna be? I can't hold these all day."

In this part . . .

We figure that you have to do something with your spare time when it's too cold or wet to work outside. So we came up with an entire part of maintenance tasks that you can perform inside your home while you wait for Mother Nature to ease up a bit. In this part, we help you care for the floors, walls, ceiling, and everything in between. Granted, it's a lot of ground to cover, but hey, it's not like you don't have the whole winter. This part also covers your home-safety systems. After all, what good is a home if you can't feel safe and secure in it?

Chapter 11

Walls and Ceilings

1t doesn't take much to mess up a wall or ceiling. And as they say, stuff happens: A missing door bumper lets the knob punch a nice round hole. A shift in the foundation results in a 5-foot hairline crack. A heavy dresser leaves dozens of dents as it's carried down the hallway. A little kid's crayon makes unpaintable purple squiggles. An area of plaster ceiling loses its grip and sags.

You get the picture: Life is hard on walls and ceilings. Luckily, most maintenance to these surfaces is well within your reach.

Cleaning Walls and Ceilings

You may not realize it, but everything in your kitchen is covered with a thin coating of grease and gummy dust. And your bathroom walls have their own coating of gunk, including hairspray, cleaning products, and stuck-on dust. And don't forget crayon marks on bedroom walls and handprints and ugly smudges galore everywhere else.

You can wipe away fingerprints, crayon, pen marks, dirt, and dust from walls, trim, and doors with almost any household cleaner and a damp cloth. If your house is relatively new, make a bucket of soapy water and wipe the walls and ceiling with a damp sponge. If your house is older, you need something that cuts through the accumulated crud: a synthetic TSP solution, like Spic And Span. (Short for *trisodium phosphate,* TSP removes greasy dirt like nothing else.) Mix up a bucketful, wipe down the walls and ceiling, and then rinse thoroughly with clean water.

Morris's wife, Carol, recommends a sponge mop for cleaning both smooth and textured ceilings (not the popcorn ones). The foam-rubber sponge holds up best. She cautions that head protection is a must. An old bath towel can be used to dry the ceiling. *Remember:* Mildew loves a wet surface. Get it dry right away! Carol loves 409, but she does use TSP in extreme cases.

 TSP (also known as liquid sandpaper) etches paint. It will eventually dull a glossy finish. A TSP cleaning should be performed only when nothing else works or when you intend to prepare a wall for painting. But be careful: If you're planning to paint your wall after cleaning with TSP, a leftover film prevents proper paint adhesion, so be sure to rinse the area thoroughly with fresh water.

Dealing with Drywall

Chances are, the walls and ceilings of your home are made of drywall (also referred to as wallboard, gypsum board, or sheetrock). Drywall is both easy to damage and easy to repair.

Drywall gets two kinds of damage: gouges and hairline cracks. Gouges are usually caused by accident — by you, an angry spouse, a guest, or the previous owner. Hairline cracks are usually caused by movement in the foundation or framing of the house, which is nobody's fault. The frame of your house expands and contracts with the seasons, as temperature and humidity levels change.

Repairing small cracks

Got a small crack? Fill it with a flexible silicone caulk. The silicone flexes as the crack widens and narrows with normal house movement. (Silicone caulking also works for little nail holes.) Caulking is easy — just follow these steps:

1. **Buy a fresh tube of silicone caulking (the paintable kind).**

   The old tube in the basement has probably dried out, making it useless.

2. **Use a caulking gun to spread a thin bead of the caulk into the crack.**

3. **Wipe the excess from around the crack with rubbing alcohol.**

4. **Coat the repair with primer.**

   Don't skip this step or you'll end up with a permanently goofy-looking, non-matching area.

5. **Repaint, as necessary.**

Don't fill a crack with drywall joint compound or spackle. Spackle's brittle-ness allows the crack to come back year after year, until you take a hammer and pound a dozen frustration holes in the wall. Or maybe that's just how we would handle it.

Filling bigger cracks

Bigger cracks require a different kind of maintenance. Here's what you need:

- ✔ 6-inch taping knife
- ✔ 10- or 12-inch taping knife
- ✔ 1 square piece of plywood or a plastic mud pan
- ✔ Drywall joint compound
- ✔ Drywall tape (paper or fiberglass)
- ✔ 220-grit sanding mesh and a drywaller's sanding block

Here's how to stop that crack dead in its tracks:

1. **Clean out the crack so there are no loose "crumbs."**

2. **Put a blob of compound on the plywood or mud pan.**

   This step makes it easy to load compound onto the knife.

3. **Apply the tape to the wall, following the instructions that are applicable to the type of tape you're using:**

   - **Paper tape:** Use the 6-inch taping knife to apply a light coat of the joint compound, about $1/8$ inch thick, directly to the crack; immediately cover the compound with the tape, being sure to center the tape over the crack; and then use the knife to lightly wipe the tape into the compound and squeegee away any compound that squishes out. The joint compound acts as an adhesive to hold the tape to the wall. Do your best to prevent ripples and bumps by using smooth, even pressure as you squeegee. You can sand any mistakes later, but sanding is a lot of work.

   - **Fiberglass tape:** Apply the fiberglass tape directly to the crack. (It has a self-stick backing.)

   Fiberglass tape is a little thicker than paper tape, so it's more difficult to make a completely invisible repair. We prefer the tried-and-true paper tape, and we think you'll get better results with it. But some people are rebels.

   If the crack is really crooked, cut the tape in short lengths so that you can follow the line as closely as possible.

4. **Apply a thin coat of compound over the tape and smooth it with the 6-inch taping knife, making sure to feather the edges.**

   Let the patch dry completely (usually overnight).

5. **Apply a second, smoothing coat using the 10- to 12-inch taping knife, again making sure to feather the edges.**

   Let the second coat dry completely.

6. **Apply a third (and, with luck, final) coat using the 10- to 12-inch taping knife, again making sure to feather the edges.**

   Let the third coat dry completely.

7. **Sand the patch until smooth.**

8. **Apply a coat of good-quality primer.**

9. **Paint to match.**

Filling holes like a pro

Joint compound alone is not enough to fill any hole larger than a quarter. You've got to put something into the hole or onto it and then use compound to make it smooth and invisible.

Holes that are too large to fill with compound, but are no more than 4 or 5 inches across, can be patched with a precut stick-on patch and some joint compound. Use a peel-and-stick patch; made of stiff metal mesh, you can place these patches over the hole and cover them with two or three coats (or more) of compound. Here's how:

1. **Cover the hole with a stick-on patch.**

   Use scissors to trim the patch so that it's about an inch larger than the hole.

2. **Smear and then smooth the compound over the entire area, feathering the edges.**

   Here, less is more. A thin layer of compound at a time is the big secret. A thick layer is difficult to sand, shows up on the wall as a bump, and may develop cracks.

3. **Let the compound dry completely, and then sand it lightly.**

4. **Smooth a second layer of compound over the patch, and let it dry completely.**

   Finish the project with a third coat of compound and allow it to dry completely. A fourth coat or "touch-up" coat may be required for an invisible patch.

5. **Sand, prime, and paint.**

Holes that are too big for a metal patch require a slightly different technique. For these holes, you have to make a patch using a chunk of drywall. The easiest way to make this kind of repair is to use drywall clips. These little metal wonders straddle the edge of the hole and create a series of little "shelves" along the back edge of the hole, providing screw-backing for a cut-to-fit patch. Follow these steps:

1. **From a piece of scrap drywall, cut a square or rectangular patch large enough to completely cover the hole.**

2. **Hold the patch over the hole and trace its outline with a pencil.**

3. **Use a utility knife or drywall saw to cut away everything inside the penciled outline.**

   Watch out for wires and pipes!

4. **Install drywall clips on all sides of the hole (no more than 8 inches apart), and secure them using the screws provided with the clips.**

5. **Insert the patch into the hole, and drive screws through the patch into the clips.**

6. **Snap off the temporary tabs of the clips (the ones that extend beyond the face of the wall).**

7. **To complete the patch, follow the finishing process for a smaller patch (see the "Repairing small cracks" section, earlier in this chapter).**

   With larger patches the only difference is that you have to apply the joint tape on all four joints of the patch (top, bottom, and sides).

Re-creating texture

If your walls have a textured surface, you need to re-create that texture on the patched area. Here's how:

✔ **For a swirly finish:** Place blobs of compound evenly throughout the patched area, and then swirl (what did you expect?) a damp sponge through the blobs until the area is evenly covered. Try to duplicate the swirls on the rest of the wall. You can use almost any implement that will duplicate the original pattern (a drywall knife, a paintbrush, a roller).

✔ **For a flattened-bumps finish:** Use spray texture in a can. Simply spray on the texture, and then use one of several spray-tip adjustments to apply a light, medium, or heavy pattern. Wait a few minutes and use a drywall knife to slightly flatten the bumps. You can also use a portable pump for larger areas. Don't rush — wiping the bumps when they're too wet will completely flatten them, and you'll have a mess.

✔ **For a bumpy finish:** Follow the procedure for the flattened-bumps finish, but omit the flattening step.

Practice your texturing technique on a scrap piece of cardboard, plywood, or drywall. You only get one whack at the real thing.

If you can't find drywall clips, there's another way to fix a cantaloupe-size cavity. Just follow the preceding steps, but instead of using clips, simply use a piece of wood. Use the same principal as the clip method; this time, though, attach a narrow strip of wood to the back of the hole in the wallboard at each side of the opening (two sides will do). Drive screws through the existing drywall and into the wood strip to create the needed backing. Half the plywood is held behind the drywall while the other half is exposed, acting as backing for the patch.

Tackling truss uplift

If your home has been plagued by constant cracks at several joints where the walls and ceiling meet, then you may have more than a simple drywall-patching problem. You may have *truss uplift*. Truss uplift results when moisture content differences exist between the upper (rafter) and lower (ceiling joist) cords of wood trusses (see Figure 11-1).

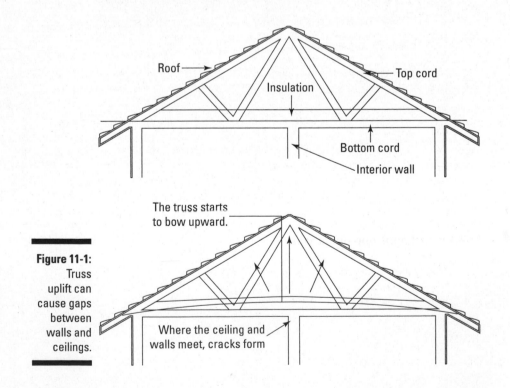

Figure 11-1: Truss uplift can cause gaps between walls and ceilings.

Moisture content differences are typical when one cord is cold and the other cord is warm. For example, the bottom cord of a truss surrounded by a well-insulated attic will be warmer than its cold rafter counterpart. The expansion of the top cord of a truss exerts an inward force on the bottom cord, which causes it to bow upward and lift away from the tops of interior partitions (hence, the term *truss uplift*).

There is no surefire means of preventing truss uplift. You can, however, eliminate the cracks at the ceiling-to-wall connection once and for all by removing all the ceiling drywall fasteners within 18 inches of the adjacent interior partition from each of the trusses. Simply use a wood block and hammer from within the attic to tap the ceiling wallboard away from the bottom cord of each truss — first on one side and then on the other — until the drywall is freed from its fasteners in that first 18 inches. With the wallboard free of the fasteners and "floating," you can repair the ceiling-to-wall crack like any wallboard crack (see "Filling bigger cracks," earlier in this chapter).

If for some reason the problem continues — even on a limited basis — we suggest installing a crown mold that is fastened only to the walls and not to the ceiling. Thus, movement can still occur, but the decorative trim conceals any seasonal cracks.

Putting the stop on nail pops

Nail pops are nail-head bumps or crescent-shaped cracks in the wall or ceiling. They occur when nails work loose, literally popping out through the surface of the drywall. Unfortunately, they happen for as long as you own your home. If you get a nail pop, you need to fix it.

You can find nail pops (and other defects) by shining a bright light at a shallow angle to the wall. Set a floor lamp with a 100-watt bulb about a foot from the wall in question, and remove the lampshade. *Voilà!* You'll be amazed at how the nail pops pop out at you.

To fix a nail pop, you need the following tools:

- ✔ Hammer
- ✔ Drill or driver
- ✔ Nail set (or large nail)
- ✔ $1^{5}/_{8}$-inch drywall screws

- 1⁵⁄₈-inch drywall nails
- 6-inch taping knife
- Drywall joint compound
- Fine-grit sandpaper
- Paint
- Paintbrush

Here's how you do the repair:

1. **Drive new drywall screws into the wall stud or ceiling joist at least 2 inches away from, and on either side of, the popped fastener.**

   The screws should pull the drywall tight against the framing, and the screw heads should slightly dimple into the drywall. Don't depend on the screws to draw the drywall tightly against the framing. Here you must use your free hand to press and hold the drywall firmly against the framing, and then install the screws.

2. **Using the hammer and nail set, drive a new nail immediately adjacent to the existing one.**

   Trying to remove the old nail can cause additional damage; resetting it minimizes the work. Try to nail the new nail into the same hole as the old one. Part of the head of the new nail will overlap the head of the old nail. Use the nail set to slightly recess the new nail (about ¹⁄₁₆ inch). The head of the new nail, combined with the adjacent screws, will prevent the old nail from slipping out again.

3. **With the 6-inch taping knife, apply a smooth, flat coat of compound over the dimpled heads of the new fasteners and the hole left by the old nail.**

   Let the compound dry completely.

4. **Lightly sand the patch with the fine-grit sandpaper.**

5. **With the 6-inch taping knife, apply a second coat of compound.**

6. **Let the compound dry, and then lightly sand it again.**

7. **Prime and paint.**

Plaster: More Trouble than You May Want

Older houses have plaster walls and ceilings with wood lath for a base. These thin strips of wood were installed on the wall framing with gaps between them, which the original plaster then filled, creating "keys" that hold the plaster in place.

If your plaster walls are in good condition, you can fix cracks and holes using patching plaster. But if your walls or ceilings are sagging and have big holes, you've got a big job ahead of you.

Fixing small cracks and holes

Cracks and tiny holes in plaster are slightly more difficult to patch than wallboard — not because the damaged area is harder to fill, but because the surface texture requires a more finite match. Refer to the "Repairing small cracks" section, earlier in this chapter, and take a little extra time to match the finish.

The major task in matching a plaster finish is to make sure to remove all excess caulk surrounding the crack and to apply a thick coat of texturing sand to the surface of the fresh caulking. You'll find small boxes of texturing sand in the paint and patching section of your hardware store or home center. Start by putting on protective goggles. Then simply place a generous amount of texturing sand in the cupped palm of your hand and blow across it and onto the fresh caulk. The sand will adhere to the caulk and help disguise the crack. Finish the job by priming and painting the patch after the caulk has had a chance to set up over night.

Dealing with sagging and other big problems

As plaster ages, as leaks occur, and as the house shifts, the ceiling plaster can loosen and sag. Finding a sag is easy. You can confirm your diagnosis by pressing against suspect areas with the flat of your hand. If the plaster feels spongy or gives, a repair is in order.

If a sagging ceiling area is not fixed, it can suddenly let go, with a huge potential for damage and personal injury. Don't wait for this to happen.

If the sagging is only slight, or covering a small area, you can reattach the plaster to the lath using long drywall screws fitted with *plaster washers* (thin metal disks through which drywall screws are threaded and then driven through the plaster into ceiling joists, wall studs, or lath). The screw/washer duo pulls the loose plaster tight against the framing, fixing the sag and stabilizing the area. The tricky thing is that you can't just wail away with the drill or driver. You've got to go slowly, tightening each screw/washer a little bit at a time, all the while pressing firmly against the plaster with your free hand so that it's gradually and evenly pulled snugly to the framing.

If the sagging is severe (more than 1 inch away from the lath), or if the sag covers a large area, the best solution is to pull down the old plaster and replaster, or cover it with drywall. Neither is an easy do-it-yourself project.

If your plaster is sagging in one place, it'll probably sag in ten other spots sooner or later. Crumbling plaster tends to become a chronic problem. Why? Your plaster simply may have reached the end of its useful life. Or maybe the original plasterers were learning on the job (not good!), you've got hidden water damage or rot (trouble!), or your foundation is unstable (big trouble!).

Whatever the underlying cause, sags and serious cracks are problems that will probably keep cropping up. You could keep repairing them, but plastering is a difficult job best done by highly skilled, expensive professionals. Instead, you probably need to think about proactively covering or replacing your slowly crumbling plaster with a fresh layer of drywall. If you elect to do that, however, it may take some time to get used to having nice straight walls, flat ceilings, and 90-degree corners.

Interior Painting: Doing the Job Right

Nothing freshens things up like a new coat of paint. But, like anything, there's a right way and a wrong way to do the job. In this section, we walk you through the steps to painting. Follow our advice, and you're sure to be pleased with the results.

Preparing to paint

You've bought your paint, you've got new brushes and rollers, you've spread out the dropcloths, and you've opened up the stepladder. You're ready to paint.

Whoa! Stop right there, Mr. or Ms. Inabighurry. You've forgotten the most important thing: surface preparation. The real secret to a beautiful, long-lasting paint job is getting the walls and ceiling really clean and perfectly smooth. The following tasks don't take that much time, but they can make the difference between a long-lasting paint job and one that you have to redo long before you're ready:

1. **Prepare the room.**

   Make sure to:

   - Remove lamps, irreplaceable knickknacks, and as much furniture as you can, and then push whatever is left to the middle of the room.
   - Remove anything attached to the walls, including pictures, window treatments, and switch and outlet plates.

- Loosen ceiling light fixtures and wrap them in plastic trash bags.

- Take off all the window and door hardware.

- Cover every inch of everything — floor, furniture, and radiators — with canvas or heavy-plastic dropcloths.

2. **Clean the surface (see the "Cleaning Walls and Ceilings" section, earlier in this chapter, for details).**

If you have mildew on a wall, you need to kill it and cover the remaining stain with a stain sealer primer made to hide stains. (See Chapter 20 for more information on killing mildew.)

3. **Prepare the surface.**

To prepare the surface, you need to:

- Fill nail holes, cracks, and other imperfections with patching compound.

- Scrape any loose or flaking paint on windows, sills, and woodwork. (See the nearby sidebar, "Removing paint from woodwork," for more information.)

- Sand patches and any bare areas on windows, sills, and woodwork.

- Lightly sand or use a deglosser to knock down the shine on glossy trim. A deglosser is essentially liquid sandpaper. It etches the existing finish that will help the new paint stick.

- Lightly sand walls if they're uneven, brush-marked, or bumpy.

- Fill gaps between the trim and the walls (especially along the baseboards and door trim) with caulk.

4. **Clean again.**

Vacuum the room to remove sanding dust and paint flakes (don't forget to do the windowsills and trim). Then wipe down everything with a tack cloth or barely damp rag. (A tack cloth is a piece of cloth that is coated in a sticky [tacky] substance so that dust and particles stick to it.)

5. **Mask the windows.**

Use wax paper or a layer of thin plastic taped to the windows to prevent paint splatters on the glass.

Use painter's tape when masking for paint prep. It contains less adhesive, which means it will be easier to remove and will cause less potential damage when peeled off. Although it's often referred to as blue painter's tape, it's available in a host of colors with varying degrees of adhesive designed to last for varying amounts of time.

Now you're ready to gather your supplies.

Removing paint from woodwork

For most woodwork, a putty knife and sandpaper remove loose flakes. But if your woodwork has 37 layers on it, try a scraper. Use a scraper designed specifically for moldings. If that doesn't work well, or if you're a little low on elbow grease, try an electric heat gun or chemical stripper. Heat guns soften the paint so that it can be scraped away. Strippers also soften the paint for easier scraping. Don't even think about using a propane torch as you would outside.

Scraping, sanding, or using a heat gun is not an option if the paint contains lead. Be safe, not sorry. Your local hardware store or home center carries a special test kit that will tell you if lead exists. The test takes only minutes, and you're always better off taking the time to check.

If your paint contains lead, and it's not peeling or flaking, your best bet is to simply give it a TSP wash and apply a fresh coat of primer and finish. If the paint is in anything but pristine condition, or if you simply want it out of your home, we suggest that you hire a professional lead-paint abatement contractor to carefully remove the paint.

Gathering your paint and painting supplies

After you've scraped, sanded, filled holes, sanded again, and cleaned, the preparation phase is complete and painting can begin, right? Not quite yet. Not until you gather your paint and painting supplies.

Selecting a primer

Primer creates a stronger bond between the paint and the wall, helps resist attack by moisture, fills small cracks, and smoothes and seals the surface so that finish coats are more uniform and lustrous, as well as longer lasting.

When you patch a spot or scrape down to bare wood, you create a rough, porous area that absorbs more paint than the area around it, creating uneven gloss and an area that is a slightly different in color than the surrounding area. Primer seals the area so this doesn't happen. A stain-killing primer also keeps mysterious dark marks, water stains, crayon, marker, and pen from bleeding through to the final finish.

If you can, use the same brand of primer and paint. Manufacturers formulate their paints and primers so that they work well together. In general, oil-based primers are the best (you can apply latex paint over them). The label on the paint will likely designate the type of primer to use. If you're still not sure, ask one of the experts at the paint store to help you select a primer.

Selecting a paint

Latex paints are the top choice for walls and ceilings. Don't let anyone tell you differently. They dry quickly and clean up with soap and water.

Sure, if latex paints aren't thin enough and wet enough to begin with, they can dry so quickly that brush marks and lap marks (also called *dry edge,* where a line left by the edge of the roller is visible) are hard to avoid. And, yeah, they don't stand up to scrapes and clunks as well as oil-based paints do. But the pluses far outweigh the minuses, particularly when you consider that latex paints contain no toxic solvents.

Check out Mythic Paint (www.mythicpaint.com). This company is the first to offer a completely 0 percent toxic latex paint — no toxic solvents *and* no toxic components.

Oil-based paints, on the other hand, are still the best choice for doors and trim. They dry slowly, giving brushstrokes time to disappear. They also dry to a very hard, durable finish. They offer greater moisture resistance, which makes them perfect for the walls and ceilings of damp areas such as the kitchen, bathroom, and laundry room. However, cleanup requires solvents, and as oil-based paints dry, they release volatile organic compounds (VOCs) into the air. (For the sake of the environment, when purchasing oil-based paint, be sure to look for a low-VOC product. Low-VOC paints contain fewer toxic chemicals.)

Buy the highest-quality paint you can afford — unless you like to paint. If you use poor-quality paint, you'll probably need to apply more than two coats — plus, you get to paint again in just a few years. Why not do the job right the first time?

Want to know just how good your paint really is? Try this test: First, have the can of paint shaken really well at a paint store. (Paint stores have machines for this.) Next, open the can and dip the tip of your index finger into the well-blended liquid. Finally, rub your index finger against your thumb. If the paint feels gritty, it contains too much filler and is of poor quality. A high-quality paint will feel silky and smooth.

How much paint should you buy? Measure the area (square footage) of your walls and ceiling, look on the can of paint to see how many square feet it can cover, and divide your room square footage by that amount. You can do the same thing for the trim.

When buying paint, err on the high side. You can always use the extra for touchups. Erring on the low side may bring you back to the store for the same color mixed on a different date. Can you spell *mismatch?*

Getting the right painting tools

When you're getting ready to paint, you need the following supplies:

- ✔ **A trim brush:** A 2-inch brush for painting door trim and other wide moldings.
- ✔ **A sash brush:** A 1½-inch angled brush made for detail painting of windows and narrow trim pieces.
- ✔ **A roller:** A fabric covered hollow cylinder (typically 9 inches long) that fits over a metal roller frame. You use a roller when you want to paint a large area, like a wall; you use paintbrushes for the detail work. The *nap* (length of the fabric) varies depending upon the desired finish. In general, use a short nap for smooth surfaces and a long nap for rough surfaces.

When buying a paintbrush, consider the following:

- ✔ **The handle should feel good in your hand.** You're going to be holding it for a while.
- ✔ **The metal piece that holds the bristles should be securely attached.**
- ✔ **The bristles should fan out, not separate, when you press them against your palm.**
- ✔ **The bristles should be smooth, straight, and have tiny split ends.**
- ✔ **The bristles should stay attached when you lightly tug on them.**
- ✔ **The brush should be appropriate for the kind of paint and surface that you want to paint.** For example, thick fluffy rollers are for rough surfaces, and tight-nap rollers are for smooth surfaces. The kind of roller you need also depends on the paint and surface in question. Ask a sales assistant for help.

Don't even think about using a sprayer to paint indoors. The same goes for power rollers. You'll make a big mess.

You may have heard some buzz about heat-reflective paint. It may be easy enough to warm up to in a laboratory, and we've witnessed impressive tests under controlled conditions, but we aren't privy to any government-approved or -recommended household uses. As far as we're concerned, the jury is still out on this one.

Painting made easy

You've bought the right paint. You've got good brushes and rollers. The room is thoroughly prepped. Everything is covered up. It's time to actually paint.

A good paint job consists of three basic steps: priming, applying a first coat of finish paint, and applying a second coat of finish paint.

Before you do anything, stir the paint thoroughly. Paint looks better and lasts longer if all its components are mixed well from the start. Three minutes is a good amount of stirring time.

Always paint a room from top to bottom. The job will go faster — and turn out better — if you follow this sequence:

1. **Paint the ceiling, using a trim brush and a roller.**

   Using the trim brush, paint a 2- to 4-inch-wide strip that feathers out toward the middle of the room. Then paint the rest of the ceiling immediately with a roller, starting in a corner and painting across the narrowest dimension of the room.

2. **Starting when the ceiling is dry, paint the walls with a trim brush and roller.**

   Do one wall at a time. With a trim brush, cut in where the walls meet the ceiling, around the doors and windows, and along the baseboards. Use a roller for the rest.

3. **Paint the windows, using an angular sash brush, and, if you prefer, a smaller brush for the dividers.**

4. **Paint the doors, using a trim brush.**

   Work quickly but carefully. Paint all the edges, but not the hinges.

5. **Using a sash brush, paint the door and window trim — edges first and then the face.**

6. **Paint the baseboards, using a sash brush.**

   Protect the floor or carpet with painter's tape or a paint shield.

Here are a few more helpful hints to getting a great-looking paint job:

- **Work with a partner if you can.** One of you can cut in the edges, and the other can follow along with the roller!

- **Use plenty of paint.** Most do-it-yourselfers try to make a brush full or roller full go too far. Hey, it ain't champagne! If you skimp on the paint, you'll end up with a room that looks yucky.

- **Two thin, wet coats of paint always flow better and, thus, dry smoother than one thick, dry coat.** Adding a bit of water to latex paint or thinner to oil-based paint will cause the paint to be thinner and wetter.

Adding a teaspoon of vanilla extract to a gallon of latex paint can make the drying process a sweeter-smelling experience. You can also try a fragrance available at the paint store.

Cleaning up right, storing smart

Latex paint cleans up with water. Wash the brush under warm water, making sure to work any paint out of the base of the bristles and the *ferrule* (the metal band). Shake or snap the brush to get the water out, and hang it up to dry, bristles down. During short breaks — lunch, siesta, poker game — cover your paintbrushes and equipment with plastic wrap to keep them from drying out.

To clean up oil-based paint or primer, use paint thinner. Fill an old coffee can with enough thinner to cover the bristles and ferrule and slosh the brush around, allowing the thinner to dissolve the paint. Remove the brush from the thinner and tap the ferrule firmly against the edge of a paint bucket (bristles pointing toward the inside of the bucket) to remove the thinned paint. Repeat this process until the brush is clean. It's a messy, stinky job. Luckily, you only need to clean your brushes once at the end of the job. When you stop for the day, wrap the brushes in plastic wrap and store them in the fridge overnight, and they'll be ready to go (once warmed to room temperature) when you start again.

To store paint (whether latex or oil-based), place a sheet of plastic wrap over the mouth of the can, and then put on the lid. Tap the lid into place snugly (use a rubber mallet or a hammer and a small piece of wood). Store the can upside-down. Your paint will be usable for years, because you've created an airtight seal.

Making Paneling Look like New

Most houses more than 25 years old have at least one room with paneling. Believe it or not, paneling was very chic at one time, and it still has its place in Dad's den, the basement rec room, and rustic homes. There are three kinds of paneling — solid wood planks, plywood sheets, and faux-finished hardboard.

Cleaning and oiling paneling

If you have solid wood or plywood on the wall, you can do a number of things to make it look like new. Cleaning is the easiest and most effective way to brighten the finish:

1. **Mix equal parts of white vinegar, turpentine, and boiled linseed oil in a small container.**

   Furniture polish won't do the job — you need something stronger.

2. **While wearing rubber gloves, dip a soft, clean, colorless cloth into the solution, wipe it on the paneling, and rub it in.**

3. **Scrub the cleaner and moisturizer into the surface until it starts to evaporate.**

4. **Finish up by wiping off the excess with a dry cloth.**

   You'll be amazed by the results.

If your wood walls are just dry, bring them back to life by wiping on lemon oil. Lemon oil is an excellent cleaner as well.

Correcting surface imperfections

To patch a small hole or surface imperfection, use wood dough, and then camouflage the repair with a color-match touch-up stick or, if you're feeling artsy, by applying a faux finish.

Faux finishing is literally an art. If it's done well, faux finishing makes the painted surface look exactly like the existing wood surface. You can't tell the area of the repair from the surrounding texture, color, or grain pattern. Faux finishing is a job for experts, though, and it's expensive. If the paneling is beautiful and isn't available anymore, a faux finish could be the least-expensive repair alternative.

If you're tired of the dark, woody look that paneling provides, but you like the texture of real wood, you can paint it. First, wash the surface with a solution of TSP (see the "Cleaning Walls and Ceilings" section, earlier in this chapter). When the surface is dry, prime it with an oil-based stain-killer primer. If you want to eliminate the grooves between the boards, fill them with vinyl spackling compound, sand, and prime. Finish the job with a good-quality latex paint.

Wondering about Wallpaper

Time is not kind to wallpaper: The edges peel and buckle, the adhesive gets tired and crumbles, bubbles develop, and the wear and tear of normal life starts to take a visible toll. Oh, and don't forget wallpaper patterns that become outrageously outdated. If replacement is in order, we can tell you how to easily remove what you have. But that doesn't mean that you have to rip it down. If it's still looking good and in style, we can help you repair everything else.

Removing wallpaper

If you've chosen to replace your wallpaper, you need to purchase a perforation tool (you can find these in the paint and wallpaper section of your hardware store, home center, or paint store) and rent a wallpaper steamer. After you have these two tools, removal is a breeze:

1. **Use the perforation tool to puncture thousands (yes, thousands) of tiny holes into the surface of the wallpaper.**

   The perforations allow the steam to penetrate to the adhesive.

2. **Use the steamer to liquefy the adhesive, working from the top down.**

   Warm, liquefied adhesive flows downward and causes the lower portion of the paper to release more quickly.

3. **Gently pull the paper off the wall.**

   Don't be in a hurry. Patience works best with this process.

4. **Remove the rest of the adhesive that remains on the wall using more steam or a liquid enzyme adhesive solvent, which can be found in the paint and wallpaper section of your local hardware store, home center, or paint store.**

   For either, you'll need a large sponge to soak up the softened gooey mess that's left on the wall.

 If your wallpaper is looking dingy, and it's washable, sponge it down with a solution of mild soap and cold water. Wipe with clean water and then wipe dry. (Be sure to test the colorfastness of the wallpaper in some inconspicuous corner before you clean it.) Read on to find out how to correct other wallpaper problems.

Fixing loose seams and clean tears

Got an edge that's coming unglued, a seam that's sticking up, or a clean tear? Here's how to fix it:

1. **Moisten the damaged area with warm water and *carefully* lift the softened wallpaper away from the wall.**

2. **Apply a thin coating of lap-and-seam adhesive (available at any wall-paper store).**

3. **Press the wallpaper back in place, matching it up exactly.**

4. **Roll the edge with a seam roller.**

   A seam roller is part of a wallpaper installation kit that you can find in the paint and wallpaper section of your local hardware store, home center, or paint store.

5. **Sponge off any adhesive that squishes out with a barely damp sponge.**

Patching wallpaper

Got a stain or a big, ugly rip in your beautiful wallpaper? If you can find a matching leftover scrap, fix it this way:

1. **Cut a square or rectangular replacement piece that's a little bit larger than the damaged area, making sure to match the pattern exactly; then attach the patch to the wall with masking tape.**

2. **Cut through both the patch and the damaged wallpaper simultaneously using a utility knife (a process referred to as *double cutting*).**

   Don't make straight cuts. In fact, making a curvy, kidney-shaped cut is best, because a curved cut patch is just about impossible to see after it's finished.

3. **Put the replacement patch somewhere safe; then use a hot-water-soaked rag to dampen the damaged bit of wallpaper and peel it out.**

   If necessary, use a perforation tool and a coat of enzyme wallpaper-adhesive solvent to loosen things up. You can buy this solvent at most hardware stores, home centers, or paint and wallpaper stores.

4. **Apply another coat of solvent, and sponge away any remaining glue on the bare spot; then clean the patch area with a clean, damp sponge and let dry.**

5. **Soak and soften the patch in a bath of warm water for about three to five minutes; when the patch becomes soft and pliable, apply a thin coating of adhesive evenly over the entire back.**

6. **Position the patch so that the pattern matches; then carefully smooth it down with a clean, damp cloth or a seam roller.**

7. **Sponge off any adhesive that squishes out.**

There you go — a fix that's nearly invisible to all eyes but yours.

Chapter 12

Floors and Interior Doors

*I*n this chapter, we take a close up look at what's underfoot. To get in the proper frame of mind, we suggest that you get out of your comfy chair and sit on the floor while you read. From that position, you can clearly see — and understand — what we're talking about. While you're on the floor, peruse the surrounding doors. At floor level, you may get a completely different perspective. On the other hand, simply reading this chapter will give you a new perspective on doors and how to maintain them.

Lucky for you, we move quickly and stick to the basics, focusing on the most important door and flooring maintenance and repair tasks.

What's Underfoot? Flooring

Roof replacement may be the single most expensive nonelective repair you can make, but flooring is a close second. Although some flooring can be reasonably inexpensive, really good, long-lasting flooring costs a bundle — making regular maintenance a must.

Vanquishing vinyl trouble

Odds are, you have resilient flooring — sheet vinyl or vinyl tile — somewhere in your house. After all, it's the most popular flooring material for kitchens, bathrooms, and laundry rooms. It's popular because it's easy to care for. And that's good for you.

This is not to say that a vinyl floor won't ever have problems. Some problems are mainly cosmetic; others are more serious. Vinyl flooring problems are not problems with the material itself but the result of some other problem. If you have a series of ridges in your floor, for example, you actually have an uneven or swollen underlayment. If your vinyl tile or sheet vinyl is coming up in places, you probably have moisture in the subfloor from a leaking pipe, spillage from the sink, or condensation from below. As tempting as it may be, you can't just cover up these problems — you have to fix their underlying cause. The following sections explain how to remedy these and other common vinyl problems.

Vinyl tile and sheet flooring manufactured prior to 1978 may contain asbestos. That's the year when the U.S. Environmental Protection Agency banned the use of asbestos in the manufacture of building products. When left alone, asbestos flooring poses virtually no risk of exposure. But when disturbed, it could release asbestos fibers into the air, which could be hazardous to your health. Therefore, be careful not to disturb old tile. If you opt for a new floor, you're almost always better off laying the new floor over the old rather than exposing yourself and your family to the risks associated with removal. If you're not sure whether your floor contains asbestos, you can have it tested by a licensed testing lab.

Scuff marks

Use an art gum eraser (one of those grayish-tan ones like you used in school) or borrow a Pink Pearl eraser from your kid's school supplies. Just rub the mark and — *voilà!* — it disappears.

For tougher scuffs, use a little paint thinner on a rag to rub the spot clean. Be careful not to go nuts with the thinner — you could remove the vinyl's no-wax finish.

After you've gotten rid of the scuff marks, stop wearing scuff-makers, like cheap plastic-soled shoes, hiking boots, and running shoes, in the house.

Persistent grubbiness

Before you know it, a vinyl floor can acquire a funky gray cast. This comes from infrequent or inadequate cleaning. Diligence is the key to avoiding this problem:

- ✔ Vacuum or sweep regularly to remove abrasive dirt and dust.
- ✔ Wipe up spills immediately.
- ✔ Mop regularly with a damp mop and 1 tablespoon of white vinegar in 1 gallon of warm water (no detergent!).

  For the best results, work on a small section at a time and dry it before moving on to the next section. If the vinegar solution is left on for an extended period and allowed to air-dry, it can dull the finish.

If regular cleaning doesn't keep the perma-dirt away, use a mop or sponge and a solution of warm (not hot) water and a few drops of liquid dish soap. Don't rub too hard. Rinse thoroughly with clean water.

Yellow discoloration

If the problem is a yellow discoloration, you need to remove and reapply wax. However, don't remove the wax more than once a year — the chemicals in the remover are hard on the vinyl. When reapplying the wax, be sure to choose a product rated for floors as opposed to a paste furniture wax. Floor wax provides maximum protection without becoming dangerously slippery. Oh, and be sure that the wax that you use is the non-yellowing type — it'll say so on the container.

No-wax vinyl floors require basically the same kind of care as the kind that requires waxing. Again, the secret to a long-lasting shine is keeping the floor clean. Stay on top of dirt and spills. And when you mop, use only a little white vinegar rinse and dry thoroughly.

Eventually, no matter how diligent you are about cleaning, your no-wax floor will lose its shine. Then, believe it or not, the best way to make it new-looking is to wax it. Use a water-based self-polishing wax. Whenever possible use a product recommended by the manufacturer. If you don't know who the manufacturer is, get a recommendation from a reputable flooring contractor in your area.

Curling vinyl tile

Curls in your hair may look great, but when they're in your vinyl flooring, they can lead to bigger problems. Curling vinyl occurs at seams and edges. The adhesive that's supposed to hold the vinyl flat is no longer doing its job and, thus, the vinyl curls up and away from the underlayment.

Aside from being unsightly, this condition presents a trip hazard. It's also a catch-all for dirt and grime. Plus, it exposes the surface below to water damage and makes the area especially susceptible to tearing. What's worse, left unrepaired, the condition will only get worse, which may turn a mole hill into a mountain.

To fix this problem, you have to remove the old vinyl tile and replace it with a new one. Follow these steps:

1. **Use a warm iron over a towel to heat the vinyl and soften the adhesive.**

   Make sure to warm the entire tile, including the edges and middle.

2. **Carefully peel out the tile using a thin scraper, and then scrape out all the old adhesive.**

3. **Apply vinyl tile adhesive (get it at your favorite home center or flooring store) all over the empty space.**

   Use a notched trowel if you have one, or apply a thin, even coat using your scraper.

   In the case of vinyl floor adhesive, less is more. Too much adhesive can cause the tile to ripple.

4. Place the replacement tile (you set aside "spares," didn't you?) carefully into the hole and press on it with a block of wood to ensure good adhesion.

5. Remove the glue that squeezes out around the edges with a solvent like lacquer thinner or whatever the glue label suggests and a soft white cloth.

6. Lay a sheet of wax paper over the repair and then place a couple of books over the tile to weigh it down until the glue fully dries (usually 24 hours).

7. Apply a clear vinyl seam sealer (also available at a home center or flooring store) around the edges.

Keep traffic out of the area for a day until the seam sealer has had a chance to set up.

Gouged, cut, or scratched sheet vinyl

In contrast to vinyl tile that has gobs of seams, sheet vinyl has far fewer seams. There is an advantage to fewer seams: fewer places to repair if something goes wrong. On the other hand, when it comes to making a patch, it can be a little trickier than replacing a single tile.

You'll need the following items:

- Clothes iron
- Towel
- Utility knife and several new blades
- Metal straightedge
- Masking tape or double-sided tape
- Putty knife
- Vinyl adhesive
- Notched trowel
- Clean rags
- Adhesive solvent
- Clear vinyl seam sealer
- A piece of vinyl slightly larger than the area you want to patch

Finding a suitable patch

Obviously, the best patch is a piece of the original flooring material and one that gives you a chance to make an unnoticeable repair. (Look for squares or distinct patterns or lines you can use to hide your cuts.) If you or the previous homeowner didn't save a scrap, you can steal a patch from underneath an appliance or from a closet floor.

To remove a piece of vinyl to use as a patch:

1. **Cut the patch carefully using a straightedge.**

2. **Peel up the patch, working slowly and using a warm iron over a towel (or a hot-air gun) and a putty knife.**

   Try not to leave too much of the backing stuck to the floor.

3. **Replace the stolen patch with any old scrap of vinyl floor. (Who's going to see it?)**

Older vinyl floors may have been waxed, and wax tends to yellow (especially in exposed locations). To make sure your patch matches the surrounding vinyl as closely as possible, remove all the wax from the entire floor using a commercial-strength wax remover (available at a janitorial supply house) and floor scrubber. It's a good idea to remove the built-up wax and re-wax every few years anyway.

Making the repair

To apply the patch, follow these steps:

1. **Place the patch over the damaged area, match up the pattern or lines exactly, and then tape the patch in place.**

   Again, it's best to place your cuts in the lines that define squares in the pattern or something (anything!) other than "blank" areas.

2. **Use a utility knife and fresh blade to cut through both the patch and the damaged area.**

3. **Set aside the patch and make sure the cuts went all the way through the damaged vinyl.**

   Carefully deepen any cuts that are too shallow.

4. **Make two corner-to-corner diagonal cuts in the repair area.**

   Doing so makes it easier to remove the damaged section.

5. **Peel back the damaged section from the middle.**

   You might have to use the old iron-and-towel (or hot-air gun) trick to loosen the glue. Work slowly and carefully. If you're using a pristine, never-been-glued patch, make sure to remove as much of the glue and stuck-down backing material as you can. If you're using a "borrowed" patch that has some of the backing torn off, it's okay if you leave some of the backing material stuck to the floor — it'll help even things out.

6. **Apply vinyl adhesive to the floor.**

   Tub-and-tile caulk works great, too.

7. **Carefully place the patch in the hole, but don't press it down.**

8. **Cover the patch with wax paper; then place several heavy books on top.**

   The bottom book should be bigger than the patch to avoid pushing the patch below the level of the surrounding floor. Let the adhesive cure for 24 hours.

9. **After 24 hours of curing time, remove the books and use mineral spirits to clean excess adhesive.**

10. **Apply clear vinyl seam sealer and let it set a day before allowing traffic in the area.**

    The key to applying seam sealer is to apply just enough to cover the seam. Again, less is more. The material is self-leveling, will bond with the vinyl, and is designed to disappear.

Sheet-vinyl bubbles

No matter how good your vinyl flooring is, or how well it was installed, bubbles or blisters will appear occasionally. Fortunately, they're usually easy to fix.

Before you do anything, make a trip to the crawlspace or basement area below the floor in question to see if moisture is rising from below and causing the bubble. If the sub-area is wet, chances are, you've got water vapor migrating into the space between the floor and the vinyl and you've got big trouble. Believe us, soon a bubble will be the least of your problems if the sub-area water problem is not resolved. If moisture is the culprit, stop here and turn to Chapter 4 for advice on how to dry out your basement or crawlspace.

If your bubble isn't caused by moisture rising from below, repairs are simple:

✔ **Plan A:** Use a large sewing needle to perforate small bubbles (1 inch or so in diameter) at their center. Make sure you go all the way through — you're making the hole to allow trapped air to escape. Then get out the old iron, towel, and books. Lay the towel over the area and use the iron (not too hot!) to soften and flatten the vinyl. Place heavy books over the area to ensure good re-adhesion. (See Figure 12-1.)

✔ **Plan B:** If Plan A doesn't work, you have to get a little glue into the bubble. To do this, you need a glue syringe. Insert the tip of the syringe into the hole you made with the needle, and squirt a couple of drops of adhesive (no more than that!) into the bubble. Place a piece of wax paper on the repair and stack the books on top. Why the wax paper? Because you don't want to accidentally glue a book to the floor!

Mildew and mold below the surface of the vinyl

If black, brown, or purple stains are visible just below the surface of the vinyl, the only way to remove the stains is to remove the vinyl. These stains are mildew and fungus that are being fed by moisture from the crawlspace, basement, or concrete slab or from water leaking beneath the vinyl from a source above it (shower, tub, sink, and so on).

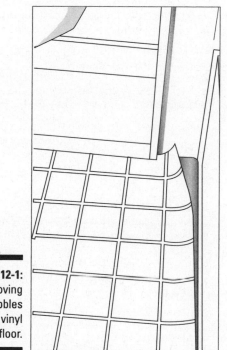

Figure 12-1: Removing air bubbles from a vinyl floor.

If you have moisture under your floor covering, you have to find the source and stop it. Check out Chapter 4 for information on how to solve a moisture problem in your crawlspace or basement and how to seal concrete. Check the various plumbing chapters in Part III on how to deal with pipe leaks.

After you solve your moisture problem, you can then deal with the stained vinyl. If the damage is widespread, you unfortunately need to rip up the vinyl (and underlayment if the vinyl is on a wood floor). *Underlayment* is a layer of plywood or particleboard that is used atop wood floors as a smoothing layer on which the vinyl is laid). On concrete floors, the vinyl is glued directly to the concrete.

✔ **To rip up the vinyl on a concrete floor:** Remove the baseboard from the perimeter of the room so that you can grip the edge of the vinyl. Pull the vinyl up by hand. This should be relatively easy because the vinyl will separate from its paper backing.

Most of the paper backing will remain stuck to the floor. Remove what's left by wetting the paper with warm water in a sprayer. Then scrape; we use a reciprocating saw with a scraper blade.

✔ **To rip up the vinyl on a wood floor:** The vinyl is glued to the underlayment, and the underlayment is stapled to the floor. Your best bet is to remove both layers at the same time. To do that, use a circular saw with the blade depth set at about ¹/₂ inch to cut the floor into 2-foot squares — like a checkerboard. (A ¹/₂-inch blade depth is enough depth to cut through the vinyl and the underlayment without damaging the substrate.) Pry up the squares using a flat pry bar.

Relaying a vinyl sheet floor covering (and underlayment if required) are tasks best performed by a flooring professional. Floor preparation, the amount and type of adhesive, and pattern cutting and placement are all key tasks that are not for the weak of heart.

Laminate love

Laminate has been one of the most popular finishes for kitchen counters for nearly half a century. Now, plastic laminate is one of the hottest products to hit the flooring market in decades. Harder than vinyl, it has the ability to match virtually any wood flooring or even ceramic tile pattern with uncanny accuracy. The reason? The floor pattern is essentially a photograph — but it's coated with a protective layer that provides years of virtually maintenance-free use, provided that you're not too rough on it.

It's like having your kitchen counters under foot — although laminate flooring has a harder finish, it can still scratch and dent.

Maintenance is simple. The first thing to keep in mind with laminate (and many other types of flooring) is to avoid abrasives, including abrasive cleaners. It also means keeping your floor clean from dirt, one of Mother Nature's most natural abrasives. Door mats, gliders under chairs, and frequent vacuuming are the easiest ways to avoid wear and tear. Next, damp-mop the floor with clean water. As you mop, keep changing the water to avoid re-depositing dirt on the floor. Never use wax cleaners, polishes, or abrasives like steel wool or scouring powder.

You can fix scratches and dents using specially designed repair sticks or fillers prepared by the flooring manufacturers. If you need such a fix, contact the manufacturer to find out what's available. If you can't locate an exact match, keep in mind that you can often mix two colors for a perfect blend. Just choose one that's slightly lighter and one that's slightly darker than the color of the spot you're trying to match.

If you've got a really big boo-boo that's ruined an entire piece, it can be successfully cut out and replaced. This procedure, however, takes practice and is best left to a trained installer.

Ceramic tile a go-go

Got ceramic tile on the floor? Need to know how to care for it? Turn to Chapter 13 and read about caring for tile countertops. Everything we describe there works well for the floor, too. If you want to install a new tile floor, you need a different book; try *Home Improvement For Dummies,* by Gene and Katie Hamilton (Wiley Publishing).

If you want your ceramic tile floor to stay looking good, never, ever use an abrasive cleanser on it. It literally sands off the finish on the tiles. Check the labels of the products you use — you'll be surprised by how many contain abrasives.

Wild things: Bamboo

Bamboo has become popular because it's renewable and inexpensive, and it lasts a long time. To keep bamboo in good condition, do the following:

- ✔ Make sure the floor remains free of dirt and dust by using a broom, dry mop, or a soft brush attachment on your vacuum cleaner.
- ✔ When cleaning, avoid excessive water — use a slightly dampened mop.
- ✔ Never use abrasive cleansers or scouring pads on your bamboo. Just about any nonabrasive hardwood cleaner is suitable for use on a bamboo floor.
- ✔ Always read the instructions by the flooring manufacturer for best results, because some cleaners may void your warranty.

Engineered hardwood

Engineered hardwood has a very thin surface and must be meticulously maintained to ensure lasting quality. Engineered floors can be touch-sanded and varnished, but they can't be deep-sanded. To keep engineered hardwood floors in good condition make sure to remove dirt and dust daily with a broom, dry mop, or soft brush attachment on your vacuum cleaner.

When cleaning any wood flooring, avoid excessive water. Use a slightly dampened mop and never use abrasive cleansers or scouring pads on a hardwood floor (engineered or not). Most engineered flooring manufacturers offer an approved cleaner. Never use a cleaner on an engineered floor that has not been approved by the manufacturer.

Keeping natural hardwood good

Properly finished wood floors are, without a doubt, the easiest of all floor surfaces to keep clean and looking good.

Keep grit off the floor. Use walk-off mats at all exterior doors to help prevent dirt, grit, and sand from getting on your wood. Laying down throw rugs or small sections of carpet just inside the entrances is a good idea.

In addition, we recommend the following for maintaining your wood floors:

- ✔ Vacuum frequently to keep abrasive dirt to a minimum.

- ✔ In kitchens, use area rugs at high-spill locations and at work stations such as the stove, sink, and refrigerator.

- ✔ Avoid ultraviolet light damage to finishes by installing window tinting or draping large windows.

- ✔ Put fabric glides on the legs of your furniture to prevent scratching and scuffing when the furniture is moved.

- ✔ Wipe up spills immediately and then wipe dry.

- ✔ Clean using a not-very-damp mop and an oil soap solution, and then immediately wipe the floor dry.

If a floor is waxed, occasional buffing helps renew the shine and remove scuffmarks that may appear in the wax coating. If the shine can't be renewed in heavily used lanes, occasionally re-waxing these areas may be necessary. You may be able to go a year or longer between waxings if you've properly cared for your floor.

For more information on how to care for or repair your wood floor, contact the National Wood Flooring Association at 800-422-4556 or 636-519-9663, or go to www.nwfa.org.

Keeping carpet clean

Carpet-cleaning professionals tell us that the most effective method of keeping carpeting clean — and making it last a long time — is to vacuum it regularly. In fact, they recommend vacuuming three or more times per week, and daily in high-traffic areas.

They also point out that the quality of your vacuum makes a difference. An upright vac does the best job of removing deep-down dirt. But a big canister vac with a beater-bar head is good, too. Whichever you prefer, the motor must be powerful enough to create enough suction to remove the dirt, sand, and debris that is ground into the carpet. If the vac has a beater bar, its brushes should be free of lint, fuzz, and threads. The suction port and hose should be checked regularly for suction-robbing blockages, and the bag should be changed frequently to ease the flow of air through the vac.

Why all this emphasis on vacuuming? Because soil is your carpet's biggest enemy. Carpets wear out because foot traffic grinds embedded dirt into the carpet fiber. And vacuuming is the best way to reduce the dirt that works its way into the carpet.

Aside from regular vacuuming, the best way to keep your carpet clean and reduce wear is to place welcome mats outside every exterior door, and rugs on the inside to catch any leftover grit before it gets farther into the house. Finally, it really pays to have everyone remove their shoes when they come into the house.

But what do you do when little Nina spills some sticky red juice in the living room? Give her a big hug, tell her that you love her, and then spot-clean!

Spot cleaning

Most of today's carpets are made with a factory-applied stain guard. So usually, a small amount of water and a drop of vinegar or club soda will get out a stain. Use a clean, white, dry cloth. Don't scrub — blot.

The most common mistakes people make when they try to spot-clean are over-scrubbing and using too much water. Scrubbing destroys carpet fibers. Excess water gets below the carpet into the pad, which leads to mildew and a funky smell.

Over time, especially after numerous carpet cleanings, the factory-applied stain guard provides little stain protection. Although a host of stain repellants are on the market, your best bet is to have an after-market stain guard installed by a professional carpet-cleaning and -dying company.

If this simple quick fix doesn't work, there are a million carpet-cleaning products you can use. Just be sure to follow the directions on the label to the letter.

Carpet cleaning

Sooner or later, your carpet will need to be cleaned. Some people like to do the job themselves, while others would rather leave the job to a professional. The pros use a variety of methods, including dry powder, foam, and steam (hot-water extraction). Most do-it-yourself carpet-cleaning machines use the hot-water extraction method: A hot-water-and-detergent solution is sucked out of a reservoir, sprayed on the carpet, and immediately extracted with a powerful vacuum. The machines aren't difficult to use — they're just loud.

Here are a few tips that will help you be a carpet-cleaning success:

- ✔ Before you head off to the hardware store to rent a machine, you need to know what your carpet is made of in order to select the right cleaning solution.

- ✔ Before you start, test the solution on an out-of-the-way spot to make sure it won't leave a stain of its own or bleach the color out.

- ✔ Read the instructions on the machine and on the detergent. Follow them exactly. This is no time to freelance.

- ✔ Don't make the mistake of using too much water or too much detergent. Excess water creates mildew, and excess detergent stays in the carpet and attracts dirt like a magnet.

- ✔ Open the windows (or turn on the air conditioning) and use a powerful fan to help speed the drying process. The quicker you get the moisture out of the carpet, the better. If you can find one, rent a carpet-drying fan from a local tool-rental company; these fans are *much* more powerful than the most powerful fan found around the average home.

Professional carpet cleaning costs less than you think. In fact, the cost of renting a machine and buying carpet-cleaning solution may not be much less. Make a few phone calls before you decide to do the job yourself. One more thing: The truck-mounted extraction machines that the pros use are way more powerful than any machine you can rent, so they get more dirt out and leave less moisture in.

De-stinking smelly carpet

Time, home life (especially cooking), and pets can make carpets stinky. You may not notice anymore, but anyone who comes into the house probably does. If your carpet has picked up a funky smell, you can try a commercial carpet deodorizer or you can go to the pantry and arm yourself with a box of baking soda. Sprinkle it into the carpet, leave it for a few hours, and then vacuum it up.

For less money and a little extra work, you can try sprinkling grated potato (yes, potato!) all over the carpet in question. Let it stand for several hours and then vacuum.

If neither of these methods works, stop trying to avoid the inevitable and call a carpet-cleaning company.

Interior Doors

As the soil around your home gains or loses moisture, it expands or contracts and the house above moves with it. When the house moves, the door frames and doors shift — sometimes moderately and sometimes excessively.

This cycle of movement occurs every winter and every spring, making door repair an ongoing maintenance issue. Besides shifting, interior doors contain several components that can fail.

Common door-maintenance tasks

Whether it's a swinging door, a bypass, or a bifold, doors or their components eventually begin to wear or shift. When this happens they rattle, won't close, and/or won't latch or won't open. It makes no difference whether the door is solid or hollow, wood, fiberglass, or metal; the typical repairs are usually treated in exactly the same way.

If your exterior doors are giving you problems, head back to Chapter 6.

Adjusting a sticking door

The most common door problem is *sticking* — when the door grabs the frame, making it hard to open or close. Sticking is caused by seasonal house movement or house settlement. If the amount of grab is slight, the easiest solution is to sand the door. Hand-sanding or machine-sanding will do the trick. Be careful, though: Too much sanding can prove to be a problem. If the original problem was caused by seasonal shift and the door moves the opposite way during the next season, you may find the resultant gap to be an eyesore.

If the grab is extreme, your best bet is to call in a repair contractor to adjust the door and frame.

Repairing a door that closes by itself

Doors that close by themselves (ghost closing — probably Casper) can be repaired easily. Here's how:

1. **Remove one hinge pin (any one you like).**
2. **Take the removed hinge pin out to the sidewalk and lay it on the concrete.**
3. **Tap it once with a hammer to bend it slightly (10 or 15 degrees); see Figure 12-2.**
4. **Put the hinge pin back in the hinge.**

    The door that once had a mind of its own will never be a problem again.

Repairing a loose hinge

Doors are heavy, and hinges are small. After years of use, hinge screws can loosen. You know what happens: You have to lift on the knob to get the door to close. Here's why: The screw strips the wood and becomes loose in its hole — and that's when the hinge starts to flop around. You can elect to use a longer screw to make this repair or you can do as we do and fix the stripped screw hole. The repair can be made with toothpicks — it's easy:

1. **Find the loose screws and remove them.**

2. **Use a few toothpicks dipped in wood glue to fill the stripped screw holes in the door or frame. Push as many of the glued toothpicks into the hole as possible and tap them into the hole with a small hammer — gently now.**

3. **Wait for the glue to dry completely.**

4. **Cut away the excess toothpicks and reinstall the old screw(s).**

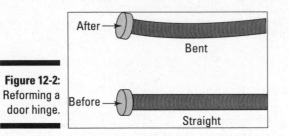

Figure 12-2:
Reforming a door hinge.

We've made this repair many times, and it works beautifully.

Replace the door on the track gently and carefully. Forcing the door into the track can bend either the door hardware or the track, which can make keeping the door on the track impossible.

Cutting to accommodate carpet

When new carpet is installed, some companies cut the door bottoms for you so that the door can open and close easily. (This also allows return air to flow back into your furnace or air-conditioning system. You'd be surprised by the amount of air that will travel through the small space between the bottom of the door and the carpet.) If your installers don't cut the bottom of the door for you, you can do it yourself. Follow these easy steps:

1. **With a pencil laid on its side on the carpet, mark a line along the entire length of the bottom of the door.**

2. **Remove the door by removing the hinge pins.**

3. **Place the door on a flat work surface or a couple of sawhorses.**

4. **Use a utility knife to make a cut along the pencil line; then place duct tape just above the cut/pencil line.**

   The slice made with the utility knife and the duct tape prevent damage to the door during the cutting process. Without these preventive measures, the cut line can easily chip and score.

5. **Use a saw to cut off the bottom of the door.**

Special tasks for different types of doors

Standard swinging doors (flush-mount doors) all end up needing the same types of repairs to resolve: sticking, swinging shut with no help, and not latching properly. After you've repaired one flush-mount door, you can repair them all. This isn't so much the case with other types of doors that have different mounting devices and unusual hinges or tracks. In this section, we cover the most common problems with other types of doors.

Double-action swinging doors

Double-action swinging doors give their hinges a real test. After your kids go through them 29 million times, treating them as if they were a new Disneyland adventure, the mounting screws loosen, and the springs within the hinge weaken in spite of the fact that you may, from time to time, shoot them with a bit of silicone lubricant.

Many of these doors use double spring-action hinges that are self-closing and allow the doors to swing in both directions. Some have stops that allow the doors to remain open when they're swung past 90 degrees. There are two main types of swinging door hinges: Some are mounted to a wood strip that you mount to the doorjamb. Others use a double-action pivot consisting of a heavy spring and a cam and are mounted either in the bottom of the door or in the floor.

Here's what you can do for either type of hinge:

✔ **Hinges in a wood strip mounted to the doorjamb:** To adjust the hinge so the doors meet flush when closed, use the spring steel adjustment rod provided with the hinge. If you've lost the adjustment rod, use the long end of a snug-fitting Allen wrench. Push or pull the adjustment rod to increase the spring tension. This allows you to remove the pin that holds the spring in place. Move the pin so that the spring is one hole tighter; then check the door alignment. You may have to make adjustments to the springs on both doors.

Because there is a lot of pull on the screws that hold these hinges in place, replace the screws with 1¹⁄₂- or 2-inch-long screws that reach into the studs behind the doorjamb.

✔ **Hinges using a double-acting pivot mounted in the bottom of the door or in the floor:** Dust and dirt are the biggest problems for these bottom-mounted spring devices. Keep them as clean as you possibly can by vacuuming frequently. If the spring is jammed, unscrew the cover plates from the hinge and vacuum. If you find any rust, scrape it off and vacuum again. Then spray the spring and the pivot with a silicone lubricant. Clean and install the cover plates.

Pocket doors

This style of door is appropriately called a *pocket door* because, when in the open position, the door neatly slides into a void space in the wall. A pocket door glides on rollers that hang from a track mounted on the frame above the door.

Old-fashioned pocket doors always seemed to fall off the track. That doesn't happen with the newer doors. But you may need to adjust the height of the doors because of changes in the floor covering. The procedures for doing this vary depending on the manufacturer and model of the door, but here are general guidelines:

1. **Remove one of the split headers that hide and trim the roller track.**

   Beneath the rollers, you find a hanger with an adjustment bolt and nut or screw.

2. **Use a thin-end wrench or a screwdriver to turn the nut or screw to raise or lower the door.**

To clean dust from the tracks, use a vacuum. Lubricate the rollers with spray silicone lubricant.

Silicone lubricant keeps the hardware locks functioning unless they become very dirty. In that case, remove the lock or lever and clean them in mineral spirits. Spray a coating of silicone on the interior parts; then reassemble.

Bypass and bifold doors

Bypass and bifold doors ride on tracks and often are derailed. To fix this common problem, do the following:

✔ **For bypass doors:** Hold the door at about a 15-degree angle into the room and then engage the rollers into the track.

✔ **For bifold doors:** Simply press downward on the roller at the top of the door and then align it with the track above. Once aligned, simply release the roller and watch it pop into the track.

Shower doors

When a snoopy guest uses your bathroom, the first thing he looks at is the shower door. Is it clean? Here's how to clean a shower door and keep it that way:

- ✔ **Using lemon-oil polish and a scouring pad, scrub the glass panels with gusto.** If the door has acrylic panels, go easy on the scrubbing or you may scratch the acrylic.

- ✔ **Scrub with sodium carbonate.** You can find a pure form of sodium carbonate, called pH Increaser, at swimming pool retailers.

- ✔ **Use a sponge and dishwashing detergent to clean the shower door (and the rest of the shower stall) after every shower.**

- ✔ **Place a couple of small suction cups that have small hooks on the inside of a shower door.** Use the pair of hangers to suspend a vinegar-soaked rag on the inside of the shower door. Reposition the hangers and rag periodically to conquer small sections at a time. This may sound funny and look terrible, but it's inside the shower, and your guests won't see it unless they're really snoopy. The vinegar will soften the mineral deposits. Really dirty shower doors may require some scrubbing with a nylon scouring pad.

If the doors get out of alignment, or the rollers come off the track, you can usually reset the doors by lifting them in the frame and resetting the rollers in the channel.

When the doors drag, or they don't stay in the bottom channel, you need to adjust the rollers. Follow these steps:

1. **Lift the outer door until the rollers clear the top track; then pull the bottom of the door out and away from the bottom channel and set it aside. Do the same with the inner door.**

2. **Clean debris from the bottom track and clean the door frames using our Easy All-Surface Mildew Remover (see Chapter 20).**

3. **Loosen the screws that hold the rollers to the door frame and adjust them to raise or lower the door as needed.**

   If the screws are rusted, replace them with zinc-coated or stainless-steel screws.

4. **Spray a dry silicone lubricant lightly on the rollers to keep them operating smoothly.**

Knobs, locks, and latches (oh my!)

How could anyone possibly write a biography about Martin without including Lewis? And what about Abbot and Costello? In the same vein, how could anyone expect us to write a chapter about doors without including door hardware? You know — knobs, locks, and latches.

Dirty knobs (not legal in every state)

Barring a damaged finish, just about the only problems you'll have with door-knobs and sliding door latches are (1) screws that loosen and (2) collected dirt that jambs up the mechanism. In our 31-plus years as contractors, we haven't ever seen a doorknob fail — at least not yet! We've found that clean-ing and lubrication can solve most problems.

When a doorknob, key lock, or sliding-door latch begins to stick intermittently, or when it isn't operating as smoothly as usual, it's probably gunked up with dirt. When this happens, most of us have the tendency to use a lubricant to solve the problem. Don't! Lubricant is used to reduce friction, not clean.

TIP

If you have a sticky doorknob, we suggest spraying cutting oil into the works. Cutting oil cleans and lubricates. Better yet, take a few moments to remove the hardware and dip it into a bath of cutting oil. Follow the bath with a spray of light machine oil — sewing machine oil is great — and reinstall the knob. Ninety-nine percent of the time, it'll operate like it's brand-new. This procedure has worked successfully for us on doorknobs and levers, deadbolts, throw bolts, and patio-door latches — just about any door hardware that we've ever had to maintain.

Someone told us your screws were loose

You reach for the doorknob, and as you grip it, you notice that it's shifted from its original position. You can see where the trim ring and the paint don't line up. You try wiggling the knob in hopes that it won't move, thinking to yourself that if it doesn't, further attention on your part won't be required. Hey, sooner or later you'll have to deal with it. The nice thing is that the maintenance is unbelievably easy.

To solve the problem, tighten the screws that hold the knob in place. Often their location is pretty obvious. Usually they can be found at the interior trim ring, although on some hardware the screws are hidden. To tighten the screws on these models, do the following:

1. **Using the blade of a small screwdriver, depress the small push-button release found in the shaft of the knob to pull the knob away from the door.**

   The push button is usually located on the underside of the knob shaft.

2. **Remove the knob and pop off the trim ring by applying pressure to a small spring lever located at the inside edge of the trim ring.**

   Alternatively, pry it off with a screwdriver. The screws — two of them — will be directly beneath the trim ring.

3. **Tighten the screws snugly in place and replace the trim ring and the knob.**

First time around, the process may confuse you slightly. After one time, you'll wonder how anything so simple ever avoided your attention.

You can keep key locks lubricated with graphite powder, but it can be a bit messy, and there's a chance that using too much could temporarily jamb the lock. However, there is an easy and inexpensive alternative: Rub a pencil onto your key. Then push the key into the lock. The lead, which is actually a graphite compound, will transfer to the lock and lubricate it. It really does a great job.

The strike plate

When is a plate big enough to hold a door closed, but not large enough to hold lunch? When it's a strike plate — that's when. If you just laughed, then you know that the *strike plate* is the small metal thing attached to the door frame that interlocks with the bolt on the doorknob when the door is closed. The strike plate is so named because it's what the bolt "strikes" as the door is being closed.

The strike plate actually serves three purposes:

- ✔ Its curved outer edge helps to gradually depress the bolt as the door closes.
- ✔ It acts as a shield preventing wear and tear to the doorframe.
- ✔ When interlocked with the bolt, it holds the door snugly to the frame. With some strike plates, this function is adjustable.

One of the major causes of door (and window) misalignment is house movement. Actually, if a house didn't move, there would probably never be a need to realign its doors. However, until homes stop shifting, doors will have to be tweaked one way or another, and the process will often have to include adjusting the strike plate to realign it with the door bolt.

Closing the door just enough for the bolt to lay on the outside edge of the strike plate can give you a good idea of why the bolt isn't interlocking with the strike plate. The bolt must rest centered between the top and bottom of the plate. If the bolt is lower than center, the plate must be lowered. If the bolt is higher than center, the plate should be raised.

Most often, the adjustment needed is extremely minor. Place a chisel into the hole in the strike plate. To lower the strike plate, hold the edge of the chisel against the bottom of the hole and tap downward on the chisel with a hammer. One light blow is all that it usually takes to move the strike plate enough to clear the bolt. Hold the chisel against the top of the opening and lightly tap upward with the hammer to move the plate up. Keep in mind that if the strike plate has to be moved more than $1/8$ inch, the door may have to be adjusted instead. In some cases you may need to adjust both the door and strike plate.

Two screws hold a strike plate in place. Slam a door often enough and the screws will definitely come loose, resulting in a door that wobbles when closed. First, try tightening the screws. If they're stripped, which is often the case, do this:

1. **Remove the screws and the strike plate.**

2. **Dip two golf tees in glue.**

3. **Drive one golf tee into each of the holes.**

4. **When the glue has dried, cut off the excess golf tees with a utility knife.**

5. **Reinstall the strike plate.**

   No more wobble!

Loving your locks

In addition to making sure that your locks are securely fastened to the door, you also need to clean and lubricate locks to keep them in good working order.

To remove the lock so that you can clean it, first unscrew the screws holding the faceplate on the inside knob and remove the knobs. Then remove the screws in the latch plate and remove the latch bolt assembly. The latch is that part of the door hardware that fits into the strike plate on the door frame when the door is closed. Clean the latch bolt assembly with mineral spirits. Lubricate the assembly with silicone spray, and then reinstall the lockset.

Bolts that hang up on the latch plate may catch on paint. Remove the paint and lubricate the bolt.

Chapter 13

Cabinets and Countertops

Kitchen and bathroom cabinets take a beating. Day in and day out, their doors and drawers are opened and closed many, many times, which gives hinges, door catches, and drawer guides a real test. Not to mention that little kids often use drawers as "steps," and have been known to create a little cheap entertainment by swinging on cabinet doors. Wheee! That much use, and that kind of abuse, is tough on cabinets. Frequent cleaning to remove dirty, oily handprints and greasy buildup can go a long way toward keeping your cabinets looking great. However, eventually you need to kick it up a notch. Luckily, most of the time all you need to do is throw on some paint, revarnish, or just repair scratches and dings. And a quick drawer-glide repair, knob replacement, or hinge adjustment can make your cabinets look and feel like new (well, *almost* new).

Countertops are pretty tough. They can be made of *plastic laminate* (a thin layer of plastic glued onto a wood-composite base), solid surface (solid plastic or solid acrylic), ceramic tile, stone (such as marble or granite), or wood butcher block. Each surface requires different care; when they're damaged, they need different cures for what ails them. In many instances, these cures also protect these surfaces and, therefore, extend their life span.

In this chapter, we look at both cabinets and countertops, even though they're made of different kinds of materials and require different kinds of care and repair. Why discuss them together? Because you find them together in the home, and, to us, that's a great reason to lump them into one chapter.

Keeping Cabinets Looking Great: Cleaning Know-How

Kitchen cabinets are magnets for grease, food bits, spills, and moisture. This slimy crud builds up, making them look dingy and dirty. As the paint or varnish on the cabinet wears, the wood beneath can become stained or even damaged.

If your cabinets aren't terribly nicked up or scratched, and they have drawers and doors that still work well, all they may need is a little TLC. In fact, a good cleaning could be just the trick to make their surfaces look new again.

Cleaning wood cabinets

To give varnished wood cabinets a super cleaning, use our Super Wood Cleaner (see Chapter 20).

This formula is not made for painted surfaces. If you have painted wood cabinets, skip ahead to the next section, "Cleaning painted wood, metal, laminate, or vinyl-covered cabinets."

After you've mixed up our Super Wood Cleaner, follow these steps:

1. **Remove all the drawer pulls and door handles from the cabinets, and cover the countertops and floors with dropcloths.**

2. **While wearing rubber gloves, wet a soft rag in the Super Wood Cleaner and ring it out well.**

3. **Thoroughly wipe all cabinet surfaces (inside and out), doing small sections at a time.**

4. **Wipe the surface dry with a clean rag.**

5. **Repeat the wiping and drying until all old wax, sticky grease film, and grubby fingerprints are gone.**

6. **Replace the pulls and handles.**

Our Super Wood Cleaner is moderately flammable. For safety's sake, don't smoke while you're using it or work with it near open flames. Don't try to reheat the mixture — mix up a new batch when it gets cold. Dispose of any leftover by letting it evaporate outside — don't pour it down the drain. Let the rags completely air-dry outside before disposing of them in the trash. (Don't keep these rags inside — they're subject to spontaneous combustion!)

Cleaning painted wood, metal, laminate, or vinyl-covered cabinets

If your cabinets are painted wood, metal, laminate, or vinyl-covered, you can clean them with warm, soapy water and a sponge:

1. **Cover the floor and countertops from spills and splashes using dropcloths.**

   If you want to do a really thorough job, remove the drawer pulls and door handles from the cabinets.

2. **Mix up a lightly soapy solution using dishwashing soap.**

   Don't go crazy — one small squirt will be plenty.

3. **With a wrung-out sponge that's wet but not drippy, thoroughly wipe the door and drawer fronts and everything in between (the face frame).**

   Get into the nooks and crannies, and don't forget the edges.

   Do one section at a time. You don't want water to sit too long on the wood or begin to dry.

4. **Remove any soapy residue with a cloth and clean water, and then thoroughly dry the cabinets with towels.**

5. **If you removed the pulls and handles from the cabinets, replace them after the cabinets are dry.**

Something Old Is Something New: Refinishing Your Cabinets

If cleaning doesn't do the trick, and your cabinets still look lousy, then it's time to cover up their flaws. In fact, a few minor surface repairs and a fresh coat of paint or varnish can make your old cabinets look new, make them easier to care for, and probably brighten up the room.

Not only does the cabinet finish look good, but it also protects the wood from moisture damage, a common problem in the places where cabinets are installed — kitchens and bathrooms.

Here's a way to get a new look for a little moolah: If your cabinets could use a little pick-me-up, but they don't quite need to be refinished, replace the drawer pulls and door handles. Nothing perks up your cabinets — and your mood — like new hardware!

One small budget, one huge success

We have friends who had a terrible-looking set of kitchen cabinets and a terribly limited remodeling budget. The cabinets were real wood, however, and our friends had to admit that they still worked fine. They tried repainting the cabinets to see if they could avoid buying new ones. And when they were done, the cabinets looked beautiful! The total cost? Less than $750! What's more, they saved more than $15,000 in what it would have cost to remove the cabinets and replace them with new ones. The bottom line: Not every kitchen remodeling job has to cost $25,000 or more. Sometimes the simplest things, like a coat of paint, can make a big difference.

Getting your cabinets ready for refinishing

Before you paint or varnish your cabinets, you have to get them ready. If you don't prepare properly, your paint will peel or your varnish will look lousy. Follow these steps:

1. **Remove the cabinet doors and drawers, being sure to label them with removable stickers so that you can get them back in the right place.**

   You may have to move or remove the refrigerator, range, or vent hood to complete the job. If so, clean behind the refrigerator, under the stove, and up inside the range hood. (Why pass up this great opportunity for a thorough cleaning?)

2. **Remove the drawer pulls, door handles, and hinges.**

   Do this job in your garage or basement workshop to minimize disruption and mess in the kitchen.

3. **If you intend to reuse the pulls, handles, and hinges, soak them in a mild solution of soap and water.**

   Don't use ammonia — it can remove the plated finish.

4. **Wash all the cabinet surfaces and the drawer and door surfaces with a mild solution of trisodium phosphate (TSP), a heavy-duty all-purpose cleaner, and wipe them dry.**

5. **Lightly sand all the surfaces you plan to paint.**

   Use 200- or 120-grit sandpaper if you intend to paint, or 400- or 600-grit sandpaper if you intend to varnish.

   The goal is not to remove all the paint or varnish, but to create a uniform surface for the new finish. So don't go nuts — just get it smooth.

6. **If you're painting, fill all nicks and blemishes with vinyl spackling compound and, when dry, sand the compound lightly. If you're varnishing, use colored putty, being careful to remove the excess from around the gouge.**

   A second application of spackle or putty may be necessary if the first coat shrinks.

7. **Vacuum the cabinets, drawers, and doors using an upholstery brush.**

8. **Wipe down the cabinets with a tack cloth or a soft cloth dampened with mineral spirits.**

Painting or varnishing . . . at last!

When your cabinets are suitably prepared (see the preceding section), you're ready to paint or varnish. Follow these steps:

1. **Cover everything with canvas or heavy plastic dropcloths.**

   Use masking tape to protect the counters where they meet the cabinets and to create a paint/no-paint edge on the interiors.

2. **If you're painting, apply a coat of oil-based primer. (Skip this step if you're varnishing.)**

   If the cabinets are dark, use a heavily pigmented shellac-based primer to conceal the color and seal in the dark stain. If you're making a big change in color, have the primer tinted at the paint store to closely (but not exactly) match the finished color.

3. **If you're painting, finish the cabinets with a high-quality, oil-based, high-gloss or semigloss enamel. If you're varnishing, apply a coat of high-quality, oil-based, glossy or satin-finish polyurethane.**

   Use a natural-bristle brush. You may want to enhance spreadability and reduce brush strokes by thinning the paint or varnish a little with mineral spirits.

4. **Cover the drawer bodies with plastic and mask the edges of the drawer bodies where they meet the fronts.**

5. **Repeat steps 2 and 3 for the doors and drawers.**

6. **Replace the hinges, pulls, and handles.**

You can make your old grungy, grimy hinges, pulls, and handles look new again by soaking them overnight in a mild solution of dishwashing liquid and warm water — about 1 tablespoon to 1 quart of water. Mix the solution in a plastic bucket and allow the hardware to soak overnight. Use a nylon-bristle brush to get into the nooks and crannies, rinse, and towel-dry. Use a fine metal cleaner and polish such as Flitz to remove stains and blemishes and provide a protective finish.

Maintaining Your Cabinets

After you have your cabinets looking good (whether you're starting with new cabinets, you've just cleaned your cabinets, or you've refinished them), you still need to do some tasks on a regular basis to keep them looking good and working well in the future. Don't worry: None of these tasks requires any special tools or materials, and together they take no more than half an hour to do.

Once a year, do the following:

- **Tighten drawer pulls and door handles.** Don't over-tighten them. One-quarter turn beyond snug should do the trick.

- **Lubricate and adjust the hinges.** Don't go crazy — a drop of fine machine oil is plenty. *Remember:* Less is more when it comes to lubrication.

- **Lubricate and adjust the drawer slides.** A little squirt of WD-40 works well on metal guides. Use beeswax or paraffin if your drawers have wooden guides.

- **Remove finger smudges.** Try spray cleaner first. If that doesn't work, try a vinegar-and-water solution (one part vinegar to three parts water). If all else fails, put a little mineral spirits on a rag, and use that to wipe off the smudges.

Making Your Lovely Laminate Last

You may know it by one of its popular brand names (such as Formica or Wilsonart), but the generic name for that slick countertop material with the rolled nosing and integral backsplash is *plastic laminate*. Common plastic laminate is nothing more than a very thin piece of plastic combined with several thin layers of resin-coated paper. A heating process is used to bond the paper and plastic, and what results is a somewhat-flexible, waterproof material that has any number of practical uses. It's cemented onto a solid surface — such as plywood or hardboard — to give it strength and support.

Cleaning and caring for your laminate

You can easily keep a laminate countertop nice and clean. All you need is water, a little soap, and a stiff nylon brush. Mix the water and the soap, and then scrub away with the brush. You'd be surprised at how dirty a countertop that looks clean really is.

After your countertop is super-clean, consider giving it a coat of car wax. Wax will protect laminate in the same way that it protects the painted surfaces of a car. Waxing takes a little effort, but at least you won't have to worry about scraping your hand on the edge of a license plate.

If you're handy with a buffer, you can use it to get an extra-glossy shine. But be very careful: Too much high-speed buffing wrecks the plastic laminate surface.

Here are a few tips that will help you keep your laminate countertops looking lovely for a long time:

- ✔ **Avoid using abrasive cleaners.** That means no Ajax, no Comet, and no Soft Scrub.
- ✔ **Don't let water stand, especially on seams and along the backsplash.**
- ✔ **Always use a cutting board.** Laminate is too soft to stand up to knives.
- ✔ **Never place a hot pan directly on the surface.**

Bursting bubbles

Laminate countertops are made of a thin sheet of plastic bonded with contact cement to a plywood or hardboard base. Sometimes the contact cement loses its stickiness, and the laminate forms a bump. Luckily, it's easy to stick the laminate back down (see Figure 13-1):

1. **Place a slightly damp towel over the bubble.**

2. **Apply low heat with a clothes iron for 10 seconds (see Figure 13-1).**

   This process softens the laminate and "re-stickifies" the contact cement.

3. **Immediately place several heavy books on the repaired spot and leave them there for 12 hours.**

   The books keep the laminate in contact with the cement as it re-cures.

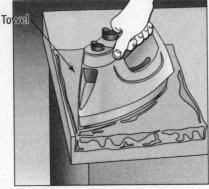

Towel

Figure 13-1:
Smoothing
out bubbles
on a
laminate
countertop.

A. Apply low heat for 10 seconds.   **B.** Leave heavy books on the repair for 12 hours.

Hiding chips, cuts, and scratches

Sooner or later, your nice laminate countertop will be chipped, cut, or scratched. This problem is more than just cosmetic — water can travel through the open area and damage the base.

When you get done yelling at the person responsible, head out to the nearest home center for a SeamFil chip-filler kit and a brand-new, well-polished putty knife. SeamFil kits come in 20 colors; mix them to match your countertop. It dries to a satin finish, and a gloss additive lets you match shiny surfaces. Just follow the directions on the package.

Neither SeamFil nor any other similar product can make a countertop gouge invisible; they just make them less noticeable. However, the repair does become water-resistant.

Caring for Super Solid Surfaces

You probably know this easy-to-care-for countertop material by one of its brand names — Corian, Avonite, and a number of others — but the generic name for it is *solid-surface countertops*. Plain and simple, solid-surface countertops require little care and are virtually impossible to permanently damage.

Because these countertops are made of a nonporous, plastic, or plastic-like material, soap and water are all you need to keep them clean.

Got some light scratches, stains, or scorched spots? The first thing you should do is go to the manufacturer's Web site and find the care-and-repair instructions. Then follow the steps to the letter, using the exact materials recommended.

Don't know the manufacturer? Don't know how to use the Internet? Forgot how to read? If all you want to fix is light surface scratches or stains, you can do the repair with a lightly abrasive cleaner like Soft Scrub and some elbow grease. If that doesn't do the job, use an abrasive sponge (such as a Scotch-Brite pad) to *lightly* "sand" the surface smooth. Don't press too hard, and make sure that the area remains wet while you work, to reduce the chances of creating new scratches.

Don't attempt this repair if your countertop has a high-gloss finish — the repaired area will not be glossy anymore.

Things get dicier if you have deep scratches, burns, and deep stains. The best answer is to call in a pro to resurface the area (and maybe the entire countertop). The next best answer, if you're feeling bold, is to *lightly* hand-sand the area using 400-grit wet/dry sandpaper. Keep the area wet while you work. Don't get carried away. Do *not* use a power sander — you'll ruin your countertop.

The manufacturer of your countertop probably offers a repair kit. If you need to undo some self-inflicted imperfection, read the instructions and do exactly what the manufacturer's instructions tell you to do.

Keeping Your Tile Terrific

Ceramic tile countertops offer a trade-off: They last forever, but they require more maintenance than other types of countertops. If you ask us, it's worth the extra work.

The tile itself is tough — it's the grout you have to worry about. *Grout* is the cement-like stuff that fills the gaps between tiles, and it readily absorbs moisture and stains.

Sealing out grout grunge

Grout sealer goes a long way toward preventing stains and keeping your beautiful new countertop looking good. The trick is, you have to wait at least 72 hours for the grout to *cure* (dry) before you can seal it.

Your local home center probably has several different brands of grout-and-tile sealer with handy sponge-tip applicators. A silicone-based sealer is best.

Sealing grout can take several hours to do depending upon the amount of tile that you have, so plan not to be in a big hurry. Follow each grout line with the sealer applicator, making sure you're getting the sealer down into the lines. (Follow the manufacturer's directions for application.) Apply a second coat 24 hours later and a third coat 24 hours after that. Big fun — but totally necessary.

Cleaning grubby grout

To clean your grout, you need a bottle of vinegar, water, and a small brass brush. (A steel brush would leave rust marks in the grout and dark scratches in the tile.) If you can't find a brass brush, grab a couple of brand-new hard toothbrushes. Then follow these steps:

1. **In a big jar, make a solution of one part water, one part vinegar.**

2. **Dip the brush in the solution and start scrubbing the grout.**

   Yes, cleaning grout takes a while. And yes, it's tedious. The vinegar, a weak acid, helps remove hard-water deposits and other hard-to-remove chemical stains.

3. **Remove the sour-smelling solution by wiping the countertop thoroughly with a damp sponge.**

If the old sauerbraten treatment doesn't do the trick, grab a bottle of hydrogen peroxide (the stuff for disinfecting cuts) and pour a generous amount all over the grout. The peroxide whitens the grout and helps dislodge stains caused by foods. Let it sit for about 15 minutes, and then scrub like crazy using a nylon scrub brush. After scrubbing, wipe down the surface with a damp sponge.

If neither vinegar nor hydrogen peroxide gets the grout nice and white, you have to scrub using a weak bleach solution — 2 tablespoons of bleach per quart of water. Open the windows, turn on the vent hood, and bring a box fan up from the basement. Wear old clothes, eye protection, and gloves. Scrub carefully, rinse thoroughly, and then rinse again.

When you're working with bleach, more is *not* better. If you use more than the recommended amount of bleach, you'll give yourself one heck of a headache and a wheezy cough. Ask any doctor: Breathing chlorine fumes is not good. And, as always, never mix other chemicals or household cleaners with bleach.

If your grout is still grubby after this all-out chemical assault, the only solution is to apply a grout stain (see the next section) or replace the grout (see "Replacing grout," later in the chapter).

Staining grubby grout

Grout stains are essentially paint. You can find them at any decent home center or tile store.

Before you apply the stain, you have to get the grout really, really, *really* clean: Clean the grout (see the preceding section), rinse it thoroughly, and allow the grout to dry overnight. Then apply the grout stain according to the manufacturer's instructions *exactly* — this is no time for creativity.

Although grout stain is a time- and energy-saving alternative to grout replacement, it doesn't last forever — you have to re-stain every year or two.

If you have just one spot that won't come clean, you can "stain" it white using white shoe polish on a Q-tip or a tiny artist's paintbrush. Wite-Out correction fluid also works well.

Replacing grout

Cracked, deteriorating grout can allow water underneath the tile, where wood rot can occur. Replacing grout will make your counters look better and last longer. How often can you kill two birds with one stone?

There are two different kinds of grout: cement-based and epoxy-based. For a number of very good reasons (cost and ease of use, primarily), you want to use cement-based grout. For thin ($\frac{1}{8}$-inch) joints between tiles, use plain unsanded grout. For wide ($\frac{1}{4}$-inch) joints, use sanded grout.

Grout comes in a rainbow of colors, and your choice has a big effect on the appearance of the finished countertop. Choose the color you want, but know that dark-colored grout hides dirt and stains better — and is easier to clean — than light-colored or white grout.

Removing the old grout and debris

Before you can do any actual grout application, you have to "saw" out old, bad grout from the joints between the tiles. You can use a grout saw to remove the old grout (as shown in Figure 13-2), but for most people, a church-key-style can-opener does the job. The really sophisticated (read: lazy) do-it-yourselfer uses a Dremel tool with a tiny grinding bit.

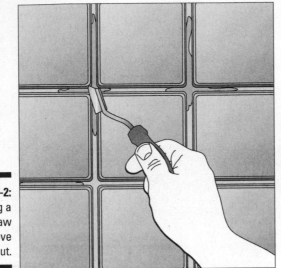

Figure 13-2:
Using a
grout saw
to remove
grout.

If you use a grout saw or can opener, work slowly and carefully. Just aim to get out the loose stuff — if you get too aggressive, and the tool slips out of the joints, you'll gouge the tiles. The same goes for doing the job with a Dremel tool. Stay focused and don't apply too much pressure. Also, be sure to wear eye protection.

When you've got all the loose grout out, vacuum the surface and wipe with a damp sponge to get up every bit of dust and debris.

Re-grouting your tile

With the grout and dust gone, it's time to get grouting! You need the following:

- Grout (powdered or premixed)
- Rubber float or squeegee
- Big sponge
- Popsicle stick
- Toothbrush
- Rags or cheesecloth

✔ Vinegar

✔ Bucket

✔ Rubber gloves (grout is caustic before it dries)

To re-grout, follow these steps:

1. **If you bought powdered grout, mix it with cold water, according to the manufacturer's directions.**

   Make only as much as you think you can use in 30 minutes, which is not a lot — typically less than a small pail. Be sure to use cold water; warm water can cause some colors to mottle when they dry.

2. **While wearing rubber gloves, apply the grout to the surface of the tiles diagonally, using the rubber float or squeegee held at a 45-degree angle to the surface of the tiles.**

   Work in a 3-foot-square area. Spread the grout liberally and force it into the joints. Use the Popsicle stick for corners and small, tough-to-reach spots. Remove excess grout with the rubber float and/or a damp sponge as you go.

3. **Let the grout set for 20 minutes or however long the manufacturer suggests.**

4. **Wipe the entire surface with a damp sponge and keep wiping until all the grout lines are even and the joints are smooth.**

   Rinse the sponge frequently.

5. **Let the grout dry for another 20 minutes.**

6. **Polish the tiles with a rag or cheesecloth.**

   Use an old toothbrush to get into the corners and hard-to-reach areas.

7. **Mix fresh grout and move on to another area, repeating steps 2 through 6 until the entire tiled surface is grouted.**

8. **When all the freshly grouted areas are dry, remove any *grout haze* (residue left on the tiles by the grout) with soft rag and a 10 percent solution of vinegar and water.**

   You may have to wipe off the haze several times before the tile surface is completely clean.

9. **Caulk where the countertop meets the walls and the backsplash and around the edge of the sink.**

10. **Seal all the joints with grout sealer (see "Sealing out grout grunge," earlier in this chapter).**

Replacing a broken tile

Got a loose tile? Dropped the big soup pot and cracked one? Worried about how it looks or that you might accidentally slash your wrist on the sharp edge? It's time for replacement!

If you're lucky enough to have a leftover tile stashed in your workbench, you're ready to go. But if you don't, you have to go on a tile hunt. Chip out a sample (read on for instructions) and take it to the biggest tile dealer you can find. If it's a standard, really common tile, they'll either have an exact match or a tile that's very, very similar in color and texture. If your tile isn't common, they probably have old partial boxes and piles of leftover discontinued tiles in the back for you to paw through. Good luck! (You're going to need it.)

If you can't find an acceptable match, consider replacing several tiles. You can randomly add tiles in a contrasting color or use *decos* (decorator tiles with pictures).

With your replacement tile in hand, grab the tools you need:

- ✔ Grout saw or Dremel tool
- ✔ Glass cutter
- ✔ Hammer and a cold chisel (the kind that isn't for use on wood)
- ✔ Electric drill with a $\frac{1}{4}$-inch masonry bit
- ✔ *Mastic* (tile adhesive)
- ✔ Putty knife
- ✔ Block of wood bigger than the tile
- ✔ Masking tape
- ✔ Eye protection

Follow these steps to replace the broken tile (and take note of how often we use the word *carefully*):

1. **Carefully remove the grout from the joints around the damaged tile using a grout saw or a Dremel tool.**

2. **Use a drill to carefully bore a hole in the center of the tile and use a glass cutter to carefully scribe an X in the tile (corner to corner).**

   Drilling a hole in the center and crosscutting the surface acts to relieve pressure when you begin to remove the tile with a hammer and chisel. Relieving pressure helps prevent damage to surrounding tiles.

3. **Use a hammer and chisel to carefully remove the tile and clean out the area behind it.**

   Carefully remove all adhesive and grout. Try not to pry underneath adjacent tiles — you could loosen them.

4. **Test-fit the replacement tile to make sure it sits well with the other tiles.**

   You want it to be slightly recessed to leave room for adhesive.

5. **Carefully spread mastic on the back of the tile with a putty knife.**

   Keep the mastic $\frac{1}{4}$ to $\frac{1}{2}$ inch from the edges for squishing room.

6. **Carefully place the tile in position, and wiggle it a little to ensure good contact between the tile, the adhesive, and the base.**

7. **Place the block of wood over the tile and give it a couple gentle taps to make extra sure the tile is flush with its neighbors and to make super sure that the adhesive is stuck to everything.**

8. **Tape the wood over the repair to protect the repair.**

9. **Wait at least 24 hours and then apply grout (see the "Re-grouting your tile" section).**

Protecting Marvelous Marble

Whether in sheets or pieces, marble is an elegant surface. Unfortunately, it's unbelievably soft. Many folks think that marble is a type of stone. It isn't — it's actually petrified calcium (old seashells) and can be easily damaged. A spill of orange juice, a few drops of hair spray, or a splash of your favorite alcoholic beverage is all it takes to damage marble.

If you see a circle on the counter where the juice glass once was, you can count on the fact that the spot has been permanently etched. You can hire someone to polish etched areas, but a better — and cheaper — solution is to keep alcohol and even the mildest acids away from marble.

 Despite your best efforts, you may end up with a stain. Here's a neat trick that you can use to clean stained marble: You'll need half a lemon and a dish of table salt. Just dip the lemon into the salt and rub the marble. Thoroughly rinse with fresh water and towel-dry. You'll be amazed by how well it works. (If you can't get your marble clean with this trick, you probably won't get it clean at all.)

Sealer goes a long way toward preventing damage. Choose a high-quality, food-grade sealer, and apply it (and reapply it periodically) exactly according to the manufacturer's instructions. You can find a marble sealer at most hardware stores, home centers, or marble fabrication shops.

Caring for Granite

Granite is one of the hardest stones. In our opinion, there is no surface that is as durable or as easy to maintain as granite. Ten years later, it shines as beautifully as the day it was installed.

All it takes to remove coffee or tea stains from granite is some warm water on a cloth or paper towel. Hot pots have no effect on granite, and cold granite is an absolutely perfect baker's surface.

To maintain your granite, simply do the following:

✔ **Keep it clean by wiping with a damp cloth.** Easy enough.

✔ **Apply a clear, penetrating sealer with a clean, soft, cotton cloth at least once a year (twice a year for kitchen counters).** The sealer prevents cooking oils, grease, and other materials from being absorbed into the granite; these substances can cause discoloration and act as a hiding place for bacteria.

You can find a granite sealer at most hardware stores, home centers, or granite fabrication shops.

Taking Care of Wonderful Wood Chopping Blocks

People who love to cook love an in-counter butcher block. Heck, anyone who ever chops an onion likes the convenience of a solid, stable cutting surface. Care of this surface is simple:

✔ **Clean** with a soapy, damp cloth; then remove soapy residue with a clean, damp cloth.

✔ **Remove stains** immediately. Remove light stains by scrubbing the area with half a lemon and some salt. Also, try simply applying lemon juice to the area and letting it sit for a minute or two. You can remove tough stains by applying a 3 percent solution of hydrogen peroxide and water. If that doesn't work, bring out the big gun — a 50 percent solution of bleach and water. Brush it on and allow it to work for 15 minutes. Rinse the area thoroughly. Never, ever, *ever* use a scouring cleanser on a butcher block.

✔ **Prevent swelling, shrinking, and warping** by not flooding the surface with water or letting water stand on the surface.

✔ **Maintain a smooth surface** by sanding out scratches and cuts with 100-grit sandpaper. (Use a sanding block.) Sand with the grain of the wood.

✔ **Protect and preserve the surface** by applying mineral oil (not vegetable oil or olive oil) monthly. Apply the oil with a soft cloth, rubbing with the grain. Allow the oil to soak in and then wipe off excess oil.

Unlike vegetable-based oils, mineral oil doesn't go rancid, and it doesn't mess up polyurethane or varnish. Mineral oil also helps prevent the wood from drying out and cracking or literally coming apart at the seams.

Chapter 14

Appliances

The kitchen is the entertainment hub of most homes. If you doubt this, just throw (or go to) a party — and watch where everyone congregates. The nicer and more inviting the kitchen, the more crowded it is. The sleek, beautiful appliances you find in the kitchen certainly add to the attraction.

In this chapter, we offer you specific tips and ideas for the safe operation, maintenance and longevity of the incredible array of marvelous and ingenious conveniences that make the kitchen the heart of the 21st-century home. We also take a look at the washing machine and dryer, two appliances that make life easier.

Note: For parts of this chapter, we sought the sage advice of our favorite appliance guru, Otto "Butch" Gross of Middletown, Maryland. Butch often appears as our appliance expert in our newspaper columns and visits our radio broadcasts from time to time — thus, he is nationally known as the lovable, all-knowing "Appliance MD."

Safety First

When it comes to maintaining and repairing appliances, you *must* respect the power of, and potential danger posed by, the natural gas in the pipe and the electricity in the wires. Always use extreme care when working inside any appliance. In the following sections, we give you the most important safety information you need when it comes to gas- and electricity-powered appliances.

Cleaning is job one

The life span of most major household appliances can be severely shortened by neglect, and, on the flip side, greatly prolonged by simple care and basic preventive maintenance. And that maintenance mostly centers on, you guessed it, cleaning. Fortunately, a few simple household ingredients, plus a little elbow grease from time to time, will keep your appliances sparkling, operating efficiently, and one step ahead of the repairman.

When it comes to choosing a cleaner to use for the different tasks, you basically have two choices:

✔ **You can use commercial cleaners.** If you do, make sure they're mild and nonabrasive; harsh cleaners can damage the glossy surfaces you're trying to clean and preserve.

✔ **You can use easy-to-make, non-caustic, homemade cleaning solutions.** You'll be surprised by how powerful simple dishwashing soap, baking soda, vinegar, lemon juice, and salt can be — and how much better than chemical cleaners they are for you, your appliances, and your home environment. (Chapter 20 shares our secret family formulas.)

Regardless of the cleaner you use, keep these points in mind:

✔ **All cleaners work best when left to sit for a while.** Generally, the tougher the stain, the longer you let it sit to work.

✔ **If you're using commercial cleaners and solvents, always read the label for the manufacturer's usage directions and special warnings.** These warnings can range from potential health hazards to potential discoloration and surface damage.

✔ **Always wear rubber gloves, protect your eyes with glasses or goggles, and have plenty of ventilation when using any type of cleaner — whether store-bought or homemade.** Even though our homemade cleaning solutions are made with natural products, they still contain mild acids that can sting and burn your eyes and skin. Commercial products can be even more dangerous and highly volatile due to caustic components and chemical ingredients that can sting, burn, and give off vapors.

The owner's manuals for your major appliances are filled with valuable information for day-to-day operation and preventive maintenance. If you can't locate a manual, contact the manufacturer and ask the customer-service department to send you one. (Some manufacturers allow you to download product manuals from their Web sites.) After you assemble a full set of manuals for every major appliance in your home, keep them in a safe place for easy reference. They'll also be invaluable to someone else who may purchase your home somewhere down the line.

Gas appliances

Natural gas has no odor itself. A heavy smell is added to the gas for one purpose: to make it easy to detect even the smallest gas leak. If you smell gas, move quickly: Open all the doors and windows, and leave immediately. If the range shut-off valve isn't within easy reach, turn off the main shut-off valve at your gas meter. (See Chapter 16 for information on how to turn off the main shut-off valve at your gas meter.)

Don't use the phone or flip a light switch. Even the tiniest spark can ignite a massive explosion. From a neighbor's home, call the gas company and the fire department.

Electric appliances

With electricity, the major danger is electric shock. (Duh!) If you ever hear a funny *zzzzzap!* sound, or a weird *pwok!,* followed by a burnt, ozone smell, you've got a problem. Something inside your appliance is sparking or *arcing* (electrical shorting). Unplug the appliance immediately and call a repairman.

At this point, anything you do will be dangerous, so stop and call a professional.

Caring for the Cooktop

Cooking can be messy. Splatters, drips, boil-overs, and spills happen. And as a result, the cooktops in many homes (including yours?) have burnt-on food, hardened mystery globs, and a few thoroughly blackened rigatoni under the burners. In this section, we give you detailed information on cleaning and maintaining your cooktop.

Cleaning up the cooking crud

For day-to-day surface cleaning of the range or cooktop, a wet, wrung-out cloth or sponge will do the job — if you wipe up spills immediately after the meal. If you don't get to a spill right away, a general, all-purpose cleaner, like our All-Purpose, Handy-Dandy Cleaner (see Chapter 20), will cut through the crud. For tougher cooked-on spills, you need a cleanser with a little more oomph, like our DIY Cleanser Scrub (see Chapter 20) or a commercial cleaner that cuts through grease. Let the cleaners sit for a while to soften those really tough stains and hardened spills.

No matter how burnt on, dried up, or crusty your cooking crud gets, never, ever, *ever* use an abrasive cleaner. You'll scratch the glossy surface, and it'll look lousy forever.

When food spills occur, immediately sprinkle them with table salt, which absorbs the moisture and makes them easy to clean up later when the stove top cools.

Whatever cleaner you use, do a thorough job. Look for nooks and crannies where crud and crumbs gather. Make sure you remove that grease film from all glossy or shiny surfaces. (You can use full-strength white vinegar or lemon juice for that.) Remember to wipe off the burner elements (when cool) and the grates. Heck, put the grates in the dishwasher every now and then. And don't forget the knobs! Pull them off and wash them in warm, soapy water. Air-dry the knobs thoroughly and completely before replacing them. Use a hair dryer to remove moisture from nooks and crannies, if necessary.

Maintaining your electric range and cooktop

There are several kinds of electric ranges and cooktops, and what you can repair and replace depends on the type you have. Here are the three types of electric ranges and cooktops:

- ✔ **Plug-in burners:** Most electric ranges and cooktops have plug-in burners, which have a tendency to collect grease and moisture down at the tips where they go into the power receptacle. This buildup leads to minor arcing that slowly builds and eventually ruins the burners. To prevent this problem, remove the plug-in burners and carefully clean the surfaces and tips with a damp rag or stiff nylon brush. If those don't do the trick, use a soapy steel-wool pad.

   Never fully submerse plug-in burners in water. Even though the metal prongs may appear to be fully dry, trace amounts of moisture usually remain on the plug-in tips and electric receptacles, which contain porcelain, an extremely porous material that absorbs water. The result: You've brought water and electricity together for a potential electric shock — and a serious zapping.

Most ranges have two 6-inch and two 8-inch interchangeable burners. When removing them for cleaning, always mark their origin so you can put them back in exactly the same receptacle.

✔ **Fixed-unit burners:** Another kind of electric burner, the fixed unit, is hard-wired and generally lifts up for cleaning underneath. The advantage to this type of burner is that the tips never corrode or burn out from dripping grease, so you don't need to concern yourself with that possibility.

✔ **Euro-style cast-iron burners:** The coating on Euro-style solid cast iron burners (also called *hobs*) wears off with use. To prevent rusting, manufacturers and dealers offer a special cleaner/sealer that you apply to a cold burner (it burns off when the burner heats). You can also use a light coat of mineral oil or cooking oil to prevent rusting, but oil smokes a bit when the burner heats. Turn on the vent fan to remove any light residual smoking or burning odor.

Always keep lightweight, inexpensive aluminum drip pans under the heating elements to prevent grease, liquids, and burned pasta from getting into the works of the range. Besides keeping a spill from shorting the burners, they also increase the efficiency of the burner by reflecting heat upward. (That's why they're shiny!)

Clean the drip pans using baking soda, rather than soap, to keep them reflective. Don't use an abrasive cleaner — you'll create a billion little scratches. Also, never line your drip pans with aluminum foil. The heat reflected off the shiny-but-wrinkly foil creates hot spots underneath a burner that will quickly end the useful life of an electric element.

Keeping your gas range and cooktop in tip-top shape

Gas burners need a little TLC, too. Very little. Cleaning and maintenance is easy — and much safer than cleaning and maintaining electric burners, because you don't have to deal with electricity.

Cleaning removable gas burners

Take out removable gas burners periodically, and clean them with a stiff nylon brush, using baking soda and hot water to keep the *ports* (gas jet holes) clean. You can remove most burners simply by lifting them out of the opening in the cooktop; you don't need any tools. If you aren't sure whether your burners are the removable type, refer to your owner's manual.

Never use any kind of soap or put your removable gas burners in the dishwasher. The chemicals in soap and dishwasher detergent trigger corrosion on burner housings, which are made of aluminum.

Cleaning nonremovable sealed gas burners

You'll know if you have a sealed gas burner — the drip pan that surrounds each burner is anchored securely to the cooktop, or the cooktop is one big piece with indentations surrounding the burners For these types of burners, the only components that can be removed for cleaning are the *burner cap* (which evenly distributes the flame) and the *burner grate* (the part that rests above the flame, on which you put the pots). Both just lift off.

Clean the burner caps with a small brush and a solution of ¼ cup of baking soda and 1 quart of warm water. Be sure to thoroughly wipe the burner caps clean, and remove all water from the gas jet port openings — first with a soft cloth, and then using a hair dryer to remove all moisture, if necessary. You'll need to up the ante when it comes to cleaning burner grates. Use an all-purpose cleanser scrub (like our DIY Cleanser Scrub — see Chapter 20) to clean these components.

Cleaning the connector tube

Between the burners is a connector tube (technically called a *flash tube*) with an opening and a pilot light or electric spark igniter. This tube is where the gas is actually ignited and carried or drawn to each burner. If you notice that one flame jet shoots farther out than the others, the opening is partially blocked and needs cleaning. In most cases, this configuration is part of the burner assembly and can be cleaned the same way the burners are (see the preceding sections).

A proper gas flame burns clear and blue. If yours burns yellow and orange, it probably is starved for air. The burners should be cleaned with a wire brush.

Opening the Door and Rolling Up Your Sleeves: The Oven

Whether your oven is gas- or electric-powered, it's going to get dirty. Really dirty. That's just how it is. And cleaning your oven will be a drag, so just take a deep breath, roll up your sleeves, and do the job right. In this section, we tell you how. We also fill you in on two other oven maintenance tasks: checking the temperature control and replacing the oven light.

Cleaning your oven

Aside from saving you embarrassment when company comes calling, a clean oven operates more efficiently by providing more even heating. A dirty oven can also prevent the door from sealing properly, which allows heat and smoke to escape.

The interior

You can clean oven interiors with commercial cleansers, steel-wool soap pads, or our People-Friendly Oven Cleaner (see Chapter 20). (***Note:*** Don't use commercial cleaners on self-cleaning ovens; see the "Self-cleaning ovens" bullet, toward the end of this section, for details.)

Here are a couple of tips to make oven cleaning easier:

- ✔ **To loosen up tough, baked-on spills, preheat the oven to 200 degrees, turn off the heat, and then put a bowl of ammonia in your oven overnight.** This strategy works well as long as you don't mind the smell of ammonia in your kitchen the next day.

- ✔ **To make it easier to reach all the way into the oven, open the door 8 to 10 inches and try lifting the door up and out.** Most ovens have special hinges that allow the door to lift right off. You can then easily clean deep into the oven interior without stretching over the lowered, open oven door. You also can comfortably clean the glass and inside surface of the door on top of a towel spread out on the countertop.

If a commercial cleaner says you must wear rubber gloves and avoid breathing fumes, it's probably very caustic and possibly toxic. It may give off harmful gases even after the cleaning is complete and the oven is again heated for use. Thus, we suggest that you avoid using commercial oven cleaners whenever possible. If you must use a commercial cleaner, follow label directions to the letter.

If the wire oven racks are severely caked with food spills, put them in a plastic trash bag, add some ammonia, and seal the bag well with a twist tie. Leave the bag outside overnight, and then either hose the racks off, hand-wash them, or run them through your dishwasher.

Here are some specific tips for the various types of ovens:

- ✔ **Electric ovens:** In electric ovens, you find two heating elements: one for broiling (above) and one for baking (below). In some models you can lift the bottom bake element for easier cleaning of the bottom of the oven. (If you're in the market for an oven, look for this handy feature.)

Many people believe that they can simplify oven cleaning by lining the bottom of their electric oven with aluminum foil to catch spills. This is a no-no! A layer of foil causes an electric oven to heat unevenly. It also shortens the life of the element by causing it to superheat in certain locations.

✔ **Gas ovens:** Like most ovens, the bottom of the gas oven is the object of most cleaning attention. Remove the bottom panel of a gas oven by lifting it out or by removing a couple of screws that hold it in place. Doing so lets you work on it in a deep sink or bathtub. It also enables you to inspect and clean the gas burner.

Over time, the bottom panel of a gas oven can become corroded or cracked. If this happens, you can replace it. Just get the proper part from the manufacturer or your local appliance parts dealer. Remove the old piece, and put in the new piece. *Voilà!*

Uneven heating, poor baking, or an odor of gas when the oven is on are telltale signs of a clogged burner. Your best bet to determine how the burner is working is to turn it on with the bottom panel off. If the flame isn't continuous along both sides of the burner, some of its holes are likely clogged. To set your burner free, turn off the oven control and carefully use a wire — such as a coat hanger — to unclog the clogged holes. Works every time!

After the gas burner is clean, check to make sure that it's burning efficiently — with a steady, blue, 1-inch cone, with an inner lighter-blue cone of about ¹/₂ inch. Adjusting the air shutter controls the air mixture and, in turn, the color of the flame. Consult your owner's manual for specific information on how to adjust the burner flame in your gas oven.

✔ **Self-cleaning ovens:** Never, never, *never* use commercial oven cleaners on a self-cleaning oven. They can pit, burn, and eat into the special porcelain surface. The result? When you reach the normal 850- to 900-degree level for self-cleaning, you can actually pop chunks of porcelain as large as 6 inches across off the oven walls. Instead, let the intended high-heat action turn food spills into carbon, which all but disappears with complete combustion, and then wipe up any minor dust-like ash residue with a damp cloth, paper towel, or sponge when the oven cools.

Manufacturers recommend removing the racks during the self-cleaning process to prevent them from turning brown. To clean these racks, use the process mentioned earlier in this section. (We strongly recommend that you consult your owner's manual for specific information on how to use your self-cleaning oven.)

When using the self-cleaning feature, don't open the oven door if you notice a flame-up or smell something burning. The oven is just doing what it's supposed to do. If you're really worried, just shut the oven off.

The lack of oxygen in the closed and sealed oven and diminishing heat level extinguish any burning in a matter of minutes.

You can clean the area surrounding the oven door gasket with any type of mild abrasive, such as our DIY Cleanser Scrub (see Chapter 20) or a commercial silver polish. Use a wide spatula or paint scraper to lift the gasket edge up to prevent rubbing up against it and possible fraying.

Many heavier-weight, porcelain-coated drip pans can be put into the oven during self-cleaning, making the cleanup of drips and spills a snap.

✔ **Continuous-cleaning ovens:** These ovens have a special rough-texture porcelain interior. Spills gradually burn off as you use the oven. A speck-led surface helps hide foods while they burn off, but these ovens may not always look clean in the process.

Combusted foods tend to remain on the oven walls. To avoid this situation as much as possible, always wipe up large spills — especially sugary or starchy foods — as soon as the oven cools. These models work best on greasy spills.

Never use harsh abrasives, scouring pads or commercial oven cleaners on continuous-cleaning ovens. These cleaners damage the special lining. Gentle cleaning by hand with baking soda and warm water works best.

The window glass

Ammonia and commercial window cleaners that contain ammonia are great for cleaning browned and discolored, oven window glass. You can also use mild abrasives and scouring pads for tough spots.

Behind the range

Occasionally you may want to clean and vacuum the back of your range and the areas behind, on either side of, and below it. On the back of a range is a metal panel that can be removed (by a professional) for service or repair. You can clean dust and grime off this panel, but don't remove it.

To clean behind the range, pull it away from the wall. If the range is electric, the cord should be long enough for you to move the appliance out and then unplug it. Gas models should have a flexible gas line that enables you to pull out the appliance.

Don't move a gas range that has a rigid gas pipe — instead, call a service professional.

To avoid damaging flooring in front of an appliance when moving it, turn an old piece of carpet upside down and place it under the appliance, or use an appliance dolly or an appliance skid pad (both available from an appliance service company).

Checking the oven temperature control

A poorly calibrated control can make it virtually impossible to conform to heating instructions on recipes. Thus, you end up with a dish that is either under- or overcooked. Yikes!

To check the accuracy of oven temperature control, put an oven thermometer on the middle rack. Set the thermometer for 350 degrees and heat the oven for 20 minutes. Write down the temperature. Check three more times at ten-minute intervals, noting the temperatures. The average temperature should be within 25 degrees of 350.

If you find that the temperature is off, recalibrate the temperature control dial by removing the oven temperature knob and doing one of the following:

✔ Loosen the screws and turn the movable disk on the backside. One notch represents 10 degrees.

✔ Turn the adjustment screw inside the hollow shaft clockwise to lower the temperature, counterclockwise to raise it. If it requires more than an eighth of a turn or is off by 50 degrees or more, have a new temperature control installed by a qualified professional.

If after you've recalibrated the temperature control, your oven still fluctuates or bakes unevenly, chances are good that your thermostat is faulty. Your best bet is to leave thermostat installation to a pro. The only tool you should pick up to make this repair is your phone.

Replacing the oven light

When the oven light burns out, turn off the power at the main circuit, remove the glass shield and, using gloves or a dry cloth, unscrew the old bulb. Only replace it with a special 40-watt appliance bulb that can stand extreme temperatures (or whatever the manufacturer recommends). If, after you've replaced the bulb, the light doesn't light, it may indicate a larger problem that needs professional attention.

Hanging Out in the Range Hood

Although it's a simple appliance, the range hood has an important job: It removes excess moisture and smoke produced by cooking. The most important range-hood maintenance task is cleaning.

Remove and clean the metal mesh filter(s) that keep grease from getting into the ductwork. Soak the filters in a sink full of hot water and liquid dish detergent. Then rinse them clean with very hot water. At least once a month (more often if you cook and operate the vent and fan frequently), inspect the filters for grease buildup. Replace worn or damaged filter screens with new ones; you can get them from an appliance repair shop or through the manufacturer.

Don't put mesh filters in the bottom rack of your dishwasher (regardless of what amateur tipsters advise). The filters may leave a greasy residue behind in your dishwasher that's hard to remove and can ultimately clog lines and affect your machine's operation. You can put them in the dishwasher after you've given them an initial once-over as outlined in the preceding paragraph.

With filters removed, wash the range-hood interior with an all-purpose cleaner (our All-Purpose, Handy-Dandy Cleaner [see Chapter 20] is good for this job), or try warm water and liquid dish detergent.

For non-vented hoods, remember to replace the disposable charcoal filter every year (or according to the manufacturer's directions).

Microwave Maintenance Mania

When it comes to a microwave oven, you can do only a few things safely. Basically, your job is to keep it clean, use it properly, and call a pro when it begins to act up.

Here's why keeping the inside of your microwave clean is so important: Stuck-on food particles eventually turn to carbon and cause arcing, which, in turn, can etch interior surfaces and could even compromise the seal around the door. Always wipe up spills promptly. Keep the interior of the oven and the area surrounding the door clean, using a damp sponge to catch spills and splatters as they occur, or an all-purpose cleaning solution for spills that have been left over long periods of time.

Never use a microwave oven for anything other than what it was designed for — cooking and heating. Using it to dry clothing, newspapers, or shoes can yield devastating results. Never run an empty microwave, and always be sure there is plenty of ventilation surrounding the unit to avoid overheating, which could cause serious damage. And only use microwave-approved containers and dishes.

Never attempt to repair an ailing microwave oven yourself. Besides the inherent dangers (the unit's capacitor holds up to 4,000 volts of electricity!), unauthorized repairs by anyone other than an authorized service tech almost always void the manufacturer's warranty. Here are some problems that require the attention of a professional:

✔ **Insufficient output:** If your microwave oven is more than 15 years old, check it for output efficiency. For 600- to 1,000-watt microwave ovens, place an 8-ounce cup of water in the oven and operate the unit on high for three minutes. The water should reach a rolling boil. If not, take the microwave to a service shop for inspection.

✔ **Radiation leaks:** Have a professional appliance-repair technician test your older microwave for radiation leakage. In addition, the pro can check other aspects of operation to determine if the microwave is safe and whether it should be repaired or replaced.

✔ **Poor heating:** Operating a microwave on a circuit that is serving other appliances not only diminishes the effectiveness of the microwave oven, but ultimately could result in an electrical fire. If lights dim when the microwave is used, consult an electrician. Whenever possible, a separate electrical circuit should be provided for the microwave oven.

✔ **Burned out interior fuse:** Appliance repair pros say the most common repair problem they find is a simple microwave fuse that gets metal fatigue after three or four years' use. At that point, even a minor power surge can cause the fuse to burn out. If your microwave quits, don't panic. It may just be an interior fuse that needs replacing by a pro.

Dishwashers

The single most important dishwasher maintenance task? Easy! Keep the interior clean. Doing so keeps all the hoses and passages clear, which, in turn, lets the machine operate freely and washes your dishes better.

The best way to clean the interior is with citric acid. Use pure citric-acid crystals, which you can find in grocery stores and drugstores. Fill your main soap cup and then run the empty dishwasher through a complete cycle. The crystals clean everything, including the unit's interior, racks, hoses, and water ports. Then, once a week, add 1 teaspoon of the acid crystals to your soap for general maintenance.

You can substitute Tang and lemonade mixes that contain vitamin C (which is citric acid) for the crystals. They work well, but with less citric acid per dose.

Here are some other tasks you can do to keep your dishwasher washing dishes:

✔ **Use the right amount of soap.** Any more than 1 tablespoon is too much and will lead to a residue buildup that's hard to remove.

✔ **Never wash anything other than dishes in your dishwasher.** Tools, clothes, sneakers, greasy range hood filters, and other "unauthorized" items can leave harmful grease and residue that clog the machine's works and inhibit proper operation.

✔ **Run your dishwasher at least once a week.** This keeps all the seals moist and prevents leaks and eventual failure.

✔ **Periodically wipe the area around the seals.** This prevents soap scum buildup, which can cause a leak.

Refrigerators and Freezers

Refrigerators are big, and they have many components to keep clean. You've got the exterior, the interior, the freezer, water lines, drain lines, and coils to worry about. Not that the maintenance they require is difficult — you just have to stay on top it to make sure the fridge does a good job of keeping everything cold.

Temperature-wise, keep the food compartment set between 34 and 40 degrees, and the freezer compartment at about 0 degrees. Generally, refrigerator and freezer controls should always be set midway initially, and then adjusted up or down as needed.

Taking care of the condenser coils

The most important thing for any refrigerator is to keep the condenser coils clean. The coils are usually located at the bottom of the refrigerator behind a removable grille; on some older refrigerators, they're located on the back of the refrigerator. Air passing over these coils is what cools the refrigerator, and if they're dirty, the unit has to work harder to do its job.

To clean the coils, first unplug the refrigerator. Remove the grille by grabbing both ends and pulling gently. Use a vacuum cleaner with a brush or crevice attachment to get as far into and under the unit as possible (being careful not to force access, which can bend condenser tubing and the thin metal coil fins). While the grille is off, also remove the refrigerator drain pan and wash it.

Typically located inside your refrigerator is an electric heater power switch. It controls small electric heaters that keep the outside of the cabinet from sweating. Only turn the switch on when it's humid and you see moisture beads. When both the weather and your refrigerator are dry, turn this switch off to save energy costs. The electric heater also helps prevent rust and nasty mold buildup.

Cleaning the gasket

The chilled air inside a refrigerator is kept there primarily by a gasket at the perimeter of the door. In good condition, it provides a good airtight seal. It can get tired and worn, or hard, and also is a prime candidate for mold. Here's how to take care of it:

- ✔ **Every six months or so, check the gasket to make sure it's in good condition.** How can you tell if your gasket is in good condition? Place a dollar bill between the gasket and the door jamb. If it's difficult to pull out, the gasket is okay. If it pulls out easily, you need to replace the gasket.

- ✔ **Wipe the gasket every few months with a wet cloth, making sure to get all the surfaces and to go completely around the door.** If the gasket seems a bit hard, apply a light coat of lemon oil, mineral oil, or any type of body lotion with lanolin.

- ✔ **As soon as you notice any mold around the gasket, remove it.** To do so, clean it with a solution of liquid chlorine bleach and water (4 tablespoons of bleach in 1 quart of hot water), and scrub well with an old toothbrush. Afterwards, completely wipe off all residue with warm water and a mild, liquid dish soap.

- ✔ **Always wipe off any food or liquid spills, drips, and runs from around the door and gaskets.** If you don't, they dry and become sticky, possibly ripping away the gasket when you open the door.

- ✔ **If the gasket has pulled away in spots, stick it back down with a little contact cement.** Use a Popsicle stick to neatly smear a small blob of glue into the gap and hold it in place for 10 seconds. Then close the door. Make sure there is nothing sticky where the gasket meets the refrigerator — otherwise, your work will be in vain.

Keeping the interior clean and fresh-smelling

To clean the interior of the refrigerator, first turn off the fridge (or unplug it) and remove all the food. Wash removable shelves and bins in the sink with liquid dish detergent and warm water. Wipe down the interior walls with an all-purpose cleanser or a solution of warm water and baking soda.

Most people know that an open box of baking soda will keep the refrigerator or freezer smelling fresh. Did you know that you can also use a small bowl with a few tablespoons of instant freeze-dried coffee crystals in it? And believe it or not, granulated cat litter also works. An added bonus: The litter eliminates food odors in ice cubes.

Defrosting the freezer and drain line

Defrost your freezer when ice begins to build up on the interior. Aside from decreasing usable freezer space, the ice can prevent the door from sealing properly. Most freezers need to be defrosted at least once and sometimes twice each year. Start by turning off the power to the freezer and removing all the contents. You can allow the ice to melt on its own or you can speed things up by placing a pot of hot water in the freezer and closing the door. Clean the interior of the freezer using the same method described for cleaning the interior.

While you're defrosting the freezer, defrost the freezer drain line leading to the drain pan, too. (This task needs to be done at least once a year.) Mold buildup starts retaining moisture, which, in turn, starts freezing and ultimately completely blocks the line. Here's how to defrost the drain line:

1. **Turn off the freezer (so that you can melt the ice in the drain line).**

2. **Put very hot water into a turkey baster and insert it into the ¹/₂-inch drain hole located at the back of the freezer floor.**

3. **Release the hot water into the line until it runs free.**

Garbage disposals

To keep your garbage disposal in good working order, keep it clean: Put ice cubes and ¹/₄ cup of white vinegar into the unit and operate it with no running water. When it sounds like the cubes are all gone, start a slow trickle of cold water. You'll probably find that the disposal's drain openings are frozen and clogged with ice, and the water will start to back up — which is good — because the churning water also washes the sides before the ice melts, the drain clears, and everything drains away. For a more thorough cleaning, sprinkle some baking soda on top of the ice cubes. To make the disposal smell fresh, add some citric-acid crystals, Tang, or a drink mix containing vitamin C, or half a lemon.

Use vinegar ice cubes as an easy means of cleaning your disposal and sharpening its blades. Pour 1 cup of vinegar into an empty ice-cube tray, fill the balance of the tray with water, and freeze until solid. Periodically pour an entire tray of ice cubes into the disposal while it's running. Just be sure to mark the tray with the vinegar ice cubes; otherwise, your guests will have an unpleasant experience next time you serve them a cold beverage!

4. **Blast in more hot water to blow out any mold buildup.**

5. **Put 2 tablespoons of chlorine bleach in 1 cup of hot water and pour it down the drain to kill off any remaining mold spores.**

All this liquid should be running into the drain pan at the bottom of the unit. Make sure it doesn't overflow, and empty and clean the drain pan when you're done.

Maintaining inline water filtration

Many, if not most, refrigerators offer automatic ice makers and water dispensers. A filter somewhere under the unit ensures clean ice and water. Typically, the only maintenance required is periodically changing the filter. Many units even have a red-light/green-light alert to tell you when the filter needs to be replaced. You can order the filters from the manufacturer, get them at an appliance parts dealer, and may even find them at your home center or the retailer that sold the unit. Consult your owner's manual to get step-by-step filter-replacement instructions.

Washing Machines and Dryers

People tend to take their washing machines and dryers for granted — until they stop working in the middle of a load. You'd be amazed by all the technology inside your washer and dryer — in fact, so much technology is involved that you can't service many components yourself. Having to call a professional is okay, though — after all, the true battle for laundry-machine longevity is fought with basic cleaning and simple maintenance, and you can do all of that yourself.

Cleaning your washing machine

Over time and multiple wash loads, mineral deposits, lime, and soap build up inside your washer and can affect the pump operation. You can avoid this buildup by using citric-acid crystals to clean tub interiors. With the tub empty, use 1 cup of citric acid instead of laundry detergent, and run your machine through a complete cycle. (Refer to the "Dishwashers" section, earlier in this chapter, for more on this cleaning method.)

Here are other problems that you can fix with just a few tools and a little know-how (or a quick call to a professional):

- **Rust stains inside the tub:** Temporary patch-ups on small nicks in the porcelain where rusting occurs can be made with a dab or two of enamel paint or clear nail polish — but these solutions are only temporary, at best. A better solution is a porcelain repair kit made for bathtubs, available at your local hardware store. It lasts longer, but not forever. If these fixes aren't sufficient, before you consider replacing your machine, try a professionally installed plastic tub liner.

- **Lint-filled drain line:** If your water outlet hose drains into a laundry basin rather than a stand pipe, cover the end with an old nylon stocking. Doing so collects 95 percent of all lint that otherwise would go into your sink's drain line. The nylon stocking filter also reduces splashing when the washer empties into the sink. When the stocking fills with lint, remove and replace it.

- **Slow-running cold water:** Turn off the water inlet valves, remove the water hoses, and clean the small screen filters, which probably are clogged with mineral buildup and small debris. The fine mesh filters are usually at either end of the hose or on the back of the washing machine's water inlet port. If debris gets past these screen filters, it can damage the pump and lead to a costly repair. Also, consider switching from rubber water inlet hoses to long-lasting braided stainless-steel hoses. They cost a little more, but both are good insurance against flooding caused by hose failure.

Keeping your dryer's lint traps lint free

Dryer lint is a big fire hazard. Plus, excess lint in the trap makes the dryer work extra hard, causing it to take forever to dry a load of clothes. To keep your lint traps lint free, do the following:

- **Clean the lint screen thoroughly after every load.** If it's clogged with lint, the air won't circulate, the clothes won't dry, and the dryer will run far longer, which wears it out faster and wastes lots of energy dollars in the process.

- **Clean the dryer duct at least twice each year.** The easiest way to clean a short dryer duct is to use a *dryer-duct cleaning brush* (a stiff-bristle circular brush attached to a flexible handle — it looks like a mini version of a brush that a chimney sweep might use) and a vacuum. Move the brush back and forth inside the duct to dislodge any lint, and vacuum out the loose debris.

✔ **Remove lint that accumulates at the bottom of the housing that contains the lint screen.** Construct a mini vacuum hose attachment using a short piece of rubber hose, the cap to an aerosol can, and some duct tape. The cap acts as an adapter that fits over the end of a wet/dry vacuum hose. Make a hole in the center of the cap the size of the outside diameter of the hose. Insert the hose snuggly into the hole and attach the two with duct tape. Attach the cap to the end of a wet/dry vacuum and insert the hose into the filter housing until it reaches the bottom (see Figure 14-1).

Taking care of the dryer vent

The dryer vent transports hot, damp air from the dryer to the outside of your house. Without it, your house would be very hot, excessively humid, and covered in a light coating of lint. The problem: All dryer vents slowly fill with lint, which impedes or blocks airflow (making the dryer inefficient) and creates a significant fire hazard. A couple of times a year, take a few minutes to clean the dryer vent. A clean vent is a happy vent.

Figure 14-1:
Removing
lint from
inside the
machine.

The easiest way to clean a dryer vent is with a dryer vent brush. It's the mini version of a chimney-sweep brush and has a round brush at one end with a flexible handle that can makes negotiating curves a breeze. You can find these brushes at most hardware stores. Use it in combination with a vacuum, and your vent will be lint free!

In addition to cleaning the dryer vent, periodically remove the flexible accordion-type exhaust hose (located between the back of the dryer and the vent at the wall or floor) and vacuum it. Better yet, don't bother cleaning the flexible vent (especially if it's vinyl). Throw it away, and replace it with a metal duct. It won't clog nearly as much, and it's a more efficient vent, making your clothes dry faster.

Not all dryer manufacturers approve the use of plastic flexible hose for venting. In fact, installing one may void the warranty. A smooth, metal vent is best. The pleats on flexible hoses (metal or plastic) create air turbulence, which results in decreased airflow. Plus, moisture collects in the pleats, attracting and holding lint.

Keeping the dryer duct free from obstruction

Most dryer ducts terminate at a hood mounted at an exterior wall. The hood contains a damper designed to open only when the dryer is blowing air through the duct. The damper prevents cold air and birds and rodents from nesting in the duct. However, crafty varmints often find a way of breaching the damper. If you've experienced such a problem, install a protective screen specially designed to solve this problem. If you already have such a device, make sure that any holes are patched so that it's doing a good job.

Mysterious dryer death: Knowing what to do

If you suddenly have a dead electric dryer, it may have burned its fuse — a totally fixable problem and much cheaper than a new unit. The fuse is a built-in safety mechanism that works only one time; after it goes off, a service technician has to fix it before your dryer will operate again.

You can prevent the dryer from burning its fuse by never opening the door in mid-cycle without first turning the dial to the air-dry mode or advancing the timer to shut off the heater. If you stop in mid-cycle, the red-hot heaters allow heat to collect inside the unit until it triggers the thermal fuse.

If you want to interrupt a drying cycle, always let the heater cool off before stopping. Otherwise you may wind up line-drying your duds for a while.

Chapter 15

Don't Get Burned: Fireplaces

(Wiley) - North Pole. Well-informed sources have it that Ol' St. Nick has been forced to replace his bright red uniform with a new one as a result of extensive soiling due to unusually dirty fireplaces last holiday season.

We're sure that St. Nick's wardrobe concerns are serious, but there are other, more critical reasons to keep your fireplace and chimney clean and in good working order. A dirty chimney not only diminishes the effectiveness of a fireplace, but, with severe neglect, could be the cause of a chimney fire — and chimney fires lead to house fires.

Failing to maintain your fireplace can lead to problems ranging from relatively minor (smoke in the house) to a catastrophic (a chimney fire). In fact, the National Fire Protection Association reports that some 64,100 residential fires were related to home-heating equipment and fireplace, chimney, and chimney connectors in 2006. As a result of these fires, 540 people died, and 1,400 people were injured. These fires may have been prevented by safer use of portable home heating equipment and with regular fireplace chimney inspection, cleaning, and repair.

Having Your Fireplace Inspected and Swept Regularly

Before modern heating systems were available, the fireplace or wood stove was the sole source of heat in a home. Although the fireplace can't compete with modern heating systems as an energy- and cost-efficient source of heat, it remains one of the most popular features in a home.

There are two basic styles of fireplace construction: masonry and prefabricated metal (also called *zero clearance*). The different fireplace styles operate in essentially the same fashion:

- Each has a *firebox* (the place where you burn the wood), a *damper* (the door that resides between the firebox and the chimney), a *flue* (chimney), and a *spark arrestor* (a screen atop the chimney that prevents sparks from getting into the air).
- Each is typically outfitted with a mesh screen and glass doors.
- In each type of fireplace, the hearth and fireplace face can be constructed of brick, stone, or another decorative finish.

Here are the key differences between masonry fireplaces and prefabricated metal fireplaces:

- **A masonry fireplace** is custom-built of bricks and mortar. The firebox is constructed of firebricks, and the flue consists of bricks or a clay or terra-cotta liner. Firebricks and the mortar that surrounds them are intended to withstand extreme temperatures.
- **A prefabricated metal fireplace** is installed and assembled on-site. The metal box contains firebrick panels (see Figure 15-1), called *refractory brick panels,* that line the sides, back, and bottom of the firebox. The flue for a prefabricated fireplace consists of a metal pipe that is concealed by a chimney constructed of plywood or another siding material.

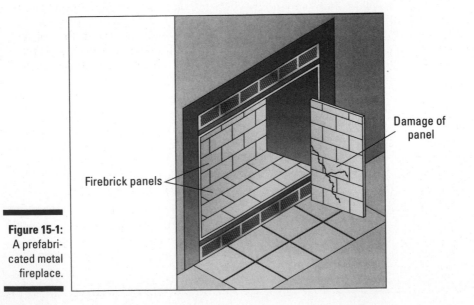

Figure 15-1:
A prefabricated metal fireplace.

Damage of panel

Firebrick panels

However you use your fireplace — as a secondary source of heat during winter or simply for its aesthetic qualities — keep in mind that a poorly maintained fireplace can spell disaster.

Failing to maintain your fireplace properly can lead to a chimney fire. Chimney fires occur when combustible deposits on the inner walls of the chimney ignite. These explosive deposits, called *creosote,* are a natural byproduct of combustion. A fire hazard exists if $^1/_8$ to $^1/_4$ inch of creosote (or more) coats the inner walls of the chimney — built-up creosote is a time bomb waiting to go off. ***Remember:*** A chimney fire can literally level your house.

One thing stops creosote from becoming a problem: a fireplace inspection and sweeping by a professional chimney sweep at least once a year or after burning one cord of wood — whichever comes first. More-frequent cleanings may be required, depending on the type of wood burned, the type of appliance, and the frequency of use. In general, an older, uncertified wood stove, or any appliance that is used frequently, requires more than one cleaning per year.

Prefabricated metal fireplaces often need more frequent cleaning. They burn cooler, allowing a higher degree of condensation of combustion deposits on the interior surface of the fireplace flue.

Fuel for the fire

The first step to having a healthy, well-maintained fireplace is to burn the right fuel. Being choosy about what you burn improves heating efficiency, helps the environment, and reduces the amount of creosote your fires produce.

Your fireplace is not an incinerator! Don't burn garbage, treated or painted wood, plastic, rubber, or any other non-recommended material. In addition to causing an unfavorable buildup on the interior of the firebox and chimney, these materials also produce noxious fumes that pollute the air (inside and outside of the home). Being careful about what you burn is the first line of defense against a catastrophic house-leveling chimney fire.

So, what's best to burn? Osage orange wood, oak, hard maple, madrone, hickory, ash, walnut, locust, apple, cherry, peach, and plum are the top-burning hardwoods. Hardwoods burn longer and cleaner with less creosote buildup in the chimney than softer woods (such as willow, poplar, pine, and cedar). Fortunately, most firewood dealers don't sell softwoods and recommend hardwoods.

Seasoning is of equal importance when shopping for wood. Unseasoned (green) wood won't burn well due to its high moisture content. When it burns, it often sizzles and pops and gives off steam. Dry, seasoned wood ignites and burns much more easily, and it causes fewer problems with condensation and creosote.

If most of your fires consist of manufactured fire logs, you'll be pleased to know that independent tests have proven that manufactured fire logs burn much cleaner than firewood.

According to the National Chimney Sweep Guild (www.ncsg.org), a national trade association comprised of chimney sweeps, a visual inspection is all that is normally required for most chimneys. In the case where a visual inspection is neither possible nor adequate, many chimney sweeps are equipped to do more elaborate inspections with a video camera and monitor referred to as a *chimscan*. A chimscan costs more than a visual inspection, but it reveals more and better information about the condition of your chimney — which is especially important when the integrity of the flue is in question due to age or damage from an earthquake or chimney fire.

Staying on Top of Fireplace Cracks

In a masonry fireplace, firebrick is used to construct the firebox. Refractory brick panels line the firebox of a prefabricated metal fireplace. In both cases, the bricks and fireclay mortar are designed to withstand extreme temperatures. However, over time, the brick, mortar, or panels can crack and crumble, creating a serious fire hazard.

Here's what you need to do to address these problems:

- **If a brick in a masonry fireplace cracks,** you need to patch it. (Head to Chapter 4 for instructions.) If the brick is crumbling, have it replaced with a new firebrick embedded in refractory mortar.

- **If the mortar joints in a firebox are crumbling,** chisel out the old mortar and replace it with new mortar (see Chapter 4). This process, known as *tuckpointing,* is the same one you follow to replace or repair mortar joints in any brick structure. The only difference is that in a firebox, you must use *refractory mortar,* which is specially designed to withstand extreme temperatures.

- **If the integrity of the majority of the firebrick and mortar in the firebox is in question,** have a qualified chimney sweep or masonry contractor inspect it. If replacement is in order, the job is best left to a pro.

- **If a panel of a prefabricated metal fireplace develops extensive cracks or is beginning to crumble,** replace it with a new panel. This is a job that most do-it-yourselfers can handle: Simply remove the old panel by unscrewing the screws that hold it in place and install the new panel; it should fit snugly against the adjoining panels. When replacing a rear panel, remove the side panels first. Refractory mortar is not generally needed, because the corners are designed to fit snugly against one another.

To make the job of finding a replacement panel easy, jot down the fireplace make and model number. (You can find these numbers on a metal plate just inside the opening of the firebox.) Give this information to the manufacturer or an installing dealer. Although replacement panels are often a stock item, a special order may be required, which can take from a few days to a couple of weeks. Don't use the fireplace until a full and final repair has been made.

Note: Repairing minor cracks and mortar joints in prefabricated metal fireplaces is essentially the same as with a brick firebox.

Dealing with the Damper

The damper is a steel or cast-iron door that opens or closes the throat of the firebox into the flue. It regulates draft and prevents the loss of heat up the chimney. To start a fire, you must have the damper in the full-open position. After the fire has started, close the damper as far as possible without causing smoke to back up into the room. Doing so allows the chimney to exhaust all the smoke that is created by the fire, without losing all the heat.

Often, a damper becomes difficult to operate or sticks in one position. One of the most pervasive causes of a stuck damper is rust, often caused when rain-water enters the chimney through a faulty or nonexistent chimney cap (see "Arresting sparks and other hazards," later in this chapter).

You can clean a dirty or rusty damper with a wire brush along with lots of elbow grease. Wear safety goggles, work gloves, a hat, and old clothing. Then, with the wire brush in one hand and a flashlight in the other, use the brush to remove soot and rust buildup (see Figure 15-2).

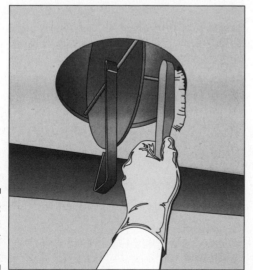

Figure 15-2:
Cleaning
your
damper.

If, after cleaning the damper, it still sticks, slide a short length of pipe — about 20 to 24 inches — over the damper handle (this extends the damper handle); then beat on the pipe with a sledgehammer to break the damper loose. If the damper still refuses to budge, use a rust and corrosion cutting oil such as WD-40 to help dissolve the rust and corrosion at the damper's hinges.

When the damper is operational, work it back and forth while applying a high-temperature lubricant at all the joints and moving parts. When it's clean and in good working order, spray-paint the damper with a black high-temperature paint to prevent future rusting.

Fireplaces without dampers or with faulty dampers can be retrofitted with new dampers. Unlike the style of damper located immediately above the firebox, a retrofit model is mounted at the top of the chimney and is operated by a long chain that hangs down the chimney.

Caring for the Outside of Your Chimney

Although caring for the inside of your fireplace, chimney, and damper is important, don't forget the outside. A chimney can be either an exposed pipe, a framed enclosure that is covered with siding (called a *sided chase*) that houses the flue pipe, or a masonry chimney.

Taking care of the flashing and flue pipe

The chimney travels from the inside of the home to the outside either through an attic and roof or out a wall. The point where the chimney exits the structure is a primary source of leaks. Thus, you should water-test the flashing that surrounds this location using a garden hose, to make sure that it's in good condition and leak-free. (Turn to Chapter 5 for instructions on how to use a water hose to discover leaks.)

Another potential problem area is the metal pipe itself. It can be attacked by rust, and the joints can become loose. To maintain the metal pipe:

1. **Use a wire brush to remove the rust.**

2. **Prime and paint the rusted area with high-temperature paint.**

3. **Use a screwdriver to tighten screws at all connections.**

4. **Install new self-tapping sheet-metal screws at locations where screws were previously installed and worked loose. (*Self-tapping screws* are ones with their own built-in drill-bit tips.)**

   Remove an existing screw and use it as an example when purchasing replacement screws.

Masonry fireplaces have a unique flashing detail called a *masonry counter flashing,* which is a secondary piece of flashing that covers the primary flashing. The counter flashing has a slight lip that's inserted into a mortar joint and then either mortared or caulked into place. Water-test the caulking or mortar annually (see Chapter 5), and repair or replace it as needed.

Apply a coat of paint to help hide otherwise unattractive flashing and prevent it from deteriorating quite so rapidly.

Sealing the deal

In areas where the climate gets unusually cold, we've actually seen unsealed brick on chimneys shatter. Water enters the pores of the brick, freezes, and then expands, causing the brick to explode.

You can prevent water seepage and the damage to bricks and mortar caused by freeze and thaw cycles by applying a coat of top-quality masonry sealer to all the brick or stone surrounding the fireplace and chimney. Apply the sealer with a pump garden sprayer, roller, or brush. Chimney sweeps usually keep masonry sealers in stock.

Arresting sparks and other hazards

A *spark arrestor* is a cage-like device with a solid cap, which is secured to the top of the chimney (see Figure 15-3). It prevents sparks and ash from escaping and causing a fire on the roof or on other potentially flammable substances. It also keeps squirrels, birds, and raccoons from nesting in the chimney. Nesting materials can cause a serious safety hazard; plus, the animals' droppings pose health risks, because diseases may be transmitted through fecal matter.

The solid cap — usually metal — prevents rainwater from entering the chimney. Rainwater can cause significant damage to the interior of a chimney by combining with the creosote to produce an acid that breaks down the flue lining and mortar. Rainwater also causes the damper to rust.

If your chimney doesn't have a spark arrestor, install one. If your chimney already has one, make sure that it's in good condition (no holes in the mesh and no rust or deterioration on the cap) and securely fastened to the top of the chimney. If you find holes (or if you accidentally make a hole or two while trying to remove rust with a wire brush), try patching the holes before replacing the entire unit. The method used to patch the spark arrestor screen is similar to the process used when patching a window screen, except that you use galvanized wire mesh rather than window screen material (see Chapter 6 for more information).

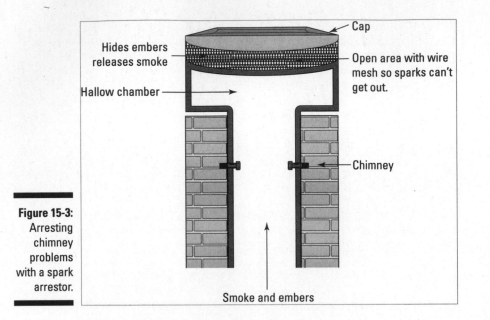

Cap

Hides embers releases smoke

Open area with wire mesh so sparks can't get out.

Hallow chamber

Chimney

Figure 15-3:
Arresting chimney problems with a spark arrestor.

Smoke and embers

You can patch a rusting chimney cap using a small piece of galvanized sheet metal that is slightly larger than the damaged area. Attach the patch using pop rivets. You'll need pop rivets, a pop-rivet gun, and an electric drill with a bit that corresponds to the size of the pop rivets. If rust is a problem, see Chapter 19 for tips on how to remove rust. After it's clean and repaired, paint the spark arrestor to prevent future rust and to slow deterioration.

Cleaning a Soot-Covered Brick Fireplace Face

Oils and soot make an otherwise handsome brick fireplace face look tired and tattered. To reduce the effect of oils and soot, regularly vacuum a brick face and hearth, and periodically wipe them down with a damp sponge. To prevent smoke from staining your fireplace face, elevate the fire by adding a layer or two of firebrick at the bottom of the firebox.

If the hearth is so soiled that you can no longer determine what material it's constructed from, then it's time for a more serious cleaning. All you need is a 10 percent solution of muriatic acid. (That's one part muriatic acid to nine parts water. Add the acid to the water, not the other way around.) Use a bristle brush to clean the affected area and rinse with fresh water. More than one application may be required for extra-dirty areas.

You can buy muriatic acid in the swimming-pool supplies section of your local hardware store, home center, or pool-supply store.

Working with acid is dangerous. Be sure to wear rubber gloves and safety goggles, and have plenty of ventilation.

Making the Most out of Glass Doors and Screens

A fireplace exhausts smoke in a sort of siphon action. When heat begins to rise through the stack, the siphon continues to draw air from within the house. The end result is that the draw in your fireplace can actually remove warm air from the home. And because fires burn oxygen, in a tightly sealed home, a fireplace drains a home of oxygen.

To offset both problems, do the following:

- ✔ **Install glass doors.** Glass doors act as dampers when the fireplace isn't being used and reduce the amount of warm air that is drawn out of the home and into the fireplace when a fire has been reduced to embers.

  Glass doors are designed for energy efficiency and not to prevent sparks from flying onto the carpet. Consequently, doors are left open when a fire is burning. There is an exception to this rule. Glass doors can be used as an added layer of protection when you need to leave the house while hot embers remain in the fireplace.

- ✔ **Add outside air ducts to the inside of the firebox.** Outside air ducts — also known as combustion air ducts — are required in the construction of all new fireplaces and can be retrofitted into existing ones. Outside air ducts provide air from the exterior of the home, leaving oxygen in the home for you to breathe. Naturally, if the fireplace draws air from ducts, it won't need to draw warm air from within the home.

  Periodically check these ducts to make sure that they're clean and free of spider webs and other debris.

Cleaning glass fireplace doors

Here is a neat trick that keeps glass fireplace doors clean and neat year-round:

1. **After the doors have cooled, spray them with glass or window cleaner or your own mixture of vinegar and water.**

2. **Spray a clean soft cloth until a wet spot is created.**

3. **Dip the wet spot into the fine gray ash left by your last fire and rub the ash onto the dirty surface.**

   The ash fills the microscopic pores of the glass, thus reducing the surface tension, making it easier to clean than ever before.

4. **After the ash has dried to a haze, buff the glass clear with a clean, dry cloth.**

Oven cleaner also works well for cleaning smoke-covered glass doors.

Make sure to wear rubber gloves and eye protection, have plenty of ventilation, and follow the manufacturer's instructions when working with oven cleaner.

Giving sluggish glass doors a pick-me-up

If your fireplace doors are operating less than smoothly, some cleaning, a little lubrication, or a slight adjustment usually fixes the problem.

Most doors can be raised and lowered or adjusted from side to side using a screwdriver or a small open-end wrench. Make a small adjustment and open and close the door until it operates smoothly. Lightly lubricate tracks, hinges, and other moving parts with a high-temperature lubricant (available from most fireplace dealers).

Because not all doors are alike (some are swinging, others are bi-fold), your best bet is to refer to the owner's manual for specific information on how to adjust the doors. If you're unable to find the manual, visit a local fireplace shop.

Screening out difficulties

A fireplace screen is essential for a safe fire. The mesh screen prevents sparks from flying onto the carpet or flooring in front of the fireplace and causing a fire.

Some screens are freestanding, others are bolted to the fireplace face, and still others are an integral part of the glass-door system. Although the freestanding models can be decorative, they offer the least amount of protection; we suggest replacing or augmenting a freestanding screen with one of the other alternatives available.

Most screens include a metal rod. As the screen and rod become dirty, the screen becomes increasingly difficult to operate. To keep the screen gliding smoothly, periodically vacuum the top of the screen and rod using an upholstery attachment, and then wipe with a damp sponge followed by a touch of high-temperature lubricant.

Just as with every other surface near the fireplace, the screen can develop a buildup of soot and oils from combustion. Rust can also be a problem. Although many cleaning products can cut the grease, some screens are just too dirty to be cleaned this way. If yours happens to be the latter, try either of the following (both are best performed in a bathtub or outdoors):

✔ **Use oven cleaner.** To get rid of rust on the screen, first remove as much rust as you can with a wire brush. (***Remember:*** Make sure to wear eye protection and gloves, and work in a well-ventilated area; outdoors is good.) Next, apply a light coat of oven cleaner to the entire surface of the screen. Allow the oven cleaner to do its thing, and then rinse thoroughly with fresh water. After the screen has dried, paint it with a heat-resistant, matte-black spray paint. Doing this every few years keeps your fireplace screen looking like new.

✔ **Use ammonia.** Remove the screens from the fireplace and place them in a large plastic trash bag. Pour in 1 cup of ammonia, seal the bag, and allow it to sit overnight. The ammonia takes all the elbow grease out of cleaning the screens. Remove the screens, rinse, and paint.

Chapter 16

Maintaining Your Home-Safety Systems

*I*n the following pages, we offer time-honored, proven safety practices blended with a host of new innovations, contemporary Carey Brothers' concepts, and the very best of today's high-tech, space-age, electronic wizardry. When all these measures are used together, they can give you greater peace of mind.

Preventing and Dealing with Household Fires

Fire has been a number-one household danger ever since the day, eons ago, when our prehistoric ancestors got the idea to bring fire indoors to heat their caves and cook their mammoths.

So what is your best defense against fire? Quite simply: good old common sense! Here are some specific strategies to employ in your home:

- ✔ Exercise great care with all flammable materials near high heat sources and be especially careful with combustible liquids (like solvents, cleaners and fuels), both when using and storing them.

- ✔ Keep space heaters at least 3 feet away from flammable items. Only buy units with tip-over shut-off switches, and never operate a space heater while sleeping.

- ✔ Don't overload electrical circuits or put too great a burden on individual outlets or lightweight extension cords.

- ✔ Don't use a bulb with a higher wattage than a lamp or fixture is rated for.

- ✔ Watch for faulty electronic equipment, malfunctioning appliances, frayed electrical cords, flickering lights, or fuses that blow and circuit breakers that trip repeatedly.

- ✔ Never smoke in bed or when you're tired or lying down, and make sure any ashes have cooled before you throw them away.

In this section, we tell you how to maintain your smoke detectors and fire extinguishers so that, if fire does strike, you and your family have the best possible chance of getting out of your house without harm.

Smoke detectors

Smoke detectors (also referred to as smoke alarms) are among the least expensive, and best, forms of protection you can buy. Check this out: A working smoke detector *doubles* your chance of surviving a fire.

For minimum coverage, have at least one smoke detector on every level of your home and in every sleeping area. Alarms can also be added to hallways outside every bedroom, the tops and bottoms of all stairways, and often-forgotten places such as basements, attics, utility rooms, and garages.

Battery-operated smoke detectors are inexpensive and easy to install. Make sure you check the batteries frequently.

AC-powered units are much more dependable than battery-powered detectors due to their direct-wired power source; they should be installed by an electrician or by someone with a good working knowledge of electricity. If you opt for an AC-powered unit, make sure you buy one that has an independent battery backup so it continues to operate when the power is interrupted (during a blackout or electrical fire, for example).

Regardless of which type of detector you have, follow these tips to maintain it properly:

- ✔ **Once a month, make sure the batteries and alarm are working.** Get up on a chair, or use a broom handle for extra reach, and push the test button. If you don't hear anything, your battery is probably dead. If after changing the battery, the smoke detector still isn't working, immediately replace it with a new one.

  All smoke detectors have a test button, which, when pushed, causes the alarm to sound. Also, most detectors have either a blinking or solid light that glows to let you know that the alarm is getting power.

- ✔ **Make sure the smoke detector is operating properly.** Once a month, put two or three lighted matches together (the wood kitchen type is best), and then blow out the flame, holding the matches so that the smoke wafts up toward the unit. (You may also use synthetic smoke in an aerosol can, which can be found at most hardware stores.) If the detector doesn't go off, and you've checked the batteries, replace the unit immediately.

- ✔ **Every six months, replace the batteries.** You can easily remember to replace the batteries if you replace them when the time changes to and from daylight saving time, in the spring and fall.

  Never remove a battery from your smoke alarm to use it in another item — like a radio, toy, or TV remote. First, you don't really know how much power those batteries still have. Second, you're likely to forget to replace it in the smoke alarm.

- ✔ **Brush or vacuum the alarm to keep dirt and dust out of the mechanism.** Do this at least four times per year or more often if you live in a dusty area. Never use cleaning sprays or solvents that can enter the unit and contaminate sensors.

- ✔ **After ten years of use, replace smoke detectors.** At that point, a smoke detector has endured more than 87,000 hours of continuous operation, and the internal sensors probably have become contaminated with dust, dirt, and air pollutant residues.

Fire extinguishers

Most fires start small. If you have a working fire extinguisher on hand, you may be able to easily and quickly put out a fire. Manufacturers of home safety products recommend having one fire extinguisher for every 600 square feet of living area. The kitchen, garage, and basement each should have an extinguisher, too. It's a good idea to keep one in your car, too.

When you're shopping for a fire extinguisher, be sure to purchase one that has a pressure gauge. Check the gauge once a month to ensure that you have a working extinguisher when you need it. If you find that the extinguisher's pressure is low, and it's a model that can't be recharged, dispose of it and replace it with a new unit.

By the way, we shouldn't have to tell you why "testing" an extinguisher by pulling the pin and squeezing the trigger is a bad, wasteful, and dangerous idea.

If you can't practice, though, how will you know how to use a fire extinguisher when you're faced with a fire? Remember this acronym: PASS.

- **P**ull the pin.
- **A**im at the base of the fire.
- **S**queeze the handle.
- **S**weep the base of the fire from side to side, starting with the closest edge and working away from yourself.

Preventing Carbon-Monoxide Poisoning

Carbon monoxide (CO) is the number-one cause of poisoning deaths in the United States. CO is an invisible, odorless, poisonous gas produced by the incomplete combustion of any fuel — such as gasoline, kerosene, propane, natural gas, oil, and even wood fires. CO in your home can be fatal, killing in minutes or hours, depending on the level of CO in the air. At low concentrations, CO produces a wide range of flu-like symptoms, including shortness of breath, mild nausea, and mild headache. At moderate concentrations, the symptoms are headache, dizziness, nausea, and light-headedness. At high concentrations, the "symptoms" are unconsciousness and death.

One telltale sign of mild CO poisoning is flu symptoms that go away when you're outside the home in fresh air.

The typical sources of CO in homes are malfunctioning gas furnaces, gas stoves, water heaters, clothes dryers, and even improperly vented fireplaces. Other major dangers include using a gasoline-powered generator in or too near the home, using a barbecue unit indoors (or in the garage) to cook or heat during a power outage, and letting a car run in the garage or carport where exhaust fumes can collect and enter the home. Making matters worse, many of today's energy-efficient homes minimize outside air exchange and cross-ventilation, giving CO no chance to exit once it enters the home.

Maintaining your carbon-monoxide detector

CO wafts through a room like perfume — only you can't smell or see it — which is why having a working CO detector in your home is critical. If you don't already have a CO detector, you should buy one. The Consumer Product Safety Commission (CPSC) recommends that every home with fuel-burning appliances of any kind be equipped with a least one CO detector. Place your CO detectors anywhere from 14 inches above the floor to eye level, and never where there is a draft (such as near a window, doorway, or stairwell).

If you have only one unit, place it in the hall outside the bedroom area of your home. Invisible, odorless, poisonous CO in concentrated form is far less likely to awaken someone who's sleeping than thick, toxic smoke is.

CO detectors can be battery operated, hard-wired, mounted directly in an electrical wall outlet, or plugged in to an electrical cord (which allows units to sit on a shelf or tabletop). If you use a unit that plugs in to a direct power source, make sure it also has an independent battery backup.

Your CO detector should have a digital display with memory that indicates and records a problem, even when it's too small to trigger the alarm. A normal low level of CO in a home is zero. Nada, zilch, zip. However, even a small reading — such as 25, 30, or 35 parts per million — indicates a problem that could escalate.

The care and maintenance of CO detectors is basically the same as for smoke detectors with regard to cleaning and frequent testing. (See the "Smoke detectors" section, earlier in this chapter, for more information.)

Because you can't test a carbon-monoxide detector using an outside source (the way you can light some matches under a smoke detector to see if it's working), you have to remember to press the test button on the CO detector once each month to make sure the detector is working.

Paying attention to sources of carbon monoxide

Don't mess around with CO. Once a year, have your heating system, vents, chimney, and flue inspected (and cleaned if necessary) by a qualified technician. And make sure that your fuel-burning appliances always are vented.

(See Chapter 10 for more information on heating and venting systems. Chapter 15 tells you all about chimney and flue inspections.)

Other maintenance procedures should include checking and correcting any signs that indicate potential CO problems, including:

- A noticeably decreasing hot-water supply
- A furnace that runs constantly but doesn't heat your house
- Soot collecting on, under, and around any appliance
- An unfamiliar burning odor
- A loose or missing furnace panel or vent pipe
- Damaged brick, chimney discoloration, or a loose-fitting chimney pipe

Keeping Your Natural-Gas Line Safe

Of all emergency preparedness efforts, gas lines deserve extra consideration — both in the event of natural disasters and for day-to-day living. Natural gas is the most potentially dangerous item in your home. Gas can cause instant flash fires and devastating explosions that can result from negligence and carelessness.

Gas lines must be properly installed, monitored, and maintained to prevent these catastrophes. Here's how:

- **Protect your gas meter.** An exposed gas meter is always susceptible to damage or being dislodged by contact. For protection from housework and gardening, and to keep gas meters located near driveways and sidewalks from being hit, place two heavy metal pipes in concrete (much like you would set a fence post) in front of and on both sides of the gas meter.

  Don't pour concrete or put asphalt around the rigid gas delivery pipe that comes up out of the ground leading to the meter. This pipe must remain in soft and pliable dirt to safely ride out any seismic activity.

- **Keep the gas-line shut-off wrench handy and easily accessible in a gas emergency.** Attach the wrench to the main line at the shut-off valve with a piece of chain and a hose clamp. If you ever have to close the main gas valve, you only need to rotate the bar on the valve one-quarter turn, so that it runs across the gas line (closed) rather than parallel to it (open).

- **Inspect all gas-line connections in your home.** Those leading to appliances, furnaces, and water heaters should only be a flexible, corrugated stainless steel or a new epoxy-coated flexible connector. You should see a shut-off valve where the gas line meets the solid gas delivery line.

If you have a rigid connection to your gas appliance, remove it and replace it with an approved flexible connector.

✔ **Always call before you dig.** There are many types of underground lines serving your home — from gas and electricity to water, telephone, and cable TV — and they're often only a few feet below the surface. So before you dig a ditch, sink a fence post, or plant a tree or bush, call your local utility companies to come out and mark where the lines are.

If you dig and hit your cable TV line, you face a slight inconvenience until the cable company can come out and repair the line. But if you hit a gas line, you may cause an explosion or fire.

Shining a Light on Electrical Safety

What are the signs of a potentially dangerous electrical problem? It's time to call the electrician when you see any of the following:

✔ Habitually flickering lights

✔ A breaker that repeatedly pops

✔ A fuse that repeatedly burns out

Any of these can signal a loose connection or an overloaded circuit, which ultimately can cause a house fire.

You should leave most electrical work to a qualified electrician.

The ground fault circuit interrupter (GFCI) was developed to help save people from getting shocked. When a short or ground fault occurs, the GFCI detects it. Any variation indicates that some of the current is going where it's not supposed to go and is creating a shock hazard. When this occurs, the GFCI trips in $1/40$ second — a short enough period of time so that most healthy people aren't injured.

Make sure that GFCIs are installed at all receptacles within 4 feet of a sink, at all exterior and garage receptacles, and at all electric fixtures over showers and tubs.

All GFCI receptacles have test buttons. Be sure to test each GFCI receptacle in your home once a month. If the test doesn't trip the breaker, replace the GFCI immediately.

Maintaining Your Burglar Alarm

Not all household dangers come from the inside. You also need to take measures to protect against those who would storm the castle, scale the proverbial stone walls, and plunder your family's treasures. A number of whole-house alarm systems are available today, and — just as with smoke detectors and carbon-monoxide detectors — these need occasional testing, checking, and tuning up:

Common sense measures to keep the bad guys at bay

A few simple guidelines can make your home as tight as the proverbial bug in a rug, affording you greater safety while you're home and when you're away:

✔ **Check all window and door locks to make sure that they're operating properly.** Install backup or secondary security locks and latches at vulnerable locations. Then use these simple protections — always.

✔ **Add a heavy-duty security storm door to outside doors.**

✔ **Toughen up sliding patio doors with pin locks and crossbars to deter forced opening.** A pin lock is a small barrel bolt that mounts on the floor against the interior of the sliding patio door frame. A thumb turn inserts the barrel or "pin" into a hole that you drill into the bottom of the center upright of the door frame. A crossbar is a fancy metal version of the wooden broom stick or closet pole that you lay in the door track to prevent the door from being opened. Instead of laying in the door track, the crossbar is attached to the interior of the sliding patio door frame (usually midway up the door) and abuts the sliding door, preventing it from being opened.

✔ **Trim back any thin shrubbery and bushes near windows and doors that may provide cover for a burglar's work-in-process.**

✔ **Add outdoor security lighting with a motion detector on/off control.** See *Home Improvement For Dummies,* by Gene and Katie Hamilton (Wiley Publishing), for more information on installing a motion detector.

✔ **Add metal security bars over windows and doors in high-risk areas, such as basement windows.** Make sure that these bars have quick-release safety latches for easy emergency escape for those inside.

✔ **Never hide a house key in an obvious location.** Even amateurs know most favorites, like under doormats, in flower pots, and inside fake rocks.

✔ **Close drapes and shades when you're out.** The goal is to prevent burglars from seeing that you're gone.

✔ **Always be on the lookout for unusual activity and new faces near your home.**

✔ **During the holidays, don't leave large displays of gifts and presents in plain view when you're out.** If your holiday involves decorating a tree, keep it well watered for fire safety, and unplug all indoor decorative lighting before leaving the house.

✔ **At least twice a year, check and replace the batteries in your alarm system.** Most alarm systems include a fail-safe battery backup.

✔ **Check the fire-sensing capability of your burglar alarm monthly.** Many systems have a fire-sensing capability; check and maintain it as outlined in the "Smoke detectors" section, earlier in this chapter.

✔ **Follow the manufacturer's instructions for maintaining and checking the keypad and the horn or siren.** Pay particular attention to all points that signal an intrusion when contact is broken.

✔ **Make sure sensitivity levels are properly set to avoid both frequent false alarms and a system that doesn't respond properly when it should.** If you experience frequent false alarms, you and your family will eventually start to ignore them — and you may ignore the alarm when you need to pay attention to it!

Before ordering and installing an alarm, check with local law-enforcement agencies to see about any restrictions or special ordinances in your area. Most police departments now discourage homeowners from installing a dialer-type alarm system that automatically calls the police or sheriff's department when activated because, during major disasters, this type of alarm completely swamps incoming lines that are needed to field calls for specific individual emergency situations.

A good alternative is to have your alarm monitored by a central reporting agency. Thus, if there is a false alarm, the police or sheriff won't be summoned, and you'll be off the hook for a false-alarm fee and the embarrassment of having the cops show up at your home only to find you in your bathrobe collecting the morning paper. Oops!

Testing the Safety Mechanisms in Your Automatic Garage-Door Opener

Garage doors are heavy, and they can close quickly, posing a danger to anyone or anything that happens to be under them when they come down. To address this safety issue, a federal law was passed in April 1982, requiring closing garage doors that are operated by automatic openers to reverse off of a 2-inch block (that is, the door must open if it meets even a small obstruction on the way down).

Even with the safety improvements mandated by the April 1982 legislation, injuries continued to occur, and safety remained an issue, resulting in a 1993 law requiring that a garage-door opener must be equipped with a monitored non-contact safety reversing device or safety edge that stops and reverses a closing garage door, such as:

- ✔ **An electronic-beam sensor that is installed at either side of the door opening:** When the beam is broken, the door stops and reverses itself.

- ✔ **A pressure-sensitive electronic rubber strip that attaches to the bottom of the door where it makes contact with the floor:** When the strip comes into contact with an object, the door automatically stops and reverses itself, avoiding injury or damage to property.

In addition to extending its life, monthly inspection and testing of the automatic opener can prevent serious injuries and property damage. Careless operation and allowing children to play with or use garage door opener controls are dangerous situations that can lead to tragic results. A few simple precautions can protect your family and friends from potential harm.

These tests are particularly important after any repairs or adjustments are made to the garage door or opener:

- ✔ **Test the force setting of the garage door opener, by using one of your hands to hold up the bottom of the door as it closes.** If the door doesn't reverse, the force is excessive and needs adjusting. Check your garage-door owner's manual — it explains how to adjust the force sensitivity.

- ✔ **Test the reversing mechanism and the pressure-sensitive rubber strip.** Place a 2-x-4-inch block of wood flat on the floor in the door's path before activating the door. If the door fails to immediately stop and reverse when it strikes the wood, disconnect the opener and use the door manually until the system can be repaired or replaced.

- ✔ **Test the electronic beam sensor.** Place a bucket or some other big object in the beam path, and activate the door. The door should not move. If it does, it needs to be repaired immediately.

- ✔ **Test the non-contact safety device.** Activate the door and wave a broom across the beam. The door should stop and reverse immediately. If it doesn't stop, it needs to be repaired immediately.

Never stand or walk under a moving door. Don't let children play "beat the door." Keep transmitters and remote controls out of reach of children and teach them that they are *not* toys. The push-button wall control should be out of reach of children (at least 5 feet from the floor) and away from all moving parts. The button should always be mounted where you can clearly see the door in full operation.

As with all mechanical components in a home, an automatic garage-door opener requires periodic maintenance to ensure safe and efficient operation. One of the best resources for garage-door maintenance is the opener owner's manual.

Maintaining your garage door

Here are common maintenance tasks that you can perform to keep your garage doors operating smoothly:

✔ **Visually inspect the garage-door springs, cables, rollers, and other door hardware.** Look for signs of wear and frayed or broken parts. Most minor repairs, such as roller replacement, can be performed by a handy do-it-yourselfer, while more complicated tasks should be handled by a qualified garage-door service technician. *Warning:* The springs and related hardware are under high tension and can cause severe injury when handled improperly.

✔ **Periodically lubricate the rollers, springs, hinges, and tracks.** Use spray silicone, lightweight household oil, or white lithium grease according to the instructions in your owner's manual.

✔ **Periodically test the balance of the door.** Start with the door closed. Disconnect the automatic-opener release mechanism so that the door can be operated by hand. The door should lift smoothly and with little resistance. It should stay open around 3 to 4 feet above the floor. If it doesn't, it's out of balance and should be adjusted by a professional.

If you don't have an owner's manual, you can usually order a replacement copy by contacting an installing dealer or the manufacturer. Some manufacturers make owner's manuals available on the Internet — all you need is the brand and model number.

Guarding Your Home against Natural Disasters

Natural disasters can befall the average home and typical family without warning. Earthquakes, tornadoes, hurricanes, floods, mudslides, blizzards, tidal waves, lightning, squalls, gales, downpours, monsoons, typhoons, whirlwinds, and microbursts can come out of nowhere and cause substantial damage to a home. You can't do anything about the weather, but you can be prepared for such emergencies — and being prepared may save your life and avert damage to your home.

The best defense against becoming a victim of a natural disaster is a strong offense — keeping your home in tip-top shape. For example, maintaining your roof can prevent shingles from being blown off and a roof leak from occurring. Installing a plumbing pipe heater can prevent hundreds or thousands of dollars in damage caused by a burst pipe due to freezing. The first step to shoring up your castle is to properly maintain your home everyday.

Your emergency preparedness kit

Once an emergency is upon you, it's too late to gather the things. So assemble the following beforehand:

✔ **A full first-aid kit:** Look for a kit that comes with instructions on how to deal with most major situations and injuries step by step. Also, watch for free first-aid training classes in your area, often sponsored by local organizations, hospitals, police departments, or fire departments.

✔ **Emergency food provisions and bottled water:** Check this kit twice a year for expiration dates and the freshness of the products it contains. When they expire, replace them.

✔ **Emergency gear:** You need a pair of sturdy shoes (to prevent injuries from rubble and broken glass), heavy socks, heavy work gloves, and clothing for keeping warm and dry for an extended period of time, both day and night. Make sure to include all these items for each member of your family. (You don't need heavy work gloves for your children, but they should have everything else.)

✔ **Portable and self-contained lighting:** You need flashlights, extra batteries, candles, a disposable butane lighter, and waterproof matches.

✔ **A radio:** How else will you hear the all clear?

When disaster is upon you

When your castle comes under siege from any of Mother Nature's natural marauders, three defensive maneuvers should take place in rapid succession:

1. **Go to your safe place.**

   Have a safe place ready in the home, such as a windowless room in the basement, and stock it with emergency survival supplies, including first-aid equipment, a radio, bottled water, and emergency food provisions. (See the nearby sidebar, "Your emergency preparedness kit.")

2. **Stay in your safe place until you get the all clear.**

   That's why you need the radio with functioning batteries! A portable phone (with extra batteries) can also come in handy at this stage.

3. **Check for damage.**

   First, check the status and well-being of your family members and nearby neighbors. Then begin a thorough home inspection to ascertain any damage that may create larger problems.

   Check especially for damaged power lines and dangerous gas leaks, which can cause fire and explosions. Next, check for electrical-system damage and downed power lines. If you see sparks, note exposed wiring, or smell overheated insulation on wiring, shut off the electricity at the main circuit breaker or fuse box. If water is present, be careful not to make contact if you suspect it may be electrically charged.

Also, ascertain any damage to water pipes and sewer drain lines. If they're damaged, turn off the main water-supply valve, avoid drinking any tap or well water, and don't flush toilets or let water drain from bathtubs, showers, and sinks.

Well in advance of any natural emergency, you should know where your valves and circuit breakers are located. Make sure that you know how to turn off all major supply lines, and show your family members how to do this, too. Many hardware stores and home centers sell an inexpensive combination dual-emergency wrench designed specifically for quick gas and water shut-offs.

For more information on disaster preparedness and recovery, go to the American Red Cross Web site at www.redcross.org.

Putting things back together

Follow these general guidelines for getting back underway after an emergency:

- ✓ **Deal cautiously with structural damage, watching for physical dangers (everything from broken glass and nails to water and wet surfaces that may be electrically charged after power resumes).** According to the American Red Cross, after drowning, the biggest flood killer is electrocution. Report downed power lines to your utility company or emergency management office.

- ✓ **Use a flashlight to inspect for damage.** Don't smoke or use candles, lanterns, or open flames unless you know that the gas has been turned off and the area has been aired out.

- ✓ **Prevent deadly carbon-monoxide poisoning by using a generator or other gasoline-powered machine outdoors and away from the home.** The same goes for camping stoves and charcoal grills.

- ✓ **Don't use appliances or motors that have gotten wet unless they've been taken apart, cleaned, and dried.** Some appliances, such as television sets, keep electrical charges even after they've been unplugged.

- ✓ **Watch for snakes and wild animals that have been flooded out of their homes.** They may seek shelter in yours.

- ✓ **Discard contaminated foods and kitchen and bath products, and boil drinking water until you're absolutely sure it's entirely safe to drink.**

✔ **Pump out flooded areas in your home as soon as possible to avoid permanent damage to the house frame.** Be sure to pump out your basement slowly over the course of several days to prevent the basement walls from caving in due to the excessive amount of pressure being placed on the walls from water-logged soil on the opposite side.

✔ **If hardwood floors get soaked, mop up excess water and debris immediately and dry the floors slowly to reduce warping.** Don't use heat for drying. (Drying finishes out too quickly can cause warping, buckling, and cracking that can otherwise be avoided if finishes are allowed to dry more slowly.) Open windows and doors and allow finishes to air-dry. Rent a high-volume fan such as those used by professional carpet cleaners to hasten the air-drying process.

✔ **If carpeting gets soaked, pick up excess water with a wet/dry vac or carpet-cleaning machine, slowly peel back wet carpet, and discard the padding.** Set up a box fan or two to completely dry the area. In most cases, carpets can be cleaned and reused; just the padding needs to be replaced.

✔ **Have a pro check all plumbing and service your septic tank.**

✔ **Call your insurance agent immediately to get the financial part of the recovery process underway.**

After immediate dangers are dealt with and relatively under control, take photos to record all damage to your home and its contents for insurance purposes. All too often, this only comes to mind once cleanup and repairs are well underway.

Part V

Out in the Great Wide Open

In this part . . .

The tale of Zorro and his mastery of swordsmanship has always thrilled us. That's probably why we got into construction — we had to find some way to be good at fencing.

Maintaining the inside of your home is only part of the equation. Outdoors there's more: the patio, driveway and walkways, decking, trellises, and, yes, fencing.

In this part, we show you how to care for everything outside, including patching, puttying, painting, staining, oiling, and caulking — tasks that add life and beauty to the outside of your home. And remember, Zorro did most of his fencing outdoors, too.

Chapter 17

Walkways, Patios, and Driveways

. . . .

In This Chapter

▶ Keeping concrete drives, paths, and patios clean and looking good

▶ Repairing concrete steps

▶ Painting and staining concrete

▶ Cleaning masonry and stone

. . . .

Rumor has it that Jimmy Hoffa's career ended one evening while wearing cement slippers. And because he hasn't been found, we can assume that the guys who mixed the concrete knew exactly what they were doing. But then again, they probably weren't too worried about the quality of their work. Most homeowners, however, are worried about the quality and condition of their concrete; specifically, they're concerned about cracks. Cracks are caused by ground movement — and that's what damages most concrete.

Although concrete bears the brunt of the traffic around most homes, masonry (brick and stone) often is used instead of, or in addition to, concrete for paths, patios, and walkways. And when they're not used on the ground, brick or stone almost always can be found as a decorative element on homes. Moreover, because concrete, brick, and stone are similar in composition, the materials and techniques used to clean and preserve one of them can, more often than not, be used to clean and preserve the others, so we've put them together in this chapter.

Whether your carport is concrete or your patio brick, cleaning, repairing, and sealing make them look good and last a long time.

Cementing Your Relationship with Concrete

This may come as a surprise to you: Your sidewalk, driveway, patio, and paths are not made of cement. Instead, they're made of concrete, which contains cement — Portland cement to be exact. Basic concrete is a mixture of rock, sand, and cement. In combination with the oxygen in water, the three dry elements bond together to make good old-fashioned concrete. You know, the stuff with cracks — the cracks you're always trying to patch.

By the way, although Portland cement was purportedly invented by Joseph Aspdin, a builder in Leeds, England, who obtained a patent for it in 1824, the use of cementing materials goes back to the ancient Egyptians and Romans. It is said to have been dubbed "Portland cement" due to its resemblance to limestone found on the Isle of Portland, England.

The following sections explain how to perform common concrete maintenance and repair tasks.

Cleaning off grease and oil stains

You probably let your vehicle rest in a garage, carport, or driveway when you're not driving it. Depending upon the mechanical condition of your vehicle, oil and grease spots soon begin to decorate the concrete in these areas. If this situation sounds familiar, you'll be pleased to know that we have a cleanup formula for you — a couple of formulas actually, depending upon the severity of the stains. In either case, wait until the area is shaded to prevent the cleaning solution from drying out too quickly.

Plan A: Using our Soda-Pop Concrete Stain Remover

This first formula may cause your neighbors to wonder whether you're playing with a full deck of cards. However, you'll soon be the envy of the neighborhood when you have the cleanest driveway on the block.

Gather the following items:

- A small bag of cat litter
- A few cans of a cola beverage (diet or regular)
- A nylon brush or stiff-bristle broom
- A mixing bucket
- Powdered laundry detergent (ammonia free)
- Liquid chlorine bleach
- Eye protection and rubber gloves
- A garden hose and running water

Then follow these steps:

1. **Completely cover the grease or oil with a thin layer of the cat litter and grind it in using the soles of your shoes.**

2. **Sweep up the cat litter and pour on enough cola beverage to cover the entire area.**

Don't just throw the oil and grease-laden cat litter in the garbage can — dispose of it as you would used motor oil, paint, or other potentially hazardous chemicals. If you're not sure how to dispose of such materials, call your local waste-management company for advice about the rules in your area.

3. **Work the cola into the affected area with a scrub brush or bristle broom, making sure to keep the entire area damp with cola. Then leave it on for about 20 minutes or until it has stopped fizzing, but don't permit it to dry.**

4. **Rinse off the cola with fresh water.**

You should see a gray stain.

5. **Scrub the gray stain with a solution of 1 cup liquid chlorine bleach, 1 cup powdered laundry detergent, and 1 gallon of very hot water.**

Make sure the detergent you use is ammonia free. Mixing ammonia with bleach creates a lethal gas, similar to mustard gas.

Plan B: Muriatic acid

If Plan A (see the preceding section) doesn't do the trick, then it's time to bring out the big gun — muriatic acid. Make a solution of one part muriatic acid to nine parts water, adding the acid to the water (not the other way around).

Working with muriatic acid is dangerous! Wear eye protection, put on rubber gloves to protect your hands and arms, and make sure that there's plenty of ventilation. Do *not* attempt this project when children or animals are present.

After you carefully mix the acid solution, follow these steps:

1. **Pour the solution over the area and work it in using a nylon scrub brush or stiff-bristle broom.**

Be careful not to splash — you don't want to damage the surrounding area.

2. **Flush the entire area with fresh water after the solution has stopped fizzing — about ten minutes.**

More than one treatment may be necessary for those stains that only professional race-car drivers can appreciate.

By the way, just before you clean your concrete is the perfect time to get that leaky engine fixed!

Cleaning up mildew: No slip slidin' away

Mildew is a fungus that grows as a surface mold on virtually any material (inside and outside of the home). Dormant mildew spores are in the air almost everywhere, and all they need to develop and prosper is a warm, damp environment, which they often find on your concrete.

In addition to its potential for causing falls, its unsightly appearance, and its often fierce odor, medical studies have shown that mildew can cause a variety of physical ailments as well, including respiratory problems, headaches, nausea, fevers, backaches, high blood pressure, and fatigue.

Many years ago, we discovered a foolproof formula to clean off mildew on all kinds of surfaces. This formula was developed by the same agency that gave us the $750 toilet seat — the U.S. government! Actually, credit should go to the U.S. Department of Agriculture's Forest Products Laboratory. Although this formula has no problem zapping mildew on concrete, it can also be used on any (non-colorfast) painted or washable surface, inside or outside.

To use this all-surface, easy mildew remover, follow these steps:

1. **Add 1 quart liquid chlorine bleach to 3 quarts warm water; then add $\frac{1}{3}$ cup powered laundry detergent.**

   Even though this solution is mild, make certain to wear safety goggles and rubber gloves, and have plenty of ventilation.

   Use ammonia-free detergent. You never want to mix bleach with ammonia because the combination of the two creates a lethal gas.

2. **Apply the solution to the affected areas using the broom.**

   Leave the mixture on long enough for the black or green stains to turn white, but don't allow it to dry — 15 minutes should be long enough.

3. **Rinse the entire area with fresh water.**

Ponding water is a primary source of mildew, so to prevent the return of mildew, make sure that you have good drainage off of your concrete surfaces. And because sunlight is a major enemy to mildew, prune and thin trees and shrubbery that shelter concrete surfaces. Proper cleaning helps fight the battle against mildew, while taking preventive steps helps win the war!

Turning up the pressure clean

When tough stains aren't the issue, and you just want to give your concrete a good once-over cleaning, use a pressure washer to eliminate the required elbow grease. You can clean just about anything with a pressure washer, including roofing, siding, window screens, decking, fencing, cars, boats, even concrete! You name it, a pressure washer will blast it clean.

Today, most home-improvement retailers stock a full line of pressure washers that range from what we classify as "toys" to heavy-duty, industrial-strength models. For a few hundred dollars, you can get all the power you need. When shopping for a pressure washer, consider the following:

✔ **The means by which the tool is powered — either by gas or electricity:** We prefer the freedom that the gas models offer; they eliminate the need to string electrical cords, especially when working in the back-40, pressure-washing a fence. The disadvantage of a gas model is that you need to fuss with gasoline and oil.

✔ **How much power you want:** Pressure washers are rated in cleaning units, or CUs. The more cleaning units, the more powerful the machine. A CU rating of 2,000 to 9,000 units is ample for virtually any do-it-yourself household-cleaning task.

Patching cracks

Aside from sprucing up the exterior appearance of your house, repairing cracks and holes in concrete also prevents water damage and improves safety. Cracks in concrete can allow water to travel into areas where it isn't invited — like a crawlspace or your basement, which can wreak havoc. Furthermore, cracks, potholes, and uneven concrete are notorious causes of nasty falls. Did you ever stop to think that a little concrete maintenance could keep you out of court as the defendant in a personal-injury case?

Frequently, extensive or severe cracks in concrete are the result of a soil condition that needs attention. For example, an inordinate amount of water may exist in the soil beside or below a path or foundation, causing the soil to expand and the concrete to crack. All the cosmetic crack repairs in the world won't correct a drainage problem like that, one that probably will result in more severe damage if left uncorrected. Address excessive moisture due to over-watering or poor drainage before making any crack repairs. Standing water, mold- and mildew-laden walls and siding, cracks in walks and walls, and difficult-to-open doors and windows are telltale signs of poor drainage.

After you take care of any long-standing drainage needs, turn to Chapter 4 for instructions on patching concrete using one of our favorite tools — vinyl concrete patch.

Only banana peels should cause slips and falls on concrete

If your concrete is clean, but it's still slippery when wet, you should slightly etch the surface using a 25 percent solution of muriatic acid. The acid removes a very, very thin layer of cement, which exposes the sand in the concrete, creating a rougher surface. The finish is similar to medium- to fine-grit sandpaper.

Simply pour the solution onto the concrete and let it stand for approximately 15 minutes before flushing the entire area with water. Allow the concrete to dry to determine if the new finish meets your expectations. More than one application may be required to achieve a coarser surface.

Warning: Muriatic acid is dangerous stuff! Refer to "Plan B: Muriatic acid," earlier in this chapter, for safety information you'll need when working with muriatic acid.

On steps, consider installing peel-and-stick, nonskid tread tape. You can purchase the tape by the foot in various widths at most home-improvement retailers. If the nonskid tread tape doesn't appeal to you, consider the newest kid on the block: a nonskid material that can be painted onto a surface. The result is essentially the same. The main difference is that, with the painted-on variety, you can customize the size by using masking tape and applying the material within the perimeter of the tape.

Got a small crack in a highly visible place? Using a masonry drill and a tube of clear or gray silicone caulk, you can easily mix up a concrete patching compound that will leave the crack virtually invisible. Follow these steps:

1. **Gather some concrete dust from your driveway.**

   Find an out-of-the-way spot in your cracked patio or step, such as just below the grade. Place a small, flat, metal pan underneath where you plan to drill. Use a masonry drill bit to drill a hole in the hidden area, and collect the dust coming out of the hole.

2. **Apply a bead of caulk to the top of the crack you want to repair.**

3. **While the caulk is still fresh, sprinkle the masonry dust over the crack and work it into the caulk with your finger.**

4. **Sweep away the excess dust and — *voilà!* — no more crack!**

Sealing concrete

Concrete is quite porous and acts like a sponge. When temperatures drop and concrete is wet, it can freeze, causing cracking and *spalling* (chipping). Rock salt used to melt snow is another primary source of deterioration of concrete.

You can minimize this damage by periodically sealing the concrete with an acrylic or silicone-based concrete and masonry sealer. A liquid concrete sealer prevents water absorption by filling the pores of the concrete. A concrete sealer lasts for six months to a year, depending upon the quality of the material, surface preparation, and climate.

Inexpensive "water seals" don't offer the level of protection that some of the pricier products do. Moreover, poor-quality sealers need to be applied again and again, and can end up costing more money in the long run.

You apply concrete sealers with a brush, roller, or pump garden sprayer. Before you begin, clean the concrete using the concrete cleaning tips mentioned earlier in this chapter.

Concrete childhood lessons

Like many children, we walked to and from school. Unlike our parents, we didn't have to walk 10 miles uphill both ways through sleet, snow, high winds, and what-have-you. However, we did have to drag ourselves a good honest mile.

Walking to and from school was one of our favorite parts of the day. We went from store to store along the main street in our little town, greeting each shopkeeper, and admired the wares. Because candy and toys were our favorites, we allowed extra time for the toy store and the corner drugstore. Believe it or not, we even found time to pop into the local hardware store, although it was off the beaten path. You see, our fascination with tools and building stuff began at a tender age.

Aside from window-shopping, one of our favorite diversions was a game that involved the lines and cracks in the concrete sidewalk, and how to avoid stepping on them — at all costs. If we stepped on a line, it would break our mother's spine, and if we stepped on a crack, it would surely break her back. Fortunately, although we accidentally set foot on many a line and crack, Mom's back never suffered in the least.

As adults, we've learned that cracks in concrete don't break your mother's back, but they can be the cause of a nasty fall. Yikes! A little concrete maintenance from time to time can save big time on repair bills and perhaps even doctor bills.

You can minimize damage caused by rock salt by rinsing the area with hot water to remove the majority of salt. Of course, unless you live in a temperate climate, you have to wait until spring to do this task.

Painting your concrete

Paint remains a popular finish for concrete porches, patios, paths, garages, carports, and basements. Painting concrete is a great idea — if the paint will stick to the concrete. You can increase the stick-to-itiveness with thorough cleaning and prep, but there are certain conditions — such as moisture — over which you simply don't have control. *Hydrostatic pressure* (moisture wicking up from below the concrete) can prevent even the best of finishes from sticking.

You can determine whether moisture is a problem by taping a 1-foot-square piece of plastic (such as a garbage bag) to the concrete. Leave it there at least 24 hours, and then remove it. If a damp spot appears where the plastic was placed or there is condensation on the underside of the plastic, paint won't stick. Consider using a clear acrylic concrete sealer (see the preceding section) or latex concrete stain (see "Staining your concrete — intentionally," later in this chapter), both of which allow moisture vapors to escape, thus improving the odds that the finish will stick.

Types of concrete paint

Three basic types of paint are available for concrete:

- ✔ **Latex:** Latex paint is the most widely used. It has excellent adhesion properties, allows water vapor to escape (prohibiting blistering and peeling), and is the most user-friendly to apply because it cleans up with water.

- ✔ **Oil-based paints:** Oil-based paints are still a favorite for porches and patios. They offer a harder, shinier, and more abrasion-resistant finish.

- ✔ **Epoxy:** Epoxy is the crème de la crème of concrete paint. It's the most durable and longest lasting. Epoxy is especially popular in basements as a means of controlling dampness. Epoxy paints generally consist of two parts which, when combined, create a chemical reaction that results in an above-average bond and highly abrasion-resistant finish.

Unfortunately, chemists haven't yet developed a paint that won't eventually sustain damage from the hot tires of cars. Over time, all types of concrete paint will bubble, peel, or chip when they suffer the wear and tear of car tires.

Doing the job right

Don't be in a hurry to paint freshly poured concrete. For best adhesion, let the concrete cure for 60 to 90 days before painting. Existing concrete is ready to go when you are.

Here are the step-by-step instructions:

1. **If necessary, remove any flaking, peeling paint on previously painted surfaces, using a chemical remover, sandblaster, or mechanical abrader.**

2. **Clean the surface.**

   Grit, grease, oil, and other contaminants inhibit the paint from sticking. (For cleaning instructions, see our concrete cleaning tips earlier in this chapter.

   If you have rust stains on your concrete, try using a concrete cleaner that contains phosphoric acid. You can buy it in liquid or jelly form.

3. **Lightly etch the surface using a 25 percent solution of muriatic acid.**

   Etching helps the paint stick better. Simply pour the solution onto the concrete, spread it out evenly, and let it stand for approximately 15 minutes. Then flush the entire area with water. (See the sidebar "Only banana peels should cause slips and falls on concrete" for more information on working with this acid.)

4. **Using a medium-to-long-nap roller cover and a nylon/polyester brush or paint pad to cut in the edges, apply concrete floor paint using the method required by the type of paint you choose:**

   - **Latex paint:** Most latex concrete floor paints are designed to be applied directly to raw concrete. Apply a first coat as a primer and a second coat to get a full and uniform finish.

   - **Oil-based paint:** These paints should be applied over a coat of oil-based concrete or masonry filler/primer (thin the primer slightly using mineral spirits to enhance the penetration and improve the bond). (*Note:* You can apply an oil-based paint over an existing oil finish, as long as the existing finish is clean and has been de-glossed with tri-sodium-phosphate [TSP] or a similar liquid paint de-glosser.) After the primer dries, apply the finish coat. Use mineral spirits for cleanup.

   - **Epoxy paints:** Epoxy typically comes in two parts that you mix together prior to application. The mixture creates a chemical reaction that makes the finish bond with the concrete for a long-lasting, durable finish.

Compared to other, more-forgiving finishes, the surface prep must be especially thorough when using epoxy, so be sure to follow steps 1 through 3 to the letter. There isn't much of a margin of error when it comes to working with epoxy.

Two to three coats of epoxy — with about 16 hours of dry time between coats — should provide a finish that will outlast you. Read the instructions on the package for specific application instructions.

Whatever type of paint you use, don't clean the surface one weekend and apply the paint the next. You don't want a week's worth of dirt and contamination to ruin the new coat of paint.

For extra protection, use paint that contains a *mildewcide* (a fungicide that prevents mildew and other fungi from growing on painted surfaces). Although mildewcide is added to many paints during manufacturing, you can add it after the fact if the paint you're using doesn't contain it — just ask about your options wherever you buy paint.

Staining your concrete — intentionally

Besides concrete floor paints, there also are concrete stains. Concrete stains are much thinner than paint so they penetrate the surface more thoroughly for better adhesion. When dry, stained concrete resembles pigmented concrete rather than a painted finish. On the other hand, because it's so thin, concrete stain is not nearly as abrasion-resistant as concrete paint, so it must be applied more frequently. Dang!

As with painting prep, the concrete should be cleaned and lightly acid-washed for maximum penetration (refer to steps 1 through 3 in the preceding section). Then mix the stain in a 5-gallon bucket and mop or roll it onto the concrete.

Repairing concrete steps

Patching crumbling concrete steps enhances the appearance and safety of your home for a fraction of the cost of new stairs. And the best part is that it's a task that most do-it-yourselfers can handle with ease.

As the weakest point of construction, the step's edge is most vulnerable to damage. Expansive soil, freeze and thaw cycles, *efflorescence* (a white powdery substance that results from mineral salts leaching to the surface of concrete; see Chapter 4), and deterioration from salt and traffic are a few of the causes of crumbling concrete stairs.

ANECDOTE

Memories from our little red porch

We grew up in a home built around the turn of the 20th century by our boat-builder-turned-contractor grandfather. Several generations were raised in that home. It boasted traditional Mediterranean architecture, a reflection of our grandfather's European roots.

Much to our chagrin, our old family home is no longer. It was sacrificed in the name of progress. (Our city called it "urban renewal.") Out with the old, in with the new. A significant piece of the hearts and souls of all the members of our family died the day that our old family home fell prey to the ravenous jaws of the indiscriminate bulldozer. All that remains some 25 years later are memories, fond memories.

Our home stood proud among those in our neighborhood. It consisted of a towering (from the eyes of children) two stories with a large basement. The building had a beige dashed plaster exterior, a red S-shaped tile roof, and vast archways flanked by stately sculpted columns. There were lots of windows, a multi-light radius-top entry door, generous architectural ornamentation, two spacious verandas at the second floor, and an ample front porch that was the first to greet each visitor to our home.

Some of the most vivid memories of our old home took place on that front porch. Many a family gathering was held there. Although the arid climate necessitated it, air conditioning was something reserved for more modern homes. Instead, we sought refuge from the sweltering heat swinging to and fro on the canvas-clad bench swing.

The porch, located a half-dozen steps above the street, was constructed of concrete and finished with a deep red paint. It was that porch wherein we had our first experience with painting. It needed a fresh coat every few years. How rewarding it was to admire our workmanship and to enjoy praise from the family!

We'll never forget that handsome red porch at our old family home. It's been 30 years since its last painting and, in our minds, it's as bright and fresh-looking as the day it was last painted.

REMEMBER

Crumbling steps frequently result from what were once small cracks that were not tended to. You can prevent most of the damage to steps by caulking, which allows the concrete to expand and contract yet prevents moisture from entering the area.

To repair concrete stairs, you need these supplies:

- Sledgehammer
- Cold chisel
- Safety goggles
- Mixing container
- Shovel

✔ Garden hose

✔ Concrete finishing trowel

✔ *Wooden float* (a wooden trowel used to tamp and work the concrete into place)

✔ Small piece of ³/₄-inch plywood to act as a form board

✔ Concrete bonding agent

✔ Ready-to-mix concrete patch material (or epoxy patch material)

✔ Tarp or plastic sheeting

✔ 1 quart of clean motor oil or concrete form-release oil

✔ At least four bricks (more may be needed)

Follow these steps to get your steps feet-worthy:

1. **Remove the loose and crumbling concrete with a sledgehammer and cold chisel. (Be sure to wear safety goggles!) Then sweep up all the debris and clean the area with the strong spray of a garden hose.**

   Isn't it just like a home fix-it expert to suggest breaking something the rest of the way before making a repair? It seems paradoxical, but to successfully repair a concrete stair — or anything else made of concrete — you must first completely remove all loose pieces and make sure that what remains is solid.

2. **Paint the raw patch area with a concrete bonding agent and allow it to set up for about 15 minutes.**

   The bonding agent is a glue that helps the new patch material adhere to the old, cured concrete.

3. **Use a circular saw or handsaw to cut a scrap piece of plywood equal to the height of the step and a few inches longer than the damaged area at either end.**

   You'll set this form board flush against the face of the step to hold the concrete patch material into place until it's fully cured.

4. **Apply a light coat of clean motor oil or form release oil on the surface of the form board facing the concrete to prevent the form from sticking and damaging the patch when removed.**

5. **Place the form flush against the face of the steps for a smooth patch.**

   The bottom of the form board should fit flat against the top of the step below.

6. **Use several bricks to hold the form boards firmly in place (see Figure 17-1).**

Figure 17-1:
Propping up
the board
with some
bricks.

7. **Mix the concrete patch material.**

   Vinyl concrete patch and polymer cement are the most popular concrete patching products because they're easy to use and they blend well with the old material. Though more expensive, epoxy patch material is the best money can buy. It's stronger and holds better — the result of a chemical reaction among the ingredients of the adhesive. The consistency of the patch material should be loose, but not runny.

8. **Using the wood float, pack the material firmly into the area, being sure to eliminate any air pockets.**

   The butt end of the float works great for this.

9. **Remove excess patch material with a wooden float and finish the patch to match the surrounding concrete with a metal concrete trowel.**

10. **When the material starts to set up (in approximately 10 to 30 minutes), cover it with a tarp or sheet of plastic.**

    Doing so holds moisture in. If the material dries too fast, it may crack or not adhere securely.

Most exterior concrete surfaces have a slightly rough finish to prevent slipping when wet. The most common finish is the broom finish. After the patch has become firm, brush it lightly once (and just once) with a broom. Or, for a small patch, use a stiff paintbrush.

11. **Until the patch has completely dried (which can take up to a week), remove the cover once a day and spray the patch with a fine mist of water and then replace the cover.**

    Leave the form board in place during the drying process to reduce the prospect of damage resulting from form removal or foot traffic.

12. **Complete the job by carefully removing the form boards, stakes, and bricks.**

Getting Things on an Even Keel

If you walk across your brick or stone path or patio and you feel as if you're on a ship on the high seas, chances are good that a little leveling is in order. Unlike a poured-in-place concrete path or patio that might need to be jack-hammered out, a brick or stone patio is one big jigsaw puzzle embedded in a layer of sand. Consequently, this is a project that you can easily do yourself by selectively removing pieces of the puzzle, shoring up the sub-base, and reinstalling the pieces. The real beauty of this project is that it can be done a section at a time, and you can take as long as you want to complete your work. It's not like you have a slab of wet concrete that must be finished before it dries hard as a rock! A few tools and a little time and it'll be smooth sailing.

Leveling settled brick patios and walkways

As a couple we know demonstrated when the repair of their sinking brick patio was featured on *Ask This Old House,* leveling and resetting a brick patio is slow, heavy work. Fortunately, it's not a complex project — just one that takes time and effort to do right.

You need the following:

- ✔ Chalk
- ✔ Crayon

- Small pry bar
- Shovel
- Hand tamper
- Rubber mallet
- 4-foot level
- Measuring tape
- Broom
- Crushed limestone
- Coarse sand
- Fine sand

Then follow these steps:

1. **Use chalk to mark out the settled area.**

2. **Starting in the middle of that area and working toward the edge, use a small pry bar to remove the whole bricks and stack them neatly nearby.**

3. **Number any partial, cut bricks using a light-colored crayon.**

   Don't use chalk — it'll rub off and make resetting a nightmare.

4. **When all the settled area's bricks are removed, explore what's underneath.**

   You should find sand. And under that you may find crushed limestone or compacted gravel. But it's more likely that you'll find dirt or clay underneath.

5. **If you find dirt or clay that's wet or loose underneath the brick, dig it out until you find solid earth.**

6. **Fill the now-low areas of the bed with crushed limestone and compact it thoroughly using a hand tamper.**

   Your wrists and hands will never be the same!

7. **Use a level to see where the top of the reset bricks will be; then use more crushed limestone (tamp it down good!) to fill the bed until there are 3 inches between the bottom of the level and the top of the bed.**

   Most patio bricks are 2 inches thick, and you want to leave room for 1 inch of sand underneath.

8. **Add 1 inch of sand, and then double-check that you still have 2 inches for the bricks.**

9. **Reset the bricks you removed earlier, working from the middle outward. Be careful to maintain the original pattern.**

   Be sure to put them in straight down to avoid jamming sand between them and messing up the spacing. Whack each brick hard a couple of times with a rubber mallet to make sure they're securely set.

10. **Sweep fine sand into the joints to fill the gaps and to lock the now-level bricks in place.**

    Save some sand to sweep in after the next rain.

Leveling and resetting stone paths

The process for fixing a sinking, uneven brick sidewalk or stone path is the same as it is for a settled patio (see the preceding section). However, in our experience, you're more likely to find just dirt underneath. Our advice when you find no stabilizing stone/sand base: Pull the whole thing up and start fresh with a proper substrate. That way you won't have to fix it again in two years . . . and then every two years after that.

Recoating an asphalt driveway

Few home-maintenance projects are easier than sealing an asphalt driveway. Mostly you need a strong back to maneuver the big, heavy buckets of sealer.

You need these supplies:

- Putty knife
- Broom
- Clean and sturdy stirring stick
- Squeegee or roller
- Hose
- Asphalt caulk
- Asphalt patch
- Asphalt sealer

When you've gathered everything you need, follow these steps:

1. **Check the weather forecast to make sure the temperature will stay above 50 degrees and there'll be no rain for the next 36 hours.**

   Cool temperatures and excessive moisture interfere with adhesion and drying.

2. **Remove debris from any large cracks using a putty knife, and thoroughly sweep the entire surface with a push broom.**

3. **Fill all cracks more than $\frac{1}{4}$ inch wide with asphalt caulk.**

   You need to use asphalt patching material to patch bigger cracks. Smaller cracks can be filled by the sealer.

4. **Prepare the surface by spraying it with water to remove any dust. Clean oil spots using one of the methods described in the "Cleaning off grease and oil stains" section, earlier in this chapter.**

5. **Allow the driveway to fully dry.**

6. **Get the sealer ready.**

   Drag the big, heavy buckets of sealer onto the driveway. Without opening them, flip them upside-down to allow the heavier goop to sink toward the top; then flip them back, crack them open, and stir thoroughly with a sturdy, clean stick. Put the lid back on the now-stirred sealer and drag one of the big, heavy buckets of sealer to your starting point.

7. **Pour out only as much sealer as will coat about 20 square feet (you'll figure out how much that is pretty quickly); then use the roller or squeegee to spread the coating across the driveway using overlapping strokes.**

   Two things to keep in mind as you apply the sealer:

   • Stir the sealer as you apply it to ensure its consistency.

   • A thick coat is not better than a thin coat.

8. **Keep dragging the big, heavy buckets around and doing 20 square feet at a time until you're done.**

   Be careful not to slop sealer onto the sidewalk or street.

9. **Let the sealer dry for at least 24 hours, and preferably 48 hours.**

   During the drying time, stay off the driveway. Put the empty buckets at the end of the driveway to prevent visitors from driving on your freshly coated and very, very handsome driveway.

For the Love of Masonry

One of our favorite children's stories is "The Three Little Pigs." In fact, we credit, to some degree, our early interest in construction to our early interest in that book. After all, the story is about three pigs who delve in to construction as owner-builders. And like most construction projects, they had their share of headaches. Enter the Big Bad Wolf! Obsessed with having a delectable ham dinner, he tried to destroy the pigs' homes.

Sadly, he was successful in demolishing the first two homes — constructed of straw and wood, respectively. However, the third little pig used brick to build his home, which foiled the wolf. Huff and puff all he might, the wolf couldn't blow down the house built of bricks. And he wouldn't have been any more successful with a home built of stone.

The only difference between brick and stone: Reinforced brick is structural, and stone is primarily decorative. However, when it comes to cleaning, repairing, and sealing, the techniques and materials used for brick and stone are the same.

We have yet to see a real, live wolf attempt to blow down a house. But efflorescence, salt air, stress cracks, and severe weathering can be as big a threat. Chapter 4 tells you how to deal with efflorescence. The following sections explain how to handle the other problems.

Dealing with stress cracks

Stress cracks typically occur in mortar joints rather than within the brick or stone itself. If stress cracks in mortar are the problem, see Chapter 4 for the lowdown on tuck-pointing.

If the problem is a cracked or broken stone or brick, you can remove it by chiseling out the mortar surrounding it. With the mortar out of the way, the brick or stone will have room to expand and can be broken up easily using a cold chisel and a small sledgehammer. Just insert a new brick or stone into the hole to replace the one removed. Then finish the job by mortaring around the brick or stone for a solid fit.

When a new mortar patch dries and doesn't match the existing shade or color, have a small amount of latex paint color-matched to the existing mortar. Use an artist's brush to paint the new mortar joints. No one will ever know where the existing material ends and the new work begins — including you!

Cleaning your masonry

The most common masonry-cleaning problems are:

- **Fungus, moss, and mildew:** One quart of household liquid bleach mixed into 1 gallon of warm water, applied with a stiff-bristle brush, usually takes care of these unsightly problems. (Don't forget to rinse the solution off with clean water.) However, sodium hypochlorite, the active ingredient in bleach, may not dissolve large masses of these types of growths. In such cases, scrape off as much of the crud as you can with a broad-bladed putty knife (or wire brush); then scrub on the killer mixture.

  When trying to eliminate fungus, it's the bleach that does the job — not the elbow grease. Make sure you give the bleach plenty of time to work before scrubbing and rinsing away. If not, fungus spores will remain and can grow back quickly.

- **Oils, soot, and mineral residue:** Oils, soot, and white, powdery mineral residue pose a slightly more difficult problem. They're embedded more deeply than moss or mildew into the pores of the masonry. You need a solution of 1 part muriatic acid to 9 parts water to get rid of this hard-to-remove crud. Add the acid to the water and apply the solution; allow it to set for about 15 minutes; then use a bristle brush to clean the affected area and rinse with fresh water. (If soot is the problem, head to Chapter 15 for ideas on how to get rid of it.)

- **Paint:** Sandblasting, wash-away, or peel-off paint removers; hand or electric wire brushing; muriatic acid washing; and power-washing are just a few of the ways that you can remove paint from masonry. Sandblasting or wire brushing is hard, messy work, and paint removers sometimes create more mess than they eliminate. Instead, we recommend power-washing. You can rent a commercial power washer for about $50 per day. It's easy to operate, mess is kept to a minimum, and you don't have to be a chemist to make it work. Be aware, however, that a power washer works fine on the outside of your home, but all that water could wreak havoc on the inside of your house. Therefore, when it comes to removing paint from brick or stone, your best bet is a chemical stripper such as Peel Away (see Chapter 15).

Applying a sealer

Applying a sealer can minimize brick or stone damage from salt air and severe weathering. It can even work to prevent efflorescence. Just as you would with concrete, you need to thoroughly clean your brick and stone before applying a sealer. See "Sealing concrete" earlier in this chapter for information on what you need to perform this task.

Chapter 18

Decks, Fences, and Retaining Walls

In This Chapter

▶ Doing right by your deck

▶ Taking care of fencing

▶ Maintaining your retaining wall's health

*E*ventually, everything on the planet deteriorates. However, some building materials last longer than others. For example, stone, brick, plaster, concrete, and aluminum (discussed elsewhere in this book) last a long time and require little or no maintenance. On the other hand, wood and wood-based composites must be regularly maintained and protected with paint or a preservative to achieve lasting quality. Why? Because wood is highly susceptible to damage caused by moisture and the sun's ultraviolet rays, whereas the other building materials aren't nearly as fragile.

So given wood's need for maintenance, why is it used in building construction? Simple: Wood is beautiful, available, very inexpensive (compared to all the alternatives), and really easy to work with.

Because of wood's susceptibility to fungus and rot, and its need for regular and ongoing maintenance, we discuss wood maintenance in great detail in this chapter. You can easily deal with wood's shortcomings and prolong the life of your wood structures with the information in this chapter.

Chapter 5 explains how to care for wood siding. This chapter focuses on other outdoor wood structures. Although you use many of the same principles and techniques to care for outdoor wood structures that you use to care for wood siding, the structures discussed here are more difficult to protect because each structure contains many pieces of wood, each piece having more than one side exposed to the elements.

Preserving Wood

Wood is wood and whether the wood is used for a deck, a fence, a gazebo, or a retaining wall, there is one common fact: Wood and water don't mix. Fortunately, you can protect your wood structures in a number of ways, as the following sections explain.

Anything that contains wood must be treated like wood. Some manufacturers of composite materials would like you to believe that their products require no maintenance, but that's just not the case. Wood composites are basically wood chips mixed with a resin. After one or two greasy barbecue spills, you'll find that composite decking stains just like the real McCoy. Composite surfaces do seem to hold up better in the beginning, and they don't splinter the way natural wood does, but composite materials can't be refinished. (That won't become important until at least ten years down the road, when replacement is your only choice.) Composite wood should be protected with penetrating oil (a wood preservative), just as solid wood should.

Paint

A painted deck or fence can be beautiful, but painting can also be a real problem. Unlike wood siding, wood in decks, handrails, fences, retaining walls, and other complex structures expose several surfaces of each piece of wood to the weather. Some of the surfaces (such as the area between a fence rail and a fence board) are inaccessible and can't be protected, which makes it difficult to achieve a complete waterproof membrane, even if you caulk.

Partially painted pieces of wood create a real problem. Even if the unpainted side doesn't get wet directly, exposed wood can absorb moisture from vapors rising from beneath. After the exposed wood absorbs moisture, the painted surface on that same piece of wood can become riddled with bubbles, splits, chips, and peeling paint. And when the painted surface has been compromised, it can no longer fully protect the wood — in fact, the damaged surface becomes a contributor to further moisture attack.

Our advice: Don't paint unless you can cover all six sides of every piece of wood. In situations where pieces of wood are sandwiched together, and the joined surfaces can't be painted, then the pieces should be joined as one by thoroughly caulking all connecting joints. If all sides can't be reached, you'll get the best protection with an oil or oil-stain finish — not with paint.

Because of the chipping, bubbling, and splitting normally associated with painted decks and handrails, we're reluctant to suggest painting. However, if you do decide to paint, do the following:

1. **Make sure that the surface is thoroughly clean and that the wood is dry.**

   Go to extremes to get the wood clean: pressure-washing, sanding, and detergent scrubbing. (Turn to Chapter 5 for cleaning instructions.)

2. **Remove all loose nails and replace them with the next larger size.**

   The larger nail will provide a like-new grip, holding loosened wood firmly in place. Use a hammer and nail punch to countersink all nails (see Figure 18-1). Fill the resultant nail hole with a high-quality, exterior-grade putty.

   Use a hinge pin (removed from a door hinge) as an oversized nail set — it's much easier for a novice to use than a common skinny tipped nail punch.

   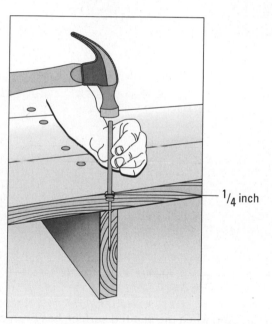

   1/4 inch

   Figure 18-1: Countersinking a nail.

3. **Fill all other holes with a high-quality, exterior-grade putty.**

   While you're applying the putty, be sure to remove all excess putty to keep sanding to a minimum.

4. **Apply a high-quality polyurethane caulk at all joints.**

5. **Prime all bare areas and puttied spots with a high-quality, oil-based primer.**

6. **Finish decks with a high-grade, oil-based finish. Handrails can be finished with a good-quality, acrylic paint.**

Remember: Be prepared to recaulk and touch up paint every year.

Never paint a wood surface that has previously been oiled. The paint won't stick, and you'll have a mess on your hands forever. After wood is oiled or oil stained, even the most minute spots of leftover paint show up like a headlight on Lover's Lane.

If you insist on painting an oiled surface (or on oiling a painted surface), you must first take the time to use a paint remover followed by thoroughly sanding the wood. Our advice? Repaint painted surfaces and re-oil oiled surfaces.

Preservative

One of the best ways to protect your wood surfaces is to use a high-quality, oil-based wood preservative — the same kind we suggest for exterior siding (see Chapter 5). Using an oil-based wood preservative with ultraviolet inhibitors keeps wood and wood-composite surfaces looking newer longer.

Unlike paint, oil doesn't lay on the surface; it penetrates deeply into the pores of the wood, preventing the attack of moisture from within. Oil also penetrates between joints and connections. With oil, there is no rigid surface layer (as there is with paint) that can bubble or split. However, oil eventually evaporates out of the wood, leaving it unprotected. If you use an oil preservative, you need to recoat your wood every 12 to 18 months.

Excessive amounts of oil can puddle, and puddled oil doesn't dry. Plus, puddling scuffs easily and can stick to furniture, feet, and shoes — meaning the destruction of interior floors. So when you oil horizontal surfaces (especially decks), take care: They're less forgiving than vertical surfaces (such as fences, posts, and rails).

Help force the oil or oil stain into the surface by going back over the entire area with a paintbrush or roller (called *back-brushing*). A China-bristle or natural-bristle paintbrush is by far the best applicator for use with oil. Don't use a nylon paintbrush with oils, oil stains, or oil-based paints.

You can also make your own wood preservative at home. You need:

- Boiled linseed oil
- Mineral spirits
- Pigment (the kind used to color paint)
- *Mildicide* (a pesticide that kills mildew; it's available at paint stores)

Mix equal parts of oil and mineral spirits. Then add pigment to the intensity you like, and stir in a package of mildicide. (Follow the instructions for the mildicide as if you were adding it to an equal volume of paint.)

When applying the preservative, don't put it on too thick. A little bit goes a long way. Don't forget to back-brush and wipe up any puddling. *Remember:* Oil and oil-stain puddles never dry. They turn into sticky, gummy messes that are nearly impossible to remove from your shoes.

Even the most clear of finishes slightly darken wood. To see how dark the wood gets, simply wet your thumb with a drop or two of water and press the wet appendage against the wood. The wet wood will look the same when oiled.

Stain

Choose a stain that's designed for the surface you want to cover:

- ✔ **Horizontal surfaces:** Well-meaning do-it-yourselfers often end up applying stains designed for vertical surfaces (such as siding, trellises, and fences) on horizontal surfaces (such as decks, porches, and steps). But if you want to stain a horizontal surface, look for a product designed specifically for decks. Deck stains are made to resist scuffing where lots of traffic is expected.

  A semitransparent, oil-based stain is a good bet. The combination of oil and a pigment protects the wood from both sun and water and hides surface irregularities. Plan to spend in the neighborhood of $35 to $55 per gallon on semitransparent, oil-based stain. A gallon covers approximately 300 to 500 square feet.

- ✔ **Vertical surfaces:** Stains designed for use on vertical surfaces are not as abrasion resistant as those made for decks. A semitransparent stain shows off the beauty of the wood because you can see through the stain. A solid-color stain won't show through, but the solid color protects the wood for a longer period of time. Solid-color stain is not like paint; it looks like paint and acts like stain — full coverage, but without the pitting, chipping, splitting or bubbling.

Always apply an oil or oil-stain finish (wood preservative) either early or late in the day when the wood is not in full sun. The thinner that helps the oil penetrate evaporates quickly on hot days and can reduce the viscosity of the oil to a glue-like mess. Oil that's too thick will end up laying on the surface. One to three very thin applications of a high-quality product may be required.

Clear finish

If you like the natural color of the wood that you want to protect, and you don't want to alter its appearance, try a clear finish. Just be sure that the clear finish that you purchase contains UV inhibitors to fight off an ultraviolet sunburn.

Beware of the popular "cure-all" water seals. Many of these products contain petroleum jelly or paraffin, which offer minimal water protection and absolutely no UV protection. Furthermore, these products have little penetration and rapidly evaporate.

Cleaning Your Wood and Composite-Wood Structures

Always keep a wood surface free of any debris. Leaves, pine needles, and dirt hold water and accelerate rot. An occasional sweeping is all that's required. You can also give your wood surfaces — oiled (clear finish), oil-stained, or painted — a good scrubbing using the following formula:

- $\frac{1}{2}$ cup liquid chlorine bleach (if moss is present)
- 1 gallon hot water
- 1 cup powdered laundry detergent

Add the bleach to the water, and then add the detergent.

Although this solution is mild, be sure to wear gloves and eye protection.

Work the solution into the surface with a stiff-bristle broom or a nylon brush. After scrubbing the surface, completely rinse it with water.

If you plan to refinish the wood after cleaning, allow the wood to completely dry before applying the finish. After it's dry, countersink any nail heads that rise above the deck's surface, or replace them with larger nails.

To get a composite-wood deck to last longer, simply keep it clean. Cleaning in spring and fall will reduce the chance for mold. Contact the wood-composite manufacturer to find out what cleaners it recommends. Some manufacturers suggest a household degreasing agent for oil and grease stains and good old household bleach for mold. In the absence of a proper cleaner, a mild detergent always works.

For more-extensive cleaning measures, read on.

Power-washing

A thorough cleaning with a pressure washer (which you can rent from a paint store or tool-rental company) saves a lot of elbow grease and makes those

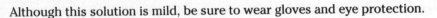

hard-to-get-to areas, like handrails and trellises, easy to clean. Pressure-washing natural wood that has turned gray can help remove discoloration and can bring the wood back to its natural color.

We were pressure-washing a home one day, when momentarily, we became engrossed in conversation and got distracted. To make a long story short, the tip of the pressure washer got a little too close to the wall. By the time we turned around to pay attention to what we were doing, the high-pressure jet of water had cut a hole completely through a $5/8$-inch-thick layer of plywood siding.

Use extreme caution when operating a pressure washer, not only to avoid damage to the surface of the wood but also to avoid personal injury.

Using a wood brightener

Severely neglected oiled or oil-stained wood may require washing with a wood-brightening product. Look for one that contains oxalic acid.

Apply the product with a nylon brush in accordance with the manufacturer's instructions. Wear protective clothing, rubber boots, gloves, and safety goggles to avoid injury.

Giving wood a facelift with sanding

If an exterior wood surface is too far gone to bring back to life with just a coat of paint or wood brightener and a coat of oil, then you may want to consider sanding. If you decide to sand it yourself, look for a power tool to help with the job. Large surfaces take forever to hand-sand. For a deck, rent a floor sander to make the job easier.

By the way, if the existing surface is painted, this would be a great time to completely remove it and convert to oil.

Countersink all nails at least $1/4$-inch deep before sanding.

For a floor sander, start with 30-grit paper and work your way up to 100-grit. For hand sanders start with 80-grit paper and work your way up to 200-grit. Regardless of the type of sander, sand first cross-grain, then in both diagonal directions, and then, finally, in the direction of the grain.

Tightening Loose Rails, Fence Boards, and Fence Posts

Loose fence rails and fence boards can be a problem. A fence can suddenly begin flopping in the wind, looking tattered and sloppy. Reattach loose rails and fence boards with nails or screws.

Be sure to use hot-dipped galvanized (not electro-coated galvanized) nails, ceramic-coated construction screws, or stainless screws. Regular shiny, non-coated nails can completely rot out in as little as a year or two.

When a fence post begins to rot at the base, the fence it supports is usually not long for this world. In the old days, when we were maintenance men on the Ark, a rotten fence post meant digging out the concrete pier surrounding the base of the post and replacing the whole kit and caboodle. Today, a pair of metal connectors, known as *fence-post repair brackets,* can be used to make such a repair.

Not every post can be reused. If the rot at the post base extends more than 8 or 10 inches above the concrete pier that holds the post in the ground, then the post should be replaced. Also, there must be at least 3 inches of concrete between the edge of the fence post and the outside edge of the concrete pier.

To repair a fence post, you need only a few items:

- 1 small block of wood
- 1 piece of scrap two-by-four, about 6 inches long
- 1 pair of fence-post repair brackets
- Hammer
- Flat pry bar
- Shovel
- Sledgehammer
- A few screws or a handful of 10d-size, hot-dipped galvanized nails

Just follow these steps:

1. **Brace the fence with the two-by-four to hold it in a plumb position until the repair can be completed (see Figure 18-2).**

   Holding the fence in an upright position, wedge one end of the two-by-four into the landscape and nail the other end of the brace to the fence near the post to be repaired. Don't drive in the nail all the way. The brace is temporary, and you'll have to remove the nail after you've made the repair.

Figure 18-2:
Bracing
your fence
for repair.

2. **Using the hammer, remove any fence boards that cover the area to be repaired.**

Use a block of wood to buffer the blow of the hammer, which reduces the chance of damaging a fence board. Lay the block against the fence board and strike the block with the hammer. The flat pry bar can be helpful here.

3. **Shovel the dirt away, exposing the base of the post and the top of the concrete pier.**

Sweep the area clean so that you can clearly see the outline of the post in the concrete. Attempting to drive a fence-post repair bracket in the wrong location can easily bend the bracket, causing the project to become more than an unhappy experience for everyone involved.

4. **Use the sledgehammer to drive in the brackets.**

As you drive the bracket into place with the sledgehammer, it crushes the post and wedges itself into the concrete. The first bracket usually goes in pretty easily. However, the second one is more difficult to install because the first bracket usually uses up all the available space between the rotted portion of the post and the pier. Be prepared to apply more force to each blow of the sledgehammer to properly seat the second bracket.

5. **Bolt, nail, or screw the brackets into the post.**

Because the brackets are tightly wedged between the pier and the post, the way in which you attach the bracket to the post usually is not terribly important. However, where substantial post damage exists, use bolts.

6. **Replace the fence boards, remove the temporary brace, and refill the post hole.**

You've just saved more than $200. Go have a beer — you deserve it!

Wood fence posts always seem to rot in the exact same place: at ground level. Why not? That's where the dirt and the water are. Make sure the earth around a fence post slopes down and away to help shed water and keep the post dryer. If you can't do that, add a sloped concrete cap to the top of the pier. Mix up a small amount of ready-mix concrete and build up the top of the pier as if you were on the beach, building a sand castle.

Remedying Sagging Gates

A sagging wooden gate is a nuisance at best, and can, at some point, become impossible to open. The problem must be pretty common, because someone has already packaged and marketed a repair kit for exactly that purpose. It's called a *gate repair kit* or *turnbuckle kit,* and it consists of a cable with corner mounting brackets and a turnbuckle. The nice thing about a turnbuckle kit is that it can be tightened or loosened to raise or lower the gate.

The kit contains:

- Two metal corner brackets with mounting nails
- Two lengths of wire cable with galvanized metal U-bolts, which are used to attach one end of each cable to one of the corner brackets and then the other end of each cable to the turnbuckle
- A galvanized metal turnbuckle

Here's how it works:

1. **Attach a metal bracket to the upper corner of the gate (on the hinge side).**

2. **Mount another bracket diagonally at the lower corner of the gate on the latch side.**

3. **Attach cables to each corner bracket and then to the two ends of a turnbuckle (see Figure 18-3).**

   As you tighten the turnbuckle, the latch side of the gate rises. As you loosen the turnbuckle, the latch side of the gate drops.

This system won't work if the upper bracket isn't placed on the hinge side of the gate.

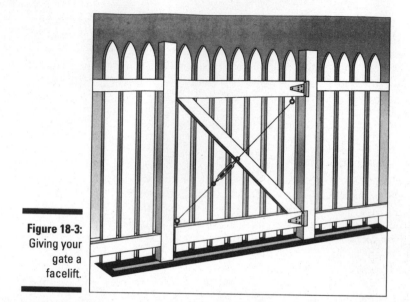

Figure 18-3:
Giving your
gate a
facelift.

Termite Treachery: Protecting Your Wood against Critters

Termites are a universal problem. And when wood buried in the ground is connected to your home — regardless of whether the buried wood is pest-resistant — that wood can act as a secret corridor from the ground to the interior of your home. A fence that has posts buried in the ground and is attached to the house, for example, can act as a termite superhighway.

To protect your home from a secret attack by termites, do the following:

- **Add a layer of sheet metal at the point where the wood and the house intersect.**

- **Wherever possible, remove dirt away from wood.** The general rule is to aim for 6 inches between the wood and the dirt. Remove enough soil to eliminate contact, making it more difficult for termites to penetrate wood structures.

- **Treat wood that has been exposed to moisture in dirt with a pesticide (such as zinc napthinate), which can be applied with a brush or sprayed on.** Pesticides help deter termites and help prevent rot.

Dirt is a world filled with tiny little insects (and some big ones, too!) and lots of moisture. Wood and water don't mix, and wood surrounded by dirt for any length of time simply rots.

Extending the Life of a Wood Retaining Wall

A wood retaining wall often doesn't get noticed until it begins to topple. The first thing we hear when someone calls us about maintenance is "Gee, the Great Wall of China has stood straight and tall for centuries." Our response is, "Yeah, but the Leaning Tower of Pisa is just about ready to fall over. It all depends on the construction, doesn't it?"

Wood retaining walls are considered temporary, but you can improve their life expectancy by keeping the wood as dry as possible. To keep your retaining wall dry, follow these steps:

1. **Dig a 6- to 12-inch-wide trench between the retaining wall and the hill it supports.**

   The trench should go to the bottom of the retaining wall.

2. **Line the bottom and both sides of the trench with burlap cloth.**

3. **Place 6 inches of drain rock over the burlap in the bottom of the trench.**

4. **Install a 4-inch perforated drainpipe (perforations down) over the first layer of rock.**

   The drainpipe should *daylight* (come out of the ground) at some point beyond the end of the retaining wall. If possible, extend the pipe so that it drains directly into the public storm-drain system.

5. **Fill the rest of the trench with drain rock to within 6 inches of the top of the dirt being retained.**

6. **Cover the rock with a layer or two of burlap and cover that with 6 inches of soil.**

   Make sure that the support posts are not in unnecessary contact with any soil and that the surrounding earth is graded to shed water away from the posts and retaining boards.

Once a year, clean the wall and post with soap and water, and apply a fresh coat of oil-based wood preservative (see the "Preservative" section, earlier in this chapter).

Chapter 19

And Then There Was Rust

Rust, the reddish-brown crust that forms on materials that contain iron, is caused by low-temperature oxidation in the presence of water. To maintain metal over very long periods of time, all you have to do is control rust. Fortunately, rust can be removed from metal year after year, layer after layer, without causing appreciable damage to the structural value of the metal. This is the main reason why metal is such a good buy in the long run.

Note that although rust can't be prevented entirely, you sure can slow it down. In this chapter, we tell you how. We also tell you how to remove that layer of rust, should it appear.

Note: Even though this chapter refers to exterior maintenance, the problems and solutions apply to interior ornamental iron as well.

Shielding Your Metals with a Protective Coat

Barbecues, patio furniture, handrails, lawn and garden equipment, steel window frames, rain gutters, and downspouts are just a few of the many metal finishes around the home that are susceptible to damage by rust.

Aside from its ugly appearance, left untreated, rust can bring any of these finishes to an early demise and lead to other damage. A rain gutter with a rusted joint, for example, can leak and allow water to travel along the wood trim at the roofline, or, perhaps down the wood siding, ultimately resulting in rot, which might cost hundreds, or even thousands, of dollars to repair. Rust also presents a safety issue. A rusted-out screw in a handrail or the rust-ravaged leg of a garden chair could send an unsuspecting guest flying to a nasty fall. Rusty outdoor power equipment leaves the operator particularly vulnerable because a rusted bolt could act as a projectile. Remember Superman and that speeding bullet? That could be you if you let rust have the upper hand.

Paint and oil are two types of coatings that you can rely on to shield a metal surface, and, therefore, prevent oxygen and water from doing their damage.

Choosing your primer and topcoat

Before you get down to painting, you need to know a few things about the primer and paint you choose.

A good paint job always begins with a high-quality primer. In this case, the primer should be made specifically for metal. Certain pigments contained in paint, such as zinc and iron oxide, adhere to metal much more effectively than other types. Ask the person at the paint store for primer and paint specifically designed for use with metal.

Whichever primer you decide to use, choose a topcoat that is compatible with the primer. In general, an oil-based finish coat is the most compatible with an oil-based primer. It also offers the greatest abrasion and weather resistance.

There are, of course, exceptions to the oil-based topcoat rule. For example, you should consider the architecture of gutters and downspouts. A flat-luster, acrylic, water-based topcoat produces a low sheen that tends to hide certain flaws, such as dents and joints. Plus, due to the inaccessibility of gutters and downspouts, more abrasion-resistant oil-based paint becomes unnecessary.

Grills, fireplaces, wood or coal stoves, heaters, and furnaces generate heat that exceeds 200 degrees. These fixtures should be topcoated with high-heat enamel paint specifically designed for use with items that are "too hot to touch." (Note that most paints emit a harmless odor the first time they're heated.)

Applying the paint

One coat each of a high-quality primer and a high-quality oil-based topcoat is all that should be required. You can apply the primer and topcoat using a brush, roller, paint pad, or sprayer.

When brushing an oil-based paint, use a natural-bristle brush. Synthetic brushes made from nylon or polyester work well with latex paints. However, they're too stiff for use with oil-based paints, often causing brush marks — not to mention loose bristles — to remain in the finished product.

Spray painting using canned aerosol spray paint or a do-it-yourself spray rig poses several advantages. Spray-painting works well on intricate designs and is smoother (without brush marks). You need to take several precautions when spray-painting:

- **Follow the necessary safety precautions.** Be sure to wear eye protection and a respirator. And never spray-paint in an area where flames or sparks could ignite volatile vapors.

- **Mask off surrounding areas with plastic, paper, or canvas to avoid damage by overspray.** Don't try spray-painting on a windy day unless, of course, your neighbor's car needs a paint job. Just be sure she's pleased with the color.

- **If you're using a spray rig, use a tip that's compatible with the paint to avoid putting too much paint on at once.** Tip sizes vary in accordance with the type of paint being used (oil based, water based, lacquer, and so on). Each type of paint has a different viscosity and, therefore, must be sprayed through a different size tip.

  Telling the various tips apart is really difficult. After you've purchased a tip for a specific use, if you plan to use it again, mark the tip with the type of paint it's for — that way, you won't have to rely on guesswork later.

- **Avoid paint runs by applying several thin coats rather than one heavy one.**

Protecting your metal with paint helps prevent rust as much as it can be prevented. However, as paint is chipped or scratched, and as it oxidizes with time and the elements, its effectiveness as a rust barrier diminishes. Eventually, moisture can make its way through the paint to the metal's surface, and rust results. To extend the life of your paint job and your ornamental iron, touch up chipped and scratched areas immediately. We keep a container of touch-up paint in the garage for each color in our homes.

Stripping Off Rust

The real secret to dealing with rust is to remove as much of it as possible before trying to apply a new finish. (You can read about applying a new finish in the preceding section.) Depending upon the configuration of the item in question, removing rust can be a tedious process that requires lots of elbow grease. In the end, your goal is to remove the rust down to bare metal. The following sections explain how.

Step 1: Removing rusted fasteners

When stripping a fixture of rust, you need to remove any rusted screws and fasteners — which is sometimes easier said than done because the rust can act as a bonding agent that can cause the fasteners and the metal structure to "freeze together" and become one.

Here are some ways you can remove rusted fasteners:

- ✔ **Saturate the fastener with cutting oil.** The cutting oil helps dissolve a small amount of the rust and acts as a lubricant to help free up some frozen connections. In combination with a screwdriver, pliers, or a wrench, cutting oil can be a favorable ally.

  Don't count on using penetrating oil to remove rust. Penetrating oil breaks down a certain amount of rust, but it isn't considered a good rust remover.

- ✔ **Use heat to remove the fastener.** A heat gun or propane torch causes a stubborn nut to expand and break loose from the bolt.

  If you plan to use heat to remove a fastener, be sure to first wipe off any lubricant or cutting oil you may have applied because the combination can cause a fire.

- ✔ **Use a drill and a hacksaw.** When all else fails, this usually does the trick.

Install rust-free replacements after you've eliminated the surrounding rust and refinished the object (see the next two sections). You can generally locate difficult-to-find replacement fasteners at machine shops. Either they'll have the items in inventory or they'll be able to fabricate a match.

There are different grades of nuts and bolts. Some are much stronger and, therefore, safer to use. Be sure to specify your use to the sales clerk to be sure that you get one that's strong enough for the task at hand.

Step 2: Getting rid of the rust

The various methods (and tools) you can use to remove rust — sandpaper, flexible sanding sponges, solvents, and so on — fall into two general categories: those that rely on elbow grease and those that rely on chemical reactions. The following sections have the details.

Whichever method you choose, be sure to wear protective gloves (to prevent metal splinters) and safety goggles (to prevent eye injuries caused by flying metal particles).

A little bit (or a lot) of elbow grease

Sandpaper, sanding tape, flexible sanding sponges, steel wool, and nylon scouring pads all work well and can be especially useful when working on tubing or twisted and curved material.

Sanding cord (industrial-strength dental floss) is a must when working around hard-to-access decorative elements, such as those you might find on a railing. As with sandpaper, sanding cord is available in a variety of grits.

A preference for plastic?

It's an age-old decision: whether to purchase an item made of steel that is strong, solid, and durable or to use a lighter, less expensive material that may be easier to maintain (like aluminum or plastic). Think about it. Would you rather sit on a plastic patio chair or one made of steel?

Many products made of steel, when properly maintained, far outlast most other materials. The bad news is that, in the short run, products made of steel are more expensive than the alternatives. *Remember:* We said in the short term. Factoring together the initial cost, the maintenance cost, and how long an item ultimately lasts is the only way to accurately measure the overall cost of anything.

In some cases, you must use steel for its strength and longevity, despite the short-term cost. Remember that some of the oldest standing structures in the United States were built from steel and continue to stand tall and beautiful after decades of existence. Can you imagine how long the Golden Gate Bridge would have lasted if it were made of wood? Would you want to chance a drive across it if it were made of plastic?

Some folks think that plastic is the solution to rust. We don't. In our opinion, plastic is not the last-forever wonder material that many believe it to be — despite the advice that Dustin Hoffman received in *The Graduate.* Plastic simply deteriorates differently than steel. Although plastic doesn't rust, it does give off *free chlorides,* which causes the plastic to become more and more brittle.

Rust is unsightly, constantly reminding you that metal is capable of deteriorating. With plastic, the process of becoming brittle isn't so apparent, but it does happen, and the deterioration that occurs is just as damaging. When plastic becomes inflexible, it doesn't spring back. Instead, it cracks. And unlike steel, "oxidized" plastic can't be repaired.

Bottom line: Don't be misled when people tell you that plastic won't disintegrate. It will. And there isn't anything that you can do to prevent it. Fortunately, plastic can be recycled, but so can steel.

By the way, we aren't anti-plastic. We both have plastic and steel products in our homes. There's just so much hype about plastic, we thought we would try to set the record straight.

In those situations where there is more rust than elbow grease can handle, we recommend the addition of a little power. A wire brush or wire wheel attached to an electric drill can make simple work of stripping rust. A bit of fine finishing with sandpaper or steel wool helps remove any residue that may remain.

Using chemical removers

Some rust simply can't be sanded or scraped without resulting in damage to the fixture. When dealing with this kind of rust, use a chemical rust remover or dissolver. These products contain ingredients that will chemically break down rust.

Rust-removal products containing gelled phosphoric acid, such as Naval Jelly, work best. You either brush the gel on (with a cheap paintbrush) or spray it on, and leave it there for 15 to 30 minutes for best results. Then simply rinse the chemical off with fresh water and dry it immediately. (**Remember:** Raw, wet steel begins to rust in minutes.) More than one application may be required, depending upon the severity of the rust.

Again, safety first. Be sure to wear rubber gloves and safety goggles, and have plenty of fresh ventilation when you're working with chemical rust removers.

Step 3: Repairing damage to the surface

Badly pitted areas can be filled with a patching compound in the same manner that wood is repaired. The difference with metal is that the patching compound must be specifically made for use with metal. Metal expands and contracts at a much different rate than wood does. A metal patch, such as Bondo, is designed to expand and contract the same way that metal does. That's why it's more likely to stay in place after you apply it — that is, unless the metal patch is on your car, in which case it's likely always on the move! You apply metal patch much like you apply spackle to wallboard when you're filling a nail hole: Simply apply the metal patch using a putty knife, allow it to dry, and sand off the excess.

After you've removed the rust and repaired any surface damage, you're ready to prime the metal. Do so within 24 hours to prevent the formation of new rust. (See the earlier section "Shielding Your Metals with a Protective Coat" for tips on priming and finishing a metal surface.)

When All Else Fails: Converting Rust

Although we recommend removing rust, there may be areas where this is simply impossible. If you can't dissolve or scrape off rust, then you have another alternative: You can convert it. Come to think of it, there are several converts in our family . . . but that's another story.

You apply rust converters directly over rust in the same way that you apply a coat of primer. The converter chemically combines with the rust, changing the rust to an inert byproduct. After the converter has cured (it doesn't actually dry hard like paint, so industry types call the combining and drying process *curing*), you can apply a fresh coat of paint directly over the converter.

One major disadvantage in using a converter in lieu of removing the rust is the likelihood of an uneven finish. The best way to guarantee a top-notch finish is to scrape, grind, patch, and sand the rust until it's smooth.

Part VI
The Part of Tens

"First of all, the stupid elves never return my phone calls, and now I find out they put the roof on without the nougat sealer."

In this part . . .

1f you think that David Letterman has the market cornered when it comes to top-ten lists, you're in for one big surprise. Old sayings have a great deal of basis in fact. For example: "Cleanliness is next to godliness." It's true, the most inexpensive home improvements involve cleaning. "A penny saved is a penny earned." So we offer alternatives to store-bought products that you can concoct yourself for "dimes on the dollar." "The early bird gets the worm." With our simple, easy-to-understand tips on skills that can save you big bucks, you won't have to worry about ending up with a "bag of worms."

Chapter 20

Ten Cleaning Solutions You Can Make at Home

In This Chapter

▶ Making your own all-purpose cleaners and mildew removers

▶ Mixing cleaning solutions for all types of surfaces

*I*f you've ever heard us on the radio, then you know that we often delve deep into the Carey Brothers' vault of valuable information to give listeners many of our secret family formulas for various easy-to-make, non-caustic, homegrown cleaning solutions. Well, in this chapter, we share these formulas with you in one, easy-to-reference place.

All-Purpose, Handy-Dandy Cleaner

You can use our All-Purpose, Handy-Dandy Cleaner to clean and freshen just about any surface. It works especially well for day-to-day cleaning of range tops and cooktops. Just mix up the following ingredients:

- 1 teaspoon borax
- ½ teaspoon washing soda
- 2 teaspoons white vinegar
- ¼ teaspoon dishwashing liquid
- 2 cups hot water

Washing soda is essentially turbo-charged baking soda. The technical name is sodium carbonate. Washing soda is a highly alkaline compound that makes a great all-purpose cleaning product and is often used as an additive to laundry detergent and other cleaning products to produce superior results.

You can replace the washing soda with baking soda and use lemon juice instead of white vinegar, depending upon what you have lying around the house. Just keep in mind that washing soda and lemon juice are a bit stronger than baking soda and white vinegar.

The secret to most cleaning formulas is hot water. It helps the various ingredients blend.

DIY Cleanser Scrub

Our formula for DIY Cleanser Scrub is especially suited for cleaning up baked-on spills on glass or porcelain ranges and cooktops when you would normally pull out the cleanser. Start with the following ingredients:

- $3/4$ cup borax
- $1/4$ cup baking soda
- Dishwashing liquid to moisten

Combine the two powders and moisten them with just enough dishwashing liquid to create a gooey paste. You can use all borax or all baking soda if you want, depending upon what you have around the house, but just keep in mind that the concoction won't be quite as strong without the borax. For a more pleasing and lingering aroma, add $1/4$ teaspoon lemon juice.

Gentle Glass Cleaner

Our Gentle Glass Cleaner works well for cleaning the glass shelving in your refrigerator, glass cooktops, and the windows in range and oven doors. You need the following ingredients:

- 2 tablespoons ammonia
- $1/4$ teaspoon dishwashing liquid
- $1/2$ cup rubbing alcohol
- Hot water

Mix the ammonia, dishwashing liquid, and rubbing alcohol, and add enough hot water to make 1 quart of cleaner. If you prefer, you can avoid the smell of ammonia by using white vinegar or lemon juice. However, these optional concoctions will cause the formula to be slightly less powerful.

For super-duper window cleaning — especially in cold weather when windows are extra dirty — add 1 teaspoon of cornstarch to the formula to boost your cleaning-and-sparkling horsepower.

People-Friendly Oven Cleaner

Our People-Friendly Oven Cleaner is a safe alternative to those conventional, caustic oven cleaners. You can also use it to clean barbecue grills and grungy pots and pans. Start with the following ingredients:

- ✔ 2 teaspoons borax or baking soda
- ✔ 2 tablespoons dishwashing liquid
- ✔ 1¼ cups ammonia
- ✔ 1½ cups hot water

Mix the ingredients, apply generously to spills, and let the solution soak for 30 minutes or as long as overnight. Loosen tough spills with a nylon scrubber, and then wipe up with a damp sponge.

Super-Duper Disinfectant Cleaner

Our Super-Duper Disinfectant Cleaner works well anywhere you would use a store-bought disinfectant, such as on appliance pulls and handles, the inside face of the refrigerator where the gasket seats, the refrigerator drip pan, counters and cutting boards, and around the opening of your clothes washer. It works especially well on all surfaces of a trash compactor — inside and out.

Mix the following ingredients and then scrub:

- ✔ 1 tablespoon borax or baking soda
- ✔ ¼ cup powdered laundry detergent
- ✔ ¼ cup pine-oil-based cleaner or pine oil
- ✔ ¾ cup hot water

For kitchen countertops, backsplashes, and the like (where there is a lot of area to cover), you can dilute with more hot water to get more coverage.

Super Wood Cleaner

To give fine wood cabinets (or furniture) a super cleaning, mix up our Super Wood Cleaner. Start with the following ingredients:

- ✔ 3 tablespoons turpentine
- ✔ 3 tablespoons boiled linseed oil
- ✔ 1 quart boiling water

This formula is not made for painted surfaces.

To create the cleaner, heat a quart of water in a saucepan and, as soon as it boils, pour the water into any old container. Then add the turpentine and the linseed oil to the water and stir vigorously. Immediately immerse a clean white cloth in the mixture and tightly wring it out. (Be sure you're wearing gloves when you do this!) Clean small areas at a time (no more than about 2 square feet), and use a clean, dry, terry-cloth towel to immediately dry the freshly cleaned area.

This mixture is moderately flammable, so no smoking or open flames while you're working. For the same reason, don't try to reheat the mixture — mix up a new batch when it gets cold. Dispose of the leftover liquid by letting it evaporate outside; don't pour it down the drain. Even the rags can be flammable — let them completely air-dry outside before disposing of them in the trash. Don't keep the rags inside — they're subject to spontaneous combustion!

Soda-Pop Concrete Stain Remover

Use our Soda-Pop Concrete Stain Remover on all concrete where the surface looks like an Indy 500 pit stop. You need the following ingredients:

- ✔ A small bag of cat litter
- ✔ A few cans of cola beverage (diet or regular)
- ✔ 1 cup liquid chlorine bleach
- ✔ 1 cup powdered laundry detergent
- ✔ 1 gallon hot water

Completely cover the grease or oil stain with a thin layer of the cat litter and grind it in with your shoes. When the mess is completely absorbed, sweep up and discard the cat litter. Cover the stain that's left with the cola beverage and use a bristle brush to work the liquid into the affected area for about 15 to 20 minutes or until the cola stops fizzing. Don't let the area dry out — use fresh water to rinse away the cola. A gray stain will be left. Add the detergent and bleach to the hot water, and scrub away the gray stain.

Although this solution is mild, be sure to wear gloves and eye protection when you work with it.

Easy All-Surface Mildew Remover

Our Easy All-Surface Mildew Remover works great on painted or other washable surfaces and costs about one-fifth the price of its store-bought equivalent. Start with the following ingredients:

- ✔ ⅓ cup powdered, ammonia-free laundry detergent
- ✔ 1 quart liquid chlorine bleach
- ✔ 3 quarts warm water

Make sure the detergent you use is ammonia free. Mixing bleach with a solution containing ammonia can release a dangerous gas that's harmful to your lungs.

Pour the water in a bucket. Add the bleach to the water, and then add the detergent. While wearing rubber gloves, stir the concoction until the detergent fully blends into the solution. Pour some of the mildew remover into a spray bottle. Spray the remover onto any area where mildew exists and allow it to sit for five to ten minutes, but don't let it dry. You'll know that the solution is working when the black mildew stains turn white. Rinse all the surfaces very well with hot water and towel-dry.

When you're working with this mildew remover, wear gloves and eye protection and make sure you have plenty of ventilation.

Special Drain Freshener and Cleaner

Our foamy Special Drain Freshener and Cleaner is great for bathroom and kitchen drains. Although it isn't meant to free badly clogged drains, it can freshen them and prevent clogging. Use this formula once a month for best results. Here's what you need:

- ✔ 1 cup baking soda
- ✔ 1 cup table salt
- ✔ 1 cup white vinegar
- ✔ 2 quarts boiling water

First, pour the baking soda into the drain, followed by the salt, and then the vinegar. The mixture will begin to foam. After a few minutes, pour the water into the drain. Let it stand overnight before using the faucet again.

Be sure to add the ingredients in the recommended order. Adding the vinegar first followed by the salt and baking soda can actually create a clog.

Universal Roof-Cleaning Formula

Use our Universal Roof-Cleaning Formula when your roof gets dirty. The concoction also gets rid of mildew or moss on your roof. You need these ingredients:

- ✔ 1 cup liquid chlorine bleach
- ✔ 1 cup powdered laundry detergent
- ✔ 1 gallon hot water

Add the bleach to the water and then add the detergent. Mix the ingredients until the soap granules dissolve. Pour the mixture into a garden sprayer. Apply the liquid onto the affected area, and keep it wet for at least 15 minutes. Use a broom to scrub the surface. Rinse with a garden hose.

A pressure washer works best. Just be careful not to damage the roof with the force of the spray. Hold the spray tip back about 12 to 18 inches from the roof.

Chapter 21

Ten Maintenance Skills You Need

Caulking lubricating, testing, painting, and more are common maintenance tasks that you'll eventually perform as a homeowner. In this chapter, we list ten universal maintenance tasks and share a few basics that we hope will help you accomplish each task as quickly and as easily as possible without sacrificing safety.

Caulking

Caulk is the stuff you pump into a gap to make it airtight or watertight. Sounds easy enough — and it is once you get the hang of it. To caulk, all you have to do is make sure that the area to be caulked is clean and dry. Open the caulk, squeeze a bead into the gap or crack, wipe off the excess, and smooth the seam with a plastic putty knife or a credit card — we use our fingers. You can clean off the excess with water or the solvent recommended for the caulk being used.

There are a million different types and colors of caulk, and knowing which to choose is important. Here are the three most common types in order of our personal preference:

- ✔ **Polyurethane:** This is our favorite all-purpose sealant and adhesive. It's flexible, paintable, and super long lasting.

- ✔ **Silicone:** This is an excellent all-purpose sealant and adhesive. It's flexible and super long lasting. Some silicone caulks are paintable.

- ✔ **Latex:** Latex caulk is a good all-purpose sealant and adhesive for little projects where water protection isn't an issue. You can paint it, but it's brittle and shrinks and cracks easily.

Regardless of which type of caulking you select, make sure that the surface you're applying it to is clean and dry — even if the caulk label claims it can be applied to wet surfaces.

Knowing How (And What) to Lubricate

A little lubrication can go a long way toward helping parts move more easily. Lubrication reduces stress on motors and equipment, which reduces operating cost and extends life. Here are common lubricants and what they can be used to lubricate:

- **Spray grease:** Good for things like the rollers, gears, or the chain on your garage door. Simply point and spray.

- **Machine oil:** Good for bearings, like you'd find in older furnaces. To apply machine oil, find the lubrication port, open it, and add a few drops.

- **Silicone lubricant:** This type of lubricant is good for sliding doors, sliding windows, and sliding screens, because it doesn't gum up. To apply silicone lubricant, clean the track and then point and spray.

- **Graphite:** Use graphite to lubricate door hardware and locks (can you spell "I don't want a broken key?"). To use graphite lubricant, place the tip of the container against the key hole and squeeze.

Anything in your home that contains a moving part is a candidate for scheduled lubrication. If you aren't sure, contact the seller or manufacturer and find out. The equipment you save will be your own!

Recognizing and Testing for Problems

You know that a smoke detector or carbon-monoxide detector with worn-out batteries provides absolutely no protection in the event of a fire. But did you also know that a water heater can explode if the pressure and temperature relief valve is stuck closed and that the explosion has the force of a stick of dynamite?

Fire extinguishers can leak and lose their charge rendering them useless in an emergency. When was the last time you took a peek at your fire extinguishers. Do you even remember where they are?

Twice a year, locate your fire extinguishers and read the pressure gauge. Once a year, pull the pin and give each extinguisher a quick test blast. Every three years, replace your extinguishers.

You can check these and other household devices easily and safely. Smoke detectors, water-heater pressure and temperature-relief valves, carbon-monoxide detectors, and fire extinguishers are examples of devices you'll find in our home-maintenance plan in Chapter 3. Many household devices are designed to be tested, so if something has a Test button, use it!

Not checking and testing a safety device places you and your family in grave danger.

Choosing the Right Tool for the Job

Nothing is more difficult than attempting a home-repair project without the proper tools. Can you spell "busted knuckles"? Not only is it important to have the right tool for the job, but that tool must be in good condition as well. A dull chisel, for example, can do more damage than good. A dull saw or the wrong saw for the job can break your back. (Did you know that there is a wrench made especially for reaching up behind the kitchen sink? Yep, it's called a sink wrench.)

So when you're tackling a job yourself, make sure you have the proper tools. Start by researching the project. Throughout this book, we tell you which tool you'll need for the job at hand. When you know which tools are needed, you can research what each does. A handy neighbor or a knowledgeable hardware-store clerk also can be helpful.

What if you don't have or can't get the proper tool? Well, some projects are best left to contractors, especially when investing in the proper tool(s) costs more than a professional repair.

Be cautious of bargain tools. A tool that breaks in your hand can hurt.

Testing an Electrical Circuit

It goes without saying that an electrical death is shocking. With an electrical circuit, it's important to ensure that your ground fault circuit interrupters

(GFCIs) are operating properly. To check, simply press the Test button to be sure that the circuit is safe. (See the earlier section "Recognizing and Testing for Problems" for info on other devices you can test.)

Make sure you know which plug or light belongs to which fuse or breaker. At any hardware store or home center, you can buy a simple circuit locator device that allows you to do this test quickly and conveniently. Then, in the event of a smoky circuit, you can turn off the breaker and prevent a fire without having to shut down the whole house.

Painting

Painting provides a protective coating to a surface, preventing rot and deterioration and making for easy cleaning. Doing it right and doing it well couldn't be more important. Outside, the ultraviolet rays of the sun and water from rain, snow, and irrigation can destroy the home's exterior. A solid coat of paint looks good, but more important, it's a barrier between your home and Mother Nature. Interior painting is equally important to protect your home against everyday wear and tear. If walls and trim are beyond cleaning, it's time to paint.

Painting well requires two basic steps:

1. **Prepare the surface.**

   Preparation (sanding, caulking, and cleaning) constitutes 80 percent of a paint job, and it's key to a good final finish.

2. **Paint.**

   Use the best paint money can buy. The longer the paint lasts, the less often you'll find yourself with a paintbrush in hand. Test paint by rubbing your thumb and index fingers together in the paint. If it's smooth and silky, it's good paint. If it fells gritty, buy something else.

If you want more information on painting, check out *Painting Do-It-Yourself For Dummies,* by Katharine Kaye McMillan, PhD, and Patricia Hart McMillan (Wiley).

Knowing How to Shut Things Off

When we covered the Loma Prieta earthquake in San Francisco two decades ago, we discovered that much of the danger to life and limb did not result from the earthquake. Instead, broken water and gas lines exposed residents to costly floods and deadly fires. Folks didn't know how to shut down these services — or even that shutting them down was important.

Here's how to shut down the major lines coming into your home:

✔ **Water:** Depending on where you live, you either have a water meter valve or a main shut-off valve. Water meters and main shut-off valves are generally located somewhere near the edge of your property. Additionally, you should have a water shut-off valve at your home. In most cases the easiest valve to shut off is the round faucet handle at your house. However, this can take almost a minute.

You may want to replace your old-style round faucet handle with a quarter-turn ball valve. In less than a second, you can have the water completely off and be on your way to safety.

✔ **Electricity:** Every home typically has one breaker (the main breaker) that shuts off all the electricity. You need to know where the main breaker (or fuse) is and how to shut the breaker off.

Never shut off a breaker when you're standing in a puddle of water.

✔ **Gas:** Find out where the gas meter is on your property and what size wrench is necessary to turn it off. Most hardware stores carry the type of wrench needed for the gas meters in your neck of the woods. We suggest purchasing such a tool and tying it to the gas meter, so you won't have to go looking for it if and when an emergency arises. (***Note:*** Modern gas-meter installations include an automatic earthquake shut-off valve.)

Make sure every member of your household knows where all these items are located and how to turn them off. When in doubt, turn everything off. Some systems may by slightly difficult to turn on later, but it doesn't ever hurt your home to turn everything off in an emergency.

Venting Moisture from Your Home

Damp air, condensation, and steam are nothing more than various forms of house-damaging water. Metal rusts, mildew thrives, wallpaper peels, and paint bubbles when any form of moisture attacks. That's why it's important to have ample ventilation.

Start with a good bath fan and a more powerful range hood. And don't forget to ensure that there is an exhaust fan in the laundry. Wherever steam is generated in your home, there should be an exhaust fan to properly remove it.

A decorative paddle fan is another important tool. Moisture often occurs in the form of condensation on windows and walls — you know "sweaty windows" and "sweaty walls." A ceiling-mounted decorative paddle fan run in reverse forces air up to the ceiling and then down the walls, absorbing moisture and preventing all forms of mildew, rot, and rust from growing on what would otherwise be a feeding ground for the fungus among us.

Replacing Filters and Cleaning Sensors

Filters and sensors exist everywhere in your home. If we asked you to name a filter, you'd probably say "furnace filter." And you'd be right — the furnace filter is one of the most important of the bunch. But there are more.

Here's our list of the most common filters and sensors and how often to clean or replace them:

- **Furnace filter:** Change monthly. Pleated filters are the best.

  To test the quality of a filter, hold the filter horizontally (like a platter) and pour regular table salt onto it. If the salt passes through, replace the filter.

- **Range-hood filter:** Clean every couple of months deepening on how often you cook and how much frying you do. (More frying equals more frequent cleaning, because grease can build up and clog the filter.)

- **Bath or laundry exhaust fan:** Clean every six months. (We know, the grate that covers the fan is not a filter per se, but a dirty cover can still wreak havoc with the system.)

- **Refrigerator filter:** Replace in accordance with the manufacturer's instructions. Besides, who wants dirty ice?

- **Smoke-detector sensor:** Vacuum twice a year. Open the unit and use your vacuum cleaner hose with a soft brush attachment. You may also use compressed air — like the kind you use to clean your computer keyboard.

- **Whole-house filters:** Change at least once a year. You may find that your water tastes better if you change the filter every six months. Filters trap debris and bacteria that can eventually affect the taste of water that passes through it.

- **Dryer filter:** Clean it every time you use the dryer, and clean the chamber that holds the filter at least once a quarter. A long skinny nozzle on the end of your vacuum cleaner hose is all it takes.

Checking On the Chimney

Nothing is as romantic as a crackling fire. And nothing can level your house faster than the explosion and raging fire from a creosote-laden chimney. Save the fireworks for the fairgrounds on the Fourth of July. Call a chimney sweep to thoroughly clean your chimney at least once a year or after every cord of burned wood.

Here are some chimney-related maintenance tasks you can do yourself:

- Make sure the damper is in proper working order by ensuring that it opens and closes easily.

- Keep birds' nests and other debris from blocking the spark arrestor atop your chimney.

- If you notice cracks in the mortar or brick, don't use your fireplace until the cracks are repaired — that is, unless you *like* loud explosions.

Index

Business/Accounting & Bookkeeping

Bookkeeping For Dummies
978-0-7645-9848-7

eBay Business
All-in-One For Dummies,
2nd Edition
978-0-470-38536-4

Job Interviews
For Dummies,
3rd Edition
978-0-470-17748-8

Resumes For Dummies,
5th Edition
978-0-470-08037-5

Stock Investing
For Dummies,
3rd Edition
978-0-470-40114-9

Successful Time
Management
For Dummies
978-0-470-29034-7

Computer Hardware

BlackBerry For Dummies,
3rd Edition
978-0-470-45762-7

Computers For Seniors
For Dummies
978-0-470-24055-7

iPhone For Dummies,
2nd Edition
978-0-470-42342-4

Laptops For Dummies,
3rd Edition
978-0-470-27759-1

Macs For Dummies,
10th Edition
978-0-470-27817-8

Cooking & Entertaining

Cooking Basics
For Dummies,
3rd Edition
978-0-7645-7206-7

Wine For Dummies,
4th Edition
978-0-470-04579-4

Diet & Nutrition

Dieting For Dummies,
2nd Edition
978-0-7645-4149-0

Nutrition For Dummies,
4th Edition
978-0-471-79868-2

Weight Training
For Dummies,
3rd Edition
978-0-471-76845-6

Digital Photography

Digital Photography
For Dummies,
6th Edition
978-0-470-25074-7

Photoshop Elements 7
For Dummies
978-0-470-39700-8

Gardening

Gardening Basics
For Dummies
978-0-470-03749-2

Organic Gardening
For Dummies,
2nd Edition
978-0-470-43067-5

Green/Sustainable

Green Building
& Remodeling
For Dummies
978-0-470-17559-0

Green Cleaning
For Dummies
978-0-470-39106-8

Green IT For Dummies
978-0-470-38688-0

Health

Diabetes For Dummies,
3rd Edition
978-0-470-27086-8

Food Allergies
For Dummies
978-0-470-09584-3

Living Gluten-Free
For Dummies
978-0-471-77383-2

Hobbies/General

Chess For Dummies,
2nd Edition
978-0-7645-8404-6

Drawing For Dummies
978-0-7645-5476-6

Knitting For Dummies,
2nd Edition
978-0-470-28747-7

Organizing For Dummies
978-0-7645-5300-4

SuDoku For Dummies
978-0-470-01892-7

Home Improvement

Energy Efficient Homes
For Dummies
978-0-470-37602-7

Home Theater
For Dummies,
3rd Edition
978-0-470-41189-6

Living the Country Lifestyle
All-in-One For Dummies
978-0-470-43061-3

Solar Power Your Home
For Dummies
978-0-470-17569-9

Internet

Blogging For Dummies,
2nd Edition
978-0-470-23017-6

eBay For Dummies,
6th Edition
978-0-470-49741-8

Facebook For Dummies
978-0-470-26273-3

Google Blogger
For Dummies
978-0-470-40742-4

Web Marketing
For Dummies,
2nd Edition
978-0-470-37181-7

WordPress For Dummies,
2nd Edition
978-0-470-40296-2

Language & Foreign Language

French For Dummies
978-0-7645-5193-2

Italian Phrases
For Dummies
978-0-7645-7203-6

Spanish For Dummies
978-0-7645-5194-9

Spanish For Dummies,
Audio Set
978-0-470-09585-0

Macintosh

Mac OS X Snow Leopard
For Dummies
978-0-470-43543-4

Math & Science

Algebra I For Dummies
978-0-7645-5325-7

Biology For Dummies
978-0-7645-5326-4

Calculus For Dummies
978-0-7645-2498-1

Chemistry For Dummies
978-0-7645-5430-8

Microsoft Office

Excel 2007 For Dummies
978-0-470-03737-9

Office 2007 All-in-One
Desk Reference
For Dummies
978-0-471-78279-7

Music

Guitar For Dummies,
2nd Edition
978-0-7645-9904-0

iPod & iTunes
For Dummies,
6th Edition
978-0-470-39062-7

Piano Exercises
For Dummies
978-0-470-38765-8

Parenting & Education

Parenting For Dummies,
2nd Edition
978-0-7645-5418-6

Type 1 Diabetes
For Dummies
978-0-470-17811-9

Pets

Cats For Dummies,
2nd Edition
978-0-7645-5275-5

Dog Training For Dummies,
2nd Edition
978-0-7645-8418-3

Puppies For Dummies,
2nd Edition
978-0-470-03717-1

Religion & Inspiration

The Bible For Dummies
978-0-7645-5296-0

Catholicism For Dummies
978-0-7645-5391-2

Women in the Bible
For Dummies
978-0-7645-8475-6

Self-Help & Relationship

Anger Management
For Dummies
978-0-470-03715-7

Overcoming Anxiety
For Dummies
978-0-7645-5447-6

Sports

Baseball For Dummies,
3rd Edition
978-0-7645-7537-2

Basketball For Dummies,
2nd Edition
978-0-7645-5248-9

Golf For Dummies,
3rd Edition
978-0-471-76871-5

Web Development

Web Design All-in-One
For Dummies
978-0-470-41796-6

Windows Vista

Windows Vista
For Dummies
978-0-471-75421-3

Available wherever books are sold. For more information or to order direct: U.S. customers visit www.dummies.com or call 1-877-762-2974.
U.K. customers visit www.wileyeurope.com or call (0) 1243 843291. Canadian customers visit www.wiley.ca or call 1-800-567-4797.